# Who Are the Major
# American Writers?

Books by JAY B. HUBBELL
published by the Duke University Press:

*The South in American Literature, 1607–1900* (1954)

*South and Southwest: Literary Essays and Reminiscences* (1965)

Also published by the Duke University Press:

*Essays on American Literature in Honor of Jay B. Hubbell,*
edited by Clarence Gohdes (1967)

# Who Are the Major American Writers?

A study of the changing literary canon by

## JAY B. HUBBELL

Professor Emeritus of American Literature
at Duke University and Chairman of
the Board of Editors of AMERICAN
LITERATURE, 1928–1954

DUKE UNIVERSITY PRESS
Durham, North Carolina   1972

Printed in the United States of America

*As a token of my deep and abiding affection*
*I dedicate this book to*
*My Wife*
LUCINDA SMITH HUBBELL
*and*
*Our Grandchildren*
LAWRENCE BAYNARD HUBBELL
DANIEL BECKLEY HUBBELL
KATHERINE HUBBELL GREEN

*The characters of prophet and critic are not always united.*
William Hazlitt, "On Criticism"

*The canon of American literature refuses to stay fixed.*
Carl Van Doren, "Toward a New Canon."

# Preface

This book has grown out of an essay, "Who Are the Best American Writers? A Study of Some Critical Polls Sponsored by American Magazines." My essay appeared in *Anglo-Americana*, edited by Karl Brunner, a volume of studies published in Vienna in 1955 in honor of the late Leo Hibler, who was the head of the English Seminar at the University of Vienna when I was a visiting professor there in 1949 and again in 1950. I have paid my tribute to this fine Tyrolese scholar, teacher, and gentleman in an essay entitled "Springtime in Vienna," published in 1965 in my *South and Southwest: Literary Essays and Reminiscences*.

Since 1955 I have found other critical polls, and I have made use of a wealth of materials not used in my essay. These include literary histories, anthologies, reviews of books, magazine articles on individual authors and on American literature in general, results of elections to the Hall of Fame for Great Americans and the American Academy of Arts and Letters, the Pulitzer, Nobel, and other literary prizes and awards, and various other attempts at ranking our authors in the order of their importance. What I have found illustrates the great changes in literary taste and fashion which have taken place in the last century and a half.

I have sometimes tried, not very confidently, to point out various historical factors that have brought about marked changes in the ranking of many of our best-known writers. My function in this book, however, is as I see it that of historian. I leave it to others to examine the materials that I have brought together and to try to explain the wide fluctuations in the reputations of such writers as Melville and Longfellow in the nineteenth century and of Scott Fitzgerald and Wallace Stevens in the twentieth.

My main concern in this book is not with the best-sellers. That subject has been admirably treated in Frank Luther Mott's *Golden Multitudes* (1947) and James D. Hart's *The Popular Book* (1949). My chief concern is with critics in positions of authority and influence: book reviewers, magazine editors, publishers and their advisers, professional critics, professors of English, anthologists, and literary historians. I have been often surprised and sometimes amazed by the failure of these "authorities" to recognize the talents of their younger contemporaries.

The record of the creative writers is better than that of the recognized "authorities." It was Poe and Melville who first saw clearly the genius of Hawthorne. In a later generation Howells was among the first to see as major American writers three very different figures: Henry James, Mark Twain, and Emily Dickinson. In this century Donald Davidson was the first critic to state publicly that Faulkner was a great novelist. The creative writers, however, have been slow to recognize the greatness of those writers whose aims and methods are different from their own. Emerson was among the first to see the greatness of Thoreau, Whitman, and Carlyle; but he could see nothing of value in the writings of Poe or even his friend and neighbor, Hawthorne. Academic critics and literary historians are often wrong about their contemporaries, but they serve to correct the critical errors of the creative writers. They know how wrong were Ezra Pound and T. S. Eliot in seeing Emily Dickinson as only "a little country bluestocking." Academic critics with the best record are minor men of letters like Bliss Perry and Brander Matthews, who had repeatedly tried their hands at creative writing before they became professors of English.

In the 1970's as in the 1920's we have with us the brash young critics who appear to assume that they alone are able to recognize beauty and truth when they see them on the printed page. They are all too ready to throw overboard the established poets and novelists and to canonize the new who must still undergo the test of time. And in this second half-century of rapidly changing literary fashions we have with us critics who cannot read with sympathy and understanding the new and original creations of a younger generation. I can only hope, rather than expect, that some of those who, young or old, read any portion of this book will become more fully aware of the difficulties encountered by any critic who sets out to appraise the merits of the living writers of his own time.

The findings reported in this book have, I think, their uses; but while writing it I have often felt as Allen Tate felt when in *Reason in Madness* he attacked the "illusion of the fixed hierarchy," "the assumption that the great writers of the past occupy a fixed position." Strange indeed seemed to him "the curious belief that the chief function of criticism is the ranking of authors rather than their use."

In an afterword, I have given, for any reader who may be interested, a brief account of my long-time personal involvement with the problem of the proper ranking of American authors in a half-century marked by shifting critical standards and fluctuating reputations.

I wish to express my grateful appreciation for important information and helpful suggestions that I have received from Professors Jackson Bryer of the University of Maryland, Clarence Gohdes of Duke University, Rayburn S. Moore of the University of Georgia, and James Woodress of the University of California at Davis. By her expert typing, and occasional retyping, Dorothy Roberts has made my task easier. My wife, Lucinda, and my son, Jay, Jr., have contributed helpful suggestions. For close and expert reading of my manuscript I am indebted to two distinguished scholars, Herbert R. Brown, Longfellow Professor of English at Bowdoin College, and Lewis Leary, Kenan Professor of English at the University of North Carolina at Chapel Hill. My manuscript is the better for their critical comments and many useful suggestions. My book is the better also for the careful reading that Mrs. Carol C. Thompson gave my manuscript when she edited it for the printer. I am, finally, indebted to the Duke University Research Council for providing much-needed clerical assistance and a subsidy in aid of publication.

With the permission of the University of Texas Press and Professor Ernest J. Lovell, executive editor of *Texas Studies in Literature and Language*, I have reprinted a large portion of my article, "1922: A Turning Point in American Literary History," which appeared in that journal in the fall, 1970 (12:481–492).

May 8, 1971

# Contents

*It is not until an age has receded into history, and all its mediocrity has dropped away from it, that we can see it as it is—as a group of men of genius. We forget the immense amount of twaddle that the great epochs produced.*

Arnold Bennett, *Literary Taste: How to Form It*

*Only a handful of writers are permanently "great," and every generation selects its own affinities in the past, the writers who are congenial to its own special nature.*

Van Wyck Brooks, *The Writer in America*

# Introduction

Sixty years ago it was generally agreed in both England and America that the greatest English poets were Shakespeare, Milton, Chaucer, and Spenser. The reputations of lesser poets, like Pope and Tennyson or Longfellow and Poe, might fluctuate; but, it was believed, the four great poets were secure in their places on the top of the English Parnassus. In 1964, four centuries after his birth, Shakespeare's primacy was conceded on all sides, but nowadays only a minority among critics would give Spenser a place among the four great English poets. Even the august name of John Milton was called in question. For many critics John Donne became a greater poet than Spenser and a much more interesting figure than Milton. Meanwhile in our own country the schoolroom poets—Bryant, Longfellow, Holmes, Whittier, and Lowell—were downgraded into third-rate authors even in their native New England. Emerson and Hawthorne, however, held their own while one by one Poe, Melville, Thoreau, Whitman, Mark Twain, Henry James, and Emily Dickinson slowly emerged as major American writers.

In 1928 an English scholar, E. E. Kellett, in an essay entitled "Critical Certainties" (in his *Reconsiderations*) complained that "the greatest difficulty in the way of confident and sound criticism" lies in "the constant shifting in the standards of taste." He gave some striking examples:

> A Cowley takes the world by storm: a generation passes, and Pope asks, "Who now reads Cowley?" Pope himself becomes the *ne plus ultra* of genius, and the *Essay on Man* is the height of the sublime. Half a century after his death it is seriously debated whether he is a poet at all. Byron's *Cain*, said Scott in 1821, "certainly matches Milton on his own ground"; in 1860 people did not stop to consider such a judgment; they smiled at it and passed on. Edgar Allan Poe expressed the deliberate opinion that Tennyson was the greatest ["noblest"] poet that

ever lived; where is Tennyson now? But this is far from all. There has been, in almost every case, a reaction against the reaction; Pope and Byron are already more or less restored to favour, and there is every sign that the restoration of Tennyson will not be long delayed. Nor may the restoration, in its turn, be final; if we may judge the future by the past, there will yet be many ebbs and flows of opinion.

The history of the fine arts provides other examples of the building up and the tearing down of the reputations of those once regarded as among the great. Sir George Grove, for example, noted that when Felix Mendelssohn visited Munich and Vienna in 1830—only three years after the death of Beethoven—he was disgusted by the ignorance of the best musicians whom he met, "Mozart, Haydn, and Beethoven utterly ignored, Hummel, Field, Kalkbrenner, accepted as classics." Many years earlier Dante had written in the *Divine Comedy*:

> In painting once laid Cimabue claim
> To hold the field; now Giotto has the cry,
> And all is overcast the other's fame.
> So doth one Guido from the other wrest
> The glory of our tongue; and he perchance
> Is born who both shall shoulder from the nest.
> Nought but a breath of wind is human fame,
> Which bloweth now from here, and now from there,
> And but for changing quarter changes name.
> *Purgatory*, Canto xi, translated by Jefferson B. Fletcher

At times the student feels that fashions in the world of literature and the other arts have no more solid foundation than fashions in dress. One is tempted sometimes to agree with Jules Lemaître, who used to remark that criticism of one's contemporaries is not literary criticism but merely conversation. "*Nothing* in our age . . . ," wrote Ben Jonson in *Discoveries*, "is more preposterous, then [than] the *running Iudgments* upon *Poetry*, and *Poets*; when wee shall heare those things commended, and cry'd up for the best writings, which a man would scarce vouchsafe to wrap any wholesome drug in; hee would never light his *Tobacco* with them."

Yet there are a handful of great writers who in age after age have held their own: Homer, Vergil, Dante, Shakespeare, Cervantes, Molière, and Goethe. Of each of these we may say as Ben Jonson wrote of Shakespeare: "He was not of an age, but for all time!" Only an erratic critic would question the greatness of the *Odyssey*, the *Divine Comedy, King Lear,* or *Faust.* It is true nevertheless that with the passing of time the critical justification of these masterpieces has shifed from one basis to another.

Literary critics often miss the mark when they pass judgment on their contemporaries. In the early nineteenth century few of the quarterly reviewers who sang the praises of Scott and Byron understood the importance of Wordsworth, Coleridge, Blake, Shelley, or Keats. Francis Jeffrey, we remember, began his review of Wordsworth's *The Excursion* with the sentence: "This will never do." When Norwegian reviewers complained that *Peer Gynt* did not conform to the rules of the poetic art, Ibsen retorted: "My book *is* poetry; and if it is not, then it shall be. The Norwegian conception of what poetry is shall be made to fit my book."

As Henri Peyre pointed out in his *Writers and Their Critics* (1944), the best literary critics were often wrong in their estimates of the great writers of their own time. Among them we find the names of Sainte-Beuve, Brunetière, Matthew Arnold, Henry James, Lowell, and Poe. Moreover, as I have noted elsewhere, Ezra Pound, T. S. Eliot, Van Wyck Brooks, Vernon Louis Parrington, and Edmund Wilson all failed to appreciate the merits of some of their greatest contemporaries and all overrated writers who are not remembered now.

Creative writers, who are often the best critics, nevertheless may miss the mark as widely as academic critics or professional reviewers. Herman Melville in an essay entitled "Hawthorne and His Mosses" saluted the author of *Mosses from an Old Manse* as the greatest living American writer. He concluded by saying: "For genius, all over the world, stands hand in hand, and one shock of recognition runs the whole circle round." Hawthorne recognized Melville's genius, but apparently no other of the great English and American authors of his time saw in *Moby-Dick* one of the really great novels of the century.

Lord Byron wrote in *Don Juan*:

> Thou shalt believe in Milton, Dryden, Pope;
>   Thou shalt not set up Wordsworth, Coleridge, Southey;
> Because the first is crazed beyond all hope,
>   The second drunk, the third so quaint and mouthy.

To the last three of these poets Byron addressed his ill-fated prophecy:

> Scott, Rogers, Campbell, Moore and Crabbe will try
> 'Gainst you the question with posterity.

The critical ratings of our literary historians are, as I have pointed out in succeeding chapters, often quite wide of the mark. This is particularly true when the elderly historian is discussing his own contemporaries. For that matter, however, older critics of all classes who undertake to rank the writers of a younger generation are peculiarly liable to be proved wrong by the passing of time. Hamlin Garland when judging American fiction of the 1920's and 1930's was no more perceptive than Professor Fred Lewis Pattee.

One cannot always rely upon the author's estimate of the value of his own achievement. In a pessimistic moment John Keats chose for his epitaph: "Here lies one whose name was writ in water." Somewhat earlier he had written a far truer estimate: "I think I shall be among the English poets after my death." Horace had good reason to boast that in his poems he had erected a monument more enduring than brass. "I shall not all die," he said. After four centuries posterity still honors the claim that Shakespeare made, perhaps not very seriously, in one of his finest sonnets:

> Not marble, nor the gilded monuments
> Of princes, shall outlive this powerful rhyme.

Chaucer was less hopeful when he wrote:

> But al shal passe that men prose or ryme;
> Take every man his turn, as for his tyme.

Throughout the nineteenth century, Americans kept looking hopefully for the great American writer whom the British insisted that the new nation must produce to prove its intellectual greatness. The literary journalists led in the search for the great American poet and—after the Civil War—for the great American novelist. They continually overrated many of the newer authors and quickly forgot them.

Somehow to many proud and sensitive Americans the ranking of our authors has seemed important. For the past hundred and fifty years our literary journalists have put into print critical estimates destined to be quickly superseded by others no more enduring; and magazine and newspaper editors have conducted polls to ascertain which of our writers are by current standards the best. They do not seem disturbed or discouraged—as some of the rest of us have been—by the wide variety of verdicts reached in such polls or by the fluctuations in the reputations of even our greatest writers.

For the reader of today it is difficult to understand how any one could ever have thought that James Gates Percival was an important poet or General Lew Wallace a great American novelist. It seems incredible that it was so long before any appreciable number of readers recognized Whitman's "Out of the Cradle Endlessly Rocking" as a great poem or Melville's *Moby-Dick* as a great novel.

Yet every middle-aged lover of literature must have wondered why his own early favorites arouse no enthusiasm in younger readers. He may feel inclined, like Sir Thomas Browne, to lament that "the inequity of oblivion blindly scattereth her poppy, and deals with the memory of men without distinction to merit of perpetuity." There are times when one is inclined to agree with Karl Shapiro, who wrote in *Beyond Criticism* (1953): "The fate of works of art is always a matter of chance. The history of art is a history of chance."

My survey of changing American literary fashions indicates that in the nature of things critical estimates can be only relative. In an essay on Burns, Robert Louis Stevenson wrote: "There is, indeed, only one merit worth considering in a man of letters—that he should write well; and only one damning fault—that he should write ill." Had Stevenson been alive in 1959, he would have been shocked to note that the Burns bicentennial passed almost unnoticed in both England and America. Scotland's great poet had not written the kind of poetry that was fashionable in 1959, and the methods of the New Critics were hardly the best approaches to such poems as "Tam o' Shanter," "The Jolly Beggars," and "The Cotter's Saturday Night."

This book is a study of the changing reputations of American writers, but its subject is only a part of the wider problem that involves the failure of intelligent men and women to recognize greatness, not only in our writers and artists, but also in our statesmen, our scientists, and our educators. Our intellectuals have been as wrong in their judgment of our statesmen as in their ranking of our authors. George Washington was unmercifully maligned by men who should have recognized his greatness; and so were Jefferson, Lincoln, and Woodrow Wilson. Jefferson's true stature was not universally recognized until the time of the New Deal, and it was not until the approach of the Second World War that Wilson's greatness was generally recognized. It was many years before the reputation of Herbert Hoover recovered from the effects of the Great Depression—the "Hoover Depression," as his political enemies labeled it. The wide fluctuations in the reputation of Lyndon Johnson point to a failure in many intelligent men and women to see that his many achievements in the Senate and the White House have earned him a place among great Americans. And, finally, in April, 1971, I am moved to wonder whether the present very able occupant of the White House will fare any better than his illustrious predecessors.

*Part One. The Nineteenth Century*

# Chapter 1. Our Literary Pioneers

> *America must be as independent in* literature *as she is in* politics, *as famous for* arts *as for* arms; *and it is not impossible but a person of my youth may have some influence in exciting a spirit of literary industry.*
> Noah Wester to John Caufield, January 6, 1783

> *We have listened too long to the courtly muses of Europe.*
> Ralph Waldo Emerson, "The American Scholar (1837)

## THE DEMAND FOR A NATIONAL LITERATURE

By 1765 the American colonists had created a body of writing which the modern literary historian finds by no means negligible. The Colonial authors, however, felt that what they had written formed only a minor part of the great literature of England. There was as yet no conscious demand for a national literature, and there was little concern about the ranking of American writers either in this country or in Great Britain.

As the Revolution approached, however, the rising tide of national feeling led youthful poets to predict a great future for an American literature. They remembered Bishop Berkeley's prophetic line: "Westward the course of empire takes its way," and his prediction, in America of

> another golden age,
> The rise of empire and of arts.

In a poem which he read at the Yale College Commencement in 1770, John Trumbull wrote:

> This land her Swift and Addison shall view
> The former honors equall'd by the new;
> Here shall some Shakespeare charm the rising age,
> And hold in magic chains the listening stage;
> A second Watts shall string the heavenly lyre,
> And other muses other bards inspire.

Trumbull saw the American future only in terms of English literature of the past; he made no claim for American authors living or dead.

After the American Revolution had given the thirteen rebellious British colonies their political independence, they began demanding a national literature more vociferously than any European country; and in Europe at that time political and cultural nationalism was a powerful force. The second war with England and the so-called "paper war" which preceded and followed it added a new stimulus to the demand. The United States was made to feel that a great literature was essential to the proof of a nation's greatness.

Americans resented most keenly the British refusal to recognize their literary and cultural pretensions. Writing in the *Edinburgh Review* in December, 1818, Sydney Smith expressed the British view:

> Literature the Americans have none—no native literature, we mean. It is all imported. They had a Franklin, indeed; and may afford to live half a century on his fame. There is, or was, a Mr Dwight, who wrote some poems; and his baptismal name was Timothy. There is also a small account of Virginia by Jefferson, and an epic by Joel Barlow—and some pieces of pleasantry by Mr Irving. But why should the Americans write books, when a six weeks' passage brings them in our own tongue, our sense, science and genius, in bales and hogsheads?

Sydney Smith was irritated by the new nation's claim that it was, in his words, "the greatest, the most refined, the most enlightened, and the most moral people upon earth"; and in the *Edinburgh Review* for January, 1820, he asked a series of embarrassing questions which taken together were intended to constitute a test of the quality of the new nation's civilization:

> In the four quarters of the globe, Who reads an American book? Or goes to an American play? Or looks at an American picture or statue? What does the world yet owe to American physicians and surgeons? What new substances have their chemists discovered? Or what old ones have they analysed? What new constellations have been discovered by the telescopes of Americans? What have they done in the mathematics? Who drinks out of American glasses? Or eats from American plates? or wears American coats or gowns? or sleeps in American blankets?— Finally, under which of the old tyrannical governments of Europe is every sixth man a Slave, whom his fellow-creatures may buy and sell and torture?

The scornful question "Who reads an American book?" demanded a speedy answer. True enough, we had a political literature of considerable importance, but in the way of belles-lettres we had—or thought we had—next to nothing. It was of no use to remind the British critic of Barlow's *The Columbiad* or the sermons of Jonathan Edwards. Where were the American Shakespeare, Milton, Pope, Scott, and Byron? Literate Americans who had little love for belles-lettres were made to feel that the new nation must proceed forthwith to produce a literature which the British would rate as excellent. Such an attitude would eventually of course result in grossly overrating American authors merely because they were American. Our writers were assigned the difficult task of providing quickly an adequate answer to Sydney Smith's embarrassing question: "In the four quarters of the globe who reads an American book?"

James Russell Lowell, who was an infant when Sydney Smith asked that embarrassing question, wrote long afterward in his *Leaves from My Journal*:

> It had been resolved unanimously that we must and would have a national literature. England, France, Spain, Italy, each already had one. Germany was getting one as fast as possible, and Ireland vowed that she once had one far surpassing them all. To be respectable, we must have one also, and that speedily. . . . Sydney Smith's scornful question, "Who reads an American book?" tingled in our ears. Surely never was a young nation setting forth jauntily to seek its fortune so dumbfounded as Brother Jonathan when John Bull cried gruffly from the roadside, "Stand and deliver a national literature!" After fumbling in his pockets, he was obliged to confess that he hadn't one about him at the moment, but vowed he had left a first-rate one at home which he would have fetched along—only it was so everlasting heavy.

What literature the new nation had produced was not what our British critics were demanding. The political writings inspired by the American Revolution, although first-rate in quality, were not to the taste of even an English Whig like Sydney Smith. The literary supply was far from meeting the demand. The first writers to be canonized as American classics—Irving, Cooper, and Bryant—were all born after Yorktown. In 1820 Americans knew nothing of the writings of William Byrd or Edward Taylor because they had not yet been published. Literary fashions were changing, and with the drift to Romanticism even the writings of Benjamin Franklin began to seem old-fashioned. His *Autobiography*, our earliest indisputable classic, had been published in this country only as recently as 1818 and in an incomplete and bowdlerized version at that. No cultivated New England Unitarian cared to resurrect the Calvinistic sermons of Jonathan Edwards, who seemed only a theologian of no literary importance. What Americans wanted was a literature that would match the magnitude of the continent and exalt the destiny of a great nation. A handful of American writers had by 1820 already found favor with some English critics, but it was not until the 1920's that the English would give to living American authors such unstinted praise as our ancestors had hoped to hear a century earlier.

There were Americans who felt that other things were more important in the New World than belles-lettres. The literature imported from London, they thought, was about all that was needed. The best of American writing was, in the words of Fitz-Greene Halleck, only "American specimens of English literature." There were also the pessimists who thought that literature and the fine arts could not flourish in the soil of the New World. In his *Poems*, posthumously published in 1800, William Cliffton had written:

> In these cold shades, beneath these shifting skies,
> Where Fancy sickens, and where Genius dies;
> Where few and feeble are the Muse's strains,
> And no fine frenzy riots in the veins,
> There still are found a few to whom belong
> The fire of virtue and the soul of song.

The exact nature of the great American literature so much desired was by no means clear, and the obstacles were many. The United States *was* not —in those days Americans still said *were*—a nation in the full sense of the word, even under the new federal Constitution. Racially the Americans were less homogeneous than the English or the French. They had no national church or royal family to bind them together. The experience of having fought a long war for their independence had not been sufficient to develop a strong feeling of unity in thirteen widely divergent states. Culturally, they were still British colonies, and London and not Boston or New York was their literary capital. It was a bold critic who would publicly praise an American book until it had been approved in England.

Few of the Americans who clamored for a national literature fully appreciated the difficulties which confronted our early poets and writers of fiction. Among the greatest was the lack of an adequate market for their writings. When young Longfellow in 1825, about to graduate from Bowdoin College, wrote to his father that he wished to be a writer, the elder Longfellow replied: "A literary life, to one who has the means of support, must be very pleasant. But there is not wealth enough in this country to afford encouragement to merely literary men . . . you must adopt a profession which will afford you subsistence as well as reputation." The lack of an international copyright law until 1891 made it difficult for an American author to get his books published. The country was flooded with cheap British reprints which brought no royalties to their authors; and most American publishers were more interested in piracy than in circulating the writings of their own countrymen. Apart from journalism there was as yet no place in America for the professional author.

Another difficulty was that while the new land supplied the writer with rich and untouched materials, it gave him no technique for handling them.

Of necessity the author had to learn from European writers how to treat these materials, and he was thus bound to seem unoriginal. Eventually, of course, this country would produce original writers like Poe, Whitman, Henry James, Mark Twain, Hemingway, and Faulkner, who would be valued by European writers and critics for their contributions to aesthetic theory or literary technique.

The United States had no literary capital, like London or Paris, where one might hear the problems of art and literature intelligently discussed and where the youthful writer or artist could find encouragement and helpful advice. "The literary man in this country has no critic," Emerson wrote in his *Journals* on October 23, 1836. It was as natural for him to wish to see and talk with Landor, Wordsworth, Coleridge, and Carlyle as it was for Washington Allston to desire to see the paintings in the Louvre and the Vatican and to study under the living masters of his art. It is not surprising that few of our nineteenth-century writers except Poe and Henry James had any clear and consistent conception of the literary art. James naturally enough gravitated to Paris and London, where he could talk with Flaubert, Turgenev, and other novelists whom he admired. If Poe and Whitman could have lived among their peers in London or Paris, they might well have discovered that their artistic ideals were somewhat narrow and their critical standards not altogether adequate.

The quest for a national literary tradition is a comparatively modern phenomenon. It is, I think, largely the outgrowth of political nationalism in a Western Europe which since the Reformation has not had a common religion to give unity to its civilization. In the last two centuries nationalism, for good and all too frequently for evil, has been one of the most powerful of all ideologies. The Romantic movement in literature brought with it a new interest in the past and glorified the ideals of folk, "race," and nation. After Napoleon's armies had overrun Germany and Italy, intelligent patriots turned to the past searching for a national spirit, a "soul," in which Germans or Italians could find a strong unifying bond. In literature they rejected whatever was not to their purpose; they wanted a usable past. Literary quality was a secondary consideration.

The definition of a literary tradition—whether national or regional—can be in the nature of the case only a kind of majority report. It stresses only those elements in the older literature which at a particular time are felt to have value, to constitute a usable past. The literature of earlier centuries— except for the omnivorous literary historian—exists only in the minds of those who actually read it and find it significant.

The Americans, however, had no literary tradition except that of England, and this seemed unsuited to the needs of the new republic. So the question arose: What was to be the dominant theme, the central motif, of the great American literature yet to be written? Was it to be political democracy, or what James Truslow Adams has called "the American Dream"? Well-bred gentlemen, like Irving and Cooper, were not disposed to glorify the "divine average" or advocate the immediate emancipation of the Negro slaves. Emerson, who often denounced the American habit of imitating all things English, could write in his *Journals*: "I suppose the evil may be cured by this rank rabble party, the Jacksonism of the country, heedless of English and all literature." And yet Emerson, though he said that he preferred the principles of the Jacksonian Democrats, chose to go along with the Whig party, which—or so he thought—had the best men. Jacksonian Democracy was not to find its poet until 1855, when Walt Whitman brought out his thin little volume, *Leaves of Grass*.

Our early writers, although they believed that in some respects their country represented a higher form of civilization than the "effete" Old World, were not clear in their own minds as to what the genuine American ideal really was. They were not sure either what traits were national as distinguished from those which were English or merely provincial. The New England character had already taken shape, and it was easy enough to distinguish the Yankee from the southerner; but provincial ignorance and prejudice made it difficult to single out those traits which were indisputably American. There was as yet no American way of writing, no conception of an American literary language as distinguished from that of the mother land.

The first notable writer to emerge, Washington Irving, hardly answered the demand for a great American writer. He spent too many years in Europe, and he wrote too little about his own country. Yet *The Sketch Book* was enough to prove to some of Sydney Smith's skeptical countrymen that an American could write excellent prose. Dickens admired and imitated him, but *The Sketch Book* and *The Alhambra* were hardly the kind of book that Americans were demanding. Irving confided to his friend Henry Brevoort: "I seek only to blow a flute of accompaniment in the national concert, and leave others to play the fiddle & French Horn."

Irving, however, was not without love for the land of his birth. He wanted to give his own country—or more accurately the state of New York—"a colour of romance and tradition." On a visit to Abbotsford he noted a little enviously that Sir Walter Scott had "tied the charms of poetry on every river hill & grey rock [and] made the desart to blossom as the rose." So far as literary and legendary associations were concerned, most parts of the United States seemed still almost a desert. The new land was still, in the words of Robert Frost, "unstoried, artless, unenhanced." In his *Knickerbocker's History of New York*, as he explained in after years, Irving attempted "to embody the traditions of our city in an amusing form; to illustrate its local humors, customs, and peculiarities; to clothe home scenes and places and familiar names with those imaginative and whimsical associations so seldom met with in our country, but which live like charms and spells about the cities of the old world, binding the heart of the native inhabitant to his home." When he could find no suitable local legend, Irving would borrow or invent one. In "The Legend of Sleepy Hollow" and in "Rip Van Winkle," which is based on an old German legend, he threw a glamour of romance and tradition over the region in which he had grown up. He was our pioneer local colorist and a creator of legends of place still without a peer in our literature. Many Americans, however, would have liked him better if he had done for Massachusetts, Pennsylvania, Virginia, and South Carolina what he had done for New York. Irving's creative imagination was stirred mainly by European literature and legend. So far as American life was concerned, he was a regional rather than a national writer.

The appearance of Scott's *Waverley* in 1814 gave a new and perhaps unfortunate direction to the popular conception of a national literature. The vague demand became a specific call for a series of romances dealing with American history. The extraordinary popularity of Scott's novels set our young writers to exploring the brief American past. Following Cooper's lead in *The Spy* (1821), Hawthorne, Caruthers, Kennedy, Bird, and Simms began adapting Scott's methods with some success to what Carl Van Doren has called the "three matters of American romance": the Revolution, the frontier, and the era of colonization. The historical romancers made their countrymen more fully aware of the American past, and that was an essential part of the process of building up a national tradition. And in the Indian and the frontiersman, whom they painted against the impressive background of the primeval forest or the lonely prairie, our novelists revealed two character types to which no European literature could point a close parallel.

It was soon evident, however, that the American past was no such rich field for the historical romancer as those Old World backgrounds which Scott had exploited in *Rob Roy, Kenilworth, Quentin Durward*, and *The Talisman*. Miles Standish and Priscilla Mullins were not impressive figures when placed beside Richard Coeur-de-Lion and Queen Elizabeth. The story of Pocahontas and Captain John Smith was no such matter of romance as the great Arthurian cycle or the marvelous legend of Troy. The American past was plebeian and commonplace; it lacked the pomp and circumstance of the age of chivalry. How was one to write a great historical romance about a nation of traders or yeomen farmers—even "the embattled farmers" who had "fired the shot heard round the world"?

Cooper and Hawthorne, who treated the American past with greater distinction than our other novelists, both came at last to the melancholy conclusion that American life, not only in the past but in the present as well, was inferior material when compared with the best that Europe had to offer. Cooper could find in the American character few salient traits, and the Indian character, he thought, was lacking in variety. Hawthorne, who often lamented his inability to portray successfully the New England life of his own time, felt it necessary, in the preface to *The Marble Faun*, to explain to his oversensitive countrymen why he had placed the scene of his romance in Italy. "No author," he said, "without a trial, can conceive of the difficulty of writing a romance about a country where there is no shadow, no antiquity, no mystery, no picturesque and gloomy wrong, nor anything but a commonplace prosperity, in broad and simple daylight, as is happily the case with my dear native land."

In spite of the many obstacles that I have mentioned, the United States had by 1850 created something like a national literature. It had also—if we leave out some of the southern states—created a strong sentiment of nationalism, and this was in great measure a literary achievement. In the Old World the sentiment of nationality had in general preceded the establishment of the state, and hence the state rested upon a solid foundation in traditions already formed. In the United States the organization of the state came before there was a nation. To create a nation out of thirteen unhomogeneous recently freed British colonies, the traditions had to be provided and the sentiment of nationality kindled. The remarkable result achieved by 1850 was, as I have said, in great measure a literary achievement; and it was accomplished by a people supposed to have little interest in literature.

The search for the great American writer continued throughout the nineteenth century. As late as 1913 John Macy concluded the opening chapter of *The Spirit of American Literature*: "The American Spirit may be figured as petitioning the Muses for twelve novelists, ten poets, and eight dramatists, to be delivered at the earliest possible moment." The debate over the value of American life as literary material also continued down into the twentieth century. Emerson and Whitman were the most notable champions of what may be called literary Americanism. Henry James, on the other hand, early discovered that he could not write his best fiction either on American subjects or while living in America. Except for occasional visits to the land of his birth he spent the remainder of his life in Europe, and he died a British subject. In the twentieth century the availability of American life found notable champions in Van Wyck Brooks and Vernon L. Parrington. Yet two of the most influential poets and critics—Ezra Pound and T. S. Eliot—cared little or nothing for American life as literary material and with a few exceptions cared little for the literature of the country of their birth. Both settled in the Old World. Eliot became a British subject. Pound, while foolishly retaining his American citizenship, broadcast propaganda in wartime for the Fascist dictator of Italy. And yet there is in the work of James, Pound, and Eliot something that can only be called American.

It is too often said that *American* writing begins with Mark Twain. This is an error. W. H. Auden, who knows the literature of his native England as well as that of his adopted America, wrote in 1957: "From Bryant on there is scarcely one American poet whose work, if unsigned, would be mistaken for that of an Englishman." With Emerson, Thoreau, and Whitman in mind Auden wrote in another connection:

> The wish for an American literature . . . has nothing to do really, with politics or national conceit; it is a demand for honesty. All European literature so far has presupposed two things: a nature which is humanized, mythologized, usually friendly, and a human society in which most men stay where they were born and do not move about much. Neither of these presuppositions was valid for America, where nature was virgin, devoid of history, usually hostile; and society was fluid, its groupings always changing as men moved on somewhere else.

> *Have the elder races halted?*
> *Do they droop and end their lesson, wearied over*
> *there beyond the seas*
> *We take up the task eternal, and the burden and*
> *the lesson,*
> *Pioneers! O pioneers!*
>
> . . . . . . . . . . . . .
>
> *Minstrels latent on the prairies!*
> *(Shrouded bards of other lands, you may rest, you*
> *have done your work,)*
> *Soon I hear you coming warbling, soon you rise and*
> *tramp amid us,*
> *Pioneers! O pioneers!*
> Walt Whitman, "Pioneers! O Pioneers!"

## LITERARY PIONEERS

In the half-century that followed the American Revolution there emerged a large number of writers whose admirers greatly overrated them. William

Cullen Bryant reviewing Solyman Brown's versified *Essay on American Poetry* in the *North American Review* in July, 1818, took occasion to protest against "the swaggering and pompous pretensions of many" American poetasters. "We make," said he, "but a contemptible figure in the eyes of the world, and set ourselves up as objects of pity to our posterity, when we affect to rank the poets of our own country with those mighty masters of song who have flourished in Greece, Italy and Britain." Bryant did not care for the ambitious epic poems of the Connecticut Wits. Timothy Dwight's *The Conquest of Canaan,* he said, would "not secure immortality to its author." Bryant found Joel Barlow's *The Columbiad* a very dull poem, but the poet's "Hasty Pudding" seemed to him "a good specimen of mock-heroic poetry." One is surprised to discover that so good a critic as Bryant labeled as "a writer in verse of inferior note" Philip Freneau, who is now regarded as the best of Bryant's poetic predecessors. Perhaps Bryant, like other New Englanders, was prejudiced against Freneau as a friend of Jefferson and a defender of the French Revolution. Or perhaps Bryant had not read "The Wild Honeysuckle" and "The Indian Burying Ground."

In 1824 and 1825 John Neal, a native of Maine, contributed five articles on "American Writers" to *Blackwood's Magazine* which in 1937 the Duke University Press reprinted in book form with editorial apparatus supplied by Fred Lewis Pattee. In his *Wandering Recollections of a Somewhat Busy Life* Neal maintained that it was Sydney Smith's question "Who reads an American Book?" that induced him to go to England to see what an American writer might accomplish there. Professor Pattee, however, points out that Neal had a more urgent motive for leaving Baltimore, where he was living at that time. In his novel *Randolph* ( 1823 ) Neal had included a sketch of the lawyer and diplomat William Pinkney that gave offense to Pinkney's son, Edward Coote Pinkney. The irascible young poet challenged Neal to a duel. Apparently Baltimore became too hot for the novelist, and he left for England.

In *Randolph* Neal had written: "Our taste is bad. Our literature is corrupt and perverted; one class of our writers are all of the sleepy, milk and water school of Addison; another intemperate and florid." In his "American Writers" Neal commented on no less than 135 authors. Edward Coote Pinkney, however, is not among them. Since Neal had with him, he says, no books or notes to refresh his memory, it is not surprising that one finds in his alphabetical dictionary of American authors a good deal of misinformation. Perhaps it was the editor of *Blackwood's* who saw to it that there is so little boasting about the excellence of our writers. Few of Neal's critical estimates seem sound today. He knew that Irving was one of the very best of American writers. He liked *The Spy,* but Cooper seemed to him "a man of sober talent—nothing

more." Benjamin Franklin "was not a man of genius"; he had "only plain good sense—nothing more." Neal found Thomas Paine "unprincipled, coarse, and wicked." Finally, Neal had some praise for three writers who, he said, would not readily pass for English authors; they were James Kirke Paulding, Charles Brockden Brown, *and* John Neal.

A better book than Neal's is Samuel Lorenzo Knapp's *Lectures on American Literature* (1829), which may be called our first history of American literature. Knapp performed a useful service in compiling much pertinent information about a great many authors; but he lacked Bryant's critical faculty, and his book is not to be compared with Moses Coit Tyler's historical works which cover much of the same ground. Knapp thought better of the Connecticut Wits than Bryant had thought. *The Columbiad* "is, indeed," he said, "a great poem." He also failed to do justice to Philip Freneau; he did not even mention Washington Allston. Although he included the forgotten Robert Treat Paine, his only reference to Thomas Paine is "the scurrilities of Paine." He appreciated Franklin's achievements as a diplomat, statesman, and scientist, but he failed to recognize his greatness as a writer. The apex of American literary accomplishment in Knapp's view was *The Federalist*. That work, he said, "stands foremost among American literary productions, whether we consider the subject, the matter, or style of the work, or its usefulness in explaining the views of those learned statesmen who achieved the second part of our independence."

For specimens of the verses written by our early candidates for literary immortality we must turn to the anthologies. The best of these, according to Poe, was John Keese's *The Poetry of America* (New York, 1840). This, he rightly thought, is better than Bryant's more conventional *Selections from the American Poets*, which also appeared in New York in the same year. The most popular of the anthologies to precede Rufus W. Griswold's was the Reverend George B. Cheever's *The American Common-place Book of Poetry* (Boston, 1831), which by 1876 had gone through twenty-four printings and numerous revisions. "Mr. Cheever's book," said Poe, "did not belie its title, and was excessively 'Common-place.'" Cheever included none of Poe's poems even in the 1849 edition which appeared in the year of the poet's death.

The most voluminous of our early anthologies was Samuel Kettell's *Specimens of American Poetry, with Critical and Biographical Notes* (Boston, 1829) in three volumes. Kettell included specimens of no less than 189 poets. Professor Pattee drily remarks: "Much trash was thus saved from oblivion." Kettell regarded Bryant as the best of the American poets; Cheever's favorite was the elder Richard Henry Dana.

There were frequent complaints from the South that southern writers had been neglected by Knapp, Kettell, Cheever, Griswold, and other northern

critics and anthologists. It is true enough that some northern critics thought of the South as an intellectual Sahara, but a main reason for the apparent neglect was the difficulty, for an anthologist working in Boston or New York, of finding adequate materials on southern writers.

There were in the South (and elsewhere) readers who had no sympathy with the demand for an American national literature. In August, 1831, the *Southern Review* of Charleston published a belated review of the works of Knapp and Kettell written by Edward W. Johnston, a southern schoolmaster, the older brother of the Confederate general, Joseph E. Johnston. The reviewer resented the way in which Knapp and Kettell had exaggerated "the early glories of New England literature," but he made no counterclaim for the South. "We do . . . in the name of the good people of the planting States utterly disclaim the having even the humble part, which is assigned us, in a separate school of writers, dignified with the title of 'American.'" In June, 1845, Johnston returned to the subject of "American Letters" in an article in the *American Review: A Whig Journal.* He wondered if the advocates of a national literature had "any idea of what 'a literature' is." He thought so little of the literature of the United States that he described the times as one of the "eras of a corrupt and feeble literature, like that in the midst of which we now are." "Halleck, Longfellow, and Bryant," he said, "are certainly the pride of all American verse; yet who will venture to say that one of them comes to the height of Thompson [James Thomson of *The Seasons*], or Collins, or Gray, or Akenside?" Johnston made no mention of Emerson or Poe, whose "The Raven" had created a sensation when it appeared in the *American Review* in the preceding January.

A much better critic was Hugh Swinton Legaré, chief editor of the *Southern Review*, which had published Johnston's earlier article. In the same quarterly for May, 1828, Legaré pronounced the popular James Gates Percival, who had sojourned in Charleston, not "a man either of great genius or of profound sensibility." He saw in Percival's poems "nothing more than a certain tender and poetic pensiveness." Legaré was equally severe with the popular Charleston poet and essayist, William Crafts. He recognized the merits of Cooper, whom he had known in Italy, and he greeted Bryant's *Poems* (1832) as "upon the whole, the best collection of American poetry which we have ever seen." Of Bryant's diction he said: "It is simple and natural—there is no straining after effect, no meretricious glare, no affected point and brilliancy. It is clear and precise. . . ." Bryant indeed was "one whom the gods have made a poet."

Who were the best American writers? In its issue of January 26, 1828, the *New-York Mirror* carried a full-page engraving with portraits of nine

"Eminent Living American Poets." Among them were John Pierpont, Charles Sprague, James G. Brooks, and Samuel Woodworth, author of "The Old Oaken Bucket." The central figure was James G. Percival, whose inflated reputation was soon to be attacked by Hugh S. Legaré and later by James Russell Lowell. Of the nine "Eminent Living American Poets" the only ones whose names are remembered today are Bryant, Halleck, and Pinkney. Washington Irving was also included, not because of his youthful verses, but obviously because he was a New Yorker and the best-known living American writer. 1828

On October 9, 1830, the *New-York Mirror* came up with a new list of the best American poets: "When we have named Bryant and Halleck, Percival, Hillhouse, Dana and Sprague, with perhaps one or two others, we have named all whose works really do their country honour." The one new name is that of the Connecticut poetaster James A. Hillhouse. A far better poet was Edward Coote Pinkney, whose name appears only in the earlier list of "Eminent Living American Poets."

By 1830 it was generally thought that the three best American writers were Irving, Cooper, and Bryant. There were, as our literary historians remind us, other authors who seem somewhat more important now than they seemed to Knapp, Neal, Kettell, and George Pope Morris, who edited the *New-York Mirror*: Washington Allston, Thomas Paine, Charles Brockden Brown, Hugh Henry Brackenridge, Philip Freneau, and of course Benjamin Franklin, Jonathan Edwards, and William Byrd.

Irving, Cooper, Bryant, and their less-known contemporaries established something like an American literary tradition. They demonstrated that American life could be successfully treated in poetry and fiction, and they pointed the way for the greater writers who were soon to follow them: Hawthorne, Emerson, Thoreau, Poe, Melville, and Whitman. They also won some recognition from readers and critics in England and on the Continent. Thackeray honored Irving as "the first Ambassador whom the New World of Letters sent to the Old." Cooper lectured his countrymen too much, but the vogue of his Leather-Stocking Tales was enormous. Even before the series was complete, there were many in Europe, like Franz Schubert dying in Vienna, who were wishing that there were more of them to read. Bryant had no great vogue overseas, but his countrymen looked upon him as the Father of American Poetry.

*This country is not destined to be always behind in the race of literary glory.*

James Kirke Paulding, "National Literature," *Salmagundi*

*Their innocence of worldly wisdom led them to undue confidence in the excellence of human nature; the simplicity of their national past blinded them to the complexity of the days even now at hand, while the sod still lies light on their graves. We used to believe them heralds of the future; already we begin to perceive that they were rather chroniclers of times which shall be no more.*

Barrett Wendell, A *Literary History of America* (1900)

# *Chapter 2. The American Renaissance, 1830-1870*

By the middle of the century many of the authors who had been so hopefully eulogized in the 1820's were being replaced by writers of a younger generation eager to make places for themselves. Nevertheless Irving, Cooper, and Bryant managed to hold on to the positions they had won in the canon of the major American writers. In the *Democratic Review* for June, 1846, the New York critic William A. Jones noted that the United States had a number of "expert story-tellers," but he ranked as "genuine originals" only Irving, Dana, Hawthorne, Brown, Cooper, and Poe. In *The Pilot* Cooper, he thought, had written the best American novel, but still Jones found his novels "abounding in faults." In the same magazine for June, 1839, Park Benjamin had discussed "Recent American Poetry" and had ranked Bryant first and after him Fitz-Greene Halleck and Charles Sprague followed by George D. Prentice, N. P. Willis, Epes Sargent, R. H. Dana, Sr., and Georgia Hill.

In the *Southern Literary Messenger* in April, 1836, Edgar Allan Poe made it clear that he thought Drake and Halleck were much overrated. In a sketch of Halleck, published in *Godey's Lady's Book*, in July, 1846, he wrote: "Our principal poets are, perhaps, most frequently named in this order—Bryant, Halleck, Dana, Sprague, Longfellow, Willis, and so on—Halleck coming second in the series, but holding, in fact, a rank in the public opinion equal to that of Bryant."

That was the popular rating. "For my part," Poe continued, "I should like to have it thus—Longfellow, Bryant, Halleck, Willis, Sprague, Dana." He added that estimating poetic capacity rather than poems actually accomplished, there were three or four poets whom he would place immediately after Longfellow and about a dozen whom he would insert between Willis and Sprague. In Poe's opinion there was not one among our literary pioneers whose writings had not been overrated. On September 4, 1838, he wrote to Nathan G. Brooks: "Irving is much overrated, and a nice distinction might be drawn between his just and his surreptitious and adventitious reputation —between what is due to the pioneer solely, and what to the writer."

The forty years between 1830 and 1870 saw not only the publication of more great books by American writers than ever before but also a great expansion of the reading public and unfortunately a marked decline in the taste of a large proportion of the reading public. The six major writers of the period as we now see them are Emerson, Hawthorne, Thoreau, Poe, Melville, and Whitman. None of these, however, quickly won a place as the peer of Irving, Cooper, and Bryant; and it was many a long year before Thoreau, Whitman, and Melville were admitted to the canon of the great American writers. As we look back on this period, it seems to have been dominated by writers who lived in Massachusetts, which except for Bryant had produced no very important writer since the time of Franklin and Edwards.

> *In this conviction that the New England mind was the New World mind, that New England literature was not a sectional utterance but a national archetype, the writers of the section consistently foresaw the alignment of the rest of the country with their culture.*
> Benjamin Spencer, *The Quest for Nationality*

## THE NEW ENGLAND LITERARY CANON

By 1865 New England had created the canon of the great American writers, but few writers outside of New England were admitted to it. The canon included Bryant, who had written his best-known poems while still living in western Massachusetts. It also included Irving and Cooper in spite of their occasional satiric treatment of the migrating Yankees who were rapidly making Upstate New York an extension of New England. The critics, anthologists, and literary historians of New England, however, could make no place for Poe, Melville, Whitman, or even for that eccentric Yankee, Henry David Thoreau. The canon included Emerson and Hawthorne and the schoolroom poets: Bryant, Longfellow, Holmes, Whittier, and Lowell. It also included on its outer fringes two literary historians: John Lothrop Motley and William Hickling Prescott, but apparently not Francis Parkman, now generally regarded as the greatest of the three.

The New England literary tradition was, as Poe, Simms, and Henry James clearly saw, a provincial rather than a national tradition. Nevertheless, the New Englanders came close to imposing it upon the rest of the country as a genuinely national tradition. Its success was due in large part to its impassioned idealism and its undoubted literary power. Emerson, Hawthorne, Thoreau, and Longfellow had no peers among writers in other sections except Poe, Melville, and Whitman; and these three were long unacceptable not only in New England but in other parts of the nation as well.

Its Puritan inheritance and its geographical isolation gave New England a unity of feeling which even the southern states lacked until after 1850. New England had a remarkably fine educational and cultural tradition. Most of its writers had attended Harvard College, and they lived in or near Boston, Cambridge, and Concord. In Boston the social standing of a writer was much higher than it was in New York, Philadelphia, or Charleston; and in no other American city was there so keen an interest in culture or ideas.

The literature of New England was in large part written by ministers or ex-ministers or by the sons of ministers, by teachers, lecturers, and reformers promoting one or another of the numerous causes obnoxious to the conservative South and to many persons in other sections as well. That literature was not greatly concerned with art, although it had a fine artist in Hawthorne and distinguished prose writers in Emerson and Thoreau. The New England writers had little patience with criticism on artistic grounds. Poe constantly chided them for their ingrained didacticism, but his criticism seemed to them merely ill-natured fault-finding. Howells, who knew and loved them, wrote in his *Literary Friends and Acquaintance* (1900): "They or their fathers had broken away from orthodoxy in the great schism at the beginning of the century, but, as if their heterodoxy were conscience-stricken, they still helplessly pointed the moral in all they did; some pointed it more directly, some less directly; but they all pointed it."

The New England writers sought each in his own fashion to make righteousness and the will of God prevail. To their southern and western readers it sometimes seemed that they were trying to make over on a Yankee model sections of the country which in actuality they knew very little about. The Abolitionists and the Transcendentalists were in fact singularly blind to the dangers of the industrial revolution then sweeping over southern New England. They were much more concerned with the sins of the distant southern states than they were with the exploitation of workers and children in their own shipyards and factories and in the Irish slums in the heart of Boston.

In the anthologies of Kettell, Cheever, and Griswold we have seen the beginnings of the New England literary canon, but other writers of that region also had a hand in the process. In "The Hall of Fantasy," which was first printed in Lowell's magazine, the *Pioneer*, in February, 1843, Hawthorne represented a number of American authors (and other persons) as attending a masked ball. Among them the narrator recognized "Mr. Rufus Griswold, with pencil and memorandum-book, busily noting down the names of all the poets and poetesses there, and likewise of some, whom nobody but himself had suspected of being there." The dig at Griswold is all very well, but how does it happen that the poets whom Hawthorne named had nearly all appeared in *The Poets and Poetry of America*, published the preceding year? Here are the authors whom Hawthorne listed with a word or more of comment about each: Bronson Alcott, Washington Allston, Orestes Brownson, Bryant, Cooper, Richard Henry Dana, Sr., Emerson, Abigail Folsom, Griswold, Halleck, George Hillard, Holmes, Irving, Longfellow, Lowell, John Neal, Charles Newcomb, John O'Sullivan, James G. Percival, John Pierpont, Poe, Epes Sargent, Catharine Maria Sedgwick, Charles Sprague, Henry T. Tuckerman, Jones Very, and N. P. Willis. Apparently Hawthorne regarded Irving and Longfellow as our best writers, but he referred to Lowell as "the poet of the generation that now enters upon the stage." Hawthorne was wise enough three years later to omit the names of all these authors when he reprinted "The Hall of Fantasy" in *Mosses from an Old Manse*.

In 1854 Hawthorne wrote from England to his publisher that Monckton Milnes had asked him to send him "half a dozen good American books, which he [had] never read or heard of before." Hawthorne explained:

> For the honor of my country, I should like to do it, but can think of only three which would be likely to come under his description—viz., "Walden," "Passion Flowers," and "Up-Country Letters." Possibly Mrs. Mowatt's "Autobiography" might make a fourth; and Thoreau's former volume a fifth. You understand that these books must be not merely good, but must be original, with American characteristics, and not generally known in England. . . . Whittier's book is poor stuff. I like the man, but have no high opinion either of his poetry or prose. Send Lowell's "Biglow Papers." He is very little known in England, and I take that to be the best thing he has written.

In Lowell's hastily written *jeu d'esprit*, *A Fable for Critics* (1848), the New England canon appears in the form which it continued to maintain down to the end of the nineteenth century. Lowell included Irving and Cooper. He even included Poe, now living in New York, but damned him with faint praise and lectured him for charging Longfellow with plagiarism. About half the writers he mentioned lived in the neighborhood of Boston. He included no writer who lived south of New York or west of the Hudson River. Here is Lowell's list: Bronson Alcott, Charles F. Briggs, Orestes Brownson, Bryant, Lydia Maria Child, Cooper, the elder Richard Henry Dana, Emerson, Margaret Fuller, Griswold, Hawthorne, Holmes, Sylvester Judd, Neal, Theodore Parker, Poe, Whittier, and Lowell himself. Without naming them he referred to Thoreau and Ellery Channing as imitators of Emerson. He brought in Margaret Fuller only to ridicule her as "Miranda."

A Fable for Critics is not one of Lowell's best poems. In later life the only part he thought well of was the apostrophe to the Bay State, and that passage has no organic connection with the rest of the poem. But Lowell was a critic as well as a poet, and A Fable contains some of the best literary criticism that any American author has ever written about his own contemporaries. It is better than Amy Lowell's A Critical Fable. With the exception of Thoreau, who had not yet published a book, Lowell singled out the best of the New England writers and praised them for qualities that they actually possessed. Nor did he give unalloyed praise to even the greatest: Emerson and Hawthorne. He later characterized Hawthorne as "the rarest creative imagination of the century." Lowell was one of the first to see that Whittier was no mere antislavery propagandist but a genuine poet. Still, he noted, Whittier sometimes mistook simple excitement for poetic inspiration.

The important American writers whom Lowell in later years failed to rate at their true value were not New Englanders. Among them were Whitman, Melville, and Mark Twain. He admired the work of his friend and protégé, William Dean Howells, but he did not share Howells's enthusiasm for realism in fiction, and he was—like most of his contemporaries—slow to recognize the merits of writers who emerged after the Civil War. Yet he admired the best of Henry James's early novels.

Lowell's reputation as poet and as critic remained high throughout the nineteenth century. In 1896 he was the chief representative of literature in Woodrow Wilson's "Calendar of Great Americans"; and he was elected to the Hall of Fame (in 1905) as soon as he was eligible. Since about 1920, however, critics of all varieties have found Lowell's criticism conventional and his once-famous odes rhetoric rather than poetry. As long ago as 1865, Emerson said to James T. Fields: "I told Lowell that his humorous poems gave me great pleasure; they were worth all his serious poetry. He did not take it very well, but muttered, 'The Washers of the Shroud,' and walked away." Lowell, however, was not always as sure of himself as he seemed to Thoreau and

Whitman. He wrote to Fields in a letter dated December 21, 1868: "As I told Howells once, the day will come when a wiser generation will drive all its literary men into a corner and make a *battue* of the whole lot." A few later critics, like Norman Foerster and Bernard De Voto, have thought better of Lowell's critical essays. Perhaps after all, however, Lowell was at his best as Ambassador at the Court of St. James's.

It was not until the 1860's that the New England canon was generally accepted in New York. On November 15, 1865, the New York *Nation* gave its rating of living American poets in a review of the Second Series of Lowell's *The Biglow Papers*. That review was written by Wendell Phillips Garrison, son of the editor of the *Liberator*.

> Without doubt, the four living American poets who fill the highest places are Emerson, Bryant, Longfellow, and Lowell. Dr. Holmes, of course, has to be mentioned when talk is made of American poetic literature, and so have Mr. Bayard Taylor, Mr. [Thomas Buchanan] Read, Mr. [Edmund Clarence] Stedman, and Mr. [Thomas Bailey] Aldrich. Whittier is in a class above these; [Henry Howard] Brownell is to be ranked above most of them; and there are Wilson [Forceythe Willson] and Howells, whose names, to be sure, are yet to be made, but who must not be omitted. For Emerson, as a philosopher, no one anticipates long remembrance; but, as a poet, it will indeed be long before his sweet and deep thoughts are let sink into forgetfulness. Bryant has written some beautiful and some eloquent poetry; not much of it is of a fashion that soon passes away—it is enduring, like an un-visited mountain. Longfellow, most admired of all, has written very many very pretty poems. As for Lowell, we do not propose to prove here (what we nevertheless hold to be not difficult of proof) that of all these writers he may be rated, all things considered, as the first.

It will be noted that the passage quoted above contains no reference to Whitman, Melville, Thoreau, or Poe.

In the publishing house of Ticknor and Fields, which in 1859 took over the *Atlantic Monthly*, the New England writers had an organization which appreciated the high quality of their writings and knew how to market them efficiently. Ticknor and Fields and their successors, the Houghton Mifflin Company, had a large part in the creation and the perpetuation of the New England literary canon. On their lists they had as many great American books as all of the leading New York and Philadelphia publishers put to-gether, and they played them up as such throughout the North, the West, and eventually in the South as well. Howells, who as a young man read their books in Ohio, once remarked: "Ticknor and Fields . . . were literary publishers in a sense such as the business world has known nowhere else before or since." The tribute is probably deserved, but Howells was a poor prophet when he went on to say: "Their imprint was a warrant of quality to the reader, and of immortality to the author." Alas! the Ticknor and Fields imprint brought no immortality to many on its list, including those southern poets, Henry Timrod and Paul Hamilton Hayne, who before the Civil War paid the house to bring out their poems.

The Houghton Mifflin Company, which held copyrights on most of the books of the popular New England writers, in 1883 launched its Riverside Literature series for schools with Longfellow's most popular narrative poem, *Evangeline*. As late as 1917 the series was selling at the rate of a million copies a year.

In the 1870's the Houghton Mifflin Company had initiated its notable American Men of Letters series of biographies under the general editorship of Charles Dudley Warner. The publishers advertised it as "Collectively, . . . a biographical history of American Literature," but the authors were much the same as those mentioned in Lowell's *A Fable for Critics*; and in its earlier years at least it might more appropriately have been called the New York–New England Men of Letters series. The authors stressed were those whom Fred Lewis Pattee later called the Big Ten, the authors who in the 1890's were always emphasized in courses in American literature: Irving, Cooper, Poe, Bryant, Emerson, Hawthorne, Longfellow, Whittier, Holmes, and Lowell. It was not until 1885, however, that the series included George E. Woodberry's able if somewhat unsympathetic life of Poe. In 1896 Albert H. Smyth's *Bayard Taylor* was finally added to represent Pennsylvania. Bliss Perry's *Walt Whitman* (1906) was one of the last books to be added to a series which also included those minor New England writers, N. P. Willis, George Ripley, Margaret Fuller, George William Curtis, and Thomas Bailey Aldrich. W. P. Trent's life of Simms, which angered the Charlestonians, had been published in 1892. This assignment had first been offered to George W. Cable. Obviously the publishers wanted a Simms biography written by a thoroughly reconstructed southerner. In 1905 Edwin Mims's *Sidney Lanier* was added as the sole representative of the New South. The poet had been dead for a quarter of a century. Among the authors represented in the new American Men of Letters series published by William Sloane Associates but not in the old are: Jonathan Edwards, Jefferson, Thoreau, Melville, Lincoln, William and Henry James, Parkman, Prescott, Mark Twain, and Emily Dickinson. It includes Emerson, Hawthorne, Bryant, and Holmes, who were in the old series, but not Whittier, Margaret Fuller, Longfellow, Lowell, or Irving.

# THE MIDDLE ATLANTIC STATES

Those older literary capitals, Philadelphia and New York, were slow to accept the New England hegemony and yield precedence to Boston. Philadelphia and New York, by virtue of their geographical position and their strong commercial ties with the southern and western states, were less provincial in their outlook. Upstate New Yorkers, especially those of Dutch descent, had no great love for the migratory Yankees who came into their state. And in New York City the literary journalists known as "Young America" were often highly critical of the New England writers. In the *Democratic Review* for May and October, 1847, William A. Jones, one of the ablest of the "Young America" critics, discussed the "New Poetry of New-England." His judgment of Emerson is curiously contradictory. While he rated Emerson as "the most original, not only of American poets, but of living writers," Jones felt compelled to add: "We cannot say that he is a great poet; that title will somehow not apply." No, he concluded, Emerson was not the great poet that Americans were looking for. That poet, he said, would not be born in New England.

In Philadelphia and New York literature was regarded less as an instrument of reform than as a means of entertainment; and New England-born lovers of the lighter varieties of literature, Joseph Dennie, N. P. Willis, and Fitz-Greene Halleck, found themselves more at home in Philadelphia and New York than they would have been in Boston or New Haven.

After a visit to Boston Poe wrote in the *Broadway Journal* for August 23, 1845, that he was surprised by the Bostonians' "ignorance of Knickerbocker authors." "The evil," he continued, "would in part be remedied, if New York were regarded as it should be, as the London of America—and if all literary enterprises were here carried into effect." New York, he noted, had better facilities for distributing books "and as a centre of opinion, it is the metropolis of the country." Such a pronouncement did not make the Bostonians love Poe any better.

The great New Englanders were not at home in New York. Emerson, in March, 1842, after a talk with Catharine Maria Sedgwick, a native of Massachusetts, who was then living in New York, wrote to his wife: "I found or fancied that there were lines of latitude & longitude which sever the mind of New York as well as the City from New England. All our questions seem new to them who live here."

The Bostonians' irritation at the cultural and literary pretensions of New

York was emphatically expressed in "Astraea: The Balance of Illusions," a poem which Oliver Wendell Holmes read before the Yale chapter of the Phi Beta Kappa Society on August 14, 1850. He first noted the provincial bias of American literary journalists in general:

> The pseudo-critic-editorial race
> Owns no allegiance but the law of place;
> Each of his region sticks through thick and thin,
> Stiff as a beetle spiked upon a pin.

Dr. Holmes next mildly ridiculed the Boston critic who

> Talks as if Nature kept her choicest smiles
> Within the radius of a dozen miles,
> And nations waited till his next Review
> Had made it plain what Providence must do.

Holmes reserved his hardest blows for the New York literati in a passage which he never reprinted in any volume of his poems:

> He cry *"provincial"* with imperious brow!
> The half-bred rogue, that groomed his mother's cow!
> Fed on coarse tubers and Æolian beans
> Till clownish manhood crept among his teens,
> When, after washing and unheard of pains
> To lard with phrases his refractory brains,
> A third-rate college licked him into shape,
> Not of the scholar, but the scholar's ape!

Rapidly growing New York City attracted writers as well as businessmen looking for larger opportunities. Halleck, Willis, and Bryant were among the first New England authors to make places for themselves there. They were soon to be followed by many more; among them, Richard Henry Stoddard, George Ripley, Horace Greeley, Margaret Fuller, Rufus W. Griswold, Lydia Maria Child, Elizabeth Oakes Smith, Seba Smith, George W. Curtis, Edmund Clarence Stedman, Thomas Bailey Aldrich, and in later years George E. Woodberry, William Crary Brownell, and many others. Of the thirty-eight writers whom Poe in 1846 discussed in "The Literati of New York City" exactly one-half were natives of New England. Among New Englanders who obtained influential positions on New York magazines and newspapers were Bryant, Willis, Curtis, Greeley, Freeman Hunt, William Trotter Porter, Charles F. Briggs, Josiah Gilbert Holland, Charles Dudley Warner, and Henry Mills Alden, to name only a few of the better-known literary journalists.

By 1865 it appeared that in cultural matters the Middle Atlantic and the Middle Western states were in a fair way to become an extension of New England. Nevertheless some of the writers from Pennsylvania and New York regarded the *North American Review* and the *Atlantic Monthly* as sectional organs rather than national literary magazines. Bayard Taylor of Pennsylvania and Edmund Clarence Stedman living in New York were as irritated by the *Atlantic's* editorial policies under Lowell, Fields, and Howells as were southern poets like Paul Hamilton Hayne and Sidney Lanier. An extreme expression of their feeling is found in a letter which in April, 1867, the Philadelphia poet and dramatist George Henry Boker wrote to Hayne: "According to the Yankee creed, Longfellow, Lowell, Holmes, Emerson and Whittier are the only poets in America, and also the only poets that New England will permit to exist."

Outsiders like Boker and Taylor, Simms and Poe often thought of the New England "school" as a mutual admiration society that ignored as "barbarians" those who lived west of the Hudson and south of New York City. Yet any one who studies the New England writers soon discovers that they were far from being a mutual admiration society. They were in fact for the most part simply unconscious of any discrimination against writers from other sections. As seen from the latitude of Boston, New York and Philadelphia were visible low on the western horizon, but Baltimore, Richmond, and Charleston were simply invisible.

With the opening of the Erie Canal in 1825 and the extension of railroads westward from Boston and New York, New Englanders flocked to the Middle West. Emerson and Lowell, lecturing in western lyceums, discovered a region and a people that hitherto had hardly existed for them. At the same time the Boston publishers were developing better methods of distributing books by the New England writers. By the middle of the century there were in the Middle West thousands of New Englanders. Everywhere they went they were founding academies, colleges, lyceums, newspapers, and magazines; and they were eager to see and hear the New England writers whose books they had read.

In 1860 William Dean Howells made the literary pilgrimage from Ohio to New England that he describes so wistfully in his *Literary Friends and Acquaintance* (1900). In his *Years of My Youth* (1916) Howells mentioned an evening he spent with the Garfield family back in Ohio after he had lived for some years in Cambridge. He was speaking of the New England poets whom he knew when Garfield interrupted him. "Just a minute!" he said.

> He ran down into the grassy space first to one fence and then to the other at the sides, and waved a wild arm of invitation to the neighbours who were also sitting on their back porches. "Come over here!" he shouted. "He's talking about Holmes, and Longfellow, and Lowell, and Whittier!" And at his bidding, dim forms began to mount the fences

and followed him up to his verandah. "Now go on!" he called to me, when we were all seated, and I went on, while the whippoorwills whirred and whistled round, and the hours drew toward midnight.

The westerners' devotion to the New England writers was still strong in 1884 when Hamlin Garland, who had grown up in Wisconsin, went to Boston because in his mind that was still the literary capital of America.

## THE SOUTH

The half century that followed the founding of Garrison's *Liberator* in Boston in 1831 was a period of controversy, armed conflict, and Reconstruction; and it was not until after 1880 that the South was willing to accept the New England canon of the great American writers.* Hawthorne, who was no reformer, had admirers among southern readers, and they liked the poems of Bryant and Longfellow in spite of their antislavery writings. Emerson, however, spoke a language which southern readers, unfamiliar with his Unitarian-Transcendentalist background, found difficult to understand. Yet even before he began making antislavery speeches, they felt that his philosophy was hostile to their way of life. There were not many bookstores in southern towns, and many of them did not carry the works of writers who openly condemned slavery. The New England writers did not come to the South to lecture, as they did in the Middle West. The South, which in cultural matters occupied a semicolonial status, was now moving half consciously toward a separate nationality and was belatedly demanding a regional literature which would defend its way of life.

Southern hostility toward the North was directed particularly at New England. Southerners came to see that the important New England writers had accepted the extreme views of Garrison and Phillips, who hated not only slavery but the slaveholders as well. In an excellent study, *The South in Northern Eyes, 1831–1861* (1958), Dr. Howard R. Floan summed up the attitude of the New England writers: "They caricatured both slaveholder and slave, without really knowing either," and again: "The Southerner was a whip-bearing villain." He concluded:

* I have discussed at much greater length the cultural and literary relations between North and South in *The South in American Literature, 1607–1900* (1954); in "Literary Nationalism in the Old South," *American Studies in Honor of William Kenneth Boyd*, ed. D. K. Jackson (1940), pp. 175–220; and in "Ralph Waldo Emerson and the South" in my *South and Southwest* (1965).

There can be little doubt that the image projected by the New England group was more vivid, less complex, and therefore more acceptable to the popular mind [in the North than that found in such New York writers as Bryant, Melville, and Whitman]. It has endured through the years with surprising tenacity. One can scarcely measure the influence of the image upon successive generations of Northerners in their view of the antebellum South.

In an address occasioned by Preston Brooks's attack on Senator Charles Sumner, Emerson said on May 19, 1856: "I do not see how a barbarous community and a civilized community can constitute one state." In the South, he said, "life is a fever, man is an animal, given to pleasure, frivolous, irritable, spending his days in hunting and practicing with deadly weapons to defend himself against his slaves and against his companions brought up in the same idle and dangerous way." In the free states, he said, life was "adorned with education, with skilful labor, with arts, with long prospective interests, with sacred family ties, with honor and justice." Lowell writing in the *North American Review* in October, 1886, gave his estimate of the culture of the antebellum South: "There were no public libraries, no colleges worthy of the name; there was no art, no science,—still worse, no literature but Simms's: there was no desire for them."

In reviewing Lowell's *A Fable for Critics* in the *Southern Quarterly Review* for October, 1849, Simms said: "This critic . . . expends all his praise upon the children of the East. He finds no others in the country, or, if he does, he dismisses them with a scornful complacency. . . ." The southern reaction to *A Fable for Critics* is apparent in the review that Poe published in the *Southern Literary Messenger* in March of the same year:

It is a fashion among Mr. Lowell's set to affect a belief that there is *no such thing* as Southern Literature. Northerners—people who have really nothing to speak of as men of letters,—are cited by the dozen, and lauded by this candid critic without stint, while Legaré, Simms, Longstreet, and others of equal note are passed by in contemptuous silence. Mr. L. cannot carry his frail honesty of opinion even so far South as New York. All whom he praises are Bostonians. Other writers are barbarians, and satirized accordingly—if mentioned at all.

It must not be imagined that all southerners condemned indiscriminately the northern writers who attacked slavery. As late as January, 1860, John R. Thompson wrote in the *Southern Literary Messenger* that "the sins of Bryant, the editor, have not deadened us to the beauties of Bryant, the poet." Even in the third year of the Civil War a minor southern writer protested against indiscriminate condemnation of northern writers. James Dabney McCabe, Jr., wrote in the *Magnolia Weekly* for September 12, 1863:

We may hold the writer an enemy, but his writings should be our friends. Because Irving was a Yankee, he is not the less fascinating, and the fact that Holmes is an Abolitionist does not diminish his wittiness. We cannot, if we would, withdraw our admiration from that which is great, and it is unjust to do so, even though it be the work of an enemy.

In the same year Whittier, who hated slavery but (he thought) not slaveholders, surprised his friends Emerson, Holmes, and Whipple by "enthusiastic praise" of one or two of Henry Timrod's wartime poems that he had seen.

The South as a whole had marked reservations about certain northern writers as late as the 1880's. The withdrawal of Union troops from the South in 1877 was followed by a movement toward reconciliation on both sides. The use of northern textbooks with writings by the New England authors helped to familiarize a younger generation with poems and stories already well-known in the North. By the time Emerson gave an address in Charlottesville, Virginia, in 1876 it was evident that he had many southern admirers. Emerson's daughter Ellen, who had accompanied him on his visit to Virginia, noted that on their way home there were many southerners on the train—going to the Centennial Exhibition in Philadelphia—who when they learned that Emerson was on the train asked to be introduced to him and brought their children to see him. She meanwhile, she wrote, had "the fun . . . of seeing all the world burn incense to Father [which] was never so great as now, just because it is the South. . . . To see people come & stand before him in the aisle of the cars & gaze at him, and bring their children & ask him to shake hands with them. People from Tennessee, Alabama, Texas. . . ." It was in 1876 also that Lanier, who wrote the centennial cantata for the Exhibition, discovered Emerson and soon afterwards wrote his best poem, "The Marshes of Glynn."

## RESIDUUM

In the 1920's there was a violent revolt amongst the young intellectuals against the literary dominance of New England. The result was a marked downgrading of the schoolroom poets: Bryant, Holmes, Lowell, Longfellow, and Whittier. Yet Emerson and Hawthorne held their own, and Thoreau and Emily Dickinson were finally given places with them as major literary figures.

It is not always remembered that even in the twentieth century New England has contributed to the national literature more than its numerical proportion of important writers. Much of the best of the new poetry came from Frost and Robinson, Amy Lowell and Edna St. Vincent Millay. To this number one might add important writers like T. S. Eliot who were born in other states and educated in New England and those who, like Wallace Stevens, have chosen to live and write in that region. There is no exaggeration in George F. Whicher's pronouncement in the introduction to his edition of *Poetry of the New England Renaissance* (1950):

> In spite of all that may be alleged in depreciation of puritanism, Victorian sentiment, and the genteel tradition, poetry by New England writers remains one of the chief glories of American literature. From Anne Bradstreet and Edward Taylor in the seventeenth century to Edwin Arlington Robinson and Robert Frost in the twentieth, the nation's singing strength has been concentrated mainly in the northeastern corner.

In "The Search for a Usable Past" (*American Heritage*, February, 1965) the distinguished historian Henry Steele Commager maintained that our image of the American past was largely created by New England writers who wrote before the Civil War. "These," he said, "were the Founding Fathers of American literary nationalism, and their achievement was scarcely less remarkable than that of the Founding Fathers of political nationalism." He continued:

> This image of the past which the literary Founding Fathers created and imposed upon Americans was very largely a New England image, and much that was distinctive about American nationalism was to be conditioned by this circumstance. It meant that Americans on Iowa prairies or the plains of Texas would sing "*I love thy rocks and rills, thy woods and templed hills*" with no sense of incongruity; that Plymouth would supplant Jamestown as the birthplace of America; that Thanksgiving Day would be a New England holiday; that Paul Revere would be the winged horseman of American history and Concord Bridge the American equivalent of the Rubicon; that Boston's Statehouse would vindicate its claim—or Holmes'—to be the "hub of the solar system." If all this was hard on the South, southerners had only themselves to blame for their indifference to their own men of letters. The most familiar of southern symbols came from the North: Harriet Beecher Stowe of New England gave us Uncle Tom and Little Eva and Topsy and Eliza, while it was Stephen Foster of Pittsburgh who sentimentalized the Old South, and even "Dixie" had northern origins.

Commager might have added that to the disgust of many an old-fashioned southerner the word "Yankee" all over the world came at last to be regarded as synonymous with "American."

*"Why don't you make your magazine what it ought to be?"*
*we once asked of a well-known editor. "Because," he replied,*
*"if we did, we should lose four-fifths of our circulation."*
Francis Parkman, "The Tale of the 'Ripe Scholar' "

## THE DECLINE IN LITERARY TASTE

In 1843 when Robert Carter and James Russell Lowell founded the *Pioneer*, Lowell declared in their prospectus that their purpose was

> to furnish the intelligent and reflecting portion of the Reading Public
> with a rational substitute for the enormous quantity of the thrice-
> diluted trash, in the shape of namby-pamby love tales and sketches,
> which is monthly poured out to them by many of our popular maga-
> zines—and to offer, instead thereof, a healthy and manly Periodical
> Literature, whose perusal will not necessarily involve a loss of time
> and a deterioration of every moral and intellectual faculty.

The *Pioneer* expired after publishing only three numbers. Poe, whose opinion of namby-pamby love tales was the same as Lowell's, wanted a magazine of his own in which, as he wrote to Philip Pendleton Cooke on August 9, 1846, "the men of genius [might] fight their battles; upon some terms of equality with those dunces, the men of talent."

The situation grew worse in the "feminine fifties." When W. D. Ticknor of Ticknor and Fields suggested to Hawthorne that it was time for him to bring out another book, Hawthorne replied, January 19, 1855: "America is now wholly given over to a d——d mob of scribbling women, and I should have no chance of success while the public taste is occupied with their trash—and should be ashamed of myself if I did succeed." "What," he asked, "is the mystery of these innumerable editions of the 'Lamplighter' [by Maria Cummins] and other books neither better nor worse?—worse they could not be, and better they need not be when they sell by the 100,000. . . ." The situation was no better in 1879 when Helen Hunt Jackson wrote to Moncure Daniel Conway that he had much better remain in London than return to the United States. In American "financial circles," she said, men looked upon literature as "an uncommonly poor way of making a living. If they had to take their choice between being Mrs. Southworth and Hawthorne they would be Mrs. S.,—unhesitatingly; she has written fifty-nine novels and made a fortune,— *that* is worth while."

What impressed Poe's biographer, George E. Woodberry, about literary New York of the 1840's was:

the mean literary poverty of the time, its atmosphere of impecuniosity, of little pay for the best work, of a log-rolling and subsidized criticism and feeble product, its environment of gossip and scandal, its deficient integrity, its undeniable vulgarity, its Grub-Street and Dunciad populace with the disadvantages of a large female immigration into these purlieus. . . . If oblivion could have been the lot of such literary mortality as is here disclosed, it would have been nothing to be sorry for.

In the New York of the thirties, forties, and fifties, one could hardly expect any general recognition of the talents of Poe or Melville or Whitman.

The great writers of the American renaissance found it difficult or impossible to make a living by what they wrote. Emerson took to the lecture platform. Longfellow, Holmes, and Lowell taught at Harvard. Hawthorne and Melville worked in customs houses. Lowell and Hawthorne held diplomatic appointments in Europe. Poe earned a scanty living by reviewing books and editing magazines. Whitman worked on various newspapers and later held a minor government post in Washington. Thoreau was a surveyor and handy man around Concord. Longfellow eventually found his writing profitable, but even he was less popular than N. P. Willis or Mrs. Sigourney.

In a study of "Taste in the Annuals," published in *American Literature* in November, 1942, Bradford A. Booth listed the number of contributions to the annuals of those American writers who had as many as 20 separate items. Those with more than 70 items were: Lydia H. Sigourney, 225; Hannah F. Gould, 153; Emma C. Embury, 128; Elizabeth Oakes Smith, 98; Nathaniel P. Willis, 94; Mrs. S. C. Egerton Mayo, 92; Catherine M. Sawyer, 90; Reynell Coates, 88; Mrs. E. F. Ellet, 80; Charles West Thomson, 73; Sarah Josepha Hale, 72. Of the American writers who are best known today Bryant had 61 items; Longfellow, 46; Hawthorne, 33; Simms, 29; Emerson, 25; Holmes and Lowell, 24 each. The popular English poetess Mrs. Felicia Dorothea Hemans had a total of 79. Professor Booth was moved to remark: "Her influence was probably the most devastating in American literature."

Except for their extraordinary vogue the subliterary books of the period were no new phenomenon, but they served greatly to confuse the literary taste of the many new members of the reading public. It is not possible to draw a sharp line separating the novels of Cooper, Hawthorne, and Mark Twain, which belong to the domain of literature, from the novels of Joseph Holt Ingraham and Augusta Jane Evans, which are not literature in any strict definition of the word. A short time after Hawthorne had written the letter to Ticknor from which I have quoted he was praising "Fanny Fern's" *Ruth Hall*. In many of the best nineteenth-century novels, in England as well as in America, one finds the same sentimental, didactic, sensational, "ideal" traits that are so conspicuous in subliterary fiction of the century. We find the same confusion of critical standards and inferior literary taste in the work of critics, anthologists, literary historians, and teachers of literature in schools and colleges. The same confusion will appear also in most of the critical polls sponsored by the *Critic* and other periodicals in the 1880's and 1890's.

And yet even though one cannot draw a sharp dividing line between what is literature and what is merely subliterary, it is to be noted that as we approach our own time more and more of our best authors write primarily for a small and sophisticated circle of readers. It was only the few who appreciated the early poems of Walt Whitman and the later novels of Henry James. In our own time the process has gone so far that most of our poets have virtually lost their audience.

> *What a curious creature Griswold is! He seems to be a kind*
> *of naturalist whose subjects are authors, whose memory is a*
> *perfect fauna of all flying and creeping things that feed on*
> *ink.*
>
> Oliver Wendell Holmes to James T. Fields quoted
> in Joy Bayless, *Rufus Wilmot Griswold*

## RUFUS W. GRISWOLD AND HIS ANTHOLOGIES

In his *Manual of American Literature* (1872) Professor John S. Hart of Princeton thus accurately characterized the most popular of our nineteenth-century anthologists:

> RUFUS WILMOT GRISWOLD, D.D., 1815–1857, without having much
> native talent, with little scholarship, and with less either of taste or
> judgment in literary matters, yet by persevering industry and by skill
> in availing himself of the help of others, not only gained distinction
> for himself, but did important service in the cause of American letters.

A native of Vermont, Griswold was a preacher and magazine editor as well as the compiler of many books. No one seems to know where or how he got the D.D. degree that appears on his title pages. The successive editions of his anthologies are a good index to the changing literary fashions of the mid-nineteenth century. Like his readers, he was slow to recognize the greatness of the newer writers. He was slow also to realize the lack of intrinsic merit in many of the literary pioneers.

The most popular of his anthologies were *The Poets and Poetry of America* (1842) and *The Prose Writers of America* (1847). By 1855 the former had gone into its sixteenth edition. He dedicated this book to the painter-poet Washington Allston, whose poems he rightly felt had not received their due from earlier anthologists. The frontispiece carried engravings of five poets whom he evidently regarded as among the very best: Bryant, Halleck, Longfellow, Dana, and Sprague. He represented Sprague by 12 poems, Brainard by 18, and Percival by 20. For his friend Charles Fenno Hoffman, whom he considered a great song-writer, he found space for 45 poems. The 1842 edition also included 20 poems by Bryant, 11 by Longfellow, 11 also by Lowell, and 12 by Whittier. Emerson, who had not yet published a volume of poems, was allotted 5; Poe only 3. In the 1847 edition Hoffman's poems dropped from 45 to 35 while Emerson's quota rose from 5 to 10 and Poe's from 3 to 5. In the 1851 edition, published two years after Poe's death, the number of his poems was raised to 14. For Griswold, however, it was not Poe or Emerson but Bryant who was "the greatest living poet who writes the English language."

Griswold had no carefully thought-out critical standards. His literary taste was on the whole conventional. In his address "To the Reader" he wrote: "Thus far the chief distinguishing characteristic of American poetry is its moral purity. May it remain so forever." What he said of Edward Coote Pinkney may help to explain why he was so slow to appreciate some of Poe's finest poems: "Pinkney's is the first instance in this country in which we have to lament the prostitution of true poetical genius to unworthy purposes." And what were these "unworthy purposes"? Griswold explained: "Pervading much that he wrote there is a selfish melancholy and sullen pride; dissatisfaction with the present and doubts in regard to the future life." What would Griswold, one wonders, have thought of Eliot's *The Waste Land* or the poems of Robinson Jeffers?

In Griswold's *Prose Writers of America* seven of the writers whom he admired most were honored with engravings by the well-known Philadelphia artist, John Sartain. The best-known of these are Irving, Emerson, and Prescott the historian. The other four are Richard Henry Wilde, John Pendleton Kennedy, Charles Fenno Hoffman, and John James Audubon, who was only incidentally a writer. The modern reader misses the names of Franklin, Cooper, Poe, Hawthorne, Melville, and Thoreau. The last three had not, however, in 1847 published their best books. In 1850, the year in which *The Scarlet Letter* appeared, Griswold ranked Hawthorne as "the greatest living American writer born in the present century." That is a verdict which posterity has been inclined to accept as its own.

Griswold was often accused of unduly favoring the writers of his native New England. On July 6, 1842, Poe wrote to a Virginia poet, Daniel Bryan: "I shall make war to the knife against the New-England assumption of 'all the decency and all the talent' which has been so disgustingly manifested in the Rev. Rufus W. Griswold's 'Poets & Poetry of America.'" Beverley Tucker's reaction was unconventional: "We, in the South, forsooth, can hardly find the name of a southern man in Mr. Griswold's collection. 'Marry, and I am glad on't. I'd rather be a kitten and cry mew, than one of those metre ballad mongers,' who are exhibited as the élite of American poets."

Yet there is no mistaking Griswold's admiration for certain southern writers, notably Richard Henry Wilde, John Pendleton Kennedy, and Philip Pendleton Cooke. In December, 1851, writing in the *International Monthly Magazine*, Griswold noted that John R. Thompson had republished in the *Southern Literary Messenger* "some pretty verses" "by the late H. S. Ellenwood, of North Carolina" and had there reiterated the conventional southern complaint about northern neglect of southern writers: "Had the gifted author been a native of Massachusetts, his name would be familiar as household words: as it is, we doubt whether one in ten of our readers has ever heard of it." In this instance Griswold had an effective reply: "He was a native of Massachusetts. His original name was Small, and he was born in Salem. . . at twenty-one had his named changed to H. S. Ellenwood, in 1820 emigrated to North Carolina. . . . We suspect that, in literature at least, all charges of 'injustice to the South,' are as ill founded as this."

Sensitive southerners found no anti-southern bias in the Duyckinck brothers' two-volume *Cyclopaedia of American Literature* (1855). Evert Duyckinck had taken the precaution of asking Simms and other southern friends to suggest names of authors to be included and to send him biographical information. For example, on February 19, 1853, he wrote to John Esten Cooke: "What is there of Virginia Revolutionary poetry? You [in Virginia] have had much literature but the light has been under a bushel. E. g. Byrd of Westover whose MSS. would have have made the fortune of a northern historical society." The Duyckincks had a high regard for Hawthorne's work and for that of their friend Melville although they did not realize how great he really was. They tried to be just also to Poe, but Griswold's forgeries that misrepresented Poe's opinion of Evert Duyckinck prevented him from giving a judicial estimate. As a source of information about American writers, the *Cyclopaedia* was far superior to anything that preceded it, and it was never completely superseded until the appearance of the *Dictionary of American Biography* (1928–1936).

> *What can we better say of him [the critic] than, with*
> *Bulwer, that "he must have courage to blame boldly, mag-*
> *nanimity to eschew envy, genius to appreciate, learning to*
> *compare, an eye for beauty, an ear for music, and a heart for*
> *feeling." Let us add, a talent for analysis and a solemn indif-*
> *ference to abuse.*
>
> Edgar Allan Poe, "Exordium"

## TWO NEW ENGLAND LITERARY CRITICS

"The literary man in this country has no critic," wrote Emerson in his *Journals* in October, 1836. That was not literally true in 1836, but it was not till later that notable literary criticism was to come from Poe, Lowell, and Margaret Fuller. And when it came, there were loud outcries from many writers who felt themselves abused by unfavorable criticism. American writers must be encouraged, not ridiculed. Even so good a poet as Longfellow found it difficult to take unfavorable criticism of his didacticism even when he must have known that it was justified.

*Margaret Fuller.* In the 1840's several writers put on record critical estimates of their contemporaries, and American readers displayed some interest in their different opinions. How good, they wanted to know, were our writers? Were any of them good enough to convince the English that we had a national literature of importance? Lowell's *A Fable for Critics*, which we have noticed, appeared in 1848. Two years earlier Poe had printed in *Godey's Lady's Book* his series of gossipy articles entitled "The Literati of New York City," which provoked a controversy. In 1846 also Margaret Fuller (1810–1850) printed a long article entitled "American Literature; Its Position at the Present Time, and Its Prospects for the Future."

For Margaret Fuller, as for Lowell, what was written outside New England had little importance. She was not, however, a member of any mutual admiration society, and she had no love for the sentimental and the meretricious that vitiated the literary estimates of Griswold and other literary journalists. In this article she had nothing to say of Poe, but in the New York *Tribune* of July 11, 1845, she had seen in Poe's tales "the fruit of genuine observation and experience, combined with an invention which is . . . a penetration into the causes of things." Even in tales that she regarded as failures she had found evidence of "an intellect of strong fiber and well-chosen aim."

Margaret Fuller did not write as well as she talked, but some of the opinions she expressed of her contemporaries anticipated the verdicts of our better critics of the twentieth century. This is all the more remarkable when we remember that she did not live to read many of the books on which the reputations of the New England authors rest. In 1846 Emerson, the oldest of the group, was only forty-three and Hawthorne was a year younger. For her Emerson was "a profound thinker" and "a harbinger of a better day." He had not yet published a volume of his poems, but she had high praise for those she had seen. Bryant, however, seemed to her as to Griswold the best of the American poets. She considered Hawthorne "the best writer of the day." She overpraised various minor writers including Ellery Channing, who incidentally was her sister's husband. She was at her best when she discussed Longfellow and Lowell.

In Longfellow's poems she found "elegance, a love of the beautiful, and a fancy for what is large and manly, if not a full sympathy with it." Of his shortcomings she wrote: "Longfellow is artificial and imitative. He borrows incessantly, and mixes what he borrows, so that it does not appear to the best advantage. He is very faulty in using broken or mixed metaphors. The ethical part of his writing has a hollow, second-hand sound." With regard to charges of plagiarism recently made by Poe and others she said:

> We have been surprised that any one should have been anxious to fasten special charges of this kind upon him when we had supposed it was so obvious that the greater part of his mental stores were derived from the works of others. He has no style of his own growing out of his own experiences and observations of nature. Nature with him, whether human or external, is always seen through the windows of literature.

With the following paragraph in mind, the late F. O. Matthiessen pronounced her estimate of Lowell "definitive":

> We cannot say as much for Lowell [as for Longfellow], who, we must declare, though to the grief of some friends, and the disgust of more, is absolutely wanting in the true spirit and tone of poetry. . . . his great facility at versification has enabled him to fill the ear with a copious stream of pleasant sound. But his verse is stereotyped; his thought sounds no depth, and posterity will not remember him.

If Margaret Fuller had lived to read Lowell's later prose and verse, she might have modified her estimate. Lowell, for his part, was unforgiving; and in *A Fable for Critics* he ridiculed her in the person of Miranda, whose appearance puts to flight the God of Poetry.

*Edwin P. Whipple.* After Lowell, Edwin P. Whipple (1819–1886) was long regarded in New England as the best American literary critic. His reputation has faded, but some of his critical estimates still stand. Like Lowell and Margaret Fuller, he did not do justice to writers who were not so fortunate as to live in New England. He could, however, see shortcomings in Emerson and Hawthorne, whom he considered the two greatest of American writers. In a long article on "The American Mind," published in 1857, he wrote:

> In treating this subject, it is important that we avoid all that blatant and bragging tone in which American conceit thinly veils its self-distrust; that a deaf ear be presented to the exulting dissonance of the American chanticleer; that the Pilgrim Fathers be disturbed as little as possible in their well-earned graves; and that the different parts of the discourse be not found, like the compositions of certain eminent musicians, to be but symphonious variations on the tune of "Yankee Doodle," or "Hail Columbia."

In the writings of Dr. William Ellery Channing and Washington Allston Whipple noted "a purified delicacy and refinement of nature . . . and a want of ruddy and robust strength." They lacked "the raciness and gusto characteristic of genius which is national."

> Our most eminent poets—Dana, Emerson, Bryant, Longfellow, Lowell —are more or less idealists, from the nature of their position. Though they may represent the woods and streams of American nature, they commonly avoid the passions and thoughts of American human nature. The haunt and main region of their song is man rather than men; humanity in its simple elements, rather than complex combinations.

In the year of the centennial, 1876, Whipple published a long survey of "American Literature," which covered the years 1776–1876. He again overpraised most of the schoolroom poets and some forgotten figures like Sprague and Percival; but again he maintained that Emerson was "the greatest of American men of letters" and Hawthorne the greatest of American writers of fiction. He saw some merit in Thoreau's writings but had no real understanding of his greatness.

Whipple's most conspicuous failures concern those writers who lived outside of New England. Like Lowell and Margaret Fuller, he failed to do justice to Melville and Whitman. Poe seemed to him "a man of rare original capacity, cursed by an incurable perversity of character," and "his critical power, when not biassed by his caprices . . . extraordinarily acute." All Whipple had had to say of the author of *Moby-Dick* was this: "Herman Melville, after astonishing the public with a rapid succession of original novels, the scene of which was placed in the islands of the Pacific, suddenly dropped his pen, as if in disgust of his vocation." Whitman, he thought, should have listened to his critics and modified "his frank expression of the relations of the sexes." *Leaves of Grass*, he said, contained "every leaf but the fig leaf." He noted that Whitman's later books of verse were not open to this objection, but still he thought that the earlier *Leaves of Grass* "if thoroughly cleaned, should . . . be considered his ablest and most original work."

Whipple was not blind to the merits of some of his younger contemporaries. He had some praise for the poems of his South Carolina friend Paul Hamilton Hayne, who dedicated a volume to him; and he thought that Henry Timrod's Magnolia Cemetery "Ode" was "in its simple grandeur, the noblest poem ever written by a Southern poet." Whipple thought well of Bayard Taylor and William Dean Howells. "The writings of William Dean Howells," he said, "are masterpieces of literary workmanship." He noted that Henry James had "a deep and delicate perception of the internal states of exceptional individuals, and a quiet mastery of the resources of style, which make his stories studies in psychology as well as models of narrative art." The western and southern humorists, he thought, suffered like Whitman from an "eccentric deviation from accredited models." He brought the same charge against Mark Twain, but he also saw that Clemens was "a man of wide experience, keen intellect, and literary culture"; and he added: "The serious portions of his writings indicate that he could win a reputation in literature even if he had not been blessed with a humorous fancy inexhaustible in resources."

# Chapter 3. Six Major Writers of the American Renaissance

> *Gainsay it who will as I now write, I am Posterity speaking by proxy—and after-times will make it more than good, when I declare that the American who up to the present day has evinced, in literature, the largest brain with the largest heart, that man is Nathaniel Hawthorne.*
>
> Herman Melville, "Hawthorne and His Mosses"

## NATHANIEL HAWTHORNE

Nathaniel Hawthorne (1804–1864), now rated as one of our three or four greatest writers, was for a dozen years or more, as he phrased it, "the obscurest man of letters in America." That misfortune was due in part to his lack of that business acumen which many popular authors seem to possess. Year after year he was publishing his fine stories and essays in giftbooks and annuals but never over his own name or even a single pseudonym. A journalist and minor poet, Park Benjamin, who knew Hawthorne, in October, 1836, reviewed in the *American Monthly Magazine* a volume of the *Token* which contained no less than three pieces from Hawthorne's hand, not one of them signed with his own name. Benjamin gave this shrewd advice to the modest author: "If Mr. Hawthorne would but collect his various tales and essays into one volume, we can assure him that their success would be brilliant—certainly in England, perhaps in this country." Hawthorne did in the following year bring out the first edition of *Twice-Told Tales*. Without his knowledge a college friend, Horatio Bridge, had guaranteed the publisher against loss. Another college classmate, Longfellow, reviewed the book in the *North American Review*.

A second edition of *Twice-Told Tales* in 1842 attracted the attention of Edgar Allan Poe, who as editor of *Graham's Magazine* was in a position to promote Hawthorne's reputation. Poe found in the tales "invention, creation, imagination, originality." His fascination with Hawthorne led him to write "The Oval Portrait," which clearly reveals Hawthorne's influence. In August, 1844, Poe wrote to Lowell: "He [Hawthorne] is a man of rare genius." Yet in 1847 Poe published in *Godey's Lady's Book* an article in which he took the strange position that Hawthorne was not an original writer but only a "peculiar" one. In the five years that had elapsed since Poe's discovery of Hawthorne had come the so-called Longfellow War over Poe's charges of plagiarism and the cooling off of his friendly relations with Lowell—two of Hawthorne's friends.

Yet Hawthorne himself was in part responsible for the change in Poe's attitude. In February, 1843, he published in the *Pioneer* "The Hall of Fantasy," which included this sentence: "Mr. Poe had gained ready admittance for the sake of his imagination, but was threatened with ejectment, as belonging to the obnoxious class of critics." That sentence was omitted when "The Hall of Fantasy" was republished in *Mosses from an Old Manse.* Yet Hawthorne on June 17, 1846, wrote to Poe, his ablest and most enthusiastic champion, a tactless letter in which he again revealed his low opinion of literary critics.

It was Melville's reading of *Mosses from an Old Manse* in 1850 that led him to write the panegyric which he entitled "Hawthorne and His Mosses." After the publication of *The Scarlet Letter,* Melville wrote to Evert Duyckinck on February 12, 1851, that he regarded Hawthorne "as evincing a quality of genius, immensely loftier, & more profound, too, than any other American has shown hitherto in the printed form. Irving is a grasshopper to him—putting the souls of the two men together, I mean." Without "the shock of recognition" that came to him from his relations with Hawthorne, Melville might never have written such a masterpiece as *Moby-Dick.*

Hawthorne's first mature novel, *The Scarlet Letter,* was a best-seller. For that popular success some of the credit must go to his friend James T. Fields of the firm of Ticknor and Fields. Hawthorne had long hoped to publish a novel, but he was still only a writer of tales when Fields visited him in Salem one cold winter day and took back to Boston "the germ" of *The Scarlet Letter.* In Hawthorne's plan that story was merely the longest in a new volume of tales which he planned to call "Old-Time Legends; Together with Sketches, Experimental and Ideal." That title, as George E. Woodberry remarked in his life of Hawthorne, is "fairly ghostly with the transcendental nonage of his genius, pale, abstract, ineffectual, with oblivion lurking in every syllable. Fields knew better than that." It was Fields who persuaded the doubting tale-writer to expand the long story into a novelette and to leave out the other tales that he had planned to include. Toward the end of his life Hawthorne wrote to Fields: "My literary success, whatever it has been, or may be, is the result of my connection with you."

Hawthorne was a modest man who was never sure that any of his books would meet with the favor of the reading public. In the memorable passage which Emerson wrote in his *Journals* just after Hawthorne's death in 1864, we find this sentence: "One day, when I found him on the top of his hill, in the woods, he paced back the path to his house, and said, 'This path is the only remembrance of me that will remain.'"

After the publication of *The Scarlet Letter*, as Clarence Gohdes has noted, "approval of Hawthorne was all but universal in British critical circles," and at the end of the century he was regarded as among American writers "the leading artist." In his discourse on Emerson in 1883 Matthew Arnold confessed that Hawthorne's subjects were not for him "subjects of the highest interest; but," he added, "his literary talent is of the first order, the finest, I think, which America has yet produced,—finer, by much, than Emerson's."

When John Morley asked Henry James to write a biography of Hawthorne for the English Men of Letters series, there was no American writer among the twenty-nine authors included in it. Published in 1879, the little book contains some admirable criticism. It is in fact the first book-length critical study of an American writer. James, however, had only recently come to his momentous decision to live and write in Europe rather than in the United States, and in *Hawthorne* he harped too much on the provincialism of New England and the barrenness of literary material in American life. The chief faults that he found in Hawthorne's masterpiece, *The Scarlet Letter*, were "a want of reality and an abuse of the fanciful element, a certain superficial symbolism." Poe before James, and W. C. Brownell after him, were also to condemn Hawthorne's excessive fondness for symbolism. There is, however, no mistaking James's admiration for the novelist who taught him that an American writer could be an artist. In the concluding paragraph of the book James wrote: "He was a beautiful, natural, original genius.... His work will remain; it is too original and exquisite to pass away. ... No one has had just that vision of life, and no one has had a literary form that more successfully expressed his vision."

In the ninety-odd years since these words were written few competent critics have denied Hawthorne a place among our greatest writers. Allen Tate, for example, writing in his *Reactionary Essays* (1936) maintained that the New England renaissance produced "two talents of the first order —Hawthorne and Emily Dickinson." In the scholars' poll of 1949 the twenty-six specialists in American literature gave Hawthorne first place with a total of 164 points. Poe was second with 163.

In his edition of *The English Notebooks* Randall Stewart wrote in 1941: "Out of the restored journals and letters a new Hawthorne will emerge: a more virile and a more human Hawthorne; a more alert and (in a worldly sense) a more intelligent Hawthorne; a Hawthorne less dreamy, and less aloof, than his biographers have represented him as being." This is the new

Hawthorne that appears in Stewart's *Hawthorne: A Biography* (1948) and in the numerous books and articles that have marked the Hawthorne revival. The varied critical tests and approaches that critics have brought to bear upon his books have not resulted in any appreciable diminution of his fame.

> *The only firebrand of my youth that burns to me as brightly as ever is Emerson.*
>
>        Justice Oliver Wendell Holmes to Sir Frederick Pollock,
>        May 20, 1930, *Holmes-Pollock Letters*

## RALPH WALDO EMERSON

The reputation of Emerson (1803–1882) was of slow growth, even in New England. As a nonconformist minister he had against him the orthodox Congregationalists and, after the "Divinity School Address" at Harvard in 1838, many of the Unitarians as well. For over a quarter of a century he was not invited to speak again at Harvard College. His antislavery opinions were long unpopular in his native Massachusetts, and the Transcendentalists with whom he associated were regarded as radicals and visionaries. Many persons who tried to read his *Essays* found his poetic, oracular, semiclerical language almost unintelligible. Outside of New England few Americans understood the Unitarian-Transcendentalist background out of which Emerson's thought had developed. His first publisher was not very efficient, but Ticknor and Fields, who took over his books from Munroe, found a market for even the lectures. The extension of the railroads to the Middle West enabled Emerson as a lyceum lecturer to win many new readers there. A younger generation understood him better; he became for them something like a prophet. By 1865 he was generally recognized in the North and West as one of the country's greatest living writers, and by the time Reconstruction came to an end in 1877 many southerners were coming to accept him at the same rating.

In Emerson's lifetime his critics raised objections and made qualifications that have been frequently repeated in the twentieth century. His doctrine of self-reliance was considered as verging upon anarchy. He was said to have no sense of evil. His temperamental optimism, especially in his old age, seemed entirely too facile. In October, 1930, James Truslow Adams the historian published in the *Atlantic Monthly* an essay entitled "Emerson Reread," in which he maintained that while Emerson's writings might have a good influence upon young readers, the too optimistic sage had little or nothing for the adult mind. Obviously, like some other critics of Emerson,

Adams did not bother to read or reread either the letters or the *Journals.* In these Emerson showed himself fully aware of many evils in American society besides human slavery.

In the essay "Experience" and in "Threnody," the poem that he wrote after the death of his six-year-old son, one feels that Emerson knew the nightmare world that haunted the imaginations of Hawthorne, Melville, and Poe. It is too often forgotten that in his earlier years Emerson knew what it was to be without a father and to be poor, and as a young man to lose two brothers and the wife that he loved passionately. It was after experiencing more than his share of sorrows that he worked out his philosophy of life, a philosophy of acceptance and not of alienation.

Matthew Arnold, upon whom Emerson had had an important influence, gave his final estimate of the sage in a lecture delivered in this country in the year following Emerson's death. He concluded that Emerson was neither a genuine philosopher nor a great poet. He was in fact not a man of letters at all but, like Epictetus and Marcus Aurelius, "a friend and aider of those who would live in the spirit." Yet illogically enough, the English critic maintained that Emerson's *Essays* was "the most important work done in prose" in English in the nineteenth century. Clarence Gohdes remarks in his *American Literature in Nineteenth-Century England* that at the end of the century Emerson "was pretty generally regarded in the better critical circles as the outstanding writer of America."

In the January and February, 1897, numbers of the *Atlantic Monthly* John Jay Chapman published a notable essay on Emerson in which he said: "As I look back over the past, the figure of Emerson looms up in my mind as the first modern man, and the City of Boston as the first living civilization which I knew." In 1900 Emerson, along with Hawthorne, Longfellow, and Irving, was elected to the New York University Hall of Fame. In 1909 the English department at Harvard granted Bliss Perry's request that he be permitted to offer a course in Emerson. They made it clear, however, that in their opinion Emerson was the only American writer worthy of such a place in the curriculum.

Emerson has frequently been criticized for a defective sense of form. His sentences are superb, but his paragraphs often lack unity and proportion. Familiar passages when we look for them turn up in essays or lectures where logically they hardly belong. Emerson himself was not unaware of his shortcomings as a stylist. In May, 1838, he wrote to Carlyle: "Here I sit and read and write, with very little system, and, as far as regards composition, with the most fragmentary result: paragraphs incompressible, each sentence an infinitely repellent particle." And yet when we read them aloud, Emerson's words never lack music, eloquence, or force; they are alive. It is no surprise to find that he has given us more familiar quotations than any other American author. When Emerson got away from the diction of the lyceum lecturer or the Unitarian clergyman, he could use colloquial American English as effectively as any of his contemporaries except for humorists like Lowell and Longstreet. He wrote in the *Journals* on June 24, 1840:

> The language of the street is always strong. . . . And I confess to some pleasure from the stinging rhetoric of a rattling oath in the mouth of truckmen and teamsters. How laconic and brisk it is by the side of a page of the *North American Review*. Cut these words and they would bleed; they are vascular and alive; they walk and run. Moreover they who speak them have this elegancy, that they do not trip in their speech. It is a shower of bullets, whilst Cambridge [Harvard] men and Yale men correct themselves and begin again at every half sentence.

Nineteenth-century readers and critics found Emerson's poems more sadly lacking in artistic form than his essays. He himself once said to J. T. Trowbridge: "I feel it a hardship that—with something of a lover's passion for what is to me the most precious thing in life, poetry—I have no gift of fluency in it, only a rude and stammering utterance." There were, however, some readers who like Longfellow found in Emerson's first volume "many exquisite poems." In March, 1883, Charles Eliot Norton wrote to George E. Woodberry: "I find him nearer to being a poet than any other American." In our time no one seems to mind Emerson's faulty rhymes—"bear" and "woodpecker," for example. We feel that his best poems justify the organic view of art, so memorably expressed in "The Poet": "For it is not metres but a metre-making argument that makes a poem,—a thought so passionate and alive that, like the spirit of a plant or an animal, it has an architecture of its own, and adorns nature with a new thing."

The two best New England poets of the twentieth century each had a high regard for Emerson's poems. Edwin Arlington Robinson told Joyce Kilmer that Emerson was the greatest American poet. In *A Masque of Reason* Robert Frost referred to "Uriel" as "the greatest Western poem yet"—an honor that Ludwig Lewisohn would have given to another of Emerson's poems, "The Problem."

Emerson is at once one of our best literary critics and one of our worst. The list of important writers who left him cold is a long one. Henry James in *Partial Portraits* noted that Emerson "could see nothing" in Shelley, Aristophanes, *Don Quixote*, Jane Austen, or Dickens. "And this," as James concluded, "is a large allowance to have to make for a man of letters." James noted that Emerson was unable to read the novels of his friend and neighbor,

Nathaniel Hawthorne, and thought them "not worthy of him." "This," continued James, "is a judgment odd almost to fascination—we circle round it and turn it over and over; it contains so elusive an ambiguity." In 1842, the year in which Poe published his famous review of *Twice-Told Tales*, Emerson wrote in his *Journals* this amazing sentence: "Nathaniel Hawthorne's reputation as a writer is a very pleasing fact, because his writing is not good for anything, and this is a tribute to the man." Years later he pronounced *The Marble Faun* "a mere mush." Edwin P. Whipple, for whom *The Scarlet Letter* was "in many respects the greatest romance of the century," remembered that Emerson, while admitting the power in the book, had added "with a repulsive shrug of the shoulders," "'. . . but it is ghastly. Ghastly!' he repeated, 'ghastly!'" The only writer of fiction that Emerson really liked was Scott. On January 31, 1841, he wrote in the *Journals*: "These novels will give way, by and by, to diaries or autobiographies." That vain hope he shared with Thomas Carlyle. Fortunately for his reputation Emerson published no detailed critical estimates of American writers.

In April, 1838, Emerson wrote in his *Journals*: "I said to Bryant and to these young people, that the high poetry of the world from the beginning has been ethical, and it is the tendency of the ripe modern mind to produce it." Wordsworth's poetry, he said, was "of the right kind." Poe's poetry obviously was not. Occasionally, as with Ellery Channing and Forceythe Willson, he greatly overrated young poets whom he liked. In May, 1837, he wrote in his *Journals* that Bronson Alcott was "the most extraordinary man and the highest genius of the time." Later when he knew Alcott better he was to write that Alcott was "a tedious archangel."

Emerson said many fine things about Shakespeare, Milton, Wordsworth, Plato, and other great writers. That was to be expected. The remarkable thing about his critical faculty is that it enabled him so quickly to see that Carlyle, Thoreau, and Whitman were among the greatest of his literary contemporaries—and in each case at a time when there were few persons who would have agreed with him.

Emerson was at times a severe critic of the literature and literary culture of his native land. In his *Journals* for May, 1839—naming Irving, Bryant, Everett, Dr. Channing, and others—he said that "all the American geniuses" lacked "nerve and dagger." Nevertheless Emerson was, among New England writers, the stoutest champion of an American literature. He continually lamented our intellectual dependence upon England. Although he was no admirer of Andrew Jackson or other leaders of the Democratic party, he thought the evil might be cured by "this rank rabble party, the Jacksonism of the country, heedless of English and of all literature." They might, he wrote in his *Journals* in June, 1834, "root out the hollow dilettantism of our cultivation in the coarsest way, and the newborn may begin again to frame their own world with greater advantage." In his essay on "The Poet" (1844) he included the following passage which, I like to think, struck the youthful Walt Whitman as a challenge to write the great American poem:

> I look in vain for the poet whom I describe. . . . We have yet had no genius in America, with tyrannous eye, which knew the value of our incomparable materials, and saw, in the barbarism and materialism of the times, another carnival of the same gods whose picture he so much admires in Homer; then in the Middle Age; then in Calvinism. Banks and tariffs, the newspaper and caucus, Methodism and Unitarianism, are flat and dull to dull people, but rest on the same foundations of wonder as the town of Troy and the temple of Delphi, and are as swiftly passing away. Our logrolling, our stumps and their politics, our fisheries, our Negroes and Indians, our boats and our repudiations, the wrath of rogues and the pusillanimity of honest men, the northern trade, the southern planting, the western clearing, Oregon and Texas, are yet unsung. Yet America is a poem in our eyes; its ample geography dazzles the imagination, and it will not wait long for metres.

> *The man [Thoreau] has stuff in him to make a reputation of; and I wish that you might find it consistent with your interest to aid him in attaining that object.*
>     Nathaniel Hawthorne to Epes Sargent, October 21, 1842

> *The country knows not yet, or in the least part, how great a son it has lost.*
>     Ralph Waldo Emerson, "Thoreau," *Atlantic Monthly,* August, 1862

## HENRY DAVID THOREAU

Thoreau (1817–1862) published only two books, and in his lifetime neither one of them attracted much attention. After receiving from his publisher the unsold copies of *A Week on the Concord and Merrimack Rivers* (1849), he wrote: "I have now a library of nearly nine hundred volumes, over seven hundred of which I wrote myself!" His masterpiece, *Walden,* appeared in 1854, but it was eight years before Ticknor and Fields were able to sell off the first printing of two thousand copies, and it was in that year that Thoreau died. By 1954 *Walden* had appeared in no less than 132 editions, and had been translated into many languages.

In 1854 the reviewers did not know what to make of *Walden*. In September, 1854, the *Southern Literary Messenger* briefly mentioned it:

A large class of readers will be pleased by the fresh rural scenes and descriptions of Mr. Thoreau, and his volume is a delightful companion for a loll under the rustling leaves of some old oak, far in the country. He paints rural scenes and habits, works and pleasures with a gusto most refreshing. The book is published in the uniform style of Messrs. Ticknor and Fields, and is very handsome. We commend it to our readers.

That was of course quite inadequate, but it was better than the verdict of the *North American Review* in Boston that the book was "more curious than useful" or that of the New York *Knickerbocker Magazine* that Thoreau was a humbug. It was *Walden* that Robert Frost had in mind when he wrote in 1922: "In one book . . . he [Thoreau] surpasses everything we have had in America."

New England critics and literary historians, though eager to praise the writers of their section, did not know what to make of Thoreau. They frequently had words of praise for his style but failed to see the significance of what he had to say. Prosperous industrial New England was not willing to admit that, as Thoreau put it, their new inventions were only "an improved means to an unimproved end." The great vogue of the nature book—one genre in which American literature has excelled—did not develop until after Thoreau's death. It was to be many years before W. H. Hudson, himself the author of some notable nature studies, would pronounce *Walden* "the one golden book in any century of best books." Emerson was the first to see that Thoreau was a major American writer. The essay that he wrote soon after Thoreau's death is an admirable portrait of the man in spite of the fact that in it he overemphasized the stoic characteristics of his friend and exaggerated his skill as a woodsman. Ten years after Thoreau's death Emerson would say at the dedication of a library building in Concord: "Henry Thoreau we all remember as a man of genius, and of marked character, known to farmers as the most skilful of surveyors . . . but more widely known as the writer of some of the best books which have been written in this country, and which, I am persuaded, have not yet gathered half their fame."

Other New England writers held a very different opinion of Thoreau. Dr. Holmes in his life of Emerson mentioned Thoreau among the queer people who were attracted to the Concord sage as "the nullifier of civilization, who insisted on nibbling his asparagus at the wrong end." After Whittier had read *Walden* he wrote to James T. Fields: "Thoreau's 'Walden' is capital reading, but very wicked and heathenish. The practical moral of it seems to be that if a man is willing to sink himself into a woodchuck, he can live as cheaply as that quadruped; but after all, for me, I prefer walking on two legs."

Lowell, the most influential American critic of the time, was slow in coming to an appreciation of Thoreau's gifts as a writer. In 1858 he omitted passages from Thoreau's "Chesuncook" when he published it in the *Atlantic Monthly*, and in return received from its author a letter that angered him. He was always inclined to see Thoreau as an imitator of Emerson, and he did not fully understand the motives that took him to Walden Pond. For Lowell "a great deal of the modern sentimentalism about Nature [was] a mark of disease." Nevertheless when in 1865 Lowell published his essay on Thoreau, he saw "fine translunary things" in him. He saw too, that "his whole life was a rebuke of the waste and aimlessness of our American luxury, which is an abject enslavement to tawdry upholstery." Of Thoreau's place in literature Lowell said: "He belongs with Donne and Browne and Novalis, if not with the originally creative men, with the scarcely smaller class who are peculiar, and whose leaves shed their invisible thought-seed like ferns." Some of Thoreau's admirers, including those of our own time, have not forgiven Lowell for failing to see him as we see him now. And yet he did see that Thoreau was primarily a writer, and no one has written a keener appreciation of Thoreau's style:

> His better style as a writer is in keeping with the simplicity and purity of his life. We have said that his range was narrow, but to be a master is to be a master. He had caught his English at its living source, among the poets and prose writers of its best days; his literature was extensive and recondite; his quotations are always nuggets of the purest ore; there are sentences of his as perfect as anything in the language, and thoughts as clearly crystallized; his metaphors and images are always fresh from the soil; he had watched Nature like a detective who is to go upon the stand; as we read him, it seems as if all out-of-doors had kept a diary and become his own Montaigne.

Lowell did not go quite so far as Walter Harding and others have gone in maintaining that "Thoreau wrote the first modern American prose"; but he did see, as some later critics have not seen, that Thoreau was primarily not a naturalist but a writer.

Henry James, who recognized the greatness of Hawthorne and Emerson, wrote in his *Hawthorne* (1879):

> Whatever question there may be of his [Thoreau's] talent, there can be none, I think, of his genius. It was a slim and crooked one, but it was eminently personal. He was imperfect, unfinished, inartistic; he was worse than provincial—he was parochial; it is only at his best that

he is readable. But at his best he has an extreme natural charm, and he must always be mentioned after those Americans—Emerson, Hawthorne, Longfellow, Lowell, Motley—who have written originally.

Clearly James did not think Thoreau belonged in the canon of the great American writers. I can find no evidence that Howells or Mark Twain held any high opinion of his books. They would not have endorsed Thomas Wentworth Higginson's opinion that *Walden* was the only American book that deserved to be reread every year.

European readers did not see Thoreau as either an eccentric or an imitator of Emerson, and they did not ask the little circle of his American admirers how to interpret his books for them. Writing in the *Westminster Review* in January, 1856, George Eliot hailed *Walden* as "a bit of true American life (not the go-ahead species, but its opposite pole) animated by that energetic yet calm spirit of innovation . . . which is peculiar to some of the finest American minds." "His observations on natural phenomena," she added, ". . . are not only made with a keen eye, but have their interest enhanced by passing through the medium of a deep poetic sensibility; and, indeed, we feel throughout the book the presence of a refined as well as a hardy mind." Robert Louis Stevenson in a notable essay in his *Familiar Studies of Men and Books* (1882) described Thoreau as "dry, priggish, and selfish" but without any tincture of misanthropy. Stevenson was later to revise his estimate of the man and to add: "Upon me this pure, narrow, sunnily-ascetic Thoreau had exercised a great charm. I have scarce written ten sentences since I was introduced to him, but his influence might be somewhere detected by a close observer." *Walden* made a profound impression upon Robert Blatchford, whose *Merrie England* had an important influence upon the policies of the British Labor Party. Somewhat later in South Africa a young lawyer named Gandhi read *Walden* and "Civil Disobedience" (in 1906) while he was slowly evolving his program of passive resistance to the British government in India. Thoreau's essay has probably influenced the course of the civil rights movement in the United States.

Thoreau's American friends and disciples managed to get into print most of his writings except the *Journals*, of which there was a ten-volume edition in 1906. Slowly, too slowly, in the twentieth century Thoreau finally came into his own. He ceased to be read merely for his descriptions of natural scenes and phenomena. The earlier anthologists had reprinted only such passages from *Walden* as "The Battle of the Ants" and "The Pond in Winter." Later anthologists have more often reprinted "Economy" and "Where I Lived and What I Lived for."

In 1896 Brander Matthews gave Thoreau the distinction of having a chapter all to himself in *An Introduction to the Study of American Literature.*

That example was followed by John Macy in *The Spirit of American Literature* (1908, 1913). In *A Short History of American Literature* (1900) Walter C. Bronson wrote: "The genius of HENRY DAVID THOREAU was not primarily literary, yet he has a secure niche in American literature." In the 1919 edition of his book Professor Bronson concluded: "On the whole, Thoreau must be classed with the minor American authors; but there is no one just like him, and the flavor of his best work is exceedingly fine." In 1916 came Mark Van Doren's book-length study, *Henry David Thoreau*. Norman Foerster's *Nature in American Literature* (1923) corrected various errors that had interfered with the understanding and appreciation of his books. In 1927 Vernon L. Parrington said of him in *Main Currents in American Thought*: "One of the great names in American literature is the name of Henry Thoreau. Yet only after sixty years is he slowly coming into his own." In an article on Thoreau entitled "One-Man Revolution," published in *Newsweek* on November 22, 1937, Sinclair Lewis referred to *Walden* as "one of the three or four unquestionable classics of American literature, published in 1854 and more modern than Dos Passos." In 1941 F. O. Matthiessen in his *American Renaissance* gave Thoreau the distinction of being discussed at great length in a book that included only four other writers: Emerson, Hawthorne, Melville, and Whitman. Critical appreciation of Thoreau's poems, which aroused no enthusiasm in his early reviewers, has increased notably since 1943 when Carl Bode brought out the *Collected Poems*. Conspicuous among writers of our time who have written admiringly and judiciously of Thoreau's genius is E. B. White.

Thoreau's admirers have sometimes overpraised him. For example, Stanley Edgar Hyman wrote in the *Atlantic Monthly* for November, 1946: "At his best he [Thoreau] wrote the only really first-rate prose ever written by an American, with the possible exception of Abraham Lincoln." When one reads passages like this, one has a better understanding of how Theodore Baird came to write in the autumn, 1962, number of the *Massachusetts Review*: "The attention to Thoreau, and admiration for him, is out of all reasonable bounds. He is, in fact, the center of a cult. At its beginning Lowell protested, and to this day he has never been forgiven." While he considered Thoreau a great writer, Baird regarded him as "an impossible egotist." Ludwig Lewisohn, who had high praise for his style, regarded him as "a clammy prig." In his *Consciousness in Concord* the late Perry Miller expressed reservations about both the man Thoreau and his writings. And in *Book Week* for November 28, 1965, Howard Mumford Jones wrote: "At his best his style is wonderful—cogent, witty, clear, sardonic, penetrating, though it lacks on the whole emotional warmth—but his writing is uneven. And to be fully persuaded that Thoreau is one of the great modern prose stylists, one must read him in extracts." It would seem that, like Poe, Whitman, Henry James and other great American writers, Thoreau will always find readers who concede his power and originality even though they are repelled by him. Thoreau was not elected to the Hall of Fame until 1960—in the first election in 1900 he got just three votes—but long before 1960 our leading critics and literary historians knew that he belonged in the canon of the great American writers. The first volume to be published in the new American Men of Letters series in 1948 was Joseph Wood Krutch's *Henry David Thoreau*.

> *For my name and memory, I leave it to men's charitable speeches, and to foreign nations, and the next ages.*
> Francis Bacon's Last Will, December 19, 1625

> *Here is the literature of the twentieth century.*
> The Goncourt Brothers, "Journal," 1876

## EDGAR ALLAN POE

The first ambition of Edgar Allan Poe (1809–1849) was to be a great poet, but the three small volumes of verse that he published in 1827, 1829, and 1831 found few readers and brought him little if any money. In the early thirties he turned to writing short stories which promised somewhat better remuneration. Yet the low scale of pay made it impossible for him to live on what he could earn by writing for magazines, annuals, and gift books. During his lifetime he was best known as a critic, but much of his criticism was regarded as harsh and prejudiced. While editing the *Southern Literary Messenger* in Richmond, his book reviews made enemies who would continue to feud with him during his later years in Philadelphia and New York. Some of his enemies long outlived him. Thomas Dunn English and Richard Henry Stoddard were still damning him half a century after his death. In *Recollections Personal and Literary* (1903) Stoddard described Poe as a misanthropist and "a curious compound of the charlatan and the courtly gentleman."*

In Victorian times nearly every author in England and America had relatives and friends who looked after his reputation, collected his scattered writings, published official biographies in which they glossed over his failings.

---

* For a historical account of Poe criticism and scholarship, see my essay in *Eight American Authors*, ed. James Woodress (rev. ed., 1971).

It was, however, no friend or relative but an enemy that edited Poe's writings and wrote the memoir which gave the world the abiding impression that he was a thoroughly bad man. Indeed, Poe was hardly in his grave before the Reverend Rufus Wilmot Griswold published under the pseudonym "Ludwig" an article in the New York *Tribune* in which he described Poe as a man without friends, envious, impious, walking the streets "in madness or melancholy, with lips moving in indistinct curses." For Griswold and his contemporaries the artistic conscience was not enough; the great American writer had to be a model of morality. Poe as Griswold, Stoddard, and English described him was the only black sheep in the American literary flock, and very black indeed he seemed to many in England and America. Griswold had some appreciation of Poe's poems and tales, but as a critic Poe seemed to him "little better than a carping grammarian." In the sixteenth edition of *The Poets and Poetry of America*, published seven years after Poe's death, he gave his most favorable estimate of Poe's achievement: "His rank as a poet is with the first class of his time." "Unquestionably he was a man of genius," he said, ". . . [but] his genius was in a singular degree wasted or misapplied."

After Poe's death in 1849 some of his northern friends—George R. Graham, N. P. Willis, Sarah Helen Whitman, and others—refuted Griswold's calumnies. His southern friends except for the "mad" Georgia poet, Thomas Holley Chivers, did little or nothing. It was left to an Englishman, John H. Ingram, to bring out a new biography and a new edition of Poe's writings that served to counteract a part of the damage Griswold had done to the dead poet's reputation. Yet it was not until 1941, when Arthur Hobson Quinn published his life of Poe, that the full extent of Griswold's forgeries was revealed. The man who did most to promote Poe's international reputation was the French poet, Charles Baudelaire.

Poe, to be sure, was in some degree responsible for his bad reputation. Although he was not the drunkard pictured by his enemies, his behavior on those occasions when he was under the influence of liquor made enemies for him. As a magazinist he thought it was good policy to charge Longfellow with plagiarism and to ridicule the "Frogpondians." He failed to realize that New England was rapidly becoming the dominant force in American literature. In an article entitled "A Hundred Years of American Verse," published in the *North American Review* in January, 1901, William Dean Howells wrote:

> The great New Englanders would none of him [Poe]. Emerson called him "the jingle-man"; Lowell thought him "three-fourths [two-fifths] sheer fudge"; Longfellow's generous voice was silenced by Poe's atrocious misbehavior to him, and we can only infer his slight esteem for his work; in a later generation Mr. [Henry] James speaks of Poe's "very valueless verses." Yet it is perversely possible that his name will lead

all the rest when our immortals are duly marshalled for the long descent of time.

Howells did not mention the essay on Poe which Lowell had published in *Graham's Magazine* in February, 1845, when he was only twenty-six years old. "Mr. Poe," Lowell wrote, "has that indescribable something which men have agreed to call genius" and, he added, "Mr. Poe has two of the prime qualities of genius, a faculty of vigorous yet minute analysis, and a wonderful fecundity of imagination." Lowell's critical comments on "To Helen" reveal him as a critic of keen discernment and admirable literary taste. It is too bad that he permitted Griswold to publish in his edition of Poe a version of the essay from which much of Lowell's earlier enthusiasm seems to have evaporated.

In the later nineteenth century Poe's reputation grew much more slowly in his own country than in Europe and Latin America. In England Poe was praised by Tennyson, Swinburne, Rossetti, and Yeats, and in France by Baudelaire, Mallarmé, Verlaine, and many others; but the chief American writers of the later nineteenth century—Whitman, Mark Twain, Howells, and Henry James—had no enthusiasm for his poetry, fiction, or literary criticism. In 1893 when the New York literary weekly, the *Critic*, polled its readers to determine "The Best Ten American Books," Emerson's *Essays* was first with 512 votes and Hawthorne's *The Scarlet Letter* was second with 493. Poe got less than twenty votes. Edmund Gosse wrote from England to express his astonishment at the exclusion of "the most perfect, the most original, the most exquisite of the American poets." "If I were an American," he continued, "I should be inclined to call it disastrous."

The conventional New England estimate of Poe appeared in *A Short History of American Literature* (1900) by Professor Walter C. Bronson of Brown University:

> There is no need to dwell upon the obvious limitations of his work—its lack of mental breadth, of moral and spiritual significance, of wholesome humanity. Poe was no sun shedding its genial beams broadcast over the earth; but he was at least an arc-light shining brilliantly, and picturesquely heightening the shadows, in the Place of Tombs.

Since the celebration of the Poe centenary in 1909 and his election to the Hall of Fame in 1910 there has been little room for doubt that Poe is a major American writer. And yet there have always been noteworthy critics who, like Yvor Winters, cannot see his importance. In January, 1937, Winters published in *American Literature* an article entitled "Edgar Allan Poe: A Crisis in the History of American Obscurantism," in which he maintained that Poe was "a bad writer accidentally and temporarily popular," whose theory and practice were both bad, and whose poetry was "an art to delight the soul of a servant girl; it is a matter of astonishment," he added, "that mature men can take this kind of thing seriously."

As long ago as 1917 the late Killis Campbell, one of the best of Poe scholars, noted the "extraordinary diversity of opinion" among critics in regard to Poe's poems and rightly attributed it mainly to "the world-old difference among critics as to the province and aims of poetry, the traditional clash between those who insist on the inculcation of moral ideas as the chief business of poetry and those who adhere to the doctrine of art for art's sake." There will probably never be anything like complete agreement among critics as to the nature and functions of poetry, drama, and fiction; and there will accordingly always be readers who find that Poe's best poems and tales leave them cold. Yet beyond doubt there will always be in Arnold Bennett's phrase "a passionate minority" who will long keep his name alive.

In 1948 F. O. Matthiessen concluded his chapter on Poe in *The Literary History of the United States*: "He [Poe] stands as one of the very few great innovators in American literature. Like Henry James and T. S. Eliot, he took his place, almost from the start, in international culture as an original creative force in contrast to the more superficial international vogue of Cooper and Irving." In 1949, one hundred years after Poe's death, the twenty-six specialists in American literature who took part in the UNESCO poll of that year gave first place to Hawthorne with 164 points and second to Poe with 163 as authors of the best American books. In 1961 Vincent Buranelli, in a book on Poe in Twayne's U.S. Authors series, concluded with the claim that Poe is "America's greatest writer, and the American writer of greatest significance in world literature."

There are of course competent critics who would not endorse any such estimate and would press the claims of such other major writers as Whitman, James, Mark Twain, Faulkner, and—if we claim him as an American—T. S. Eliot. There would, I think, be general agreement with Richard Wilbur's comment on Poe's tales in his 1959 Library of Congress lecture on "The House of Poe": "Poe is a great artist, and I would rest my case for him on his prose allegories of psychic conflict. In them, Poe broke wholly new ground, and they remain the best things of their kind in our literature. . . . I think that he will have something to say to us as long as there is civil war in the palaces of men's minds."

Unlike Lowell or Arnold, Poe wrote no formal critical essays on major writers or aesthetic problems. As a magazinist, his primary duty was to review books, most of which had only an ephemeral importance. Imbedded in his reviews, however, there are memorable passages in which he praised a little-known author like Nathaniel Hawthorne, ridiculed a poetaster like W. W. Lord, or expounded his theories of the short story and the lyric poem or the function of literary criticism.

The literary theories that Poe worked out for himself are such as fitted neatly into the demands of the American magazine in his time. What he valued most in verse and prose was the brief lyric and the short story. They could each be read at a single sitting. Novels and epic poems were too long for that, and so they lost the unity of effect which Poe regarded as indispensable to artistic success. Yet when Poe criticized *Paradise Lost* as only a series of poetic passages interspersed with barren stretches of versified prose, we suspect him of rationalizing. One cannot help remembering that in *Tamerlane* and *Al Aaraaf* he had attempted the long narrative poem with no great success and that his longest prose narrative, *Arthur Gordon Pym*, had been regarded as a failure.

Poe was a professional writer with high standards at a time when most other writers had little appreciation of sound criticism. But he was also a journalist with a keen eye for effects that were not always scrupulous. He liked to "kick up a dust," and he thought it good journalism to accuse the popular Longfellow of plagiarism. (On that subject his attitude bordered on the insane.) He almost invariably overpraised the work of women writers, and he made enemies needlessly by impaling such small fry as Theodore S. Fay, the author of *Norman Leslie.* His long series "The Literati of New York City" he professed to regard as primarily literary gossip concerning authors about whom the public was curious; but he found that the public took them seriously.

By his own account Poe once told an audience "made up chiefly of editors and their connexions" that "they had been engaged for many years in a system of indiscriminate laudation of American books—a system which, more than any other one thing in the world, had tended to the depression of that 'American literature' whose elevation it was designed to effect." Poe himself, however, especially in his later years could not refrain from literary logrolling of the kind that he condemned.

Much of our best American criticism has come from poets and writers of fiction like Poe, Lowell, Henry James, Howells, T. S. Eliot, and John Crowe Ransom. The creative writer, however, can be singularly obtuse when he is judging a writer whose fundamental aims and methods are different from his own. If Henry James in the nineteenth century and Yvor Winters in the twentieth could miss the mark in their judgment of Poe by so wide a margin, Poe himself greatly undervalued Wordsworth, Carlyle, and Emerson. He overpraised many women poets, and he greatly exaggerated the merits of minor writers when he discussed La Motte Fouqué's *Undine* and Richard

Hengist Horne's *Orion*, which at one time he regarded as a greater poem than *Paradise Lost*. Poe was at his best when he early recognized the genius of Dickens, Tennyson, and Mrs. Browning and among American writers Hawthorne, Longfellow, Lowell, Longstreet, and many others.

In spite of his ill-advised attack upon Longfellow as a plagiarist, Poe did not underestimate the importance of Longfellow's poetry. It was his reading of the "Hymn to the Night" in a newspaper that led him to "the firm belief that a poet of high genius had at length arisen amongst us." In 1843 he wrote: "Longfellow is unquestionably the best poet in America." When he attacked Longfellow for continual moralizing, he was trying to establish a proper basis for poetic criticism. Poetry for him was "the rhythmical creation of Beauty" and Longfellow was guilty of "the heresy of the didactic."* A poem should be written for the poem's sake and not to teach a moral. Poe's criticism is in the main the criticism of a skilled craftsman. It anticipates the methods of critical analysis of the New Critics of the twentieth century, and it is often amazingly good.

Poe's first reading of *Twice-Told Tales* in 1842 prompted him to write: "Upon the whole we look upon him [Hawthorne] as one of the few men of indisputable genius to whom our country has as yet given birth. As such it will be our delight to do him honor." In 1847 he wrote that Hawthorne was "the example, *par excellence*, in this country, of the privately-admired and publicly-unappreciated man of genius." Later, one regretfully notes, he could argue that Hawthorne was not original but only "peculiar." After the so-called "Longfellow War" and Poe's break with Lowell, his antipathy to New England led him to modify his earlier estimate. He remembered no doubt the derogatory passage about his criticism which he had read in Hawthorne's "The Hall of Fantasy" in Lowell's *Pioneer*. He remembered also the letter he received from Hawthorne in June, 1846, in which the New Englander wrote so untactfully to the critic who had done more than any other to promote his reputation: "I care for nothing but the truth; and shall always much more readily accept a harsh truth, in regard to my writings, than a sugared falsehood." What was the point in saying that to his ablest champion? Did he think that Poe's review of *Twice-Told Tales* contained any "sugared falsehoods"? In the last paragraph of his letter Hawthorne once again indicated his low estimate of literary criticism along with his appreciation of Poe as a writer of tales: "I confess, however, that I admire you rather as a writer of tales than as a critic upon them. I might often—and often do—dissent from

* Among some metrical experiments in Longfellow's *Works*, III, 306, I find this couplet:

> "In Hexameter sings serenely a Harvard Professor;
> In Pentameter him damns censorious Poe."

your opinion in the latter capacity, but could never fail to recognize your force and originality in the former."

Poe's literary criticism, which had much to do with giving him a bad name among his contemporaries, seems, however, to some twentieth-century critics his best claim to fame. Richard Henry Stoddard's verdict was: "Poe is no critic." In our time, however, Edmund Wilson has written: "His literary articles and lectures . . . surely constitute the most remarkable body of criticism ever produced in the United States."

> *The fame I've got has not in all respects sufficed*
> *And rediscovery would have its fitness.*
> Archibald MacLeish, "Sentiments for a Dedication"

> *The problem of the professional writer is not identical with*
> *that of the literary artist, but when a literary artist is also a*
> *professional writer, he cannot solve the problems of the one*
> *function without reference to the other.*
> William Charvat, *The Profession of Authorship*
> *in America, 1800–1870*

## HERMAN MELVILLE

A strange case and one difficult to explain is that of Herman Melville (1819–1891). His first books, *Typee* (1846) and *Omoo* (1847), were widely read. Yet even in these stories of adventure Melville antagonized the orthodox by suggesting that the influence of white missionaries and traders upon the noble savages of the South Seas was an evil influence. *Mardi* (1849) puzzled Melville's readers. It began like another *Typee*, but it soon became a fruitless quest for the lost Yillah—the symbol of one knew not what—and finally became a satire upon American and European manners and morals. It is dangerous for a popular writer to disappoint the expectations of his readers, even if in so doing he presents them with a strange new masterpiece. And in 1851 Melville did just that when he published *Moby-Dick*. The real meaning of the book was obscure, and there was about its leading character a suspicion of blasphemy. Melville's British publisher felt impelled to bring out a sadly bowdlerized version.

The book was written while Melville was seeing much of his new friend and neighbor in the Berkshires, Nathaniel Hawthorne, whose *Scarlet Letter* had brought him fame a year earlier. In a letter to Hawthorne, noting his own fading reputation, Melville stated his belief that literary fame is "the most transparent of all vanities." The reading public, if it remembered him, he said, would think of him only as "the man who lived among the cannibals." In an earlier letter, while trying to finish writing *Moby-Dick*, he had written to Hawthorne: "What's the use of elaborating what, in its very essence, is so short-lived as a modern book? Though I wrote the Gospels in this century, I should die in the gutter." In 1851 when American readers of fiction were predominantly women, Melville had chosen to write a novel in which there are no important women characters and no "love interest." Even in the twentieth century *Moby-Dick* has not been a favorite with women readers.

Hawthorne was one of the few American authors to see that Melville was a writer of genius. On August 29, 1850, he wrote to Evert Duyckinck:

> I have read Melville's works with a progressive appreciation of the author. No writer ever put the reality before the reader more unflinchingly than he does in "Redburn" and "White Jacket." "Mardi" is a rich book, with depths here and there that compel a man to swim for his life. It is so good that one scarcely pardons the writer for not having brooded long over it, so as to make it a great deal better.

The next year after he had read *Moby-Dick* Hawthorne wrote: "What a book Melville has written! It gives me an idea of much greater power than his preceding ones." In the mid-fifties a fire in the Harper warehouse destroyed all but 60 copies of *Moby-Dick*, yet the publishers did not bring out another edition until 1863. There was a third printing in 1892, a year after Melville's death.

*Pierre* (1852) marked a new low in the author's reputation. Perversely Melville was giving his readers not a story of adventures in the South Seas but a curious novel of manners which by its suggestion of incest shocked many who tried to read it. In February, 1853, Fitz-James O'Brien, himself the author of some good short stories, published in *Putnam's Magazine* a warning to Melville: "He totters on the edge of a precipice over which all his hard-earned fame may tumble." In January of the preceding year the *Democratic Review* had announced: "Mr. Melville has survived his reputation." Melville in his "probings at the very axis of reality" had failed to give his readers—and his reviewers—the kind of fiction they wanted.

Melville's later novels fared little better than *Pierre*. Obviously he could not support his family on the income they brought him. He tried writing short stories for magazines with only moderate success. He tried lecturing. He tried to secure a diplomatic appointment. Finally in 1866 he got an appointment as an inspector in the Customs House in New York. On July 4, 1868, the Richmond weekly, *Southern Opinion*, quoted the New York correspondent of the

Cincinnati *Times* as saying that the Customs House "appears to be a kind of hospital for literary invalids." He continued: "Herman Melville, who delighted the publick with his 'Typee' and 'Omoo,' and ended with such trash as 'Pierre' and the 'Confidence Man,' has enrolled himself in the service of Uncle Sam. He is thoroughly written out, and so very unpractical that he needs some such position to live."

After nearly twenty years Melville resigned his position. Before he died he wrote but did not publish *Billy Budd*, now regarded as one of his greatest books. In the years that followed the Civil War Melville had written more verse than prose. The long and difficult *Clarel* (1876) added nothing to his reputation. Even his stirring *Battle-Pieces* (1866) had made little impression. When he died in 1891, there were few who remembered him, and many of those who had read his earlier books thought he had died long before.

The twentieth century, which "rediscovered" Melville, thought he had been completely forgotten. That was not the case. Melville had continued to be read by a few discerning judges like Robert Louis Stevenson and Robert Buchanan, who in 1885 called Melville "the one great imaginative writer fit to stand shoulder to shoulder with Whitman on that continent [America]." In the Stedman-Hutchinson *Library of American Literature* (1888–1890) there are five of Melville's poems and a short story; but in the New York *Critic*'s poll of its readers in 1884 to select our "Forty Immortals" Stedman did not vote for Melville—nor apparently did any one else. Stedman's son Arthur, who visited Melville in order to get a photograph for *The Library of American Literature*, liked the man and his books well enough to write several articles about them. In Melville's last years there were signs of a coming revival of interest in his books. A Canadian scholar, Archibald McMechan, wrote to Melville asking for information he could use in writing about the great sea stories. Melville, at work on *Billy Budd*, was still disinclined to promote the sale of his own books. "My books will speak for themselves," he said to Titus Munson Coan, "and all the better if I avoid the rattling egotism by which so many win a certain vogue for a certain time." That attitude does honor to a writer of great integrity, but still one wishes that in his old age Melville might have enjoyed a modicum of the praise that has been heaped upon his books in the twentieth century. Soon after Melville's death there were new editions of *Typee, Omoo, White-Jacket*, and *Moby-Dick*; but the real Melville revival was not to come for another quarter of a century.

Melville's discovery of Hawthorne had moved him to write: "For genius, all over the world, stands hand in hand, and one shock of recognition runs the whole circle round." Hawthorne recognized the greatness of *Moby-Dick*, but I find nothing to indicate that the other major writers of either England or America experienced that "shock of recognition." He was not admitted to the New England canon of the great American writers. As Willard Thorp remarks, "The hegemony in letters had passed to New England, and the Brahmins had no use for him." Nor, so far as I know, did Henry James, Mark Twain, or William Dean Howells ever recognize his genius. Even his good friends the Duyckinck brothers did not quite know what to make of him. Richard Henry Stoddard, who worked at the New York Customs House with Melville, did not know what to make of him either. In his *Recollections Personal and Literary* (1903) he wrote: "Whether any of Melville's readers understood the real drift of his mind, or whether he understood it himself, has often puzzled me." Stoddard mentioned four of Melville's novels but showed little enthusiasm for any one of them. He did not mention *Moby-Dick*, but did rate Melville as "one of our great unrecognised poets." This estimate, however, was based not on *Clarel* or the magnificent prose poetry of *Moby-Dick* but on *Battle-Pieces*, Melville's poems of the Civil War. Another contemporary, Thomas Wentworth Higginson, reviewing Julian Hawthorne's biography of his father and mother in the *Atlantic Monthly* for February, 1885, wrote: "In some cases the letters are given so fully as to give the impression of 'padding,' as where we have nine consecutive pages of not very interesting epistles from Herman Melville." Colonel Higginson obviously did not see Melville as an important writer, and yet to him more than to any other person we owe the publication of the poems of Emily Dickinson. Melville had no such able critics to promote his fame as Hawthorne had in Poe, Edwin P. Whipple, and Melville himself; and Harper and Brothers, unlike Ticknor and Fields and the Houghton Mifflin Company, made little effort to advertise his books and keep them in print.

In our time the academic literary historians have made much of Melville, but they were very slow to recognize his greatness. In *An Introduction to the Study of American Literature* (1896) Brander Matthews merely mentioned *Typee* along with Dana's *Two Years before the Mast* as books "not to be classed as fiction." In 1900 Barrett Wendell barely mentioned him and misspelled his first name. In *A Manual of American Literature* (1909), edited by Theodore Stanton, Sutherland Northup gave to Melville a single page in which the author of *Moby-Dick* was described as "a follower of Cooper— though at some distance in point of quality." Melville was not included in W. C. Brownell's *American Prose Masters* (1909) or in John Erskine's *Leading American Novelists* (1910). In 1913 John Macy, who gave separate chapters to Irving, Lowell, and Whittier, barely mentioned "Herman Melville's 'Moby Dick,' a madly eloquent romance of the sea." As late as 1919 Professor Percy H. Boynton of the University of Chicago published a history of American literature in which Melville's name does not appear. It was in the same year that in the August number of the *Review* Frank J. Mather, Jr., published the earliest comprehensive survey of Melville's writings. In 1922–1923 Constable and Company in London brought out in twelve volumes Melville's *Works*, to which in 1924 they added four more volumes. The Melville revival was on, in England as well as in America. D. H. Lawrence gave a chapter to Melville in his *Studies in Classic American Literature* (1923), and there is an illuminating discussion of *Moby-Dick* in E. M. Forster's *Aspects of the Novel* (1927). In 1926 John Freeman's *Herman Melville* was added to the new English Men of Letters series. In his opening sentence he referred to Melville as "the most powerful of all the great American writers."

Various scholars on the English staff of Columbia University had played a major role in the "rediscovery" of Melville. Professor W. P. Trent, who in 1902 edited *Typee*, in 1903 published *A History of American Literature*, in which he pronounced *Moby-Dick* "on the whole [a] genuine work of genius." "The breath of the sea is in it and much of the passion and charm of the most venturous of all the venturous callings plied upon the deep. It is a cool reader that does not become almost as eager as the terrible Captain Ahab in his demoniacal pursuit of Moby Dick, the invincible whale, a creation of the imagination not unworthy of a great poet." Trent qualified his praise by saying: "If it were not for its inordinate length, its frequently inartistic heaping up of details, and its obvious imitation of Carlylean tricks of style and construction, this narrative of tremendous power and wide knowledge might be perhaps pronounced the greatest sea story in literature." In 1917 in the first volume of *The Cambridge History of American Literature*, of which Trent was editor-in-chief, one of his former pupils, Carl Van Doren, wrote: "Too irregular, too bizarre, perhaps, ever to win the widest suffrage, the immense originality of *Moby-Dick* must warrant the claims of its admirers that it belongs with the greatest sea romances in the whole literature of the world." In *The American Novel* (1921 and 1940) Van Doren discussed Melville in greater detail and concluded: "And while Melville at home has had somewhat slighter praise [than in England], an acquaintance with his work is a sign by which it may be learned whether any given American knows the literature of his country." In 1921 also appeared Raymond Weaver's *Herman Melville: Mariner and Mystic*; this Columbia University dissertation was the first published biography of Melville. Weaver also edited the Constable edition of Melville's *Works*. A notable contribution to Melville scholarship was another Columbia dissertation, Charles R. Anderson's *Melville in the South Seas* (1939). Still another Melville scholar who had his graduate training at Columbia is Lawrance Thompson, author of *Melville's Quarrel with God* (1952).

By 1940 there was a small but very able group of scholars at work on Melville. A fine detailed study of his work appeared in F. O. Matthiessen's *American Renaissance* (1941). Since that time many scholars have contributed notably to the elucidation of various problems connected with Melville's life and writings. Unfortunately, however, as is the case with Poe, Whitman, Eliot, and Faulkner, much of what has been put into print has contributed only to what Jay Leyda described in 1951 as "the bog of Melville interpretation . . . with its thick growth of wild guesses." He asked: "Is there anyone in American literature who has attracted such a swarm of myths and apocrypha as has Melville?" After reading some of the various theories of symbolism in *Moby-Dick*, one feels disposed to agree with E. M. Forster that Melville himself did not quite know what the White Whale symbolized.

There is little doubt in any one's mind now about Melville's place in the American literary pantheon: he is one of the ten or twelve of our greatest writers, and *Moby-Dick* is surely one of our half-dozen greatest works of fiction. Yet as we look back upon the curious chart of his reputation, it is difficult to account for the blindness of so many nineteenth-century writers who had grown to maturity before he died. Why were there not hundreds of readers who, like Justice Oliver Wendell Holmes, knew they were reading a great book? On May 18, 1921, he wrote to Sir Frederick Pollock: "Did I mention *Moby Dick*, by Herman Melville? I remember him in my youth. It seemed to me a great book. . . . It shook me up a good deal. It's wonderful already that a book published in 1851 doesn't seem thin, now. Hawthorne did when last I read *The Scarlet Letter*. Not so *Moby Dick*."

In an article on "Herman Melville" published in the *Saturday Review of Literature* for April 27, 1929, Frank Jewett Mather, Jr., stated that about twenty-five years earlier, after visiting Melville's daughter Elizabeth, he had hopefully written to "the American publishers [the Houghton Mifflin Company?] whose list is heaviest with our classics, and proposed a modest biography in one volume. The answer," he added, "was friendly but decisive: Herman Melville was a hopelessly bad risk, and one that no prudent publisher could undertake even to the extent of a few hundred dollars." The first biography of Melville, as Mather noted, was published by a firm "which had no long list of American worthies and was willing to bet on an unsure thing." Furthermore, Mather suggested that it is "to the lasting discredit of our publishing trade" that Melville's collected works were first published by an English house.

We understand and like Melville better because the climate of social and critical opinion has changed. We are indifferent to those things that disturbed or irritated readers in his own time: his pessimism, his religious heterodoxy, his mysticism, his abrupt changes in style and mood, his failure to write conventional romances or sentimental domestic novels.* On the other hand, some of our critics are inclined to overrate Melville now because they prefer writers who were in a sense alienated from the society in which they lived. The critics, one hopes, are not transmitting to posterity a new conventional image of a great writer who in reality had no desire to be regarded as an alien in his own country.

> *Shut not your doors to me proud libraries,*
> *For that which was lacking on all your well-fill'd*
> *shelves, yet needed most, I bring.*
> Walt Whitman, "Shut Not Your Doors"

## WALT WHITMAN

Jacksonian democracy was slow in finding its poet. In the first number of the *Democratic Review* (October, 1837) the editor, John O'Sullivan, wrote: "The vital principle of our literature must be democracy. . . . All history is to be rewritten; political science and the whole scope of moral truth have to be considered in the light of the democratic principle."

That was the attitude of the literary nationalists. Others held a different view of the American literature problem. In 1837 when Samuel Langtree urged John Quincy Adams to write for the *Democratic Review*, the old statesman declined on the ground that "literature was, and in its nature must always be, aristocratic; that democracy of numbers and literature were self-contradictory."

The American demand for a great national literature began before Walt Whitman (1819–1892) was born, but it seemed to him in the 1850's that our literature was still imitative and undemocratic. He was determined to write the great American poems that his master Emerson in 1844 had called for in his essay on "The Poet":

I look in vain for the poet whom I describe. . . . We have yet had no genius in America, with tyrannous eye, which knew the value of our incomparable materials. . . . Oregon and Texas are yet unsung. . . .

* The best explanation of Melville's failure to succeed as a professional writer of fiction is found in the three chapters on Melville in William Charvat's posthumously published study, *The Profession of Authorship in America, 1800–1870*, ed. Matthew J. Bruccoli (1968).

America is a poem in our eyes; its ample geography dazzles the imagination, and it will not wait long for metres.

No "matter" of European romance for Whitman.

> Come Muse migrate from Greece and Ionia,
> Cross out please those immensely overpaid accounts,
> That matter of Troy and Achilles' wrath, and Aeneas',
>     Odysseus' wanderings,
> Placard "Removed" and "To Let" on your snowy Parnassus,
>
> . . . . . . . . . . . . . . . . . . . . . . . .
>
> For know a better, fresher, busier sphere, a wide, untried
>     domain awaits, demands you.

In 1840 Alexis de Tocqueville included in the first book of volume 2 of his *Democracy in America* certain passages that seem prophetic of Whitman. Although the Americans had no literature, he predicted that they would eventually have one, and it would be quite different from the literatures of the Old World. Moreover, it was possible, he felt, to suggest what the literature of a democratic nation would be like. The American literature of the future would show little regard for order or regularity, and the formal elements would be slighted. The language of literature would also be altered by democracy, and the distinction between "vulgar" and "refined" words would cease to be drawn. The shaggy idiom of *Leaves of Grass* would have seemed to de Tocqueville a logical result of democracy.

"I readily admit that the Americans have no poets," de Tocqueville said; "I cannot allow that they have no poetic ideas." "Democracy, which shuts the past against the poet, opens the future before him." "Democracy," as de Tocqueville saw it, gave men "a sort of instinctive distaste for what is ancient." "The ideas of progress and of indefinite perfectibility of the human race belong to democratic ages. . . . Among a democratic people poetry will not be fed with legends or the memorials of old traditions. The poet will not attempt to people the universe with supernatural beings, in whom his readers and his own fancy have refused to believe. . . . All these resources fail him, but Man remains, and the poet needs no more." "The principle of equality," he concluded, "does not, then, destroy all the subjects of poetry; it renders them less numerous, but more vast."*

When the first slim edition of *Leaves of Grass* appeared in 1855, Whitman concluded his preface with this confident assertion: "The proof of a poet is

---

* Much of the two preceding paragraphs is taken from an editorial which I wrote in the year of the Whitman Centennial, "De Tocqueville and Whitman," *Nation*, CIX (Nov. 22, 1919), 655. My quotations are from the 1945 edition of *Democracy in America*, ed. by Phillips Bradley.

that his country absorbs him as affectionately as he has absorbed it." Bitter indeed must have been his disappointment at the reading public's neglect of the successive editions of his book. As late as 1888 he would write in "A Backward Glance o'er Travel'd Roads:"

> That I have not gain'd the acceptance of my own time, but have fallen back on fond dreams of the future. . . . that from a worldly and business point of view "Leaves of Grass" has been worse than a failure—that public criticism on the book and myself as author of it yet shows mark'd anger and contempt more than anything else. . . .

In *Good-bye My Fancy* (1891), one of his very last books, Whitman included a brief essay entitled "Old Poets," in which he wrote: "Lord Bacon says the first sight of any work really new and first-rate in beauty and originality always arouses something disagreeable and repulsive." With the many denunciations of *Leaves of Grass* in mind Whitman added: "People resent anything new as a personal insult." That was the only way he could explain what had happened.

With the conspicuous exception of Emerson, those American writers who stood highest in the public estimation failed to appreciate *Leaves of Grass*. The long list includes Lowell, Holmes, Longfellow, Whittier, Howells, Mark Twain, and (for a long time) Henry James. When Thomas Wentworth Higginson asked Emily Dickinson whether she had read *Leaves of Grass*, she replied: "I never read his book but was told that he was disgraceful." Higginson himself said that it was no discredit to Whitman "that he wrote 'Leaves of Grass,' only that he did not burn it afterwards." America, said Higginson, did not need "new literary forms . . . but only fresh inspiration, combined with cultivated taste." Even Howells, who described the poet as "the gentlest person," of "the greatest benignity" and "spiritual purity," could not reconcile his personal impression of the man with "what denies it" in *Leaves of Grass*. "His verse," he said, "seems to me not poetry, but the materials of poetry."

In Edith Wharton's *The Spark* (1924) a young man who admires Whitman's poems has an elderly friend who often talks of a big bearded man who had befriended him while he was in a Washington hospital during the Civil War. The young man decides that the wonderful man is none other than the Good Gray Poet; and so with book in hand he visits the old man and informs him that his nameless friend was the great American poet Walt Whitman. But after listening to the young man while he reads some of Whitman's poems, the old man says: "He was a great chap, I'll never forget him—I rather wish, though," he adds, in his mildest tone of reproach, "you hadn't told me that he wrote all that rubbish."

Whitman had ample reason for feeling that his countrymen had rejected him as their spokesman. He consoled himself by remembering the praise heaped upon him by a few friends and admirers. In Concord there were Emerson, now revered as a sage, and his young friend Henry David Thoreau. Emerson wrote to Whitman: "Henry carried your book around Concord like a red flag—defiantly, challenging the plentiful current opposition there!" Other friendly admirers were Moncure Daniel Conway, Bronson Alcott, John Burroughs, and William Douglas O'Connor; the last two published important books in the poet's behalf. Whitman was destined for many years to be read chiefly by a small circle, his "little phalanx" of intimate friends in Camden, and by British intellectuals like Robert Louis Stevenson, William Michael Rossetti, Algernon Charles Swinburne, and John Addington Symonds. A few Europeans hailed him as a prophet or the originator of a new art form. Americans in general disliked his free verse and his unconventional poetic diction. On the printed page Whitman's poems did not look like poetry. The diction, too, was unconventional, for the poet had worked hard to rid his verses of "the stock 'poetical' touches" which the average reader considered the proper language of poetry.

It was not enough to write chants praising democracy in general terms; what Whitman's American readers wanted was portraits of individual men and women and stories of their achievements. Even Emerson, who in 1855 had written to the poet: "I greet you at the beginning of a great career," was in 1871 sending word to Walt that he had expected him to "make the songs of the nation" but was disappointed to find that he was content merely to "make the inventories." *Leaves of Grass* might be the Bible of American democracy, but it was not literature of, by, or for the people. The America that Whitman celebrated was not the America of the popular imagination. It was an idealized America, compounded of various elements drawn from the past and the present and blended to form an idealized future which the poet projected for his native land. His view of the function of the American poet was akin to that of Archibald MacLeish, who wrote in *A Time to Speak* (1940): "Poetry alone imagines, and imagining creates, the world that men can wish to live in and make true."

In "A Backward Glance o'er Travel'd Roads" (1888) Whitman wrote: "No one will get at my verses who insists upon viewing them as a literary performance, or attempt at such performance, or as aiming mainly toward art or aestheticism." The poet was of course right in rejecting current literary standards represented by critics like Thomas Bailey Aldrich and Josiah Gilbert Holland; but if *Leaves of Grass* is not to be judged by the best literary tests available, how shall we judge it? Whitman, however, was eminently right when in the same essay he asked: "Has not the time arrived when . . . there must imperatively come a readjustment of the whole theory and nature of Poetry?" In a brief entry in *Specimen Days* he had written: "Has it never occur'd to any one how the last deciding tests applicable to a book are entirely outside of technical and grammatical ones, and that any first-class production has little or nothing to do with the rules and calibres of ordinary critics? or the bloodless chalk of Allibone's Dictionary?"

It was Whitman's treatment of sex that more than any other one thing turned away from *Leaves of Grass* men and women who might otherwise have read it with some appreciation of its merits. In this the midmost of mid-Victorian times Americans, as Mrs. Frances Trollope and other British observers have testified, shrank from any frank treatment of sex in literature. Whitman battled courageously for greater freedom of treatment, but it was too soon. The battle was not to be won in this country until the twentieth century, and it was refought over the novels of Theodore Dreiser, James Branch Cabell, and James Joyce and in the pages of the *American Mercury* and other magazines. The poet's reputation would have developed more rapidly if he had taken Emerson's very practical advice to leave out the "Children of Adam" poems in his 1860 edition. American readers, especially among women, did not like sex stripped of sentiment. Whitman did not suspect that his own sexual instincts were not exactly normal. While no one has ever brought forward any evidence that Whitman was guilty of homosexual practices, it seems clear that, as Bliss Perry once put it, the poet carried into manhood something of the bisexual attitude of the child. The "Children of Adam" poems, which celebrate "amativeness," or sexual love, are inferior to the "Calamus" poems, which glorify "adhesiveness," or the attraction of man for man. In fact, the best of the "Children of Adam" poems, "A Woman Waits for Me," in its earliest known form had as its subject not a woman but a man. "Calamus" contains some of Whitman's finest poems, but the doctrine of "adhesiveness" is no firm basis for American democracy.

That Whitman was finally admitted in 1930 to the Hall of Fame for Great Americans was due mainly to the persistent urging of the passionate minority who recognized and loved great and original poetry. His reputation developed first among intellectuals, the literary radicals who were dissatisfied with both the form and the content of conventional verse. Whitman had no influential publisher eager to promote his fame as the Houghton Mifflin Company in Boston was promoting the fame of the New England poets; but in England as well as in America Whitman had friends and disciples—as Melville had not —who were willing to fight to make the world accept *Leaves of Grass* as the creation of a poet and prophet.

The New England Brahmins, who had ignored Melville, rejected Whitman even more emphatically than they had rejected Poe. Whittier, it is said, threw into the fire his copy of *Leaves of Grass*. Lowell on December 7, 1863, wrote to a minister who thought Lowell had given a copy of Whitman's book to the Harvard College Library: "It is a book I never looked into farther than to satisfy myself that it was a solemn humbug." That verdict from the outstanding American literary critic of the time! Whitman once remarked to Horace Traubel and other friends: "Lowell is one of my real enemies. He never relaxed in his opposition; Lowell never even tolerated me as a man. He not only objected to my book; he objected to me."

In *Over the Teacups* (1891), his last book, Oliver Wendell Holmes commented briefly on *Leaves of Grass*. The Autocrat was discussing a subject for which he had no enthusiasm, American literary nationalism:

> If it means dispensing with punctuation, coining words at will, self-revelation unrestrained by a sense of what is decorous, declamations in which everything is glorified without being idealized, "poetry" in which the reader must make the rhythms which the poet has not made for him, then I think we had better continue literary colonists. I shrink from a lawless independence to which all the virile energy and trampling audacity of Mr. Whitman fail to reconcile me.

In a different mood Dr. Holmes wisely concluded: "But I suppose I belong to another age, and must not attempt to judge the present by my old-fashioned standards."

In November, 1880, a younger critic, Thomas Bailey Aldrich, soon to succeed Howells as editor of the *Atlantic Monthly*, wrote to Edmund Clarence Stedman, who had published the first important American critical essay on Whitman: "I admire his color and epithets and lyrical outbreaks when I can forget the affectation which underlies it all. . . . There is something unutterably despicable in a man writing newspaper puffs of himself. I don't believe a charlatan can be a great poet."

In 1900 Barrett Wendell allotted to Whitman a chapter of fourteen pages in his *Literary History of America*, but in the verses of this "literary eccentric" he found "a complete confusion of values." Wendell, who was no democrat, objected to Whitman's creed, which seemed to the critic that "as God made everything, one thing is just as good as another." After quoting a famous passage from the "Song of Myself," Wendell commented: "In an inextricable hodge-podge you find at once beautiful phrases and silly gabble, tender imagination and insolent commonplace,—pretty much everything, in short, but humour." Wendell quoted a long passage from "Crossing Brooklyn Ferry," which seemed to him one of Whitman's best poems, and added this comment:

> The eight preceding stanzas are very like this,—confused, inarticulate, and surging in a mad kind of rhythm which sounds as if hexameters

were trying to bubble through sewage. For all his faults, Whitman has here accomplished a wonder. Despite his eccentric insolence both of phrase and of temper you feel that in a region where another eye would have seen only unspeakable vileness, he has found impulses which prove it, like every other region on earth, a fragment of the divine eternities.

In his conclusion Wendell wrote: "The spirit of his work is that of world-old anarchy; its form has all the perverse oddity of world-old decadence; but the substance of which his poems are made—their imagery as distinguished from their form or their spirit—comes wholly from our native country." Regretfully, Wendell noted that the older America perished in the Civil War; the new America, he said, was not yet "mature enough for artistic record." Possibly, however, Whitman would be remembered as the man who pointed out "the stuff of which perhaps the new American literature of the future [might] in time be made."

In 1900 another Harvard professor, George Santayana, philosopher, poet, and essayist, set forth his estimate of *Leaves of Grass* in an essay entitled "The Poetry of Barbarism." For Santayana, as for Lord Macaulay and Thomas Love Peacock before him, the earliest poets were the greatest. From the time of Homer down to the end of the nineteenth century, said Santayana, "we see the power of idealization steadily decline." The modern poets, he thought, were "things of shreds and patches"; they were "incapable of any high wisdom, incapable of any imaginative rendering of human life and its meaning." In Whitman's poems Santayana found a "wealth of perception without intelligence and of imagination without taste." He also noted in them a "lack of distinction, absence of beauty, confusion of ideas, incapacity permanently to please." Whitman had thrown overboard the "double discipline," which had been "formed partly in the school of classic literature and polity, and partly in the school of Christian piety"; and the result was a return to something like "barbarism."

Santayana, however, was by no means blind to some of Whitman's better qualities; he gave him credit for "a profound inspiration and a genuine courage." He added: "The absence of any principle of selection or of a sustained style enables him to render aspects of things and of emotion which would have eluded a trained writer. . . . He has accomplished, by the sacrifice of almost every other good quality, something never so well done before." Reluctantly Santayana conceded that in Whitman's case "notoriety [had] become fame."

During his lifetime Whitman and his friends had good reason for their distrust of academic critics, but in 1905 Professor Curtis Hidden Page could say in his *Chief American Poets*: "The question whether Whitman's work is properly to be called poetry at all or not still exists only in a few academic circles." Two years earlier Professor William Peterfield Trent in *A History of American Literature* had discussed Whitman with greater understanding and sympathy than any of his predecessors. For Trent there was in Whitman nothing of the "virulent form of modern decadence" that Max Nordau in *Degeneration* professed to have found. Nor could Trent agree with Santayana that Whitman saw only the surface of things. "Whitman was in many respects the voice of a long silent element of the people of the United States," and "he interpreted their emotions to others if not to themselves." In spite of the great unevenness of his work, Whitman, he said, "seems not only a far better man and truer poet than his censors are willing to admit, but too large a man and poet for adequate comprehension at present."

In 1906 the Houghton Mifflin Company of Boston added to its American Men of Letters series Bliss Perry's biography of Whitman. Perry was a native of New England and was soon to become a professor at Harvard and thus a colleague of Wendell and Santayana, but he knew better than they that Whitman belonged in the canon of the great American writers. Said he: "Whitman . . . is sure, it seems to me, to be somewhere among the immortals. . . . Upon the whole the most original and suggestive poetic figure since Wordsworth . . . no American poet now seems more sure to be read, by the fit persons, after one hundred or five hundred years." In 1918 when volume 2 of *The Cambridge History of American Literature* appeared with a chapter on Whitman by Emory Holloway, one of Trent's former students, the effect was to give a kind of official sanction to the poet's final achievement of a place in the canon of the great American writers.

Before Whitman died in 1892, he was on his way to becoming a figure in world literature. *Leaves of Grass* was being translated into the chief European languages, and it had begun to influence the work of European poets. The intellectuals found in *Leaves of Grass* the kind of poetry they had been led to expect from America. It was a little barbaric perhaps but certainly not reminiscent of Wordsworth or Tennyson, and it bore no resemblance to the poems of Longfellow, which they felt might have been written in the vicinity of the British Museum. The image of America that Whitman's poems conveyed seemed just what a European critic might have expected from his reading of Rousseau, Chateaubriand, de Tocqueville, and Fenimore Cooper. Whitman's literary nationalism had its parallels in various European countries. The Transcendental phase of his philosophy, though he was slow to realize it, derived through Emerson, Coleridge, and Carlyle from the ancient Neo-Platonic philosophers and the poets and the sages of India and the Near East. In his old age Whitman began to realize something of his indebtedness to the long literary tradition which derives ultimately from Greece, Rome, and Palestine. In these later years, conscious of his European admirers, he began to see himself as in some sense a world poet. It was in these years that he wrote "Passage to India" and "Song of the Universal."

After about 1915 Whitman's reputation grew more rapidly in his own country. He became a symbol for the younger poets and novelists who were in rebellion against the Victorian tradition and were revising the canon of the great American writers. In 1915 Van Wyck Brooks wrote in *America's Coming-of-Age*: "Whitman—how can I express it?—precipitated the American character. All those things which had been separate, self-sufficient, incoordinate—action, theory, idealism, business—he cast into a crucible; and they emerged, harmonious and molten, in a fresh democratic ideal, which is based upon the whole personality." In 1919, the year of the Whitman centennial, H. L. Mencken spoke for many besides himself when he wrote in *Prejudices, Third Series* that Whitman was "the greatest poet that America has ever produced." In 1930 the poet was finally admitted to the Hall of Fame for Great Americans. In the same year appeared the posthumous third volume of *Main Currents in American Thought*, in which V. L. Parrington proclaimed Whitman "a great figure, the greatest assuredly in our literature." The first volume to be published in the American Writers series was Floyd Stovall's *Walt Whitman* (1934). Whitman was now beginning to find more of the many readers he had hoped to find in his own country during his lifetime. The Book-of-the-Month Club, which used the 1940 Doubleday edition of *Leaves of Grass* as a "dividend," distributed no less than a quarter of a million copies during the next five years.

The Great Depression turned the minds of many American writers to political and economic problems, and some of them came to regard literature as primarily an instrument for promoting reforms in government. In the early 1930's two left-wing literary historians, V. F. Calverton and Granville Hicks, did their best to make Whitman into a Marxist poet. In his *Whitman* (1938) Newton Arvin came close to enrolling the poet as a member of the Socialist Party of the Depression Era. In the summer, 1939, number of the *Partisan Review* James T. Farrell protested: "Whitman has already been retrospectively admitted to the Communist Party and the People's Front, and such a business surely constitutes an abortion on both history and literary criticism."

In the twentieth century Whitman's influence is evident chiefly in the work of the lesser poets: Edgar Lee Masters, Robinson Jeffers, Hart Crane, James Oppenheim, Stephen Vincent Benét, Carl Sandburg, John Gould Fletcher, and various others. Directly or indirectly he has had an influence upon several American writers of fiction, notably Thomas Wolfe. Scholars, however, have found little evidence of any strong influence upon the work of Robert Frost, Edwin Arlington Robinson, T. S. Eliot, or the Fugitive poets of Vanderbilt University. Eliot was slow in coming to an appreciation of Whitman, and he thought that *Leaves of Grass* had little influence upon his own poetry or that of Ezra Pound. Pound once said that twenty years earlier he had read as many as thirty well-written pages in *Leaves of Grass* but that now he was unable to find them. It seems evident, however, from various references to Whitman in Pound's earlier writings that his own poems had been influenced by Whitman's. On February 1, 1909, he wrote: "From this side of the Atlantic I am for the first time able to read Whitman. . . . I see him America's poet . . . the only one of the conventionly [*sic*] recognized 'American Poets' who is worth reading."

The New Critics were inclined to conclude that Whitman's poems did not withstand close scrutiny like the novels of Henry James, whose reputation was rising as Whitman's was declining. Literary nationalism went out of fashion. In 1939 the *Partisan Review* in a symposium on "The Situation in American Writing" asked various well-known writers whether they thought that "Henry James's work [was] more relevant to the present and future of American writing than Walt Whitman's." Katherine Anne Porter, as I have noted in the chapter on James, chose James. As to Whitman she wrote:

> I am always thrown off by arm-waving and shouting, I am never convinced by breast-beating or huge shapeless statements of generalized emotion. In particular, I think the influence of Whitman on certain American writers has been disastrous, for he encourages them in the vices of self-love . . . , the assumption of prophetic powers, of romantic superiority to the limitations of craftsmanship, inflated feeling and slovenly expression.

Outside of those countries where English is spoken Whitman's vogue in the twentieth century has been far greater than that of Henry James. The 1955 centenary of *Leaves of Grass* brought forth not only Gay Wilson Allen's admirable biography, *The Solitary Singer*, but also numerous tributes and special studies which made it clear that Whitman was still a major figure. His literary nationalism no longer deeply interests our critics, but his poetic power and his philosophy of life still have a strong appeal.

As we look back to his formative years, one wonders at the audacity of the self-educated—and badly educated—young journalist who dared to dream of writing great American poems and, strange to say, succeeded in doing just that. In the winter, 1952, number of the *Kenyon Review* the poet-critic Randall Jarrell published an article entitled "Walt Whitman: He Had His Nerve." Jarrell rated this most unlikely of poets along with Emily Dickinson and Herman Melville (in the prose poetry of *Moby-Dick*) as one of the three greatest of all American poets.

Whitman wrote many pages about the nature and function of poetry in America, but it is not easy to single out what is significant as one reads his clumsy and wordy attempts to explain them. "As a critic of his own work," writes his best biographer, Professor Allen, "he was always inept and totally unable to discriminate between his artistic achievements and failures." Until 1928, when Norman Foerster published his *American Criticism*, few persons had taken Whitman seriously as a literary critic. Foerster carefully formulated the critical principles underlying *Leaves of Grass* which were to have an important influence upon the writers of a younger generation.

Whitman is our most original poet, but on the whole his literary taste seems conventional. His favorite nineteenth-century British poets were Scott and Tennyson. The greatest of all poets, however, were Shakespeare and Homer even though they celebrated aristocratic heroes and not the "divine average." On November 24, 1889, the *Critic* printed Whitman's response to a query the editors had sent to various authors: Whether any living American poet deserved a place among the thirteen "English inheritors of unassail'd renown: Chaucer, Spenser, Shakespeare, Milton, Dryden, Pope, Gray, Burns, Wordsworth, Coleridge, Byron, Shelley, and Keats." Whitman replied: "Of the thirteen British immortals mention'd—after placing Shakspere on a sort of pre-eminence of fame not to be invaded yet—the names of Bryant, Emerson, Whittier and Longfellow . . . deserve in my opinion an equally high niche of renown as belongs to any one of the dozen on that glorious list." These four American poets, so Whitman wrote in a late essay on "Old Poets," all had the "distinctive American quality," as apparently Lowell and Holmes did not. Whitman was somewhat uncertain about the relative merits of the four poets. Once at least he placed Bryant at the head of the list; and yet over and over he insisted that no American writer was greater than Emerson. In a brief essay entitled "Emerson's Books, (The Shadows of Them)," he belittled his own indebtedness to Emerson. Emerson's writings were "always a *make*, never an unconscious growth." "Cold and bloodless intellectuality," he said, "dominates him." Whitman at times wondered whether Emerson really knew or felt "what Poetry is at its highest, as in the Bible, for instance, or Homer or Shakspere." In a revealing sentence he complained that "for a philosopher, Emerson possesses a singularly dandified theory of manners." Emerson was a gentleman in the best New England tradition; Whitman was not, or he never would have printed without Emerson's permission the famous letter he had received from Concord in 1855.

In weighing the literary achievement of Edgar Allan Poe, Whitman finally concluded that Poe probably belonged "among the electric lights of imaginative literature, brilliant and dazzling, but with no heat." Poe's theory that strictly speaking there is no such thing as a long poem seems to have convinced Whitman that he himself should not attempt a poem of great length. In November, 1875, when at long last a monument was erected over Poe's grave in Baltimore, Whitman was the only important American poet to be present for the ceremony.

Whitman was a better critic of poetry than of fiction, and he held a low opinion of his two greatest American contemporaries. Henry James, he said, "is only feathers to me." Of Mark Twain he remarked to Horace Traubel in the late 1880's: "I think he mainly misses fire; I think his life misses fire; he might have been something; but he never arrives."

# Chapter 4. The Later Nineteenth Century

> *The situation of American literature is anomalous. It has no centre, or, if it has, it is like the sphere of Hermes. It is divided into many systems, each revolving around its several sun.*
>
> James Russell Lowell, "Edgar Allan Poe," *Graham's Magazine*, February, 1845

## GENERAL CHARACTERISTICS

The new literary era differed from its predecessor in many ways. The New England–New York area was no longer producing the great majority of important writers. Except for Sarah Orne Jewett and the still unknown Emily Dickinson, the important younger writers who were living in New England were outsiders; and the literary aims of Howells, Henry James, and Mark Twain were widely different from those of Emerson, Hawthorne, Longfellow, and Thoreau. New writers came from the South, the Middle West, and even from the Far West; moreover, they did not form anything like a "school." No two American authors could differ more widely than Henry James and Mark Twain, or Emily Dickinson and Walt Whitman. Constance Fenimore Woolson, who had been born in New England and brought up in the Middle West, wrote to Paul Hamilton Hayne on February 13, 1876, while she was living in the South: "I spoke of myself as a "Philistine," because I do not seem to belong to anybody, or any class. The Boston writers, young and old, hang together; the New York journalists and magazine people have their own creed; and the southern, ditto. Whenever I hear any of these people talk, or receive letters from them, I perceive this."

For the most part the older writers of New England had come from good families that had sent their sons to Bowdoin and Harvard. Few of the important writers of the new generation were college-bred; and many of them, like Howells, Harris, and Mark Twain, had got much of their education in the printer's shop and the newspaper office. They came into literature through the medium of journalism, and they profited by the criticism they received from the editors of the *Atlantic Monthly*, the *Century*, and other magazines. Fortunately for their contributors, these magazines were able to offer higher prices than the earlier magazines, gift books, and annuals had been able to pay to Hawthorne and Poe. With the enactment of the International Copyright Act of 1891 the financial status of the American writer notably improved.

In 1874 Edmund Clarence Stedman said in an interview in Washington: "The New England school of literature, centering in Boston, has been a brilliant one, marked by originality and power, but it has been a feature of a single generation, not destined to be succeeded by another of equal importance. Just as the literary metropolis shifted from Edinburgh to London, so now it is shifting from Boston to New York." Stedman's pronouncement did not please the Bostonians. His friend Thomas Bailey Aldrich, who had recently moved to Boston from New York, wrote to him: "Gad, these Bostonians are not thin-skinned on the subject—they haven't any skin at all!"

The older writers of New England who lived into the 1880's and early 1890's continued to be honored as no American writers have been honored before or since; and the long-established canon of the great American writers continued practically unaltered even beyond the end of the nineteenth century. And yet none of these men had much influence upon their immediate successors. In May, 1881, George E. Woodberry published in the *Fortnightly Review* an article entitled "The Fortunes of Literature under the American Republic," in which he said:

> Irving, it is true, had imitators, who came to nothing; but our fiction does not seem to be different because Hawthorne lived, no poet has caught the music of Longfellow, no thinker carries forward the conclusions of Emerson. These men left no lineage. They are not connected with their countrymen even by the secondary tie of calling into being a body of literature with power to enter effectively into the nation's life, to shape the character and determine the expansion of its thought.

As we shall see, the polls conducted by the *Critic* and other periodicals reveal the continued dominance of the New England writers. Everybody read *Tom Sawyer* and *Huckleberry Finn*, but there were not many who rated these books as literary masterpieces. Few except the highly sophisticated cared much for the novels and tales of Henry James. Some of the southern writers were widely read and admired, but not many critics were willing to admit Sidney Lanier or George W. Cable to the canon. In the 1890's Howells stood higher in the opinion of the literary critics than either Henry James or Mark Twain. They, like Emily Dickinson, had to wait for the twentieth century to canonize them, along with Poe, Melville, Thoreau, and Whitman.

In "Toward a New Canon," published in the *Nation* on April 14, 1932

Carl Van Doren thus described "the canon of American literature" as it was seen in the early twentieth century:

> Bearded and benevolent, the faces of Bryant, Longfellow, Whittier, Lowell, Holmes, and sometimes (rather oddly) Whitman, looked down unchallenged from the walls of schoolrooms. Emerson was the American philosopher, Irving the American essayist, Cooper the American romancer, Hawthorne the American explorer of the soul, Poe the American unhappy poet (unhappy on account of his bad habits), Thoreau the American hermit, Mark Twain the American humorist (barely a man of letters), Henry James the American expatriate, and Howells the American Academy. Here were fifteen apostles set in a rigid eminence, braced by minor figures grouped more randomly about them.

"New York," wrote Howells in 1900, "is a mart and not a capital, in literature as in other things." In New York the literary outlook was different, even to editors and publishers who had grown up in New England. They needed a nationwide market for their wares, and they saw that what their readers wanted was not Transcendentalist poems, essays, and lectures but entertainment in the form of novels and short stories. Much of the new American literature was regional in its subject matter, but it was as never before directed to a nationwide audience. In New York and Philadelphia editors of magazines were quick to note the emergence in the South and the West of new writers whose work seemed promising. They noted also in all sections a great increase in the number of potential purchasers of books and magazines. In September, 1881, *Scribner's Monthly* in welcoming the writers of the New South said: "New England has many advantages, but New England is no longer king. Her great literary school is dying out. . . . The South and the West are hereafter to be reckoned upon in making up the account of our literary wealth, and the North will welcome with no stinted praise and no niggardly hand the best that the South can do."

During the period of Reconstruction the South, defeated and embittered, was reluctant to accept those northern writers who, like Emerson, Lowell, and Whittier, had denounced the South as semibarbarous. The demand for a distinctive southern literature continued for a decade or two. Hopefully a few men and women launched southern literary magazines designed to publish materials that northern editors found unacceptable. With inadequate financial resources, however, they soon found themselves unable to compete with *Harper's* and the *Atlantic Monthly*. By 1880 the northern editors had discovered that their readers liked the romantic and nostalgic stories of the Old South written by the new generation of southern writers. In December, 1888, Albion W. Tourgée, a northern novelist who had spent several years in

North Carolina, wrote in the *Forum*: "Our literature has become not only Southern in type, but distinctively Confederate in sympathy."

Northern and southern writers worked together in an effort to promote reconciliation between the sections. Emerson in old age journeyed down to Virginia to show his good will. In "Under the Old Elm" Lowell paid tribute to the Old Dominion as the mother of Washington. Bayard Taylor befriended Sidney Lanier, and there developed a notable friendship between Whittier and Paul Hamilton Hayne. The friendly aid and encouragement of northern writers and editors meant much to lonely poets and writers of fiction in the poverty-stricken South. Southern readers gradually discovered that there was much in Emerson's *Essays* that seemed beautiful and true. In 1877 Lanier found in Emerson a congenial and powerful influence, and not long afterward he wrote "The Marshes of Glynn." By that time the South was coming to accept the New England writers at the valuation placed upon them in the North and West.

The demand for a great national literature which in the early nineteenth century had taken the form of a demand for a great American poem now became an insistent clamor for the great American novel. Or so one infers from the attitude of many literary journalists. Readers who in the fifties and sixties had failed to see in *Leaves of Grass* the great American poem, in the eighties failed to find in the best books written by Henry James, Howells, and Mark Twain the answer to their prayer for the great American novel.

It was indeed a large order that American novelists were asked to fill. As Herbert R. Brown has described it in "The Great American Novel" (*American Literature*, March, 1935), that much-desired masterpiece was to be "at once radiantly fresh and maturely wise, tender as a young virgin and stalwart as a pioneer, as towering as Niagara and as powerful as the Mississippi, romantic and realistic, didactic and scientific, and withal a tale which should hold children from play and old men from the chimney corner." Competent critics like Howells, Henry James, and Thomas Sergeant Perry ridiculed the whole idea, but the delusion resulting from the confusion of aesthetic values with national pride and patriotic feeling continued even beyond the end of the century.

Why, one wonders, did the literary journalists never ask themselves what (in their sense of the word) are the great English novel, the great French novel, and the great Russian novel? *Tom Jones* is a great English novel and so are *Vanity Fair* and *David Copperfield*, but none of them gives us the whole significance of English life and thought. There are great French novels, but did Balzac even in the many volumes of his *Comédie humaine* embody the essence of French life and thought? Leaving to one side the great novels of Turgenev and Dostoevski, one might argue plausibly enough that Tolstoy's *War and Peace* is the great Russian novel, but what then shall we do with his *Anna Karénina*, which is probably an even greater novel? And do any of the nineteenth-century Russian novels adequately describe those aspects of Russian life and thought that came to play the dominant role in the Russia of Lenin and Stalin?

The impact upon literature and the fine arts which accompanied the worldwide drift toward democracy led to results such as Walt Whitman and other democrats neither understood nor approved. Alexis de Tocqueville, who had much to say about "the tyranny of the majority," observed in 1840 that while democracy had infused a taste for reading in the common people, it had resulted in "the sale of books which nobody much esteems." In the 1850's American literature reached a highwatermark in the work of Emerson, Hawthorne, Thoreau, Melville and Whitman. Yet these years were, in Fred Lewis Pattee's phrase, the "feminine fifties." *The Scarlet Letter* found many readers, but few persons bought copies of *Moby-Dick*, *Walden*, or *Leaves of Grass*. The reading public, wrote Hawthorne in 1855, cared only for cheap novels written by women.

By 1870 advances in public education and improved methods of printing and distribution had brought about another increase in the number of men and women able to read books and magazines. The increase was unfortunately chiefly on the lower intellectual level. In the seventies good taste reached its nadir. In cultivated Boston, where Emerson, Whittier, Holmes, and Lowell were honored as writers have seldom been honored anywhere, the public library in 1872 reported that the authors whose books were most in demand were Mrs. E. D. E. N. Southworth, Mrs. Caroline Lee Hentz, and Mrs. Mary Jane Holmes. Publishers of books had discovered a profitable market among the half-educated, and these novelists and others were giving the undiscriminating what they wanted to read. Publishers were simply not interested in bringing out new editions of *Moby-Dick*, *Walden*, or *Leaves of Grass*.

As one notes the increasing popularity of subliterary fiction in both England and America, one may well wonder why so many of the more intelligent read the novels of Augusta Jane Evans and Mary Elizabeth Braddon rather than the novels of George Meredith and Henry James. One may wonder also how many more readers would have bought novels by Hawthorne and George Eliot if Mrs. Southworth, Elinor Glyn, and their fellows had never published a book.

Literature, like its sister arts, had for centuries been developing its techniques, its traditions, and its critical standards under the patronage of the aristocracy, royalty, or the church. Artists and authors alike had for the most part created their masterpiece for the rich and powerful who in the main also comprised the educated and cultivated minority. In the late nineteenth century the serious writer faced the acute problem—still unsolved in the twentieth century—of holding to high standards and yet finding it possible to live on the income from his books. If he cannot support himself and his family on his royalties, he must resort to something like "moonlighting." How among the many millions who buy an occasional book can he find the "fit audience . . . though few" who will recognize his talent? And if his attitude toward the society in which he lives is one of "alienation," how can he expect it to support him?

## BOOK SALES IN THE UPPER MISSISSIPPI VALLEY IN 1887

On August 27, 1887, a New York weekly, the *Critic*, printed an article by Charles H. Sergel entitled "The Comparative Popularity of Authors." The figures given in the article were obtained, we are told, from an unnamed "wholesale bookstore, whose trade extends over the northern half of the Mississippi Valley," and they cover a period of five years. The figures are not numbers of books sold but percentages. Thus E. P. Roe, whose books top the list, was rated at 1000 while other writers are represented by lower figures in proportion to the sales of their books all the way down to Walt Whitman's 2 and Henry James's 1. I do not think that the sales of books by the same writers would have been very different in New England, the Middle Atlantic states, or the South. It seems obvious, however, that the high rating of Will Carleton was due in large part to the fact that his poems deal with life in the Middle West.

Sergel called attention to the fact that among American writers of fiction seven of the ten most popular novelists were women. He added, however, that the most popular single novel was *Ben-Hur*, and suggested that Lew Wallace "would stand far higher on the list if, instead of only two novels, he had written as many as E. P. Roe or Mrs. [Mary Jane] Holmes." The reader who looks in vain for the name of Mark Twain needs to be reminded that his books were sold only by subscription.

The New England poets are all on the list, but Longfellow (345) and Whittier (139) outsold Emerson, Holmes, and Lowell. Poe (5) and Bret Harte (22) surprisingly enough appear only among the poets. Among writers of fiction Hawthorne got 50 points and Cooper 52. With 14 points Frank R. Stockton was tied with Cable and Howells. All three of them were outranked by Helen Hunt Jackson (30) and Frances Hodgson Burnett, whose *Little Lord Fauntleroy* (1886) was a best-seller. The names of Melville and Thoreau do not appear anywhere on the list.

British authors were widely read. Dickens with 800 points was second only to the invincible E. P. Roe; Scott with 232 points was outselling Mrs. Stowe, who had only 122. Among the poets Tennyson (272) was outranked only by Longfellow (345). The forgotten Owen Meredith (223), outranked only by Tennyson and Shakespeare (242), rated higher as a poet than Byron (117), Scott (114), Burns (103), Thomas Moore (97), or Mrs. Browning (75). It is a little surprising to find that Macaulay (155) was more widely read than Prescott (35), Bancroft (29), or Motley (7). Francis Parkman, now considered the greatest American historian of his time, got only 2 points. The forgotten Josiah Gilbert Holland rated 160 points while Whitman got only 2 points and John Keats and Henry James each only 1. The Americans in the Upper Mississippi Valley who bought these books were no doubt less sophisticated and not so well educated as the readers of the *Critic*, whose various polls are soon to be considered; and yet its readers were as much at sea as to the merits of *Ben-Hur* as those who bought the book in the Upper Mississippi Valley.

PROSE FICTION

| American | | British | |
|---|---|---|---|
| E. P. Roe | 1000 | Dickens | 800 |
| Mrs. Mary J. H. Holmes | 342 | Scott | 232 |
| Louisa M. Alcott | 282 | George Eliot | 84 |
| Harriet Beecher Stowe | 122 | Thackeray | 74 |
| May Agnes Fleming | 110 | Bulwer | 66 |
| Lew Wallace | 100 | Stevenson | 40 |
| Marion Harland | 79 | William Black | 12 |
| Mrs. E. D. E. N. Southworth | 61 | R. D. Blackmore | 10 |
| A. W. Tourgée | 54 | Wilkie Collins | 5 |
| Fenimore Cooper | 52 | Charles Reade | 4 |
| Nathaniel Hawthorne | 50 | Fielding | 1 |
| Edward Eggleston | 46 | Richardson | 0 |
| Marion Crawford | 41 | Smollett | 0 |
| Helen Hunt Jackson | 30 | | |
| Frances Hodgson Burnett | 18 | | |
| G. W. Cable | 14 | | |
| Frank R. Stockton | 14 | | |
| W. D. Howells | 14 | | |
| T. B. Aldrich | 6 | | |
| Henry James | 1 | | |

## Poetry

| American | | British | |
|---|---|---|---|
| Longfellow | 345 | Tennyson | 272 |
| Will Carleton | 215 | Shakespeare | 242 |
| Whittier | 139 | Owen Meredith | 223 |
| Bryant | 28 | Byron | 117 |
| Alice and Phoebe Cary | 25 | Scott | 114 |
| Bret Harte | 22 | Burns | 103 |
| Emerson | 15 | Moore | 97 |
| J. G. Saxe | 15 | Mrs. Browning | 75 |
| Benjamin F. Taylor [?] | 14 | Milton | 66 |
| Lowell | 13 | Jean Ingelow | 53 |
| Holmes | 10 | Mrs. Hemans | 47 |
| Aldrich | 8 | Goldsmith | 36 |
| Bayard Taylor | 6 | Wordsworth | 27 |
| Poe | 5 | Shelley | 23 |
| Stedman | 4 | Pope | 19 |
| Whitman | 2 | Cowper | 19 |
| | | Chaucer | 19 |
| | | Robert Browning | 8 |
| | | Gray | 3 |
| | | Spenser | 2 |
| | | Swinburne | 2 |
| | | Keats | 1 |

## History

| American | | British | |
|---|---|---|---|
| Prescott | 35 | Macaulay | 155 |
| Bancroft | 29 | Gibbon | 96 |
| Motley | 7 | Hume | 42 |
| Parkman | 2 | Rawlinson | 12 |
| McMaster | 2 | Green | 10 |
| | | Carlyle | 9 |
| | | Buckle | 1 |
| | | Lecky | 1 |

## Miscellaneous

| | |
|---|---|
| J. G. Holland (complete works) | 160 |
| Washington Irving (complete works) | 39 |
| O. W. Holmes (prose) | 27 |
| Herbert Spencer | 7 |
| Darwin | 4 |

# THE PHILADELPHIA *WEEKLY PRESS* POLL (1885)

In the summer of 1885 the Philadelphia *Weekly Press* took a poll of its readers, asking each of them to name (1) his favorite story-teller and (2) his favorite poem. On another page I have reprinted the results of the poll as given in the *Literary World* of Boston for August 8, 1885. The two writers of fiction who stood highest were Harriet Beecher Stowe, with 113 votes, and the Reverend E. P. Poe, with 112. Henry James, who so much wanted to be widely read, got only 3 votes. Surprisingly enough, his friend William Dean Howells won third place with 91 votes. Fourth place went to the Scottish novelist William Black, with 65 votes. Mark Twain, who had published *Huckleberry Finn* earlier in the year, got 43 votes. Bret Harte, who had passed the peak of his popularity and was now living abroad, got 14. Albion W. Tourgée, whose novels of the Reconstruction South were widely read, got 12 votes. George W. Cable, whose most recent books had not been well received, got 9. Edward Eggleston got only 2 votes, the same number that was given to the great English novelist, Thomas Hardy. The absence of such names as Scott, Dickens, Bulwer-Lytton, Hugo, and Dumas is due to the provision that only living novelists were eligible. I do not know why the *Weekly Press* poll did not mention Lew Wallace, whose *Ben-Hur* was a notable best-seller. By and large the favorite story-tellers of those who took part in the poll were English and American women. Among the favorites were Mrs. E. D. E. N. Southworth, 36; Elizabeth Stuart Phelps (Mrs. Ward), 30; Louisa May Alcott, 28; Mary Jane Holmes, 26; and "Pansy" (Isabella Alden), 18.

The readers of the *Weekly Press* made it clear by their ballots that their favorite poet was Longfellow. Five of his poems garnered a total of 220 votes: *Evangeline*, 125; "A Psalm of Life," 55; *The Song of Hiawatha*, 26; "The Bridge," 7; and *The Courtship of Miles Standish*, 7. Bryant's "Thanatopsis" was third with 80 votes, but second place went to Thomas Gray's "Elegy Written in a Country Churchyard," 113. "The Raven" got 58 votes, but Poe was apparently no one's favorite story-teller. Whittier had 3 poems on the composite list; Josiah Gilbert Holland, 2; and Lowell, 1. Among the American poets we find no mention of Emerson, Thoreau, Jones Very, Fitz-Greene Halleck, Bayard Taylor, Thomas Bailey Aldrich, Edmund Clarence Stedman, Henry Timrod, or Sidney Lanier. The best-loved of the British poets were Tennyson, Scott, and Burns. Milton's great epic got 40 votes, but it would seem that there were no votes for poems by Wordsworth, Keats, Shelley, Blake, Arnold, Rossetti, Swinburne, or Robert Browning.

The Philadelphia *Weekly Press* has been taking the vote of its readers on a number of questions. Two of them were literary: (1) Who is your favorite living story writer? and (2) Which is your favorite poem? On the first question 127 writers were voted for as follows:

| | | | |
|---|---|---|---|
| H. B. Stowe | 113 | Samuel L. Clemens | |
| E. P. Roe | 112 | (Mark Twain) | 43 |
| W. D. Howells | 91 | J. T. Trowbridge | 40 |
| Wm. Black | 65 | Mrs. Southworth | 36 |
| Elizabeth Stuart Phelps | 30 | Wilkie Collins | 36 |
| Louisa M. Alcott | 28 | Mrs. Oliphant | 22 |
| Mrs. Holmes | 26 | Miss Braddon | 21 |
| Miss Muloch | 15 | Ouida | 17 |
| Bret Harte | 14 | "Pansy" | 16 |
| | | Albion W. Tourgée | 12 |

Among the other votes received were the following: R. D. Blackmore, 4; Frank Stockton, 7; Mrs. A. D. T. Whitney, 5; Augusta J. Evans, 7; Marian [*sic*] Harland, 7; James Park, 3; Jules Verne, 3; Edward Eggleston, 2; E. E. Hale, 1; O. W. Holmes, 6; Julian Hawthorne, 5; Oliver Optic, 9; George Macdonald, 8; Bertha Clay, 13; Rebecca Harding Davis, 8; George W. Cable, 9; Mrs. Frances H. Burnett, 8; Charles Egbert Craddock, 8; Mrs. Henry Wood, 5; Thomas Hardy, 2; Henry James, 3; T. B. Aldrich, 1; Mary Cecil Hay, 5; Donald G. Mitchell, 1; Mrs. A. L. Wister, 1.

On the second question 178 poems were voted for:

| | | | |
|---|---|---|---|
| Evangeline | 125 | The Raven | 58 |
| Gray's Elegy | 113 | Psalm of Life | 55 |
| Thanatopsis | 80 | Lady of the Lake | 43 |
| Paradise Lost | 40 | O, Why Should the Spirit | |
| Hiawatha | 20 | of Mortal Be Proud | 30 |
| Lucile | 16 | Snow Bound | 17 |
| Home, Sweet Home | 13 | In Memoriam | 17 |
| Maud Muller | 12 | Enoch Arden | 15 |
| Cotter's Saturday Night | 10 | Barbara Frietchie | 12 |
| Childe Harold | 8 | Lalla Rookh | 11 |
| Courtship [of] Miles Standish | 7 | Locksley Hall | 8 |
| The Deserted Village | 5 | Pope's Essay on Man | 9 |
| | | Iliad | 3 |

Other poems receiving votes were: Star Spangled Banner, 10; Ancient Mariner, 2; Vision of Sir Launfal, 4; Midsummer Night's Dream, 2; Curfew Shall Not Ring Tonight, 14; Sheridan's Ride, 3; Charge of the Light Brigade, 4; Bitter Sweet, 6; Burns's Farewell to Highland Mary, 7; Marmion, 4; Kathrina, 6; The Bridge, 7; Burial of Sir John Moore, 4.

*The practice of classifying authors and ticketing them with their relative rank is doubtless amusing to those who do it . . . but it is scarcely more conclusive than debate on the ancient question, "Which is preferable, summer or winter?"*
Henry C. Vedder, *American Writers of To-day*

THE COUNT. *But is it a good play, Mr. Bannal? That's a simple question.*
BANNAL. *Simple enough when you know. If it's by a good author, it's a good play, naturally. That stands to reason. Who is the author? Tell me that; and I'll place the play for you to a hair's breadth.*
Bernard Shaw, *Fanny's First Play*

## THE *CRITIC*'S POLLS (1884, 1893)

During Matthew Arnold's lecture tour of the United States in 1883 the *Century Magazine*, remembering the critic's essay on "The Literary Influence of Academies," published a brief history of the French Academy under the title "The Forty Immortals." A Boston reader wrote to the editors of the *Critic* suggesting a poll of its readers to select forty Americans who might constitute an American academy of arts and letters. The Bostonian's suggestion led the *Critic* to embark on a series of polls designed to select the greatest American writers and their best books. The *Critic*, which was probably the best American literary weekly of its day, was edited by Jeannette and Joseph Gilder, whose brother Richard Watson Gilder was editor of the *Century*.

On April 12, 1884, the *Critic*, after polling its readers, published "Our Forty Immortals" and suggested them as a nucleus for a possible American academy of letters. Later the *Critic* listed forty more of the names suggested by its readers. The first three places went to the surviving members of the New England "school": Holmes with 130 votes, Lowell with 128, and Whittier with 125. George Bancroft the historian was fourth with 121 votes. The greatest of the New England historians, Francis Parkman, got only 34 votes and was ranked fortieth. Howells won fifth place with 119 votes; Bret Harte was eighth with 105 votes. Walt Whitman, who was a regular contributor to the *Critic*, was twentieth with 76 votes, two notches below the forgotten Richard Henry Stoddard and James Freeman Clarke. George W. Cable was twelfth with 87 votes, outranking Henry James, who got 86 votes, and Mark Twain, who got only 84. Apparently no one voted for Herman Melville, and probably few of the *Critic*'s readers knew that he was still living in the city where the magazine was published.

On April 19 the *Literary World* of Boston reprinted the names of the second as well as those of the first forty "immortals" and commented: "As to the first of these lists it has a decidedly New England, not to say Bostonian, complexion, and suggests that the sceptre of literary leadership may not yet have departed to New York after all."

Edmund Gosse, writing in the London *Speaker*, suggested that the United States might possibly have as many as eighteen writers worthy of the high honor but certainly not so many as forty; and he complained that he could not find in the *Critic's* list the name of Thomas Nelson Page, whom he would have included "for the sake of those exquisite Virginian tales of his."

### The First Forty

1. Oliver Wendell Holmes, 130
2. James Russell Lowell, 128
3. John Greenleaf Whittier, 125
4. George Bancroft, 121
5. William Dean Howells, 119
6. George William Curtis, 118
7. Thomas Bailey Aldrich, 111
8. Bret Harte, 105
9. Edmund Clarence Stedman, 104
10. Richard Grant White, 102
11. Edward Everett Hale, 100
12. George W. Cable, 87
13. Henry James, 86
14. Mark Twain, 84
15. Charles Dudley Warner, 84
16. Henry Ward Beecher, 83
17. James Freeman Clarke, 82
18. Richard Henry Stoddard, 82
19. William Dwight Whitney, 77
20. Walt Whitman, 76
21. Asa Gray, 69
22. Noah Porter, 66
23. John Fiske, 62
24. Theodore A. Woolsey, 57
25. A. Bronson Alcott, 55
26. Julian Hawthorne, 55
27. John Burroughs, 52
28. Mark Hopkins, 52
29. Thomas Wentworth Higginson, 49
30. John G. Saxe, 49
31. Octavius Brooks Frothingham, 48
32. George F. Fisher, 47
33. Moses Coit Tyler, 45
34. Charles A. Dana, 44
35. Donald G. Mitchell, 41
36. Alexander Winchell, 38
37. Edwin P. Whipple, 37
38. George Parsons Lathrop, 36
39. William Wetmore Story, 36
40. Francis Parkman, 36

### The Second Forty

41. Phillips Brooks, 33
42. George Ticknor Curtis, 33
43. William A. Hammond, 32
44. E. L. Youmans, 32
45. Austin Fling, Jr., 31
46. William Graham Sumner, 31
47. James D. Dana, 30
48. John G. Dalton, 29
49. Parke Godwin, 28
50. Henry C. Lea, 28
51. F. Marion Crawford, 27
52. Richard Watson Gilder, 27
53. Albion W. Tourgée, 27
54. Edward Eggleston, 25

55. W. W. Godwin, 25
56. Joaquin Miller, 25
57. John Townsend Trowbridge, 25
58. Henry Cabot Lodge, 24
59. Charles Eliot Norton, 24
60. John Bach McMaster, 23
61. Francis J. Child, 22
62. James Parton, 21
63. Joel Chandler Harris, 21
64. Joseph Cook, 20
65. Edgar Fawcett, 20
66. John Hay, 16
67. Charles Godfrey Leland, 16

68. Brander Matthews, 14
69. Whitelaw Reid, 14
70. Hubert Howe Bancroft, 13
71. George Henry Boker, 13
72. Arthur Sherburne Hardy, 13
73. William Winter, 13
74. Horace E. Scudder, 12
75. Andrew D. White, 12
76. Will Carleton, 11
77. William T. Harris, 11
78. Henry H. Hudson, 11
79. David Swing, 11
80. Charles A. Young, 11

In its issue of July 19, 1890, the *Critic* announced the names of "Nine New 'Immortals' " who had been chosen to replace those who had died since 1884. These new "immortals" were chosen not by the readers of the *Critic* but by the surviving members of the original forty. Here are the nine with the number of votes given to each of them:

Richard Watson Gilder, 17
Phillips Brooks, 15
Charles Eliot Norton, 15
Francis James Child, 12
Frank R. Stockton, 11

Henry Charles Lea, 10
Andrew D. White, 10
Joel Chandler Harris, 9
Horace Howard Furness, 8

The editors of the *Critic* noted that three of the thirty-one surviving academicians did not vote: "George Bancroft, who was very feeble; Mr. [Walt] Whitman, who is a disbeliever in 'close corporations'; and Mr. [Henry] James, whose absence is unaccounted for." James, as the *Critic* failed to note, had in 1886 declined the invitation of the *Pall Mall Magazine* to take part in a poll to select the one hundred best books.

On August 21, 1890, the New York *Nation* analyzed the final list of the immortal forty and announced that, whether one classified the writers according to the states in which they were born or those in which they now lived, "New England and New York, it seems, still furnish the bulk of the recognized authors of the nation. . . ." Of the total number no less than twenty-five had been born in New England, seventeen in Massachusetts alone; and fourteen were graduates of Harvard.

On July 17, 1886, the editors of the *Critic* with the assistance of some twenty writers had published a list of "A Hundred and Twenty-five Great Authors," in which the only American names were those of Emerson, Franklin, Hawthorne, Holmes, Irving, Longfellow, and Lowell. The list did not include the names of Whitman, Melville, Poe, Henry James, or Mark Twain. A week later, however, the *Critic* included all five of them—even Melville—in its list of "A Hundred American Authors," arranged in alphabetical order. In 1886 the South was the most popular background in American fiction and the list included Cable, John Esten Cooke, Harris, Lanier, Mary Noailles Murfree, and William Gilmore Simms.

On July 31 the *Critic* printed a letter from Donald G. Mitchell ("Ik. Marvel"), whose name had appeared in "A Hundred American Authors." Mitchell found himself embarrassed because there were names in the list which he did not know. He added prophetically: "It appears to me that in making it you have been treading on slippery ground. . . . Fifty years would—I should say—make grievous excoriations of your list."

Undiscouraged, the *Critic* in the spring of 1893 took a poll of its readers to select "The Best Ten American Books." On May 27 the results were announced: (1) Emerson's *Essays*, 512 votes; (2) Hawthorne's *The Scarlet Letter*, 493; (3) Longfellow's *Poems*, 444; (4) Mrs. Stowe's *Uncle Tom's Cabin*, 434; (5) Holmes's *The Autocrat of the Breakfast-Table*, 388; (6) Irving's *The Sketch Book*, 307; (7) Lowell's *Poems*, 269; (8) Whittier's *Poems*, 256; (9) Lew Wallace's *Ben-Hur*, 250; and (10) Motley's *Rise of the Dutch Republic*, 246. A little later the *Critic* rearranged its list to indicate the total number of votes given to each writer. As a result, Hawthorne took first place; Emerson, second; Lowell, third; and Irving, fourth.

In its issue of June 3, 1893, the *Critic* extended its list to include twenty writers who got fewer votes than the first ten. Mark Twain was fifteenth with 72 votes; Whitman was twenty-eighth, with 24; and Thoreau was thirtieth and last with only 20. The *Critic*'s readers could not muster as many as twenty votes for Poe, Melville, or Henry James. In the June 3 issue the editors pointed out that American literature was still largely the creation of the New England writers:

> Of the first ten authors in this list, it will be observed that eight are New Englanders; while of the remaining twenty, fourteen were natives of the New England States. Of the whole number fewer than 27 per cent. were born elsewhere than in New England. Only ten of the thirty are living, and of these five are New Englanders.

The editors of the *Critic*, reflecting on their readers' choice of "The Best Ten American Books," gave their own reaction: "The most extraordinary omissions from this list are, to our thinking, the poems of Emerson and Poe and the Autobiography of Franklin."

Edmund Gosse, writing to the *Critic* on June 3, 1893, expressed his surprise that "among these thirty [who received as many as twenty votes] does not occur the name of the most perfect, the most original, the most exquisite of the American poets [Poe]." He added:

> The omission is extraordinary and sinister. If I were an American, I should be inclined to call it disastrous. While every year sheds more lustre on the genius of Poe among the most weighty critical authorities of England, of France, of Germany, of Italy, in his own country prejudice is still so rampant that he failed to secure a paltry twenty votes when Wallace (who on earth is, or was Wallace?) secures 252, Mrs. Jackson 57, and Mitchell (who is, or was, Mitchell?) 42. You must look to your own house, but it makes one wonder what is the standard of American style.

The omission of Poe and the inclusion of *Ben-Hur* in the list of the ten best American books indicates a failure on the part of the *Critic's* readers to distinguish between popular fiction and the work of a major American writer. A generation later in *The Spirit of American Literature* (1913) John Macy was to pronounce *Ben-Hur* "fit work for a country clergyman with a pretty literary gift" but "a ridiculous inanity to come from a man who had seen the things that Wallace saw [in Shiloh and other battles of the Civil War]!" To Macy the book was an "example of what seems to be the American habit of writing about everything except American life." And yet in the very year that Macy's book was published, Harper and Brothers sold to Sears, Roebuck and Company one million copies of *Ben-Hur*. This, as Frank Luther Mott pointed out in *Golden Multitudes* (1947), was "the greatest book-order in publishing history." No one can be sure just what qualities in a book make it a best-seller, but James D. Hart's suggestion in *The Popular Book* (1949) is probably as accurate as any. *Ben-Hur*, he said, "combined the historical values of Scott and the moral worth of Mrs. Stowe, the two previous novelists who had battered down almost the last prejudices against fiction."

> *The principle of universal suffrage, however applicable to matters of government . . . is by no means applicable to matters of taste. . . . The highest efforts of genius, in every walk of art can never be properly understood by the generality of mankind.*
>
> William Hazlitt, "Why the Arts Are Not Progressive"

## LITERATURE'S POLL, 1899

In February, 1899, the editor of *Literature*, John Kendrick Bangs, announced the results of a poll he had taken of its readers asking them: "What ten of our many authors do the readers of *Literature* consider to be most worthy to become charter members of the American Academy?" Apparently only about a hundred readers voted, each of them naming ten writers. A few of them wanted to vote for Rudyard Kipling. Others objected to Bret Harte and Henry James because they had chosen to live outside the United States. Here are the twenty writers who headed the list:

| | | | |
|---|---|---|---|
| William Dean Howells . . . | 84 | George W. Cable . . . . . | 45 |
| John Fiske . . . . . . . | 82 | Charles Dudley Warner . . | 43 |
| Mark Twain . . . . . . | 80 | Donald G. Mitchell . . . . | 36 |
| Thomas Bailey Aldrich . . . | 74 | Henry Van Dyke . . . . . | 36 |
| Frank R. Stockton . . . . | 59 | James Whitcomb Riley . . . | 36 |
| Henry James . . . . . . | 56 | Richard Henry Stoddard . . | 34 |
| S. Weir Mitchell . . . . . | 51 | Mary Wilkins Freeman . . . | 27 |
| Bret Harte . . . . . . . | 51 | Margaret Deland . . . . . | 21 |
| John Burroughs . . . . . | 49 | Richard Harding Davis . . | 19 |
| Edmund Clarence Stedman . | 46 | Bronson Howard . . . . . | 11 |

Francis F. Browne, founder and editor of the *Dial*, which was then published in Chicago, reprinted the complete list in its June issue and added some rather severe comments on the whole procedure. E. C. Stedman, he thought, would have been a better choice than Howells to head the list. It was, he said, nothing but "critical ineptitude that could set Mr. Riley above Mr. Stoddard," and he asked why the popular Frank R. Stockton should outrank Henry James, Bret Harte, and Stedman. Browne scanned the list in vain for the names of Dr. Edward Everett Hale, Colonel Thomas Wentworth Higginson, and "the most typical academician we have, Mr. Charles Eliot Norton." Browne concluded: "It is because no form of popular vote would ever, by any possibility, single out the men most deserving of this sort of distinction that the *plébiscite* Academy can never be anything but a rather bad jest."

In the fall of the following year, after seeing the results of the first election to the Hall of Fame for Great Americans, Rebecca Harding Davis wrote in the *Independent* for October 25:

> The voting habit is a chronic disease now among Americans. . . .
> For the plebiscite is the voice of God—it cannot err.
> For example: At intervals of a few months some editor calls upon his readers to decide now and forever, by vote, which American poet or artist, short story or water-color, is and ever shall be the foremost and best. A hundred or two votes are taken from among the eighty millions of Americans, amid breathless excitement in the breasts of the editor

and the voters. A decision is reached by the majority of these voters and is announced as final; but a month or two later another editor holds another election and we are all at sea again, and know not who are our true demigods, and Fame gives uncertain squawks through her trumpet, not knowing what she is bidden to say.

> So an election to the French Academy is not inevitably the reward of literary excellence. In every generation there is at least one of the best authors who is pointedly left out, and is said to occupy the forty-first armchair—the number of the immortals being limited to forty. . . .
> While great writers are not seldom left in outer darkness, others are admitted whose literary production is of the slimmest.
>
> Albert Guérard, *Literature and Society*

## THE AMERICAN ACADEMY OF ARTS AND LETTERS

In 1898 the Social Science Association created the National Institute of Arts and Letters. With its two hundred members the institute proved unwieldy, and at the suggestion of Edmund Clarence Stedman it created the American Academy of Arts and Letters with a membership limited to thirty (later raised to fifty) to be chosen from its own body. The academy came into existence in 1904, just twenty years after the *Critic* had begun its series of polls. The first seven members, elected by secret ballot in 1904, were William Dean Howells, Augustus Saint-Gaudens, Edmund Clarence Stedman, John La Farge, Mark Twain, John Hay, and Edward McDowell. Among the writers elected in the next four years were Thomas Bailey Aldrich, Richard Watson Gilder, Joel Chandler Harris, William James (who declined), Edward Everett Hale, George W. Cable, Thomas Wentworth Higginson, Donald Grant Mitchell, Henry Van Dyke, William Crary Brownell, Julia Ward Howe, F. Hopkinson Smith, F. Marion Crawford, Hamilton Wright Mabie, Bronson Howard, Brander Matthews, and Thomas Nelson Page. At the first organized meeting in November, 1908, Howells was elected president. In his presidential address in December, 1909, Howells, who well knew how precarious a thing is an author's reputation, said:

It is possible that, by an oversight, which we should all deplore, some artist or writer or composer whose work has given him the right to be of us is not of us. It is also possible that time will decide that some of us who are now here were not worthy to be here, and by this decision we must abide. But until it is rendered, we will suffer with what meekness, what magnanimity, we may the impeachments of those contemporaries who may question our right to be here.

There was some justification for the complaints of various critics that New Englanders bulked much too large in the membership of both the institute and the academy. In 1916 the Congress finally granted a charter to the academy, but there was considerable opposition to that action. Representative Charles Henry Sloan of Nebraska made the point that the "50 men named in one-sixteenth part of the United States" represented "less than one-third of the population of the United States." "This," he said, "is how I would dispose of it. I propose to introduce an amendment that these people, to whom this bill attributes all the brains of America, and who have seen fit to reside in this little province in the northeast, let it be called the Academy of Northeastern America."

The academy was severely criticized on the ground that it represented only outmoded and reactionary artists and writers. On April 26, 1912, John Macy wrote in the preface to *The Spirit of American Literature*:

> The National Institute of Arts and Letters announced the Forty American Immortals, the first roster of an absurd Yankee imitation of the French Academy. Twenty-eight men, "chosen from among the greatest living American writers" (that is, of course, men past middle age), were elected to immortality on the score of literary achievement. On the roll are exactly three men who have made literature—Mr. Henry James, Mr. Howells, and Mr. James Whitcomb Riley. . . . there is no other genius that one would nominate for a place in it, except Mrs. [Edith] Wharton and Mrs. [Mary Wilkins] Freeman, who cannot be admitted because they are women.

The gulf that separated the literary generations was to become very obvious in 1923 when the academy moved into the magnificent building given by Archer Huntington and proceeded, in a four-day festival, to honor the memory of James Russell Lowell, who had died in 1891. The long-time secretary of the academy, Robert Underwood Johnson, said that, after Emerson, Lowell was "the foremost American man of letters."

The National Institute of Arts and Letters was a conservative body, too. In 1928 Wilbur Cross, who was to serve as its president from 1931 to 1936, denounced Gertrude Stein and James Joyce as the "bores" of contemporary literature. The charge came from a fine scholar who was not only editor of the

*Yale Review* but the author of a widely-used history of the English novel.

In 1930 Sinclair Lewis, a graduate of Yale and the first American to receive the Nobel Prize for Literature, denounced the academy in his Stockholm address. He conceded that the academy had among its members "so admirable and courageous a scholar as Wilbur Cross and several first-rate writers: the poets Edwin Arlington Robinson and Robert Frost, the free-minded publicist James Truslow Adams, and the novelists Edith Wharton, Hamlin Garland, Owen Wister, Brand Whitlock and Booth Tarkington." Lewis then proceeded to list those American writers who should have been and were not members of the academy: Theodore Dreiser, H. L. Mencken, George Jean Nathan, Eugene O'Neill, Edna St. Vincent Millay, Carl Sandburg, Robinson Jeffers, Vachel Lindsay, Edgar Lee Masters, Willa Cather, Joseph Hergesheimer, Sherwood Anderson, Ring Lardner, Ernest Hemingway, Louis Bromfield, Wilbur Daniel Steele, Fannie Hurst, Mary Austin, James Branch Cabell, Edna Ferber, and Upton Sinclair. The American academy, said Lewis, "does not represent literary America of today—it represents only Henry Wadsworth Longfellow."

In later years the various awards sponsored by both the academy and the institute have in many instances gone to writers whom their members were loudly condemning in the 1920's. The Gold Medal awarded by the institute went in 1950 to Mencken and in 1957 to Dos Passos. The Award of Merit Medal established by the academy in 1940 was given to Dreiser in 1944 and to Hemingway in 1954. The William Dean Howells Medal established by the academy in 1921, after being awarded to Mary Wilkins Freeman, Willa Cather, Pearl S. Buck, Ellen Glasgow, and Booth Tarkington, was in 1950 awarded to William Faulkner.

If the record of the American academy is not very impressive, neither is that of its model, the French academy, of which Albert Guérard wrote in *Literature and Society* (1935):

> Molière was [not a gentleman but] a "mountebank," appearing on the stage in broad farcical roles; in his lifetime, he could not be thought of as a candidate. After his death, he was admitted in effigy, and his bust bears the handsome apology: "nothing was lacking to his glory; *he* was lacking to ours." Diderot, the hackwriter and Bohemian, Rousseau the vagabond, in spite of their increasing prestige, were not eligible. Neither was Balzac, ever in fear of the sheriff; nor Alexandre Dumas, whose life was a Christmas Pantomime, all glittering tinsel and paste. Zola knocked most insistently at the inexorable door; it became a perennial jest of literary Paris. . . . He was invariably, almost unanimously blackballed.

*Fame, as a noble mind conceives and desires it, is not em-
bodied in a monument, a biography, or the repetition of a
strange name by strangers; it consists in the immortality of a
man's work, his spirit, his efficacy, in the perpetual rejuvena-
tion of his soul in the world.*

George Santayana, *Reason in Society*

## THE HALL OF FAME FOR GREAT AMERICANS

The Hall of Fame for Great Americans has its home on University Heights
in New York City in a beautiful building designed by Stanford White. The
endowment that made it possible was a gift to New York University from
Mrs. Finley J. Shepard (née Helen Gould). At its first election in the fall of
1900 the one hundred electors chose twenty-nine great Americans, of whom
the first seven were, in order: Washington, Lincoln, Webster, Franklin, Grant,
Marshall, and Jefferson. Some of these men had written materials of more
than ephemeral importance, especially Lincoln and Franklin; but they were
not elected to the Hall of Fame as writers, nor were Jonathan Edwards and
William Ellery Channing, who were also elected in 1900. The four who in
that year were chosen as great American writers were, in order: Emerson,
who got 87 votes; Longfellow, 85; Irving, 83; and Hawthorne, 73.* Only persons who had been dead for ten years were eligible, and consequently Lowell
and Whittier were not admitted until the second election in 1905. Among the
names of the seven writers elected in 1910 were those of the historians George
Bancroft (53 votes) and John Lothrop Motley (51). Francis Parkman was
not elected until 1915; William Hickling Prescott and Henry Adams are still
not in the Hall of Fame. Other writers elected in 1910 were Bryant (59),
Cooper (62), Holmes (69), Harriet Beecher Stowe (74) and—at long last—
Edgar Allan Poe (69). At the first election in 1900, Poe had received only
38 votes while Longfellow got 85 and Irving, 83. President Hadley of Yale

* Not long before the Hall of Fame held its first election, two newspapers, the Min-
neapolis *Times* and the Brooklyn *Eagle*, asked their readers to name the best American
writers. In an article entitled "Guesses at Fame" (*Independent*, August 16, 1900), Thomas Wentworth Higginson reported the order in which seven American authors were
ranked:

|  | Brooklyn *Eagle* | Minneapolis *Times* |
|---|---|---|
| Longfellow | 7 | 14 |
| Irving | 13 | 9 |
| Emerson | 15 | 12 |
| Hawthorne | 18 | 22 |
| Bryant | 20 | 17 |
| Jonathan Edwards | 26 | 39 |
| Poe | 33 | 37 |

explained why, he thought, Poe had not been elected: "Poe wrote like a drunkard and a man who is not accustomed to pay his debts." In 1905, when Lowell got 59 votes and Whittier 53, Poe got only 42. When Poe's election was announced, Walter Hines Page was moved to write: "Edgar Allan Poe might be described as the man who made the Hall of Fame famous. He made it famous for ten years by being kept out of it, and he has now given it a renewed lease of fame by being tardily admitted to it."

One of the electors, Edmund Clarence Stedman, had been so much disturbed by his colleagues' refusal to elect Poe and Cooper that in an article entitled "Poe, Cooper and the Hall of Fame," published in the *North American Review* in 1908, only a few months before his death, he made this eloquent appeal to the college of electors:

> On your consciences, fellow judges, whether you are realists or dreamers, jurists, scholars or divines, pay some slight regard to that voice of the outer world, which one of our own writers termed the verdict of "a kind of contemporaneous posterity"; note that there is scarcely an enlightened tongue into which Poe's lyrics and tales have not been rendered,—that he is read and held as a distinctive genius, in France, in Spain, Germany, Italy, Russia, Scandinavia,—that the spell of his art is felt wherever our own English speech goes with the flags of its two great overlands. Fame! Is there one of us still unconscious of Poe's *fame?*

Mark Twain was elected to the Hall of Fame only ten years after his death, but Walt Whitman, who had died in 1892, had to wait until 1930 before he was admitted. As Charles B. Willard points out in *Whitman's American Fame* (1950), the poet got only 10 votes in 1915 when Louisa May Alcott got 44 and Helen Hunt Jackson, 25. In 1920 Whitman got 20 votes; Louisa May Alcott, 57; and Helen Hunt Jackson, 37. On November 9 of that year the New York *Times* commented in an editorial: "Whitman was a great writer and he has become famous, but that is not enough to get him into the Hall of Fame." In 1925 Whitman got 44 votes. He was finally admitted in 1930, when 64 of the 106 electors gave him their votes. The ceremony of admission took place on May 14, 1931. Mr. Willard remarks: "In this academic setting, enthusiast, scholar, and creative writer joined in dedicating this belated memorial to the man and poet whose fame they had been building for forty years."

In 1922—at a time when a new canon of the great American writers was beginning to take shape—the rules governing election to the Hall of Fame were changed so that no person was eligible until he had been dead for twenty-five years. This no doubt is a partial explanation of the fact that no writers were chosen in the elections of 1925, 1935, 1940, 1955, and 1965; and yet it is evident that before 1915, electors were more inclined to choose writers than their successors have been. In 1945 Thomas Paine (51 votes) and Sidney Lanier (48) were elected. In 1960 Thoreau (63 votes) was elected ninety-eight years after his death. In 1900 only three of the electors had voted to admit him.

The electors, chosen by the New York University Senate, are divided among the following groups of American citizens: "1. Actual or former University or College Executives, 2. Historians or Professors of History or Literature, 3. Scientists, 4. Authors, Editors, and Artists, 5. Men and Women of Affairs, 6. Actual or former High Public Officials, and 7. Actual or former Justices, national or state." The names chosen by a majority of the electors have to be approved by the University Senate. In the early days there were among the electors no less than six honorary representatives of theological seminaries in the vicinity of New York City. Perhaps they had something to do with the tardiness of the electors in admitting to the Hall of Fame three writers who were widely regarded as literary black sheep: Paine, Poe, and Whitman.

No one who has examined the long list of the members of the college of electors from 1900 to 1965 would question their general intelligence or their competence in their respective fields; but among the seven classes of electors only a portion of the second and fourth categories have any special qualifications for selecting the best writers. College presidents, scientists, judges, and men of affairs when called upon to pass judgment upon the merits of an American author whose books they probably have not looked into for twenty years would come up with a verdict that was a decade or two behind the times. And if the puzzled elector asked the advice of friends and associates, is there any assurance that he would be any the wiser? Imagine an educator, a justice of the U. S. Supreme Court, or a scientist (in a field where he has no "controls") called upon to pass upon the claims of Melville, Howells, or Emily Dickinson. He has probably not read *Moby-Dick*, or *A Modern Instance*, or a poem by Emily Dickinson since he left college thirty or more years ago. Is it any wonder that even yet the electors have not voted to admit Melville, Howells, or Emily Dickinson? These writers, whom critics and scholars now rate among our greatest, are little read outside the colleges and universities. Emily Dickinson got only 14 votes in 1940, 6 in 1945, 7 in 1950, 14 in 1955, and only 11 in 1960. Melville has not fared much better with 24 votes in 1935, 23 in 1940, 5 in 1945, 9 in 1950, 16 in 1955, and 22 in 1960, fewer than he had received a quarter of a century earlier. Howells got 2 votes in 1950, 3 in 1955, and none in 1960. Obviously the college of electors has not heard that Howells is a major American writer. Henry Adams got 1 vote in

1955 and only 3 in 1960. Henry James, who is apparently not eligible since he resided outside the United States and died a British subject, nevertheless got 2 votes in 1945, 10 in 1950, none in 1955, and 4 in 1960.

The college of electors has it in its power to confer honor but not fame. Poe and Whitman each enjoyed a worldwide fame long before being admitted to the Hall of Fame. And it is sad to note that in the earlier years the electors chose too many writers whose laurels have withered, while Emily Dickinson and Herman Melville are still outside the Hall of Fame.

> *To the generation of the seventies the inhibitions of the gen-
> teel tradition were all-powerful, and the little Boston group
> set themselves up as a sort of final jurisdiction over American
> letters!*
> Vernon L. Parrington, *Main Currents in American Thought*

## SOME END-OF-THE-CENTURY CRITICAL ESTIMATES

*George E. Woodberry.* George Edward Woodberry (1855–1930) was a native of Massachusetts and a graduate of Harvard. After some years as a professor of literature, first at the University of Nebraska and later at Columbia University, he retired from teaching to devote his time to writing. He published several volumes of poems and essays in criticism. His lives of Emerson, Hawthorne, and Poe are among the best literary biographies of his time.

On November 17, 1900, Woodberry published in *Harper's Weekly* "A Century of Achievement," much of which in 1903 he reprinted in *America in Literature,* from which my quotations are taken. The book is not a formal literary history but a summary of literary achievement in the various sections of the United States. In the chapter dealing with the West, Woodberry played up Bret Harte and Lew Wallace, but he displayed no enthusiasm for Mark Twain. The best that had been written about the South, he said, came from the pens of outsiders like Thackeray and Mrs. Stowe. *Uncle Tom's Cabin* he considered "the one book by which the Old South survives in literature, for better or worse." He added: "And yet it may eventually prove that the song of Dixie is the most immortal contribution that the South has given to the national literature." Such pronouncements make one wonder, as in the case of Barrett Wendell and other northern literary historians, just how much Woodberry had read of, say, Simms and Kennedy or Timrod, Lanier, and Cable.

Woodberry, however, cannot be accused of not having read the writings of Poe, whom he regarded as "the one genius of the highest rank, who belongs to the South." He could find no American trait in Poe, but he praised his originality and power. He held it against Poe that he was, as Woodberry phrased it, "the only poet, so far as I know, who is on record as the defender of human slavery." Woodberry might have been less severe if he had known that the long defense of slavery included in the Virginia edition of Poe's *Works* was actually written by Beverley Tucker.

Emerson and Hawthorne seemed to Woodberry, as they seemed to Barrett Wendell in 1900, "the greatest [American] writers of the last century." He singled out "Bryant, Irving, Cooper, Emerson, Hawthorne, Longfellow, Lowell, and Poe" as "the authors whom the nation as a whole regards as its great writers in pure literature, and none besides." Woodberry did not include Whittier or Holmes, whom he described as a "town wit," or Thoreau, a "leader" among "the describers of nature." Emerson, Hawthorne, and Poe were, he thought, "unique each in his own kind." Yet he regarded Lowell—not Poe—as "our only critic of the first rank." In Whitman's *Leaves of Grass* Woodberry found "a few fine lyrics" and a "natural poetic force without art." He concluded: "A poet in whom the whole nation declines to find its likeness cannot be regarded as representative, though he may smack strongly of some raw earth in the great domain." Clarence Gohdes, a fine critic, maintained that Woodberry's critical estimates were "vitiated by a New England strabismus." Other handicaps were his antipathy to realism and a mistaken conception of the Ideal.

Woodberry was struck by the "complete failure of this literature [of the American renaissance] to establish an American tradition—none of its authors left any successors in the same line. . . . apparently, it is only from a new growth that literature may now be anticipated." "What if it be true," he once remarked, "that our older literature was merely a back-flow from Europe, and the future really is rooted in Mark Twain and Missouri?" Woodberry did not single out among the greatest American books of the nineteenth century *Walden, Moby-Dick, Huckleberry Finn, The Rise of Silas Lapham, The Portrait of a Lady, Leaves of Grass,* or the *Poems* of Emily Dickinson. Melville and Emily Dickinson are not mentioned in his book.

Woodberry in his later years was not in sympathy with those American writers who were establishing a new literary tradition. On May 18, 1911, after living abroad for several years, he wrote to one of his former Columbia students, John Erskine, that he had come to feel that the United States was

a backward nation, in all those things that are in a region above the material and mechanical parts of life and civilization. . . . The democracy in which I was bred was of the souls of men; but the fruit here seems to be of their bodies—comfort and mechanical convenience—admirable but not what we believed in. . . . I am unhappy here, and the country has not the least use for me, or my books, or for poetry at all, and the only instrumentality that counts here is money, and I have not got it. . . . The honor of literature with us is an auction-sale—the owner is dead and gone.

*Edmund Clarence Stedman.* Edmund Clarence Stedman (1833–1908) was not only a better critic than his friend Woodberry; he was, after Lowell and Howells, probably the best critic of American literature in the later nineteenth century. He was a native of Connecticut, but he spent most of his mature life in New York City, where he earned his living as a Wall Street broker. Stedman's ambition was to be a great poet; but with few exceptions his verses, like those of his friends Bayard Taylor and Richard Henry Stoddard, seem feeble and derivative. It was not a favorable time for the writing of poetry as he emphasized in an essay entitled "The Twilight of the Poets."

Stedman's estimates of American writers are found chiefly in a book of critical essays, *Poets of America* (1885), and in two anthologies: *An American Anthology* (1900) and *A Library of American Literature* (11 volumes, 1888–1890), edited by Stedman and Ellen M. Hutchinson. Like his contemporaries, Stedman overrated most of the poets of New England. Lowell, for instance, was for Stedman "our representative man of letters," "our most brilliant and learned critic," and also the author of "our best native idyl," our best example of dialect verse, and "the noblest heroic ode that America has produced—each and all ranking with the first of their kinds in English literature of the modern times."

Stedman's essays on Poe and Whitman, both of which aroused opposition, are probably his best. Josiah Gilbert Holland, who published the two essays in the *Century Magazine,* had little regard for Poe and none at all for Whitman. The essay on the author of *Leaves of Grass,* which it took some courage to write, contributed markedly toward establishing Whitman as an important American poet, but Stedman's judicial appraisal was too lukewarm to please some of Whitman's disciples. It also displeased some of Stedman's friends. After reading the essay, Thomas Bailey Aldrich, soon to succeed Howells as editor of the *Atlantic Monthly,* wrote to Stedman on November 20, 1880: "Whitman's manner is a hollow affectation, and represents neither the man nor the time. . . . That he will outlast the majority of his contemporaries, I haven't the slightest doubt—but it will be in a glass case or a quart of spirits in an anatomical museum."

In the early seventies Stedman, like Aldrich and other eastern writers, felt that "the taste of the newest generation of book-buyers" was being corrupted by the humorous stories and poems in dialect coming out of the West. "The whole country," he said, ". . . is flooded, deluged, swamped, beneath a muddy tide of slang, inartistic bathers [bathos], impertinence and buffoonery that is not wit." In later years, however, the supposedly "genteel" Stedman was an admirer of Mark Twain. After reading *A Connecticut Yankee* in manuscript he wrote to the author on July 7, 1889: "My belief is, on the whole, that you have written a great book, in some respects your most original, most imaginative,—certainly the most effective and sustained." He was, he said, "most impressed by the magnificently riotous and rollicking imagination and often poetry, of the whole work." Stedman suggested only a few minor changes, and the grateful author accepted them.

In 1919 another anthologist, Louis Untermeyer, was to describe Stedman's *An American Anthology* (1900) as a "gargantuan collection of mediocrity and moralizing" which contained "perhaps sixty pages of genuine poetry and no more than ten pages of what might be called American poetry." Stedman's purpose, however, as he explained in his introduction, was not to compile "a Treasury of imperishable American poems." It was, as he indicated in his subtitle, to give "Selections Illustrating the Editor's Critical Review of the Poets and Poetry of Our Land." Stedman certainly included too many verses by the older New England poets, by belated romanticists like Taylor, Stoddard, Woodberry, and Gilder, and by many forgotten poetasters from every section of the United States. Yet in his introduction he made it clear that in his estimation the three greatest and most influential American poets were Emerson, Poe, and Whitman. The figures in his frontispiece, clustered around Bryant as the central figure, were Longfellow, Lowell, Whittier, Holmes, Poe, Whitman, and Lanier (but not Emerson). In 1900 other critics would have excluded Lanier, Whitman, and probably Poe. In the *Anthology* Stedman gave nine pages to Poe, seven to Lanier, and twelve to Whitman. He also included five of the forgotten Melville's poems and five by the still obscure Edwin Arlington Robinson. Thomas Bailey Aldrich protested vigorously in a letter to Stedman against his giving to Lanier in his frontispiece the place of honor which Aldrich thought rightly belonged to Fitz-Greene Halleck, "whose 'Burns,' 'Marco Bozzaris,' and 'Red Jacket' are poems which promise to live as long as any three pieces in the anthology." Lanier, he said, belonged "in the rear rank of minor poets."

Stedman was, as I said in the beginning, one of the best American critics of his time, but he mistakenly assumed that there are critical standards that do not change. In 1885 he concluded his *Poets of America* by stating his conviction that the future historian of American literature would "test his poets and their bequests by the same unswerving laws" that Stedman thought he had employed. He dedicated his book "To the Younger Writers of America," little thinking that in the 1920's a still younger generation would discard his books and his critical standards as the work of an outmoded Victorian.

In 1931 William Allen White (1868–1944), one of the "Younger Writers of America" to whom Stedman had dedicated his book, commented on the subtle changes in literary fashion that had taken place in his own lifetime:

> When the popular fiction of the last quarter of the old century was written and published I read it; I enjoyed it; it seemed to me, some of it, splendid and beautiful. It seemed to reflect life between the words. ... Now as I re-read those old books I find that their charm has vanished; the vividness, the truth and glamour of the pages have gone dead and run drab and saddened. Truth has changed. Man's theory of beauty has changed. His manners and morals have changed. And so the parables of another generation, written to carry home its truth, its sense of beauty, its moral conventions, its tricks and its manners, seem stale and stilted and outworn.[*]

Stedman of course could not foresee the literary revolt of the 1920's; yet in a mood of depression a year before his death he wrote to the youthful Percy Mackaye: "Assuredly I am a buried man in this twentieth century, and it is only now and then when a pick like yours touches my tomb that I indulge in posthumous exclamations."

*Other Critical Estimates.* The publication of Stedman's *American Anthology* in the closing year of the nineteenth century prompted various critics to attempt some evaluation of the nation's literary achievement. On October 16, 1900, the Chicago *Dial*, founded and still edited by Francis F. Browne, praised the anthology in an editorial entitled "A Century of American Verse." The editor wrote: "The best dozen of our American poets are probably Bryant, Emerson, Holmes, Longfellow, Poe, Whitman, Whittier, Lanier, Taylor, Mr. Aldrich, and Mr. Stedman." Two weeks later, however, the *Dial* published "Tendencies of American Literature in the Closing Quarter of the Century," in which Charles Leonard Moore expressed his opinion that "there are twenty contemporary verse-writers who have done more and better poetry than Lanier." Of Emily Dickinson, not even mentioned in Browne's editorial, Moore wrote: "Some of Emily Dickinson's rugged rhythms, with their gleams of profound insight and their revelations of personality almost as strong and strange as Emily Bronte's, are like to live."

In January, 1901, Oscar Lovell Triggs, whose "Variorum Readings" of *Leaves of Grass* is well known to students of Whitman, published in the

---

[*] "Fiction of the Eighties and Nineties," *American Writers on American Literature,* ed. John Macy, 1931.

*Forum* "A Century of American Poetry." He had high praise for Stedman's *American Anthology*. Of the 573 poets whom Stedman had included, just two, he thought, were "major poets measured by almost any standard"; they were Poe and Whitman. But, he added, "Bryant, Emerson, Lanier, Riley, and Emily Dickinson have significance hardly less than the [two] major writers."

> Edgar Poe and Walt Whitman are conspicuous among American poets for their striking originality and intensive force. They belong to the order of Makers: each created a distinctive style; each contributed something precious that had not been in the world before; each gave evidence of unique experience and new heights of vision; each has had a wide influence, inspiring other poets and becoming the founder of a school—the one of Symbolism and the other of Democratism.

In 1900, when Stephen H. Wakeman began building up his superb collection of American literature, he limited himself to his nine favorite authors. These included the seven writers enshrined in the New England literary canon: Bryant, Emerson, Hawthorne, Holmes, Longfellow, Lowell, and Whittier. The only author included who was not a New Englander was Poe. Wakeman, however, had the good judgment to include Thoreau, who in 1900 got only three votes from the one hundred men in the college of electors of the Hall of Fame for Great Americans. In 1900 no other collectors would have included Melville or Emily Dickinson, but one wonders why Wakeman included no living writers like Howells, Mark Twain, or Henry James.

In its issue of December 1, 1900, the *Outlook* printed an article entitled "The Greatest Books of the Century," which gave the results of a poll of eight well-known Americans and two Englishmen: James Bryce, Henry Van Dyke, Arthur Twining Hadley, Thomas Wentworth Higginson, William DeWitt Hyde, Edward Everett Hale, George A. Gordon, A. M. Fairbairn, William J. Tucker, and G. Stanley Hall. The judges were asked to name "the ten books of the century ending this month which have most influenced its thought and activities." The two books that stood highest on the judges' composite list were Goethe's *Faust* and Darwin's *On the Origin of Species*. The writings of Emerson and Mrs. Stowe's *Uncle Tom's Cabin* were much higher on the list than any other books by American writers. Six of the ten judges named Emerson and five Mrs. Stowe. Unfortunately, perhaps, as Van Dyke pointed out, the *Outlook* editors' instructions took "account of books, not by the standard of perfection, nor by the test of popularity, but by the measure of influence"— and influences are notoriously difficult to measure. Hadley noted that the judges were asked to pick books "for their results rather than for their merits." He accordingly ruled out George Eliot's *Middlemarch* although he considered it a greater novel than *Uncle Tom's Cabin*, which he included among the ten. Ambassador Bryce, who ruled out Emerson, Carlyle, and Ruskin because their influence seemed to him limited to English-speaking countries, was the only judge to include a book written in London by a German Jew whose influence since 1900 has been enormous: *"Karl Marx's treatise called Das Kapital* became, soon after its publication, a sort of Bible for the Socialists of Continental Europe. Its force is not spent, nor can we tell as yet how far its doctrines may continue to work."

> *Professors of literature are learned but not critical men. . . .*
> John Crowe Ransom, *The New Criticism*

> *It takes a great wrench in our minds to realize that possibly literature is not identical with what the Professors have been handing down from generation to generation.*
> Albert Guérard, *Literature and Society*

## LITERARY HISTORIANS

There was little teaching of American literature in our colleges and universities until long after the Civil War. There was, however, sufficient interest in the subject to induce a few teachers to prepare textbooks designed for use in academies, public schools, and colleges. These early self-taught specialists in American literature usually treated that literature as only a minor part of the literature of the British Isles. Their literary taste was in general old-fashioned, and they were as a rule not very hospitable to the original writers among their own contemporaries. Too often the academic historians were content merely to repeat the critical estimates of their predecessors.

Most of our early literary historians and anthologists were New Englanders—all honor to them!—but of too many of them one may say as Woodrow Wilson said of the New England non-literary historians of the republic: "From where they sit, the whole of the great development [of the United States] looks like an Expansion of New England." For these men the literary history of the United States was primarily the story of the rise and decline of the New England "school." The New England historians made room for Irving and Cooper, but they could not see Poe, Melville, or Whitman as worthy of a place in the canon of the great American writers. Simms and his fellows of the slaveholding South were now hopelessly discredited, and the historians had no intention of questioning the justice of the accepted opinion. The New England historians were unaware of the real significance of that Yankee rebel,

Henry David Thoreau; and they failed to see how far superior Emerson and Hawthorne were to Whittier and the three Cambridge poets.

The best of our early literary historians, Moses Coit Tyler (1835–1910), worked only in the Colonial and Revolutionary periods and thus did not have to face the difficult problem of ranking the nineteenth-century poets and writers of fiction. Tyler's books have not yet been susperseded, and one can only admire the industry, the intelligence, and the literary judgment of a scholar, largely self-taught, who did not have access to the vast materials in American libraries that now seem indispensable. More clearly than any of his predecessors, Tyler saw how superior Jonathan Edwards and Benjamin Franklin were to their American contemporaries. Yet Tyler, too, treated the New England divines with greater sympathy and understanding than he brought to William Byrd and other writers from the southern and Mid-Atlantic colonies.

*John S. Hart.* John S. Hart, LL.D. (1810–1877), who in 1872 gave at Princeton one of the first—if not the very first—of college courses in American literature, published in the same year *A Manual of American Literature for Schools and Colleges.* He had already published a study of Spenser and had edited *The Female Prose Writers of America,* of which the fourth edition appeared in 1864. The *Manual* is rather a compilation than an orthodox literary history. Hart included not only numerous minor writers picked up by Knapp, Neal, and Kettell but many more. He gave fuller treatment to writers of the Middle Atlantic and southern states than his New England predecessors had given.

The "literary pioneers" bulk too large in Hart's *Manual.* He thought that Halleck's "Marco Bozzaris" was "probably the best war lyric in the language." Irving seemed to him "on the whole the brightest and dearest name in the annals of American literature"; but Hawthorne, he said, deserved a place "beside the great masters, not of the age only, but of all time." For Professor Hart, Longfellow was "by general consent the most distinguished living representative of the poetical literature of the country" and "clearly our American Poet Laureate." Yet Whittier seemed to him "our leading lyric poet." Hart gave two pages to Whitman and thought more highly of his poems than one might have expected from an academic critic in 1872. He was impressed by Thoreau's "wonderfully acute power of observation, and his fine taste and skill in word-painting." He went on to suggest—not that Thoreau was one of our best prose writers—but that "he might have made a first-class naturalist." To Herman Melville, Hart gave just one-third of a page, and he failed to mention *Moby-Dick.* Melville's best books, he thought, were his earliest. He singled out *Typee* and *Redburn,* which Melville had regarded as a potboiler. "Melville," said Hart, "is a writer of forcible and graceful English although in some of his works he lapses into mysticism." Like most of our nineteenth-century literary historians, Hart disliked Poe's literary criticism. His estimate of Poe's poems became the conventional one of the later nineteenth century: "[Poe] was endowed with poetical gifts of the rarest and most wonderful kind. Had he united with these gifts high moral principle, and a power of will and of persistent labor, such as marks all true greatness, he might have made for himself a name above that of any yet known to American letters."

*Henry A. Beers.* In 1887 Professor Henry Augustin Beers (1847–1926) of Yale University published *An Outline Sketch of American Literature,* which in 1892 was superseded by his *Initial Studies in American Letters.* Beers was also author of a life of N. P. Willis and of an important early study of the Romantic movement in English literature. His shortcomings as a literary critic are those of the academic mind of his own time. For Beers, Lowell was "the foremost of American critics and one of the foremost of American poets." His verdict on Poe was much the same as those of Hart and Griswold: "The defect in Poe was in character, a defect which will make itself felt in art as in life. If he had had the sweet home feeling of Longfellow or the moral fervor of Whittier, he might have been a greater poet than either." Beers noted rather regretfully: "In the place of moral feeling [Poe] had the artistic conscience." He failed to note the lack of the artistic conscience in many of the minor writers whom he overpraised. Beers made no mention of Melville. He had, however, some appreciation of Howells and Henry James. He thought Cable "the most important figure of the New South." He did not know what to make of the conflicting estimates of Whitman. He was not without appreciation of Thoreau's writings, but he was repelled by the "inhumanity" which seemed to him the "most distinctive note in Thoreau."

Beers was impressed by the British vogue of Artemus Ward and Mark Twain, but he did not see how far superior the one was to the other. He noted that they were much more widely read than those other humorists, Lowell and Holmes, and he added: "And though it would be ridiculous to maintain that either of these writers takes rank with Lowell and Holmes . . . , still it will not do to ignore them as mere buffoons." Beers made no mention of either *Tom Sawyer* or *Huckleberry Finn.*

Some thirty years after publishing his book, Beers admitted that he had modified his opinion of Mark Twain. In the early 1920's he wrote to Fred Lewis Pattee:

> I care very little for Whitman and nothing at all for Joaquin Miller, *Arcades Ambo*—barbarians both. . . . Mark Twain was also a kind of barbarian but different. . . . [In my literary history] I failed to do justice to Mark Twain, and was taken to task for it by Howells one evening

when he dined here. Howells was right, of course, and yet I have never understood his unqualified admiration for Clemens. Mark was so vulgar and Howells so refined!

*Charles F. Richardson.* A better historian than Hart or Beers was Charles F. Richardson (1851–1913), who in 1882 became professor of English at Dartmouth College. Before coming to Dartmouth he had been for a short time on the editorial staffs of the *Independent* and the *Critic*. He was among the earliest to offer a college course in our national literature. The two volumes of his *American Literature* appeared in 1887 and 1889. For his critical standards Richardson was in large measure indebted to Matthew Arnold and to Taine.

Of the early American poets Philip Freneau seemed to him by much the best. "The House of Night," he thought, was the best poem written in America before 1800. Richardson did not hesitate to express unconventional opinions of the New England poets. Whittier, he said, was "Not one of the chief American poets." Among the minor poems of Dr. Holmes, he said, "I find just half-a-dozen that stand out." Only two of the six that he singled out now seem among Holmes's best: "The Last Leaf" and "The Deacon's Masterpiece." What literary historian today would pass by a poem like "Dorothy Q" and praise "The Voiceless," "Homesick in Heaven," and "Aestivation"? Richardson gave Melville only half a page. He apparently thought that Melville had written his "brisk and stirring tales of the sea" merely because the public liked stories of adventure. One wonders just how many of Melville's books Richardson—and the other literary historians—had actually read.

For Richardson, Hawthorne was "clearly enough the greatest author yet produced in America," a writer who seemed "both relatively and absolutely great." He defended Emerson's poems in spite of their irregularities. More than any other American poet, he said, Emerson "tests and almost defies the laws of poetics." Like most other nineteenth-century critics, Richardson undervalued Poe's critical writings, but he stoutly defended Poe's "mental integrity." "All charges of literary dishonesty," he wrote, "may be dismissed from his case." Strangely enough, Richardson thought he had found some of Poe's "cheapest jingles" in "Israfel," "For Annie," and the Song to Ligeia. He quoted some lines from "For Annie" and boldly pronounced them "doggerel." Possibly they are—Louis Untermeyer years later was to express a similar opinion of some lines in "For Annie"—but I can find no "cheap jingles" in "Israfel," which is generally rated as one of Poe's finest poems.

Richardson had no higher opinion of the western humorists than Beers expressed. He apparently thought that Artemus Ward, Josh Billings, and Petroleum V. Nasby were better than Mark Twain. He wrote: "Bret Harte, Artemus Ward, Nasby, and the various professional newspaper 'wits' have been put, by the half-educated, into the representative seats that belong to Emerson and Hawthorne." There are other critical lapses which strike the reader of today who looks into Richardson's book. One wonders why he failed to see how far superior Lincoln's "Gettysburg Address" was to the long oration delivered on the same occasion by Edward Everett. Like Beers, Richardson thought highly of Howells and James. He was perhaps right in regarding *A Modern Instance* as Howells's "strongest" novel; but why, one wonders, did he select *The Bostonians* rather than *Daisy Miller* or *The Portrait of a Lady* as "James's masterpiece"? In 1889 it was felt that the great American novel must have its locale in the United States, and that is apparently why Richardson selected a novel that James did not include in the New York edition of his novels and tales.

*Barrett Wendell.* *A Literary History of America* (1900) by Barrett Wendell (1855–1921) is one of the most engagingly written of our literary histories, but its proportions are truly astonishing. In his 530 pages of text Professor Wendell gave to the West a chapter of only 15 pages; to "Literature in the South" he gave just 20. The remainder is devoted to New York, Pennsylvania, and New England—mostly New England. After discussing the New York writers, Wendell remarked: "In the work of the earlier New York school, and even in the work of Poe . . . nothing was produced which touched seriously on either God's eternities or the practical conduct of life in the United States." "For the serious literature of America," he concluded, "we must revert to New England." The unjust accusation that Bernard De Voto once brought against Van Wyck Brooks is certainly applicable to Wendell: "The inability to credit the reality of any portion of the country except New England . . . was central in the literary tradition which he accepted." Wendell had been one of Lowell's students, and the canon of the great American writers as he saw it was much the same as that embodied in *A Fable for Critics* half a century earlier. So marked is the bias in Wendell's book that Fred Lewis Pattee, himself a native of New England, remarked that it should have been entitled "A Literary History of Harvard University with Incidental Glimpses of the Minor Writers of America."

For Wendell the two greatest of our writers were Emerson and Hawthorne; the only other eminent figures were Longfellow, Lowell, Holmes, and Whittier. Wendell did not include Thoreau among our eminent writers, but he noted that though "no maker of immortal phrases" like Emerson, "he did possess in higher degree than Emerson himself the power of making sentences and paragraphs artistically beautiful." Wendell made no mention of Emily Dickinson, Jones Very, George W. Cable, or even Lincoln as a writer. (His low estimate of Walt Whitman I have noted elsewhere.) Wendell mentioned

Melville only to misspell his given name and to say that he "began a career of literary promise, which never came to fruition." One wonders whether Wendell ever read any of Melville's books. His discussion of William Gilmore Simms is obviously based upon a reading of Trent's biography and just one of Simms's eighty-odd books, *The Yemassee.*

Yet there are some surprises in Wendell's book. He found Sidney Lanier a "truly lyric artist" and placed him "among the truest men of letters whom this country has produced." He hailed *Huckleberry Finn* as a "masterpiece" and went so far as to assert that it was "a book which in certain moods one is disposed for all its eccentricity to call the most admirable work of literary art as yet produced on this continent."

William Dean Howells found Wendell's book so unsatisfactory that in the *North American Review* for April, 1901, he made public his objections under the title "Professor Barrett Wendell's Notions of American Literature." Howells had lived in New England and had known and loved its greatest writers; but as author, editor, and adviser to publishers he was fully aware— as Wendell was not—of the great change which had come over the national letters since the Civil War. Anticipating Pattee's pithy phrase, he wrote: "If he [Wendell] had called his book 'A Study of New England Authorship in its Rise and Decline, with Some Glances at American Literature,' one could not have taxed him with neglect, though one might still have found him wanting in proportion." Howells complained that Wendell, who had written a biography of Cotton Mather, had given one fourth of his space to the early New England writers. In Howells's opinion Franklin was the only one of them that had any literary importance. Wendell's worst failure was his neglect of "the truly American period which has followed the New England period of our literature." Wendell, said Howells, had not only neglected important writers from the South, the West, and the Middle Atlantic states, but he had failed to do justice to "the rise of American fiction since the war."* In American literature both early and late Howells found qualities that were not—as Wendell seemed to think—of Puritan origin: a "literary conscience, the wish for purity and the desire for excellence." Finally, Howells saw that Wendell was an Anglophile, and he resented the "priggish banality" that led the historian to write: "When her majesty came to the throne. . . ."

Wendell may have been "the Last of the Brahmins," but he was an honest critic and he was capable of reversing his earlier estimates. This is evident in his various discussions of Poe, who was so generally underrated in New England. In a commencement address on "American Literature" delivered at Vassar College in 1893, Wendell had pronounced Poe "fantastic and meretricious

---

* Van Wyck Brooks, who studied at Harvard, remembered that Wendell had pronounced Stephen Crane's *The Red Badge of Courage* "sensational trash."

throughout." "As one knows him better," he said, "one does not love him more." At that time Wendell believed that, as he said, "only New England has expressed itself in a literary form which inevitably commands attention from whoever pursues such inquiries as ours." Seven years later in his *Literary History* Wendell devoted fifteen pages to a discussion of Poe. He still regarded him as somewhat "meretricious" but admitted that "genius he certainly had." The New England writers were, as Wendell unduly emphasized, gentlemen of good family, but Poe was, he mistakenly thought, "always a waif and a stray, essentially a Bohemian." Poe, one remembers, had complained years before that Rufus Griswold had included in his anthologies certain writers whose chief claim was their wealth or social position.

In 1909 Wendell journeyed down to Charlottesville to deliver the principal address on the evening of January 19 as part of the University of Virginia's observance of the Poe centenary. Here for the first time he conceded to Poe a high place among American writers. Perhaps during his year at the Sorbonne he had been impressed by Poe's "constantly expanding fame," or was he merely trying to say what the amenities of the occasion seemed to require? I think not, for when later in the year he revised and published the address, he made no essential change in what he had said in Charlottesville. He wrote: "Not only all of us here assembled, not only Virginia, and all New York, and all New England, and all of our American countrymen beside, but the whole civilized world instantly and eagerly recognize the certainty of his eminence." "So long as the name of America shall endure, the name of Poe will persist, in serene certainty, among those of our approved national worthies." He praised the poet's "consummate craftsmanship" and his "supreme artistic purity" and said nothing about his "meretriciousness." It appears that nine years after publishing his *Literary History* Wendell had gained a new perspective on American literature. "The literature of New England, in brief," he now said, "American though we may gladly assert it in its nobler phases, is, first of all, not American or national, but local."

*William Peterfield Trent.* The first important literary historian to come from the South was William Peterfield Trent (1862–1939), a native of Virginia, who from 1900 until his death in 1939 was professor of English at Columbia University. At the University of Virginia he had been a classics major; at Johns Hopkins his graduate work was in history and English. In 1892, while teaching at the University of the South and editing the *Sewanee Review* (of which he was the founder), he had published a life of William Gilmore Simms in the American Men of Letters series. The biography gives an excellent picture of the man Simms, but Trent undervalued Simms's robust Revolutionary romances on the ground that, unlike *Waverley* and *The Heart of Midlothian*, they were not "ennobling." Trent was at that time a somewhat over-reconstructed young southerner who had gone out of his way to set other southerners right on controversial issues.

In 1903, when Trent published *A History of American Literature*, he appended to his title the dates 1607–1865. He felt that "it was impossible to deal satisfactorily with living writers" or even with writers like Whittier, Holmes, and Lowell, "who have seemed almost a part of our generation." With the earlier writers Trent felt himself on somewhat firmer ground. He made much more of the antebellum southern and western humorists than his predecessors had done, and he recognized in William Byrd "a real man of letters who, in a more favorable environment, might have become a fairly eminent, if not a great writer." Trent noted that many European critics regarded Poe as our best and most influential writer, and one surmises that he agreed with them. He gave higher ratings to Thoreau, Melville, and Whitman than any of his predecessors. He had no very high opinion of Thoreau's poems, but he found his prose style "more sustained and varied and thoroughly satisfying than that of any of his contemporaries." Trent had obviously read not only the two books that Thoreau published but also *Cape Cod, Maine Woods*, and the rest of the eleven-volume Cambridge edition of Thoreau's works. He concluded his discussion of Thoreau: "He is a cosmopolitan-provincial, a Concord-Greek, an archangel-faun—in other words, a sheer, inexplicable, indescribable genius."*

Like other literary historians, Trent overrated Lowell, but he came nearer to recognizing the greatness of Melville than any of his predecessors. He pronounced *Moby-Dick* not only Melville's masterpiece but "on the whole, [a] genuine work of genius":

> If it were not for its inordinate length, its frequently inartistic heaping up of details, and its obvious imitation of Carlylean tricks of style and construction, this narrative of tremendous power and wide knowledge might be perhaps pronounced the greatest sea story in literature. The breath of the sea is in it and much of the passion and charm of the most venturous of all the venturous callings plied upon the deep. It is a cool reader that does not become almost as eager as the terrible Captain Ahab in his demoniacal pursuit of Moby Dick, the invincible whale, a creation of the imagination not unworthy of a great poet.

*John Macy.* When John Macy (1877–1939) published *The Spirit of American Literature* (1908; revised edition, 1913), it was evident that a new

---

* In *Great American Writers* (1912) by Trent and John Erskine I find this sentence: "The Transcendentalist who stood nearest to Emerson was Henry David Thoreau, whose reputation not improbably will equal or surpass Emerson's" (p. 126).

generation had begun to attack the New England canon of the great American writers. Macy himself, though born in Michigan, had grown to manhood in Massachusetts. He had for a time been a teacher, but he did not have the academic attitude toward American literature. "The American spirit in literature," he said, "is a myth." Most of our books, he added, "are eminent for just those virtues which America is supposed to lack. Their physique is feminine; they are fanciful, dainty, reserved. . . . Our poets are thin, moonshiny, meticulous in technique." The notable exceptions were "our most stalwart men of genius, Thoreau, Whitman, and Mark Twain." *The Spirit of American Literature* seemed to H. L. Mencken in 1917 "by long odds the soundest, wisest book on its subject."

In his preface Macy attacked his academic predecessors for perpetrating "traditional values." "It is perplexing," he wrote, "to find in our current manuals no mention of Father Tabb, but a full page about Anne Bradstreet; a chapter on Bryant but only a page about Sidney Lanier; extended accounts of Charles Brockden Brown and William Gilmore Simms, but only half a page about Mark Twain." Macy devoted a chapter to Henry James and another to his brother William but none to "that dreadful bore," Jonathan Edwards.

*The Spirit of American Literature* is avowedly "a collection of appreciative essays" and not "a formal history or bibliographical manual." Nevertheless, Macy was confident that the only "first-rate man of letters of the older days" whom he had not discussed was Francis Parkman. Separate chapters are given to Irving, Cooper, Poe, Emerson, Hawthorne, Longfellow, Whittier, Holmes, Lowell, and Thoreau; but there is no chapter on Bryant. Whitman, Howells, Mark Twain, and Sidney Lanier are also given separate chapters. Among writers who failed in "workmanship" Macy merely mentioned "Herman Melville's 'Moby Dick,' a madly eloquent romance of the sea." Macy had high praise for Edith Wharton and Theodore Dreiser, but he did not discuss their work in detail. It is surprising to find in the index no mention of either Henry Adams or Emily Dickinson.

In 1931 Macy, still dissatisfied with the academic historians, brought out a symposium entitled *American Writers on American Literature*. More than a dozen of the thirty-seven contributors were or had been professors; and if I am any judge, their essays are superior to most of those written by the men of letters. The result is a symposium by contributors of widely varying competence. There are separate chapters on four writers who were given none in Macy's earlier book: Melville, Lincoln, Henry Adams, and Jonathan Edwards. There is, however, no chapter on Bryant, who Macy hoped might be "disposed of in a paragraph or two." There is no separate chapter on William James or on Emily Dickinson; but her poems are sympathetically and competently discussed in four or five pages in a chapter written by George F. Whicher. In his essay on Hawthorne, Louis Bromfield singled out Whitman, Poe, and Hawthorne as "American writers who have passed the test of time and the perspective of distance and emerged as great men." He added: "The same century produced several others, notably Emerson, Melville, Mark Twain and William Dean Howells, whose title to greatness, of the same nature, remains in dispute." Bromfield made no mention of Thoreau or Emily Dickinson. Llewellyn Jones in his chapter on "Contemporary Fiction" made no mention of Ernest Hemingway or William Faulkner. In a period of transition like the twenties and thirties, the creative writers could be as wide of the mark in their estimates as the academic literary historians.

The editor of *American Writers on American Literature* stated that the book contained "many opinions" with which he did not agree. That circumstance no doubt confirmed Macy in the rather low opinion of literary criticism that he had expressed in an essay entitled "The Critical Game." "The function of criticism at the present time, and at all times," he said, "is the function of all literature: to be wise, witty, eloquent, instructive, humorous, original, graceful, beautiful, provocative, irritating, persuasive . . . it must in some way be good writing." "There is," said Macy, "no other sound principle to be discovered in the treatises on the art of criticism or in fine examples of the art."

*Every anthology is a confession of faith, the faith of an individual, of an age, of the spirit of that age and a revaluation of some past in the terms of some present. This revaluation is one of the continuous processes of every civilization. It has become more rapid and more aware of itself in modern times.*
Ludwig Lewisohn, "Introduction," *Creative America: An Anthology*

## ANTHOLOGISTS

Two widely-used anthologies were published by the Houghton Mifflin Company, which held the copyrights on many of the best books by the older writers of New England. They were *The Chief American Poets* (1905), edited by Curtis Hidden Page, and *The Chief American Prose Writers* (1916), edited by Norman Foerster.

*Poetry.* In *The Chief American Poets* Professor Page included nine poets, of whom six were New Englanders: Bryant, Emerson, Longfellow, Lowell, Holmes, Whittier, Poe, Whitman, and Lanier. The modern reader looks in vain for the name of Emily Dickinson. In Page's mind, it would seem, the two greatest American poets were Poe and Whitman. Poe seemed to Page "the only American poet (as Hawthorne is our only prose writer) who can justly be said, in any strict and narrow use of the word, to have had genius." Page noted that in nearly all of Lowell's poetry there is lacking "something of charm . . . something of poetic suggestiveness. . . . He lacks, usually, just that last touch of genius. . . ." Why, then, did Page feel that he had to include Lowell among the major American poets? Perhaps he lacked the courage of his own convictions. More probably he felt that prospective buyers of his anthology would want to see Lowell represented. Even as late as 1905 Lowell's reputation as poet, critic, and essayist was so great that no anthologist could safely deny him a place in the canon of the great American writers —especially in a text published by the firm which held the copyrights on Lowell's writings and those of other New England poets.

In 1936 Harry Hayden Clark brought out his *Major American Poets,* an anthology of the same general scope as Page's. By 1936 the old New England poets had been down-graded even in academic circles, but Professor Clark included them all along with Poe, Whitman, and Lanier. The new names in *Major American Poets* are those of Philip Freneau, Emily Dickinson, Vachel Lindsay, and Edwin Arlington Robinson. Clark thus commented on the poets represented in his anthology: "The present book includes the ten generally recognized major American poets, along with Freneau to illustrate the neglected but important early development of our poetry as inspired by scientific deism, and along with Robinson and Lindsay to represent two contrasting aspects of the modern temper in the East and the West, respectively."

One suspects that copyright difficulties may account for Clark's failure to include more poets of the twentieth century; and yet, one wonders, why in 1936 did he include Vachel Lindsay rather than Carl Sandburg (as a western poet) or Robert Frost, T. S. Eliot, Ezra Pound, or Wallace Stevens? It would seem that Clark's literary taste in 1936 was somewhat old-fashioned, like that of the professors of English who adopted his book as a text in their classes. Three poets who compiled anthologies that appeared before 1936—Conrad Aiken, Louis Untermeyer, and Mark Van Doren—gave far fewer pages to the schoolroom poets of New England than Clark devoted to them.

*Prose.* The writers whom Norman Foerster included in *The Chief American Prose Writers* were Franklin, Irving, Cooper, Poe, Hawthorne, Emerson, Thoreau, Lowell, and Holmes. "The nine writers represented in this volume," said the editor, "have become, by general consent, the American prose classics." Yet in 1916 Foerster was well aware that with the passing of time there would come changes in the American literary canon. "Others," he said, "such as Brockden Brown, Bret Harte, Whitman, Prescott, Mark Twain, and Mr. Howells, to name but a few among many who have achieved high distinction, are not far below the unquestioned nine; perhaps some of them will, as time goes on, displace certain of the elect. . . . As it stands . . . the book may pretend to a certain finality." Foerster, I hasten to add, gave Whitman a conspicuous place in his *American Criticism* (1928); and in the various editions of his *American Poetry and Prose*, first published in 1925, he included many prose writers and poets not represented in *The Chief American Prose Writers* or *The Chief American Poets*.

Other critics would not in 1916 have agreed with Foerster as to the nine best American prose writers. In 1909 William Crary Brownell included in his *American Prose Masters* only six writers: Cooper, Emerson, Hawthorne, Poe, Lowell, and Henry James. In 1910 John Erskine included in his *Leading American Novelists* the six writers whom, he said, "time has sifted . . . for special remembrance": Brockden Brown, Cooper, William Gilmore Simms, Hawthorne, Harriet Beecher Stowe, and Bret Harte. Why, the modern reader may well ask, did neither Foerster, Brownell, nor Erskine include Melville, Mark Twain, Howells, Sarah Orne Jewett, or Stephen Crane? And why was Brownell the only one to make a place for Henry James?

In the 1960's our anthologists had a different alignment of major American writers. In 1962, for example, Professors William M. Gibson and George Arms included in their *Twelve American Writers* nine writers from the nineteenth century and only three from the twentieth. The nineteenth century is represented by Emerson, Thoreau, Hawthorne, Poe, Melville, Whitman, Henry James, and Emily Dickinson. Not one of the five schoolroom poets is included. Irving and Cooper are gone, too. For the twentieth century Gibson and Arms chose only Eliot, Frost, and Faulkner. They did not include either Robinson or Lindsay, who were in Clark's *Major American Poets* in 1936.

# Chapter 5. Four Major Nineteenth-Century Writers

*It is the fate of many thinkers to make their thoughts so common to all the world that what they have to say seems nothing new to the generations succeeding their own. None but their contemporaries can know them to have been prophets, with fresh truth to reveal.*

Howells, "Introduction," *Living Thoughts from the Writings of Charles Kingsley*

## WILLIAM DEAN HOWELLS

In 1860 on his first visit to New England Howells (1837–1920) was the guest of James Russell Lowell at a dinner in the Parker House in Boston where the other guests were James T. Fields and Oliver Wendell Holmes. It was then that the Autocrat, "with a laughing look" at Lowell, said: "Well, James, this is something like the apostolic succession; this is the laying on of hands." A few years later the young middle-westerner was indeed to become heir to the Brahmin literary tradition. As assistant editor and later as editor of the *Atlantic Monthly* Howells almost never rejected a manuscript sent him by the New England authors whose contributions had made the *Atlantic* the best literary magazine in the United States. He did nevertheless manage to get from writers in other sections more good articles than his predecessors had obtained.

Although Howells, as he once said, did not like writing literary criticism and thought that he did not do it very well, he was probably the most influential American literary critic of his time. He did more than any other critic to introduce to American readers the important European writers of fiction and drama. Among them were Goldoni, Galdós, Valdés, Flaubert, Maupassant, Zola, Turgenev, Dostoevski, Tolstoy, Ibsen, and Björnson.

After interviewing Howells in 1907, Theodore Dreiser accurately described him as "the lookout on the tower straining for a first glimpse of approaching genius." In the same year Howells himself was to write in his "Recollections of an Atlantic Editorship": "To feel the touch never felt before, to be the first to find the planet unimagined in the illimitable heaven of art, to be in at the dawn of a new talent, with the light that seems to mantle the written page: who would not be an editor for such a privilege?" Howells gave substantial encouragement to nearly every important writer of fiction who emerged between 1865 and 1900. His greatest services were to two American writers whose genius he was quick to recognize, Henry James and Mark Twain; but there were many others whom he found praiseworthy. Among them were John W. De Forest, Hamlin Garland, Edward Bellamy, Harold Frederic, George Ade, Harold W. Fuller, Robert Herrick, Booth Tarkington, and Stephen Crane.

Howells, whose first ambition had been to be a great poet, was a better judge of fiction than of poetry. George Parsons Lathrop, who as assistant editor had worked with him on the *Atlantic Monthly*, told L. Frank Tooker, one of the editors of the *Century Magazine*, that he "never understood Mr. Howells's tests of availability in poems . . . he thought them erratic and not understandable." One of Howells's mistakes was in rejecting Sidney Lanier's long poem, "Corn." Paul Hamilton Hayne, who thought that Howells liked only poems of "a Wordsworthian stamp," felt somewhat bitter when Howells rejected his powerful narrative poem, "Cambyses and the Macrobian Bow," because the dénouement—more tragic than in the analogous William Tell legend—was too horrible for the taste of the champion of realism.

Howells nevertheless was, as I have noted elsewhere, quick to recognize Emily Dickinson as a great poet. Of the older American writers he loved best Hawthorne, Longfellow, and Lowell. He did not care greatly for Thoreau, Melville, or Poe. In 1860, when he met Walt Whitman, he found that the "apostle of the rough, the uncouth," was in reality "the gentlest person," "of the greatest benignity" and "spiritual purity." Yet Howells could not, even in 1900, reconcile this personal impression of the man "with what denies it" in *Leaves of Grass*.

Howells was quick to recognize the merits of Henry James and Mark Twain. His literary taste and critical standards were more catholic than those of either of these writers, neither of whom had any use for the writings of the other. Better than other critics, Howells understood the nature of the American literature problem. In discussing the question of a national literature in the "Editor's Study" in *Harper's Magazine* for November, 1891, he wrote: "It has been noted that our literature has always been distinguished by two tendencies, apparently opposite, but probably parallel: one a tendency toward an elegance refined and polished, both in thought and phrase, almost to tenuity; the other a tendency to grotesqueness, wild and extravagant, to the point of anarchy." In the first class Howells placed Longfellow, Lowell, Holmes, Aldrich, and Henry James; in the second, Artemus Ward, James Whitcomb Riley, and Mark Twain. Philip Rahv would have classified them as "pale faces" and "redskins."

On December 5, 1866, Howells after a long walk and talk with Henry James, then only twenty-three years old, wrote to E. C. Stedman that the younger writer was a "very earnest fellow" and "extremely gifted," "gifted enough to do better than any one has yet done toward making us a real American novel." Yet, Howells added almost prophetically: "I suspect that he must in a great degree create his audience." Howells printed much of James's early work in the *Atlantic* even though he knew that most of its readers had little enthusiasm for James's stories. The mature James was fully aware of what Howells had done for him. On February 19, 1912, he wrote to Howells:

> You showed me the way and opened me the door; you wrote to me, and confessed yourself struck with me—I have never forgotten the beautiful thrill of *that*. You published me at once—and paid me, above all with a dazzling promptitude; magnificently, I felt, and so that nothing since has ever quite come up to it. More than this even, you cheered me on with a sympathy that was in itself an inspiration.

Howells's article, "Henry James, Jr.," published in the *Century Magazine* in November, 1882, irritated British literary journalists because Howells had maintained that "the new school" of fiction writers, of which James was "the chief exemplar," was artistically superior to old-fashioned novelists like Thackeray and Dickens. "These great men," he said, "are of the past—they and their methods and interests. . . ." "We cannot deny [to Henry James]," he said, "a very great literary genius." In 1916, the year of James's death, Howells wrote in his introduction to *Daisy Miller*: "It is not yet known to the ignorant masses of educated people that Mr. James is one of the greatest masters of fiction who has ever lived."

In the fall of 1869 Mark Twain called at the office of the *Atlantic Monthly* to express his appreciation of an unsigned review of *The Innocents Abroad* which had appeared in that magazine. For Mark Twain the *Atlantic* was "the recognized critical Court of Last Resort in this country." There he discovered that it was Howells who had written the review. The two quickly became friends, and Howells became also Mark Twain's best critic and his most trusted adviser. He knew, as often Mark Twain did not, the difference between great fiction and worthless burlesque. As an editor and adviser to publishing houses he knew also what might offend readers of the *Atlantic* and *Harper's* and purchasers of books sold by subscription.

In their edition of the *Mark Twain–Howells Letters* (1960) Henry Nash Smith and William M. Gibson express their conviction that these letters "complete the destruction of the once widely held belief that Howells as an editor emasculated Mark Twain's vigor of expression and partially kept him from fulfillment." In fact, what Howells was chiefly concerned with when he read one of Mark Twain's manuscripts was "consistency of tone, verisimilitude, and the need to eliminate irrelevancy and to keep burlesque from becoming mere horseplay." In 1883 Mark Twain was working alternately on *Huckleberry Finn* and a burlesque that Bernard De Voto was to pronounce "almost lethal" in its dullness. Howells had to tell Mark Twain that this burlesque fell "short of being amusing." During Mark Twain's lifetime Howells published two admirable critical appraisals of his friend's work: in the *Century* in September, 1882, and in the *North American Review* in February, 1901. The two books that Howells liked best were *A Connecticut Yankee in King Arthur's Court* and *Huckleberry Finn*. Not many months after the death of his friend in 1910 he published *My Mark Twain*, which is undoubtedly the finest tribute one American writer has paid to the memory of another. For Howells, Mark Twain belonged with "the great humorists of all time, with Cervantes, with Swift, [and] with any others worthy of his company; none of them was his equal in humanity."

The New England writers who preceded Howells had been poets and romancers. He wanted to write the realistic novels of American life that they had not written. His first long work of fiction, *Their Wedding Journey* (1872), appeared when he was thirty-five years old. As in the case of Henry James, one may wonder whether Howells was a born story-teller; but, again like James, he worked at his trade and made himself a thoroughly competent novelist. All the while he continued to review books and to write critical essays and reviews championing the cause of realism. In 1895 Henry C. Vedder wrote in *American Writers of To-day*: "Mr. Howells is easily the first living American novelist"; and in February of the following year the *Bookman* stated that Howells was "universally admitted to hold the primacy among living American men of letters." In the same year, however, Henry James in praising *The Landlord at Lion's Head*, said to Owen Wister at Rye that it was just possible that "six-and-a-half Americans know how good it is."

In his old age Howells was highly honored. He was president of the American Academy of Arts and Letters from 1908 until his death in 1920. In 1912 President William Howard Taft, also a native of Ohio, attended a dinner at Sherry's given in honor of Howells on his seventy-fifth birthday. Said he: "I have traveled from Washington to New York to do honor to the greatest living American writer and novelist."

Howells's vogue nevertheless had already passed its peak. In a letter written to Howells on his seventy-fifth birthday, Henry James noted that his old friend's reputation had declined, but he predicted: "Your beautiful time will come." In 1915 Howells wrote to James: "A change has passed upon things, we can't deny it; I could not 'serialize' a story of mine now in any American magazine. . . . I am comparatively a dead cult with my statues cut down and the grass growing over them in the pale moonlight."

In 1917 H. L. Mencken wrote in his *Prejudices, First Series* that Howells really had "nothing to say for all the charm he gets into saying it. His psychology is superficial, amateurish, often nonsensical; his irony is scarcely more than a polite fastidiousness, his characters simply refuse to live." Mencken had read so little of Howells's fiction that, as James Woodress points out, of the five Howells titles listed by Mencken as novels, two are plays and one a volume of poems. The future author of *The American Language*, however, was perceptive enough to pay a well-deserved tribute to Howells as a stylist:

> What remains of Howells is his style. He invented a new harmony of "the old, old words." He destroyed the Johnsonian periods of the Poe tradition, and erected upon the ruins a complex and savory carelessness, full of soft naivetés that were sophisticated to the last degree. Like Mark Twain, but in a diametrically different way, he loosened the tightness of English, and let a blast of air into it. He achieved, for all his triviality, for all his narrowness of vision, a pungent and often admirable style.

In *The American Novel*, which appeared in 1921, the year after Howells's death, Carl Van Doren included a discussion of the novelist's work that revealed a thorough knowledge of his many-sided achievements. Two years later in *The Roving Critic* Van Doren said in effect that Howells was a major writer in the "Silver Age of Our Literature." "Where else, indeed," he asked, "may be found another representation of American life during half a century as extended and accurate as that in Howells's total work?" Van Doren conceded that a great part of what Howells had written would not survive: his occasional reviews, his travel books, his farces, and even his "more formal criticism." What would survive, said Van Doren, would be a few of the novels and such autobiographical books as *A Boy's Town, Years of My Youth*, and *Literary Friends and Acquaintance*. "*My Mark Twain*," he said, "is the most exquisite tribute yet paid by one American man of letters to another."

> Doubtless a few of his novels will easily survive the rest—*A Modern Instance, The Rise of Silas Lapham, Indian Summer, A Hazard of New Fortunes, The Kentons*, and that exquisite triumph of art and temper, *A Chance Acquaintance*. Of this last Howells himself said that it made him more friends than any of the others; he thought *A Modern Instance* the strongest, and he liked *Indian Summer* best.

Van Doren was a critic and a literary historian with a mind of his own, and he could not accept the current rating of Howells as an outmoded Victorian. Howells, however, continued to be neglected and maligned by young intellectuals who refused to read his work. Even so intelligent a critic as Van Wyck Brooks had not discovered the real Howells when in 1920 he published *The Ordeal of Mark Twain*. In 1930 when Sinclair Lewis accepted the Nobel Prize for Literature in Stockholm, he said: "Mr. Howells was one of the gentlest, sweetest, and most honest of men, but he had the code of a pious old maid whose great delight was to have tea at the vicarage." A truer estimate of Howells appeared in the same year in the posthumous third volume of Parrington's *Main Currents in American Thought*:

> Not an original genius like Mark Twain, far from a turbulent soul like Herman Melville, Howells was the reporter of his generation—the greatest literary figure of a drab negative age when the literary impulse was slackening, and the new was slowly displacing it. . . . A humane and lovable soul, he was the embodiment of all that was kindly and generous in an America that was not wholly given over to the ways of the Gilded Age—an America that loved beauty and served culture even amidst the turmoil of revolution.

By 1937, the year of the Howells centenary, critics were beginning to realize that the conventional conception of the novelist was all wrong. In that year Newton Arvin wrote that the vitality of Howells's works was "more evident, at the moment of his centenary, than it has ever been before."

By 1950 a Howells revival was in full swing. In that year appeared two significant books of selections from Howells: Henry Steele Commager's *Selected Writings* and the American Writers series of selections edited by Clara and Rudolf Kirk. Commager, an American historian, found in the writings of Howells "the most comprehensive and faithful transcription of middle-class America that can be found in our literature." He considered the works of Howells much closer to reality than the work of the twentieth-century naturalists and irrationalists who have "concentrated on the misery, poverty, dullness and frustration of life in America." "We have," he said, ". . . fallen into the habit of supposing that realism requires a photographic reproduction of the dull, the shabby, the sordid, the passionate, the violent." He asked: "Is it not rather the writers and artists who have been so ostentatiously alienated from their society who need to be explained than Howells?"

In *Howells: His Life and World* (1959) Van Wyck Brooks praised Howells as a significant writer who had written "ten or a dozen novels destined to be read in a long future." In 1920 Brooks had written in *The Ordeal of Mark Twain*: "And in this man of marvelous talent, this darling of all the gods and all the graces, he [Mark Twain] had encountered once more the eternal, universal, instinctive American subservience to what Mr. Santayana calls 'the genteel tradition.'" In the spring of 1960 in an article entitled "The Dean's Comeback" (*Texas Studies in Literature and Language*) James Woodress felt justified in asserting that Howells "finally has become a major American writer." Howells, however, has not yet been admitted to the Hall of Fame for Great Americans, and his books are little read outside the colleges and universities. In a sense we may now say that his "beautiful time" has come, but not many critics rate him as the equal of the two friends for whom he did so much, Mark Twain and Henry James.

Why, one wonders now, was it so difficult in the twenties and thirties for American critics to understand Howells and to appreciate his merits? Changes in literary fashion had much to do with it no doubt. The realism of the commonplace had given way to naturalism with its strong emphasis upon violence, passion, unreason, the subconscious mind, and primitive rather than civilized human types.

Howells was in fact, as he admitted in *My Literary Passions* (1895), inclined to be squeamish. As a boy he had been disillusioned to find that writers whom he had admired were "drunkards, and adulterers, and unchaste, and untrue. I lamented over them," he said, "with a sense of personal disgrace in them. . . ." Twenty years later he was to write to Joyce Kilmer: "I like you, my dear young brother, not only because you love beauty, but decency also. There are so many of our brood I could willingly take out and step on." And yet as Everett Carter and others have pointed out, it is true that in his portrayal of men and women Howells, like Henry James, wrote with a freedom that sometimes brought down on him the disapproval of literary critics and magazine editors.

Howells's reputation has suffered greatly from the misinterpretation of an unfortunate phrase that he used in *Criticism and Fiction* (1891). "Our novelists . . . ," he said, "concern themselves with the more smiling aspects of life, which are the more American. . . ." Howells was commenting on Dostoevski's *Crime and Punishment* and thinking of life in Czarist Russia when he wrote that "whoever struck a note so profoundly tragic in American fiction would do a false and mistaken thing." Thirty years later Robert Frost was to write in *New Hampshire* (1923):

> How are we to write
> The Russian novel in America
> As long as life goes so unterribly?
> There is the pinch from which our only outcry
> In literature to date is heard to come.
> We get what little misery we can

Out of not having cause for misery.
It makes the guild of novel writers sick
To be expected to be Dostoievskis
On nothing worse than too much luck and comfort.

There is little or no false optimism to be found in Howells's books and essays, particularly in those written after his discovery of Tolstoy. In *A Traveler from Altruria* he revealed himself as a forceful critic of American life and thought.

In an essay on Howells published in *Harper's Weekly* in 1886 Henry James noted that Howells was "animated by love of the common, the immediate, the familiar and vulgar elements of life." "He adores," he said, "the real, the natural, the colloquial, the moderate, the optimistic, the domestic, and the democratic. . . ." That was the kind of America that Howells knew better than any other American novelist of his time. James continued: "If American life is on the whole, as I make no doubt whatever, more innocent than that of any other country, nowhere is the fact more patent than in Mr. Howells' novels, which exhibit so constant a study of the actual and so small a perception of evil." James noted that in Howells's novels "the only immoralities are aberrations of thought, like those of Silas Lapham, or excesses of beer, like those of Bartley Hubbard."

Howells described the American life that he knew. Such aspects of American life as would have attracted an American Zola he wisely left to a later generation that included Dreiser, Dos Passos, Farrell, Lewis, Faulkner, Steinbeck, and Hemingway. They were aware of sordid and tragic sides of American life that Howells had not witnessed or experienced. Few if any of these novelists, it is sad to remember, ever understood or appreciated the great debt which all of them owed to the champion of realism.

> *I shall dine late; but the dining-room will be well lighted, the guests few and select.*
>
> Walter Savage Landor
>
> *And I may dine at journey's end*
> *With Landor and with Donne.*
>
> William Butler Yeats

## HENRY JAMES

Henry James (1843–1916) was not a born story-teller like Scott or the elder Dumas; but he had a keen intelligence and great ambition, and he made himself into a first-class writer of fiction. The process took him a good many years. His early stories and reviews reveal his indebtedness to the authors whose books he read and reviewed: Goethe, George Eliot, Balzac, Mérimée, George Sand, and various others. James was indebted also to the novelists whom he came to know while living in Paris: Flaubert, Daudet, Zola, and Turgenev. It was, however, the example of Hawthorne that had convinced him that an American could be an artist. He owed much also to William Dean Howells, with whom he spent long hours discussing "the true principles of the literary art." Howells printed a number of James's early stories in the *Atlantic Monthly* even though he knew that not many of its readers appreciated the quality of James's fiction.

James had mastered his craft by 1879, the year of his *Daisy Miller, An International Episode*, and his critical study of Hawthorne. In 1881 he published *The Portrait of a Lady*, one of his best novels. In November of the following year Howells published in the *Century Magazine* an article on "Henry James, Jr.," in which he ascribed to his friend "a very great literary genius" and pointed to him as a leader of "the new school" of fiction writers who, he said, were better craftsmen than Dickens and Thackeray had been.

James's early novels found readers both in book form and in the magazines where they appeared as serials; but only rarely was he to have the many readers he hoped for, and few American literary critics displayed any great enthusiasm for his novels. Americans did not like his obvious preference for England as a place in which to live and write. They could not see in any of his international novels the answer to their prayer for the great American novel.

James, who was by no means lacking in patriotic feeling, was disturbed when he discovered that he could not write his best fiction either on American themes or while living in this country. On January 16, 1871, he wrote to Charles Eliot Norton:

> Looking about for myself, I conclude that the face of nature and civilization in this our country is to a certain point a very sufficient literary field. But it will yield its secrets only to a really grasping imagination. . . . To write well and worthily of America one need even more than elsewhere to be a *master*. But unfortunately one is less!

James knew little about life in his own country west of the Hudson River or south of New York City. When he visited Saratoga and Newport, he found only women and children whose husbands and fathers were at work in Boston or New York. In *The American* (1877) he gave a leading role to a young California businessman, but obviously the novelist knew nothing about how Christopher Newman had made his fortune. James once confessed: "Before the American business-man . . . I was absolutely and irredeemably helpless, with no fibre of my intelligence responding to his mystery." Now the American businessman was and still is probably our most interesting and characteristic type, as Howells, Dreiser, and Lewis have repeatedly demonstrated. It is just as well perhaps that James chose to live in Europe. The England that attracted him, however, was not the great industrial nation of the nineteenth century but the England of leisure-class men and women, of country houses, of artists and writers; it was also the England of English literature which had attracted Irving and Hawthorne before him.

When in 1879 James published his *Hawthorne* in the English Men of Letters series, he dwelt at length on the thinness of American life as material for literature and deplored the provincialism of the region and the country in which Hawthorne had lived and written his best books. James was in reality defending his own decision to live in the Old World rather than the New. He took his cue from the preface to *The Marble Faun*, in which Hawthorne had complained of "the difficulty of writing a romance about a country where there is no shadow, no antiquity, no mystery, no picturesque and gloomy wrong, nor anything but a commonplace prosperity, in broad and simple daylight." James proceeded to enumerate what seemed to him "the items of high civilization" which were absent from the texture of American life:

> No State, in the European sense of the word, and indeed barely a specific national name. No sovereign, no court, no personal loyalty, no aristocracy, no church, no clergy, no army, no diplomatic service, no country gentlemen, no palaces, no castles, nor manors, nor old country-houses, nor parsonages, nor thatched cottages, nor ivied ruins; no cathedrals; nor abbeys, nor little Norman churches; no great Universities nor public schools—no Oxford, nor Eton, nor Harrow; no literature, no novels, no museums, no pictures, no political society, no sporting class —no Epsom nor Ascot!

For cultivated Bostonians James's indictment was almost as embarrassing as Sydney Smith's "who reads an American book?" had been to an earlier generation. Was America still a cultural desert? Walt Whitman of course would have thanked God that the New World had none of the aristocratic fripperies that seemed so important to the expatriate novelist. Howells protested that even in the absence of those "dreary and wornout paraphernalia" which to James seemed so essential, "we have simply the whole of human life left." James strongly dissented. "It is," he wrote to Howells, "on manners, customs, usages, habits, forms, upon all these things matured and established, that a novelist lives. . . ." He would agree with Howells only when America had produced a novelist of the stature of Balzac or Thackeray.

None of James's American critics, it seems, remembered a little poem beginning: "Amerika, du hast es besser," in which in his old age Goethe had congratulated the young republic that it had no robber barons or ruined castles and had urged American authors to write of the living present. A local-colorist from the South defended the Bostonians against James's charges of provincialism. Joel Chandler Harris, who regarded James as "the most delightful literary snob of the period," propounded his own theory "that no enduring work of the imagination has ever been produced save by a mind in which the provincial instinct was the controlling influence." It seemed to Harris that "the provinciality which gives us Hawthorne, Holmes, Whittier, Howells, Harte, and Lowell ought to be as well worth nurturing and cultivating as the exquisite culture which has given us (and the rest of the universe) Mr. James."

Harris or Howells should have reminded James that in his discussion of *The Marble Faun* he had written:

> Hawthorne forfeited a precious advantage in ceasing to tread his native soil. Half the virtue of *The Scarlet Letter* and *The House of the Seven Gables* is in their local quality; they are impregnated with the New England air.... [In his descriptions of the streets and monuments of Rome Hawthorne] incurs that penalty of seeming factitious and unauthoritative, which is always the result of an author's attempt to project himself into an atmosphere in which he has not a transmitted and inherited property.

Did James when he deserted his own country make the great mistake of his literary career as H. L. Mencken, V. L. Parrington, and Van Wyck Brooks have argued? Could he have written better novels if he had continued to live in the United States? In his old age James was not sure that his decision to live in Europe had been the right one. Hamlin Garland in *Roadside Meetings* (1930) stated that James said to him at his home in Rye in 1906: "If I were to live my life over again, I would be an American. I would steep myself in America, I would know no other land. I would study its beautiful side. The mixture of Europe and America which you see in me has proved disastrous." Five years later James expressed a similar opinion in a conversation with Amy Lowell.

Edith Wharton, who knew James better than most of his literary friends, ridiculed the notion that he had been wrong when he made his decision to live in Europe; but then Mrs. Wharton, one remembers, had chosen to make her home in France. Was she not in effect defending her own expatriation? James himself in later life felt that it was better that American writers of fiction should remain in America. He once wrote of Mrs. Wharton: "She must be tethered in native pastures, even if it reduces her to a back-yard in New York." On another occasion he wrote that if Mary Wilkins Freeman should sail for Europe, he "would positively have detectives versed in the practice of extradition posted at Liverpool."

The American student of James notes with some surprise that a number of British writers have sharply questioned the value to a novelist of "the items of high civilization" which to him seemed so important. In 1934 Wyndham Lewis, after quoting that famous list of things lacking in American life, concluded: "All that baronial scenery catalogued by Henry James is today in England either non-existent, or so shrunken, unimportant and discredited that we may say it would be a handicap, instead of an asset, to have it behind one at the moment of writing."

In Somerset Maugham's *Cakes and Ale* (1930) the fictitious novelist Edward Driffield maintains that "Henry James had turned his back on one of the great events in the world's history, the rise of the United States, in order to report tittle-tattle at tea parties in English country-houses." "Poor Henry," says Driffield, "he's spending eternity wandering round and round a stately park and the fence is just too high for him to peep over and they're having tea just too far for him to hear what the countess is saying."

Virginia Woolf in an essay on "American Fiction" wrote in 1925: "The English tradition is formed upon a little country; its centre is an old house with many rooms each crammed with objects and crowded with people who know each other intimately, whose manners, thoughts, and speech are ruled all the time, if unconsciously, by the spirit of the past." It was better, she thought, for American writers, like Whitman and Sherwood Anderson, not to stand in awe of English literature and not to try to write like Englishmen.

> The choice has to be made—whether to yield or to rebel. The more sensitive, or at least the more sophisticated, the Henry Jameses, the Hergesheimers, the Edith Whartons, decide in favour of England and pay the penalty by exaggerating the English culture, the traditional English good manners, and stressing too heavily or in the wrong places those social differences which, though the first to strike the foreigner, are by no means the most profound. What their work gains in refinement it loses in that perpetual distortion of values, that obsession with surface distinctions—the age of old houses, the glamour of great names —which makes it necessary to remember that Henry James was a foreigner if we are not to call him a snob.

The debate over James's decision to live in Europe was renewed in 1925, when Van Wyck Brooks brought out *The Pilgrimage of Henry James*, in which with all the skill of a practiced lawyer he argued that James's writing had suffered greatly from his expatriation. The whole question now seems somewhat academic. No one can ever know what James might have written if he had chosen to make his home in Missouri, Louisiana, or California. We do know, however, that he left us some of the best novels and short stories written in English during his lifetime.

After two great wars in which Americans fought alongside Englishmen, we do not so loudly condemn writers who, like T. S. Eliot, have chosen to live and write in England. It is easier now for Americans to sympathize with the point of view that James on October 19, 1888, expressed in a letter to his brother William: "I can't look at the English-American world, or feel about them, any more, save as a big Anglo-Saxon total. . . ." He wanted, he said, to treat "the life of the two countries as continuous or more or less convertible, or at any rate as simply different chapters of the same general subject." He aspired, he said, "to write in such a way that it would be impossible to any outsider to say whether I am at a given moment an American writing about England or an Englishman writing about America . . . and so far from being ashamed of such an ambiguity I should be exceedingly proud of it, for it would be highly civilized."

American readers would have liked James better if he had more often spiced his novels with satire as he did in *An International Episode*. The English, as James quickly discovered, did not like being satirized "from the American point of view." "Their conception of the normal in such a relation," he wrote to his mother on January 18, 1879, "is that the satire should be all on their side against the Americans. . . ." For his part James liked the English too well, he said, "to go into the satire-business." Many Americans would have agreed rather with James's father, who, as he wrote late in life, hated the "hideous class distinctions" of the English and "the consequent abject snobbery or inbred and ineradicable servility of its lower classes." There were Americans also who felt as Henry Adams felt when he wrote in *The Education*: "All through life, one had seen the American on his literary knees to the European; and all through many lives back for some two centuries, one had seen the European snub or patronize the American; not always intentionally, but effectually. It was in the nature of things."

The kind of recognition that James hoped for and never achieved is suggested in a single sentence in "The Real Thing" (1893). The narrator has been employed to supply illustrations for a deluxe edition of the writings of Philip Vincent, "the rarest of novelists—who, long neglected by the multitudinous vulgar and dearly prized by the attentive . . . had had the happy fortune of seeing, late in life, the dawn and then the full light of a higher criticism, and estimate in which on the part of the public there was something really of expiation." Possibly James dreamed of a day when, like Neil Paraday in "The Death of the Lion" (1894), he might wake up "a national glory."

When these two stories were published, James was still vainly trying to write a successful play. When after five years he returned to prose fiction, he was to write novels and tales which only the few discriminating readers would care for. On January 5, 1895, he wrote to Howells: "A new generation that I know not, and mainly prize not, has taken universal possession." The magazines, he thought, no longer wanted his stories. He continued: "I have always hated the magazine form, magazine conditions and manners, and much of the magazine company." (As a matter of fact, however, the *Yellow Book* was already printing some of his best stories. Its editor, Henry Harland, another American expatriate, was willing to allow James enough space to print in a single issue a story comparable in length to the French *nouvelle*.) In December, 1902, James wrote to Howells: "The *faculty of attention* has utterly vanished from the general Anglo-Saxon mind, extinguished at its source by the big blatant *Bayadère* of Journalism. . . ."

For the 1907–1917 edition of *The Novels and Tales of Henry James* in twenty-six volumes published in both London and New York, James labored long and hard in revising his earlier books; and he wrote that admirable series of prefaces which R. P. Blackmur has praised as "the most remarkable piece of literary criticism in existence." The prefaces are in general, as James wrote to Howells on August 17, 1908, "a sort of plea for Criticism, for Discrimination, for Appreciation on other than infantile lines—as against the so almost universal Anglo-Saxon absence of these things; which tends so, in our general trade, it seems to me, to break the heart."

The edition was not a financial success. In 1915 James wrote that his royalties from his English and American publishers had brought him only about £50. A year before his death he wrote to Edmund Gosse: "That Edition has been, from the point of view of profit either to the publishers or to myself, practically a complete failure. . . . I am past praying for anywhere; I remain at my age . . . and after my long career, utterly, insurmountably, unsaleable. . . ." James continued: "The edition . . . has never had the least intelligent critical justice done it—or any sort of critical attention paid it."

In fairness one must look at James's novels from the point of view of the publisher. Walter Hines Page, one-time editor of the *Atlantic Monthly* and one of the founders of the publishing house of Doubleday, Page and Company, included in *A Publisher's Confession* (1905) an essay entitled "Why 'Bad' Novels Succeed and 'Good' Ones Fail," in which he stated that "half the publishing houses in the United States [had] lost money" on the novels of Henry James. "And novels," he concluded, "after all have less to do with literature than they have to do with popular amusement."

In an essay on "Henry James and the Artist in America" (*Harper's*, July, 1948), W. H. Auden noted that European critics were bewildered by James's repeated complaints of a lack of popular success. His attitude seemed to Auden characteristically American since it suggested a belief that an author's "sales and profits are an accurate indication of value." Auden continued: "I have never met a serious European writer who, outside of the need to pay his creditors, took the slightest interest in the opinion of any but a few friends whose critical minds he admired and trusted."

James had cause to complain that even some of his most intelligent friends failed to appreciate what he was doing. H. G. Wells repaid James's expert advice and criticism by publishing *Boon*, a satire in which he publicly branded James as "extraordinarily futile" and "an unmitigable mistake." Even James's brother William did not care for Henry's later phase. After reading *The American Scene*, he wrote on May 4, 1907:

> Give us one thing in your older directer manner, just to show that, in spite of your paradoxical success in this unheard-of method, you can still write according to accepted canons. Give us that interlude; and then continue like the "curiosity of literature" which you have become. For gleams and innuendoes and felicitous and verbal insinuations you are unapproachable, but the core of literature is solid. Give it to us *once* again! The bare perfume of things will not support existence, and the effect of solidity you reach is but perfume and simulacrum.

On November 23, 1905, Henry James had written to his brother, who disliked *The Golden Bowl*:

> Let me say, dear William, that I shall greatly be humiliated if you do like it, and thereby lump it, in your affection, with things, of the current age, that I have heard you express admiration for and that I would sooner descend to a dishonored grave than have written.

In these later years when James felt his work so little appreciated in both England and America he too often failed to remember that there were important novelists and literary critics who had publicly expressed their admiration for him as a great writer. In 1896 James G. Huneker called James the "master of living American novelists." He added: "I am tempted to say the greatest of American fictionists until I remember Hawthorne." In January, 1905, Joseph Conrad published in the *North American Review* "Henry James: An Appreciation," in which he praised the master as "the historian of fine consciences." In the same year Elizabeth Cary published the first book devoted to a discussion of James's writings, *The Novels of Henry James: A Study*. In April of that year the *Atlantic Monthly* printed an essay by the able American critic, William Crary Brownell. The essay reappeared in his *American Prose Masters* (1909); James was the only one of the six "masters" still living. The essay began: "If any career can be called happy before it is closed, that of Mr. Henry James may certainly be so called." James's career, he said, had been "quite free from any mistake"; he had "scrupulously followed his ideal." Brownell had no enthusiasm for "the *chevaux-de-frise* of James's later style." Nevertheless he believed that James would occupy a "very nearly unique niche in the history of fiction." "There is," he added, "no question of its eminence or of his powers." Those powers, he concluded, were such as to "make it impossible to measure him otherwise than by the standards of the really great novelists and of the masters of English prose."

If Brownell's praise did not persuade James that he had earned a place among the great novelists of England and America, he might have remembered that on November 30, 1886, James Russell Lowell had written him: "You have grown steadily ever since I knew you and have conceived more original characters and situations than all the [modern] English school put together. . . ." On August 27, 1889, Lowell wrote again: "You are doing work of extraordinary excellence. . . ." Lowell was, as he said, "partial to romance," but he added: "I know what's good when I see it all the same."

The outbreak of the First World War gave James the harrowing feeling that the European civilization which he so overvalued had finally betrayed him. On July 31, 1914, he wrote to Sir Charles Phillips: "The unthinkability of anything so blank and so infamous in an age that we have been living in and taking for our own as if it were a high refinement of civilization . . . finding it after all carrying this abomination in its blood, finding this to have been what it *meant* all the while. . . ."

That was his initial reaction to the war. He was deeply disappointed that his own country did not immediately come to the aid of the England and the France that he loved so well. He became a British citizen because, as he once explained, he wished to be able to say "We" when discussing the war with his English friends. Had the war led him to believe that he was already essentially English? Howells, who knew him intimately, insisted that "through all the perversities of his expatriation, and his adoration of foreign conditions and forms" James remained "an inalienably American soul." At any rate, James gave instructions that his remains should be taken to Mount Auburn Cemetery in Cambridge, Massachusetts, where Longfellow, Lowell, and Holmes were buried. It was in Cambridge that James's literary career had begun. As a writer he belongs to both England and America. On his tomb there is this memorable inscription: "Henry James, O.M. / Novelist, Citizen of Two Countries / Interpreter of His / Generation on Both / Sides of the Sea."

Henry James died on February 28, 1916. Before the year was out, three book-length studies of his writings had appeared. They were written by Rebecca West, Joseph Warren Beach, and Ford Madox Hueffer (who later changed his surname to Ford). In 1918 the *Little Review* devoted its August number to Henry James. Ezra Pound and T. S. Eliot were among those who contributed to it. In 1920 Percy Lubbock published a two-volume edition of

James's *Letters*, and the next year in *The Craft of Fiction* he paid his tribute to James as a master of technique.

In 1925 came Van Wyck Brooks's *The Pilgrimage of Henry James*, which rekindled the old controversy over James's expatriation. In the third volume of *Main Currents in American Thought* (1930) Parrington labeled James "the last refinement of the genteel tradition, the complete embodiment of its vague cultural aspirations." In 1932 and 1933 V. F. Calverton and Granville Hicks found James's novels of no great significance because they had not been written to promote the Communist revolution in America.

In the early 1930's, however, there were foreshadowings of the coming James revival. In 1930 appeared Miss Cornelia Kelley's important study, *The Early Development of Henry James*. In 1931 Leon Edel brought out the first of his many contributions to James scholarship, *Les années dramatiques*. The new interest in Henry James extended to other members of the James family. In 1932 came C. Hartley Grattan's *The Three Jameses* and in 1934 both Austin Warren's *The Elder Henry James* and Anna R. Burr's *Alice James*. In 1934 also Edith Wharton published her reminiscences of the master in *A Backward Glance*. In that year, too, the *Hound and Horn* devoted its April–May number to the work of Henry James. Among the contributors were Francis Fergusson, Edna Kenton, and Edmund Wilson, whose analysis of "The Turn of the Screw" was to call forth many other essays on that notable *nouvelle*. Meanwhile as American resentment of James's expatriation slowly declined, scholars and critics were learning that the traditional conception of the man James was quite inaccurate. In the words of Leon Edel, author of the monumental biography of the novelist, "The image of Henry James as a figure uprooted and forlorn—disconnected from his homeland and adrift between countries—has given way slowly to the upright figure we now know, the citizen of the world, who nevertheless remained distinctively American."

The James revival is in some ways a curious thing. During the Great Depression when so many of our writers were denouncing the capitalist system and flirting with Russian communism, who would have expected a renewed interest in a Victorian novelist concerned not with the proletariat but with the lives of well-to-do American travelers and British aristocrats living on inherited estates? Who that had been reading the work of Thorstein Veblen, John Dos Passos, or William Faulkner could find the time or the patience to wade through James's verbose stories of the manners and minor morals of people living in country houses or vacationing in Switzerland? And what reader familiar with the theories of Sigmund Freud, the novels of Ernest Hemingway, or the plays of Eugene O'Neill could tolerate the voluminous novels of an old bachelor, who seemed both ignorant and squeamish in matters pertaining to sex?

And yet in a world where ruthless dictators were preparing to plunge the world into a Second World War a reader could find in the novels of Henry James a lost world of stability and security where the more fortunate had leisure to consider the lesser problems of conscience and conduct.

In the 1940's James was to find an increasing number of readers who possessed "the faculty of attention" and had received expert training in the art of reading. In the 1940's the New Critics were becoming a power in university English departments, and more and more professors were applying to James's novels, tales, prefaces, and critical essays the lessons they had learned from I. A. Richards, Ezra Pound, T. S. Eliot, E. M. Forster, Cleanth Brooks, Robert Penn Warren, and the master himself. They took an especial delight in analyzing James's later novels, which made no appeal to the great mass of readers of fiction. The lofty position which James was now coming to occupy on the slopes of Parnassus was, as Rayburn S. Moore has well said, "primarily the result of scholarship and criticism, not of popularity among the 'multitudinous vulgar.'"

In the forties it was becoming more and more obvious to those who studied James's work that his theories and technique had had a great influence upon other writers of fiction in both England and America. Among them are such diverse figures as William Dean Howells, Joseph Conrad, H. G. Wells, Owen Wister, Edith Wharton, Willa Cather, Ellen Glasgow, and Katherine Anne Porter.

In 1939, when James's reputation was rising and Whitman's was beginning to decline, the *Partisan Review* in a symposium on "The Situation in American Writing" asked various writers whether Henry James's work was "more relevant to the present and future of American writing than Walt Whitman's." Katherine Anne Porter replied: "For myself I choose James, holding as I do with the conscious, disciplined artist, the serious expert against the expansive, indiscriminately "cosmic" sort. James, I believe, was the better workman, the more advanced craftsman, a better thinker, a man with a heavier load to carry than Whitman."

James's best critics and warmest admirers have not hesitated to point out serious shortcomings in the work of the master. Edmund Wilson noted that James was "short on invention," old maidish about sex, and ignorant of many aspects of life. He said of James's later style: "He never seems to be aware of the amount of space he is wasting through the roundabout locutions or quite gratuitous verbiage with which he habitually pads out his sentences. . . ."

Edith Wharton regarded James's later novels, "for all their profound moral beauty [as] lacking in atmosphere, more and more severed from that thick nourishing human air in which we all live and move." Deeply interested in James's "technical theories and experiments," she once asked him:

"What was your idea in suspending the four principal characters in 'The Golden Bowl' in the void? What sort of life did they lead when they were not watching each other, and fencing with each other? Why have you stripped them of all the *human fringes* we necessarily trail after us through life?"

He looked at me in surprise, and I saw at once that the surprise was painful, and wished I had not spoken. I had assumed that his system was a deliberate one, carefully thought out, and had been genuinely anxious to hear his reasons. But after a pause of reflection he answered in a disturbed voice: "My dear—I didn't know I had!"

In *Henry James and the Jacobites* (1963) Maxwell Geismar denounced the James cult and repeated the traditional objections: his adoration of things European, his desertion of his own country, his ignorance and fear of sex, his excessive concern with technique, and his lack of substance. No doubt too many of James's admiring critics have looked at his novels only through his eyes and have discussed them only as the work of a skillful craftsman; and yet it remains true, as Edmund Wilson maintained: "Henry James is a great artist, in spite of everything." For F. R. Leavis, writing in *The Great Tradition* (1948), the greatest English novelists were Jane Austen, George Eliot, Joseph Conrad, and Henry James. He added: "To insist that James is in the English tradition is not to deny that he is in an American tradition too. He is in the tradition that includes Hawthorne and Melville." James, I think, would have been satisfied with that estimate and with Leavis's conclusion: "It is a measure of the greatness of Henry James's genius that discussion should tend to stress mainly what he failed to do with it. But what achievement in the art of fiction . . . can we point to in English as surpassing his?"

R. P. Blackmur, Alfred Kazin, and René Wellek have all rated Henry James as the best American critic of his generation. So he is if one thinks only of his many illuminating comments on the art of fiction. Yet any one who carefully examines his critical comments on American writers is more likely to agree with T. S. Eliot, who wrote in 1918: "James was emphatically not a successful *literary critic*. His criticism of books and writers is feeble."

James's criticism of American writers suffers from his ignorance of both life and literature in his native land. In addition he shared with Poe the limitations of the creative writer who attempts to evaluate writers whose aims and methods are different from his own. He was, as we should expect, a better critic of fiction than of poetry. What he had to say of masters like Balzac and Turgenev is always enlightening. His little book on Hawthorne is one of the classic pieces of American literary criticism. He is at his best also when he writes about Howells, whom he understood better than other critics. James was not without some appreciation of the New England writers, but his view of their milieu was quite different from that found in Matthiessen's *American Renaissance* or Brooks's *The Flowering of New England*. In an essay on Emerson in 1888 he referred to "the frugal, dutiful, happy but decidedly lean Boston of the past" as "a kind of achromatic picture." In the same essay, as I have noted elsewhere, he wrote of Thoreau: "Whatever question there may be of his talent, there can be none, I think, of his genius. It was a slim and crooked one, but it was eminently personal. He was imperfect, unfinished, inartistic; he was worse than provincial—he was parochial; it is only at his best that he is readable."

While James recognized the merits of such competent local colorists as Constance Fenimore Woolson and Sarah Orne Jewett, he felt in 1898 that in the dialect stories of their contemporaries "colloquial speech [arrived] at complete debasement." It was, he thought, "a part, in its way, to all appearances, of the general wave of curiosity on the subject of the soul *not* civilized that has lately begun to roll over the Anglo-Saxon globe and that has borne Mr. Rudyard Kipling, say, so supremely high on its crest." If James had ever written an essay on Mark Twain, what would he have said of "the soul *not* civilized" of Huckleberry Finn?

James had a good deal to say about Emerson, Hawthorne, Longfellow, and Lowell but little or nothing about Irving, Cooper, Melville, Emily Dickinson, or Mark Twain. His judgment of Poe shows no more insight than the conventional comments of the New England literary historians. In *Hawthorne* he admitted that Poe was "a man of genius," but he pronounced Poe's literary criticism "probably the most complete and exquisite specimen of provincialism ever prepared for the edification of men." In an essay on Baudelaire in 1876 James had written: "An enthusiasm for Poe is the mark of a decidedly primitive stage of reflection." Poe's poems were in his opinion "very valueless verses"; later he changed the epithet to "superficial." To Andrew Lang, who was an admirer of Poe, he said: "I suppose I made a mistake." In *The Golden Bowl* (1904) he referred to *The Narrative of Arthur Gordon Pym* as "a wonderful tale . . . which was a thing to show, by the way, what imagination Americans *could* have—the story of the shipwrecked Gordon Pym. . . ."

Henry James came finally to see Whitman as a great poet, but it took him a long time. In 1865, when he reviewed *Drum-Taps* for the New York *Nation*, he began: "It has been a melancholy task to read this book; and it is a still more melancholy one to write about it." The book, he said, was neither good verse nor acceptable prose. James pictured the Intelligence as saying to the poet: "We look in vain . . . through your book for a single idea. We find nothing but flashy imitations of ideas. We find art, measure, grace, sense sneered at on every page. . . ." Again the Intelligence lectures the poet: "To become accepted as a national poet, it is not enough to discard everything in particular and accept everything in general, to amass crudity upon crudity, to discharge the undigested contents of your blotting-book into the lap of the public. You must respect the public which you address; for it has taste, if you have not."

In *A Backward Glance* (1934) Edith Wharton gave a memorable brief description of an evening when in his old age Henry James read aloud from *Leaves of Grass*:

> All that evening we sat rapt while he wandered from "The Song of Myself" to "When lilacs last in the dooryard bloomed" (when he read "Lovely and soothing Death," his voice filled the hushed room like an organ adagio), and thence let himself be lured on to the mysterious music of "Out of the Cradle," reading, or rather crooning it in a mood of subdued ecstasy till the fivefold invocation to Death tolled out like the knocks in the opening bars of the Fifth symphony . . . [but] finally James, in one of the sudden humorous drops from the heights, flung up his hands and cried out with the old stammer and twinkle: "Oh, yes, a great genius; undoubtedly a very great genius! Only one cannot help deploring his too-extensive acquaintance with the foreign languages."

> *At how long an interval Mark Twain shall be rated after Molière and Cervantes it is for the future to declare. All that we can see clearly now is that it is with them that he is to be classed,—with Molière and Cervantes, with Chaucer and Fielding, humorists all of them, and all of them manly men.*
> Brander Matthews, "An Appreciation" (1899)

## MARK TWAIN

American writers were slow to learn to write like Americans. The spell of English literature was too strong. Hawthorne, for instance, was an accomplished stylist, but for our taste today he wrote too much like nineteenth-century Englishmen. Emerson had a fondness for the earthy talk of teamsters and farmers, but his essays are too reminiscent of the rhetoric of the lyceum lecturer and the Unitarian minister. Lowell in *The Biglow Papers* was the earliest of our eminent men of letters to make effective use of the New England dialect; but the first notable humorists to write in dialect were newspapermen: Seba Smith, who wrote the "Jack Downing" letters from Maine, and Augustus Baldwin Longstreet, the author of *Georgia Scenes*. Our various regional dialects, whether southern, western, or New England, do not vary greatly from one another. In the aggregate they represent the speech of uneducated Americans of the backwoods in all sections; they are the basis of what in the twentieth century H. L. Mencken was to call "the American Language."

The southern and western humorists were men of some education, most of whom came from states to the east or the north. They were fascinated by the speech and the behavior of those whom they encountered in the semi-frontier regions of the South and the West: adventurers, braggarts, gamblers, fools and rascals, sharpers and their victims, tellers of tall tales, and notable hunters and scouts like David Crockett and Daniel Boone. Among the legendary characters that figure in their tales are Mike Fink, King of the Keelboatmen; Simon Suggs, who robs a congregation at a camp meeting; and Ransy Sniffle, the Georgia victim of hookworm who never comes fully alive except when he is fomenting or witnessing a fight. Some of the humorists were themselves accomplished raconteurs, and no doubt many of the tales they wrote out for publication had already been shaped as they were told to eager listeners. Even in their written form, the oral tradition is still strong. These humorous sketches and tales were written not for backwoodsmen but for more sophisticated readers on the Atlantic seaboard. The humorists were in a sense pioneer realists and local colorists, forerunners of Joel Chandler Harris and Mark Twain; and like them they often satirized the sentimental, the romantic, and the bombastic.

Most of our best-known writers of the early nineteenth century had no high regard for any humorists except Lowell and Holmes, Brahmins from the neighborhood of Boston. There was, however, a Yankee from Vermont who had a different idea. William Trotter Porter (1809–1858), who had spent much time in the South, was editor of the *Spirit of the Times*, a sporting magazine in which many of the best southern humorous sketches first appeared. Porter reprinted some of the best pieces in two collections: *The Big Bear of Arkansas* (1845) and *A Quarter Race in Kentucky* (1846). In the preface to the earlier collection he announced: "A new vein of literature, as original as it is inexhaustible in its source, has been opened in this country within a very few years." Though Thomas Bailey Aldrich and Edmund Clarence Stedman thought otherwise, Porter confidently asserted that the newspaper humorists had "conferred signal honor on the rising literature of America."

The sketches of the humorists, first appearing in one newspaper, were quickly copied in many another news sheet. In his boyhood Samuel Langhorne Clemens (1835–1910) no doubt read many of them—in addition to literature of a more respectable sort—and probably set some of them in type for his brother Orion's paper, the Hannibal *Journal*. The first of his writings to attract wide attention was "The Jumping Frog of Calaveras County," which he wrote out to please Artemus Ward. The manuscript arrived in New York too late to be included in Ward's book; but when it was printed in the *Saturday Press* on November 18, 1865, it was copied far and wide. Mark Twain thus got his first taste of nationwide fame, but that was not the kind of reputation that he wanted. On January 20, 1866, he wrote to his mother and sister expressing disappointment that the New York people should single out a "villainous backwoods sketch" which he had written only because Artemus Ward had asked for it. He thought more highly of articles that in 1864 and 1865 he had printed in the *Californian*, which seemed to him "the best literary weekly in the United States." Bret Harte, who also wrote for the *Californian*, on November 10, 1866, wrote in the Springfield, Massachusetts, *Republican*:

> He [Mark Twain] has shrewdness and a certain hearty abhor[r]ence of shams which will make his faculty serviceable to mankind. His talent is so well based that he can write seriously and well when he chooses, which is perhaps the best test of true humor. His faults are crudeness, coarseness, and an occasional Panurge-like plainness of statement. I am particular in these details, for I believe he deserves this space and criticism, and I think I recognize a new star rising in this western horizon.

*Innocents Abroad* (1869) was a popular success, but few besides Howells and Harte praised it for its literary qualities. The New York *Nation* made no mention of its literary merits, and Josiah Gilbert Holland called its author a "mere fun-maker of ephemeral popularity."

In 1870, after Mark Twain married Olivia Langdon and became part-owner of the Buffalo *Express*, he still saw himself as a newspaperman and a humorous lecturer rather than a man of letters. In 1872 he published *Roughing It* and settled in Hartford, Connecticut. In the following year appeared *The Gilded Age*, a novel that he had written in collaboration with his new neighbor, Charles Dudley Warner, a well-known man of letters. Mark Twain was now discovering his true métier in fiction. In *The Adventures of Tom Sawyer* (1876) he began to exploit his richest mine of literary materials, the memories of his youth. Born in Missouri of southern parents, he had spent his formative years in the western South; and he found that what he remembered of his life in the Mississippi River country served him better than his recollections of California and Nevada. With his journalistic training Mark Twain was always sensitive to changes in literary fashions which affected his market, and in the early eighties he could not fail to note the extraordinary popularity of stories of the Old South. Indeed, some of the best of them were being written by two of his friends, George W. Cable and Joel Chandler Harris. There are no more memorable descriptions of Southern life than those in *Huckleberry Finn* and the earlier chapters of *Life on the Mississippi*. The life of the Old South that Mark Twain knew was more primitive than that portrayed in Thomas Nelson Page's *In Ole Virginia*, but the South that he knew was not frontier country. The American frontier had passed on westward by the time Mark Twain was born.

Memorable also are some of the scenes in *Pudd'nhead Wilson* (1895), in which belatedly Mark Twain returned to the southern scene. Before that time, however, the vogue of southern stories had waned; and there was under way a revival of historical romance led by Robert Louis Stevenson. Mark Twain had made use of a romantic period in English history in *The Prince and the Pauper* (1882). *Joan of Arc*, which for a time he considered his best book, came in 1896. A better book was the satiric *A Connecticut Yankee in King Arthur's Court* (1889), a favorite with Howells and Stedman. He lived on until 1910, but apart from *The Mysterious Stranger* and "The Man That Corrupted Hadleyburg" his later published writings have little importance.

In its issue of October, 1898, the *Critic* asked: "Who are the four most famous of living authors?" and in answer to its own query named Tolstoy, Zola, Ruskin, and Mark Twain. It is true nevertheless, as Howells maintained in his *My Mark Twain* (1910), that in his own country "polite learning [had] hesitated his praise."

> In proportion as people thought themselves refined they questioned that quality which all recognize in him now. . . . I went with him to see Longfellow, but I do not think Longfellow made much of him, and Lowell made less. . . . It was two of my most fastidious Cambridge friends who accepted him with the English, the European entirety—namely, Charles Eliot Norton and Professor Francis J. Child.

Until after the end of the century few of the literary historians recognized Mark Twain as a major American writer. Richardson and Beers failed to see that he was any more important than Josh Billings and Petroleum V. Nasby. Even W. P. Trent, who was among the first scholars to see the importance of the western and southern humorists, could not in 1903 rank Mark Twain as the equal of those Cambridge humorists, Lowell and Holmes; and he regarded the author of *Joan of Arc* as greatly inferior to Scott as a historical romancer. Mark Twain is not included in William Crary Brownell's *American Prose Masters* (1909) or John Erskine's *Leading American Novelists* (1910), and there are no selections from his works in Norman Foerster's *The Chief American Prose Writers* (1916).

In 1900, however, Professor Walter Bronson of Brown University had ranked Twain as the "greatest writer of the West," greater he felt than Bret Harte. "Time," he said, "will winnow much chaff from his pages, but much of great merit will remain." In 1900 also Professor Barrett Wendell of Harvard wrote that "in certain moods one is disposed for all its eccentricity to call [*Huckleberry Finn*] the most admirable work of literary art as yet produced on this continent." In 1904 Professor Richard Burton wrote that the United States possessed "one living writer of indisputable genius . . . Mark Twain." Professor William Lyon Phelps of Yale was also among the first scholars to praise Mark Twain as a major American writer. Before Mark Twain's death in 1910 three universities had bestowed honorary degrees upon him: Yale in 1901, Missouri in 1902, and Oxford in 1907. In 1915 Fred Lewis Pattee in *A History of American Literature since 1870* wrote: "His generation bought his books for the fun in them; their children are finding now that their fathers bought not, as they supposed, clownish ephemera, but true literature, the classics of the period." In 1921 Stuart P. Sherman's chapter in *The Cambridge History* seemed to give official sanction to Mark Twain's rank as a great American writer, and in the same year Carl Van Doren in *The American Novel* gave it as his opinion that the two greatest American novels were *The Scarlet Letter* and *Huckleberry Finn*.

One of the first American critics to see Mark Twain as a major writer was a professor of English at Columbia University, but it is perhaps well to remember that it was not until his fortieth year that Brander Matthews (1852–1929) began his distinguished career at Columbia University. He had tried his hand at writing verse, fiction, and literary and dramatic criticism; and he had spent many months in France and England. He was not only a great teacher but a man of letters as well. In his "Memories of Mark Twain" (in *The Tocsin of Revolt*, 1922) he recalled that he had read "The Jumping Frog" story at the age of fifteen and from that time on he had followed Mark Twain's literary career with keen interest. He recalled also that soon after its publication he had "had the pleasure of reviewing [*Huckleberry Finn*] for the London *Saturday Review*, hailing it as one of the masterpieces of American fiction."

For the Uniform Edition of Mark Twain's writings in 1899 Brander Matthews wrote an introductory essay entitled "Biographical Criticism" (reprinted later as "An Appreciation"). Mark Twain, he noted, had "ripened in knowledge and power since he first attracted attention as a wild Western funny man." And yet, he added, "In many of the discussions of American literature he is dismissed as though he were only a competitor of his predecessors, Artemus Ward and John Phoenix, instead of being what he is really, a writer who is to be classed—at whatever interval only time may decide—rather with Cervantes and Molière." Mark Twain's best books, Matthews felt sure, were not those with romantic European historical backgrounds but those which dealt with the life the author knew at first hand in the Mississippi River country. *Huckleberry Finn,* he said, is "the finest of his books, the deepest in its insight, and the widest in its appeal." It is, he asserted, "very much more than a funny book, it is a marvelously accurate portrayal of a whole civilization." "No American author," he added, "has at his command a style more nervous, more varied, more flexible, or more various than Mark Twain's. His colloquial style," he continued, "should not hide from us his mastery of all the devices of rhetoric."

> Consider the tale of the Blue Jay in "A Tramp Abroad," wherein the humor is sustained by unstated pathos; what could be better told than this, with every word the right word and in the right place? And take Huck Finn's description of the storm when he was alone on the island, which is in dialect, which will not parse, which bristles with double negatives, but which none the less is one of the finest passages of descriptive prose in all American literature.

*Huckleberry Finn* was a great popular success, but there is scant evidence to show that American literary critics recognized it as a masterpiece. Like other books sold by subscription, this novel was not widely reviewed. The *Century Magazine,* however, assigned it to a very competent reviewer, Thomas Sergeant Perry, who saw that it was a much greater book than *Tom Sawyer.* Perry was a native of New England, but the book drew more unfavorable criticism from that section than from any other. The Concord, Massachusetts, library banned the book as "rough, coarse, and inelegant, dealing with a series of experiences not elevating. . . . It is the veriest trash." In Boston both the daily *Transcript* and the weekly *Literary World* approved the verdict of the Concord library committee. In Springfield the *Republican* branded the book as "trashy and vicious."

> The trouble with Mr. Clemens is that he has no reliable sense of propriety. His notorious speech at an *Atlantic* dinner, marshalling Longfellow and Emerson and Whittier [Holmes] in vulgar parodies in a Western miner's cabin, illustrates this, but not in much more relief than the "Adventures of Tom Sawyer" did, or these Huckleberry Finn stories do. . . . They are no better in tone than the dime novels which flood the blood-and-thunder reading population.

Professor Arthur L. Vogelback, who quoted this passage in his study of the reception of *Huckleberry Finn* (*American Literature*, November, 1939), concluded:

> In these indignant comments, it is, of course, easy to identify the genteel tradition. Critics who used such words as "vulgar," "coarse," "inelegant," in condemning the book, indicated by implication the qualities they deemed necessary to literature—"refinement," "delicacy," and "elegance."

One thinks of a Pudd'nhead Wilson epigram that Mark Twain inserted in *Following the Equator* (1897): "There are no people who are quite so vulgar as the over-refined ones."

Among men of letters in England and America there were a few who publicly recognized *Huckleberry Finn* as a contemporary classic. Conspicuous among them was William Dean Howells. That small number, however, does not include Matthew Arnold, for whom Mark Twain was only a vulgar funny man, or Henry James, who regarded him as a writer for immature minds. Joel Chandler Harris, who in 1908 was to refer to Mark Twain as "not only our greatest humorist but our greatest writer of fiction," in November, 1885, wrote in the *Critic* that "there is not in our fictive literature a more wholesome book than 'Huckleberry Finn.'" It teaches, he added "the lesson of honesty, justice, mercy." After reading these words in the *Critic*, Mark Twain wrote to thank Harris for "the good word about Huck, that abused child of mine, who has had so much mud flung at him."

In England in 1883, before the publication of *Huckleberry Finn*, Thomas Hardy had asked Howells: "Why don't people [in America] understand that Mark Twain is not merely a great humorist?"* On August 3, 1886, Brander Matthews had a talk with Robert Louis Stevenson which he briefly described in *These Many Years* (1917): "What I remember most vividly was the high appreciation of 'Huckleberry Finn' that he expressed, calling it a far finer work artistically than 'Tom Sawyer,' partly because it was a richer book morally; and he wound up by declaring it to be the most important addition to the fiction of our language that had been made for ten years." Andrew Lang, though he said he would not read *A Connecticut Yankee*, praised *Huckleberry Finn* in the *Critic* for July 25, 1891, as "a nearly flawless gem of romance and humor." Bernard Shaw had praise for Mark Twain's books.

* A year earlier Professor John Nichol of the University of Glasgow in his book on *American Literature* had asserted that Mark Twain had done "perhaps more than any other living writer to lower the literary tone of English speaking people."

Rudyard Kipling, on his first visit to the United States, went out of his way to see Mark Twain. A decade later he wrote to his American publisher, Frank Doubleday: "He [Mark Twain] is the biggest man you have on your side of the water by a damn sight, and don't you forget it. Cervantes was a relation of his."

In 1920 when Mark Twain was elected to the Hall of Fame for Great Americans, his status as a major American writer seemed assured. The college of electors, however, had not reckoned with the young intellectuals who were now systematically denigrating the standard British and American authors of the nineteenth century. It was in 1920 that one of the ablest of the young literary radicals launched a devastating attack in *The Ordeal of Mark Twain*. Van Wyck Brooks saw in Mark Twain one of the most gifted of all American writers, one who might have developed into a great satirist like Swift or Cervantes. Brooks, whose appreciation of humor in literature was rather weak, was a social rather than an aesthetic critic, and he looked to American writers to take the lead in bringing about a transformed social and economic order. He saw in Mark Twain the victim of a society that failed to stimulate and nourish its geniuses.

The three persons who in Brooks's view were most to be blamed for Mark Twain's failure were his mother, his wife, and his friend and adviser, William Dean Howells. Of his mother Brooks wrote: "Jane Clemens, in short, was the embodiment of that old-fashioned, cast-iron Calvinism which had proved so favorable to the life of enterprising action but which perceived the scent of the devil in any least expression of what is now known as the creative impulse." Olivia Langdon, argued Brooks, did her best to make of her husband not a great writer but a gentleman and a money-maker. Said Brooks: "From the moment of his marriage his artistic integrity, already compromised, had, as a matter of fact, been irreparably destroyed. . . ." Brooks in 1920 had not discovered how wrong he was when he wrote of Howells: "He [Mark Twain], this divided soul, had sought the great leader and had found only an irresponsible child like himself, a child who told him that you had to sneak off behind the barn if you wanted to smoke the pipe of truth."

The indictment was a formidable one. Brooks had ransacked Mark Twain's books and published letters and Paine's huge biography, and with great skill he had marshaled numerous details in support of his thesis. He explained the pessimism and cynicism which are so conspicuous in Mark Twain's later writings and conversation: "That bitterness of his was the effect of a certain miscarriage in his creative life, a balked personality, and arrested development . . . which for him destroyed the meaning of life." In the 1935 edition of *The Ordeal* Brooks was less sharply critical of Mark Twain.

Brooks's book caused critics and scholars to take sides in a debate that continued intermittently for years. Various scholars brought forth convincing evidence that Brooks's vivid portraits of Mark Twain's mother and wife were distorted and inaccurate. As to Brooks's thesis that Mark Twain could not in an American environment become the great literary leader that Brooks had hoped for, Clarence Gohdes's comment is not irrelevant: "As a thinker, Mark Twain is too inconsistent and too shallow to be of much importance."

The most persistent of Brooks's critics was Bernard De Voto, who in 1938 became custodian of the Mark Twain Papers. He pointed out various errors in Brooks's indictment and gave his own interpretation of Mark Twain's significance: "Mark Twain was a frontier humorist. His literary intelligence was shaped by the life of the frontier and found expression in the themes and forms developed by the humor of the frontier." De Voto, himself a product of the West, chose to make little of Mark Twain's southern background and to ignore the fact that Mark Twain had had no experience of frontier life until he was twenty-six years old. De Voto would not have agreed with Fred Lewis Pattee, who in a book of selections from Mark Twain's writings wrote in 1935: "The Mark Twain that has endured was born in New England. He needed restraint, literary ideals, suggestion, and publication in adequate magazines." "What," said Pattee, "would he have written had he remained in San Francisco?"

DeLancey Ferguson, after a study of revisions in the manuscript of *Huckleberry Finn*, concluded that whether made by Mark or Livy the revisions "are not the dilution of grim realism to make it meat for babies; they are the work of a skilled craftsman removing the unessential, adding vividness to dialogue and description, and smoothing incongruities." Mark Twain, he concluded, was not a folk humorist but a highly skilled man of letters.

Too much has been made of the pessimism of the aging Mark Twain, and we do not need to go to the Freudians for an explanation of it. How indeed could any one expect important results to come from the application, by an amateur like Brooks, of Freudian methods to a writer who could not be questioned or examined by a competent physician? Mark Twain was deeply grieved by the deaths of those he loved most: a son, two daughters, and his beloved wife. There was in addition a business failure followed by bankruptcy and the need once again to return to the lecture platform that he had come to hate. Not to be overlooked also are his declining health and energy and frustrations concerning his later writings. The world in which he spent the last decades of his long life was immeasurably remote from the world in which he had grown up; and neither his own country nor the rest of the civilized world was fulfilling the promise that in his early manhood he thought he had seen. As Henry Nash Smith wrote in 1958: "He had bet too much on the doctrine of Progress and the belief in an orderly benign universe to be able to emulate the younger writers who in his old age were finding literary capital in the master image of the Waste Land and were beginning to produce a whole literature of alienation."

The great humorists of other nations and ages have been pessimists also; witness Molière and Swift. There were pessimists among Mark Twain's predecessors and contemporaries. Harry Levin has emphasized "the power of blackness" in Poe, Hawthorne, and Melville, authors who could not share the optimistic attitude of Emerson and Whitman. There were pessimists among Mark Twain's contemporaries, notably Henry Adams, Ambrose Bierce, Thomas Hardy, Samuel Butler, and the aging Carlyle. There is a strain of pessimism in Edward Fitzgerald's *The Rubáiyát of Omar Khayyám* and in James Thomson's *The City of Dreadful Night*. Meanwhile in the United States writers who are not to be classed as pessimists—Lowell, Howells, and Whitman—had lost much of their faith in the innate goodness of human nature and now saw that the republic was not fulfilling the promise of its earlier years.

Since his death in 1910 critics of every variety have had their say about Mark Twain's life and writings: impressionists, formalists, symbolists, New Humanists, Marxists, Freudians, and various others. They have pointed to artistic defects in even the greatest of his books, and they have noted that the great bulk of his published work has little intrinsic importance; and yet for most of them he is still one of our greatest writers. For the literary critic Mark Twain poses two special problems. First, he was a great humorist, and Brooks and other critics with little taste for humor have had great difficulty in assessing the value of his books. In the second place, Mark Twain was and still is enormously popular, and this disturbs the modern critics who seem to value only those writers whom they regard as alienated from society. This, it seems to me, is a main reason why they have made so much of his pessimism.

Mark Twain's influence has been greatest on writers of fiction, and it is greater than that of any other American writer except Henry James. Hemingway doubtless spoke for others besides himself, notably Faulkner, when in 1935 he wrote in *The Green Hills of Africa*:

> All modern American literature comes from one book by Mark Twain called *Huckleberry Finn*. If you read it you must stop where the Nigger Jim is stolen from the boys. That is the real end. The rest is just cheating. But it's the best book we've had. All American writing comes from that. There was nothing before. There has been nothing as good since.

*If fame belonged to me, I could not escape her—if she did not, the longest day would pass me on the chase—and the approbation of my Dog, would forsake me then.*

Emily Dickinson to Thomas Wentworth Higginson, June 7, 1862

# EMILY DICKINSON

On March 20, 1876, Helen Hunt Jackson (H.H.) wrote to Emily Dickinson (1830–1886): "You are a great poet—and it is a wrong to the day you live in, that you will not sing aloud." On September 5, 1884, H.H. was still lamenting that her friend was unwilling to publish. "What portfolios of verses you must have.—It is a cruel wrong to your 'day and Generation' that you will not give them light." She asked the poet to name her as literary executor, but Emily Dickinson was then suffering from a nervous collapse from which she never fully recovered, and H.H. was to die the following year.

The "little manuscript volume" of Emily Dickinson's poems mentioned in H.H.'s earlier letter had apparently been copied from the poet's letters to Thomas Wentworth Higginson. He more than any other person deserves credit for the eventual publication of some of the finest poems written in America. This minor man of letters was a graduate of Harvard, a friend of the Cambridge poets, an Abolitionist, and a Unitarian minister. He was also a regular contributor to the *Atlantic Monthly*. In April, 1862, Emily Dickinson read in that magazine his "Letter to a Young Contributor," and she promptly sent him four of her poems with a note asking: "Are you too deeply occupied to say if my verse is alive?" She had obviously been struck by Higginson's advice: "Charge your style with life" and "tolerate no superfluity that can be struck out." In later letters she was to ask whether or not she "had told it clear." On June 7, 1862, she made bold to ask: "But, will you be my preceptor, Mr. Higginson?" Two years later she was to write: "You were not aware that you saved my life. To thank you in person has been since then one of my few requests." This she was able to do in August, 1870, when he visited the Dickinson home in Amherst.

As her "preceptor," Higginson at first, he says, tried "to lead her in the direction of rules and traditions." In those mid-Victorian years who would not have been disturbed by her unconventional syntax and imperfect rhymes? His final estimate of her poems appears in an article he published in the *Christian Union* for September 25, 1890: "One can no more criticize a faulty rhyme here and there than a defect of drawing in one of Blake's pictures. . . . When a thought takes one's breath away, who cares to count the syllables?" While Higginson and Mrs. Mabel Loomis Todd were preparing the poems for publication, he wrote to her: "You are the only person who can feel as I do about the extraordinary thing we have done in recording this rare genius. I feel as if we had climbed to a cloud, pulled it away and revealed a new star behind it."

Higginson was no admirer of Melville or Whitman, but he was a better critic than most of his literary contemporaries. He thought that Thoreau's *Walden* was "the only book yet written in America that bears an annual perusal." He was the first person to write an appreciative essay on the Negro spirituals. Colonel Higginson had heard many of them sung in South Carolina by Negro soldiers under his command during the Civil War. He could see defects in two of the greatest New England writers: "Both looked into the realm of passion, Emerson with distrust, Hawthorne with eager interest; but neither thrilled with its spell, and the American poet of passion is yet to come." So in 1870 Higginson wrote in an *Atlantic Monthly* essay on "Americanism in Literature." He was in time to recognize in the poems of Emily Dickinson a lyric passion lacking in her New England predecessors.

In the twentieth century too many of Emily Dickinson's critics and biographers—including her niece Martha Dickinson Bianchi, Amy Lowell, and the able editor of her poems, Thomas H. Johnson—have berated Higginson for not praising Emily Dickinson as highly as they thought she deserved. This is quite unfair, as Anna Mary Wells points out in her biography of Higginson, *Dear Preceptor* (1963): "The nineteenth-century writers we admire all went against the main current of their time, and Higginson was essentially a part of it." As Miss Wells notes, Higginson had "that way of viewing things, which was the common property of his generation . . . [but] he had also much more, not only peculiar talent but personal integrity and an independence of spirit rare in any age."

Before Roberts Brothers published a volume of Emily Dickinson's poems in 1890, Higginson had approached the Houghton Mifflin Company about bringing out a small book of her lyrics. They flatly refused. That firm was making money from the writings of the established New England poets and writers of fiction, and had no interest in promoting the crude verses of an unknown and eccentric Yankee spinster. H.H. had earlier appealed to Thomas Niles of Roberts Brothers to publish Emily Dickinson's poems. He, however, finally concluded that, as he wrote to Higginson in June, 1890, "it would be unwise to perpetuate Miss Dickinson's poems. They are quite as remarkable for defects as for beauties and are generally devoid of true poetical qualities." Roberts Brothers had an adviser in Arlo Bates, author of novels, verses, and a treatise on composition, who in 1893 was to become professor of English in the Massachusetts Institute of Technology. He was of the opinion that Higginson and Mrs. Todd had not revised Emily Dickinson's poems nearly enough. He wrote: "There is hardly one of these poems which does not bear marks of unusual and remarkable talent; there is hardly one of them which is not marked by an extraordinary crudity of workmanship."

The wonder is that Roberts Brothers ever published any of Emily Dickinson's poems. They did in fact bring out three volumes of the poems in 1890, 1891, and 1896 containing a total of 449 poems; and in 1894 Harper and Brothers published a volume of her letters which contained 102 poems or parts of poems. There would have been a fourth volume of the poems in the late 1890's but for the unfortunate quarrel that arose between Mrs. Todd and Emily's sister Lavinia.

After the appearance of the first two volumes in 1890 and 1891, an anonymous writer in the Boston *Transcript* mentioned as among the "fads of the time—Browningese, Ibsenese, or, to name the latest, Dickinsonese." Neither the editors nor the publishers had expected anything like the favorable reception given the poems by the reading public. That public, unlike the literary critics, was not greatly troubled by imperfect rhymes or unconventional grammar and syntax.

Among the friends of the Dickinson family were two able journalists of the Springfield *Republican*, Samuel Bowles and Josiah Gilbert Holland. Both Bowles and Holland were intelligent men who were not blind to the force and beauty of some of the lines in Emily's poems; but with their conventional notions of poetic technique and the proper diction of poetry they felt that her poems should not be published. Holland, minister, novelist, journalist, and poet, was one of the most popular and best-paid writers of the time. Emily Dickinson was not, however, the only great American writer whose work he failed to appreciate. Soon after Bryant's death in 1878 he wrote in *Scribner's Monthly*: "Of one thing we may be reasonably sure, viz., that when the genuine geniuses of this period shall be appreciated at their full value . . . their countrymen will have ceased discussing Poe and Thoreau and Whitman." Yet Holland was to publish in his magazine some of the best fiction to come out of the South and the West; and he was in September, 1881, to salute Sidney Lanier as "a rare genius."

The poetic rules and conventions of the 1870's irked three of the best poets of the time: Whitman, Lanier, and Emily Dickinson. On March 15, 1874, in a letter to his wife Lanier explained his difficulties with "My Two Springs," a poem he had written in her honor:

Of course, since I have written it to print, I cannot make it such as *I* desire, in artistic design: for the *forms* of today require a certain trim smugness and clean-shaven propriety in the face and dress of a poem, and I must win a hearing by conforming in some degree to these tyrannies,—with a view to overturning them in the future.

Lanier was to some extent willing to conform to the conventions, but Emily Dickinson, like Walt Whitman, was not; and so she apparently—after Higginson had advised against publication—made no effort to get her poems published. She wrote:

> Publication is the auction
> Of the mind of man.

"How can you," she wrote to H.H., "print a piece of your soul?"

Emily Dickinson's failure to observe the conventional rules was roundly condemned by Thomas Bailey Aldrich, poet and writer of fiction, who in 1881 succeeded Howells as editor of the *Atlantic Monthly*. In January, 1892, he published in the *Atlantic* an unsigned article, "*In Re* Emily Dickinson," of which a revised version appeared in his *Ponkapog Papers* (1903). In the earlier version Aldrich began by referring to an anonymous English critic who had said that Emily Dickinson might have become a fifth-rate poet "if she had only mastered the rudiments of grammar and gone into metrical training for about fifteen years." If she had undergone such training, said Aldrich, "she would, I am sure, have become an admirable lyric poet of the second magnitude." Aldrich could not resist the temptation to rewrite one stanza of a poem already revised by Mrs. Todd or Colonel Higginson. As it appeared in the *Poems* of 1890 the stanza read:

> I taste a liquor never brewed
> From Tankards scooped in pearl;
> Not all the vats upon the Rhine
> Yield such an alcohol.

Here is Aldrich's first version:

> I taste a liquor never brewed
> In vats upon the Rhine;
> No tankards scooped in pearl could yield
> An alcohol like mine.

His second version is no improvement upon the first:

> I taste a liquor never brewed
> In vats upon the Rhine;
> No tankard ever held a draught
> Of alcohol like mine.

Time was to bring in its revenges. In 1930 the poet Genevieve Taggard was to write in her *Life and Mind of Emily Dickinson*: "Idiotic meddler! What has he dared to do to one of the most delicious lines in the English language!"

Aldrich, whom some critics regarded as the best of the younger poets, was a meticulous craftsman who had no patience with the metrical irregularities of Whitman, Lanier, or Emily Dickinson. A belated romanticist, he disliked the early poems of Kipling, the novels of Zola and Hardy, and the writings of Josh Billings and other American humorists. As editor of the *Atlantic Monthly* he was less hospitable to the newer writers than Howells had been.

In the early 1890's those two irreverent young poets who wrote *Songs from Vagabondia*, Bliss Carman and Richard Hovey, amused themselves by satirizing Aldrich, Woodberry, Gilder, and other old-fashioned critics who held positions of authority or influence:

> When shall the Golden Age of Song
> Return to earth again?
> When all the dilettante throng
> Is silenced or is slain
>
> When Tommy Aldrich is tabooed
> And Woodberry's forgot;
> When Gilder knows bad verse from good
> And stops accepting rot.

In 1896 Carman wrote of the poems of Emily Dickinson:

> The conviction remains that Emily Dickinson's contribution to English poetry (or American poetry if you prefer to say so) is by far the most important made by any woman west of the Atlantic. It is so by reason of its thought, its piquancy, its untarnished expression. She borrowed from no one; she was never commonplace, always imaginative and stimulating, and finally the region of her brooding was that sequestered domain where our profoundest convictions have their origin, and whence we trace the Puritan strain within us.

Carman added what might have served as a warning to later students of Emily Dickinson's life and writings:

> This New England woman was a type of her race. A life-long recluse, musing on the mysteries of life and death, she had that stability of character, that strong sanity of mind, which could hold out against the perils of seclusion, unshaken by solitude, undethroned by doubt. It would never, I feel sure, occur to anyone with the least insight into the New England conscience (with its capacity for abstemiousness, its instinct for being always aloof and restrained rather than social and blithe) to think of Emily Dickinson as peculiar or her mode of life as queer.

William Dean Howells was a better judge of fiction than of poetry, but he did not fail to recognize the greatness of Emily Dickinson's poems. In a review in *Harper's Magazine* in January, 1891, he wrote:

If nothing else had come out of our life but this strange poetry, we should feel that in the work of Emily Dickinson, America, or New England rather, had made a distinctive addition to the literature of the world, and could not be left out of any record of it; and the interesting and important thing is that this poetry is as characteristic of our life as our business enterprise, our political turmoil, our demagogues, our millionairism.

It was Howells's reading aloud to Stephen Crane in April, 1893, of some of Emily Dickinson's poems that prompted the younger author to try his hand at writing poetry.

At the turn of the century most of the literary historians were ignoring Emily Dickinson's poems. She is not mentioned in Barrett Wendell's *Literary History of America* (1900). In the same year Professor Walter C. Bronson of Brown in *A Short History of American Literature* gave Emily Dickinson just three lines and a half. He noted that "The minor poets are legion"; then he added: "A rarer vein is that of EMILY DICKINSON (1830–1886), whose condensed little poems on nature and life startle and stab by their erratic originality of thought and phrase." In 1919 when he published a revised version of his *Short History*, Bronson made no change in his text. In 1912, however, he had included seven of her poems in his *American Poems* (1625–1892). Emily Dickinson is not mentioned in Professor Percy H. Boynton's *A History of American Literature* (1919).

Edmund Clarence Stedman was a better critic than the academic literary historians. In 1900 he included twenty-two of her poems in *An American Anthology*. (He also included seven poems written by Emily's niece, Martha Gilbert Dickinson, better known as Madame Bianchi, who had visited him apparently because she wanted her own poems in *An American Anthology*.) The inclusion of Emily Dickinson's poems brought from Horace Howard Furness, who was probably the best Shakespearean scholar in America, this indignant protest:

> But, O man of taste, severe and pure, could you not withstand the pressure, doubtless put on you, to include the bawbling idiocy of [Emily Dickinson]? I have never seen so many of her—(I don't know what to call 'em, verses they are not) her *words* gathered together and I thought I was reading a back number of the *Opal* published by the inmates of the Bloomingdale Lunatic Asylum—I screamed with laughter over them, and then heaved a bitter sigh that within the covers which held Emerson, Bryant, and Lowell there should be bound up such (pardon the word) Rot. But I know it was not your fault. You couldn't help it. Heaven alone can pardon those who first put such drivelling into print,—man cannot or at least this man cannot.

In reply Stedman offered this somewhat lame defense:

> The selections that move you to Homeric laughter were all, among
> hundreds, that were *structural* in the least; yet read them a second
> time and there *is* something in them, though they *were* originally dis-
> covered by T. W. H[igginson]. whom sacredly *inter nos*, Clarence
> King books as "sired by a second-class Greek damned by a Puritan
> mother."

One wonders whether if Stedman had seen Emily Dickinson's poems in the
form in which she left them, he would have found any of them worthy of
inclusion in his huge anthology.

By 1914, when Madame Bianchi brought out a volume of new Emily
Dickinson poems, *The Single Hound,* the new poetry was attracting attention,
and a keen interest in the poet soon developed. Madame Bianchi, aided by
Alfred Leete Hampson, brought out other volumes: *Complete Poems* (1924),
*Further Poems* (1929), *Unpublished Poems* (1936), and *The Poems of Emily
Dickinson* (1937). The editing was inaccurate and confusing. The Dickinson
family, one regrets to say, gave little or no help to competent investigators
who requested it. An Amherst College professor, the late George F. Whicher,
who got no help from Madame Bianchi, managed nevertheless to write what
was, when it was published in 1938, by far the best life of Emily Dickinson.

Meanwhile there had been much speculation about Emily Dickinson's
withdrawal from the world and the supposed love affair that precipitated it.
The critics, preoccupied with Freudian psychoanalysis and the new attitude
toward sex, felt certain that Emily Dickinson was suffering from a puritanic
suppression of her natural instincts. The critics failed to note that in her second letter to Colonel Higginson she had written: "When I state myself, as the
representative of the Verse—it does not mean—me—but a supposed person."
Mrs. Todd, who thought that Emily Dickinson cared more for her poems
than for any man, had issued a warning in her preface to the *Poems* of 1891:
"She had tried society and the world, and found them lacking. She was not
an invalid, and she lived in seclusion from no love-disappointment. Her life
was the normal blossoming of a nature introspective in a high degree, whose
best thought could not exist in pretence." Years later Allen Tate was to write:
"All pity for Miss Dickinson's 'starved life' is misdirected. Her life was one
of the richest and deepest ever lived on this continent."

Until 1945 there was no published volume in which Emily Dickinson's
poems were printed exactly as she had written them. In that year Mrs. Milli-
cent Todd Bingham brought out in *Bolts of Melody* the poems which had
remained in her mother's possession after the quarrel between Mrs. Todd
and Lavinia Dickinson. It was not until 1955 that Thomas H. Johnson pub-

lished his admirable three-volume edition of the *Poems* with a new biography to accompany them. Aided by Theodora Ward and others, Johnson had succeeded in arranging the 1,775 poems in something roughly approximating the order in which they were written. Johnson included the many variant readings among which too often the poet had made no final choice. In 1957 there was a new edition of the *Letters* which included no less than 1,049 separate items, and in 1960 Jay Leyda brought out in two volumes *The Years and Hours of Emily Dickinson.*

These indispensable books gave a new and strong stimulus to critical and scholarly studies, of which one of the most notable is Charles R. Anderson's *Stairway of Surprise* (1960). The new materials, however, left certain questions without complete answers. There was still room for speculation and research concerning the men whom Emily Dickinson admired (her "tutors") and perhaps loved. Students were bothered by the many variant readings found in the manuscripts. The poems often begin magnificently, but too many of them seem not to find a fit conclusion. Was Emily Dickinson merely a "private poet" writing for no audience but herself? Many of the poems are of course only personal messages written to be included in letters to relatives and friends. John Crowe Ransom suggested that not more than one in seventeen of her poems would become "a public property." That would mean a hundred poems, which is a larger number than other major American poets have achieved in that domain. Anderson wrote in the preface to his book: "Her really fine poems do not seem to number more than a hundred, her great ones about twenty-five."

In the last half-century we have seen marked changes in literary fashions and in theories of poetry and criticism, but these have had no great influence upon the reputation of Emily Dickinson. It is clear that she is not only a major American writer but in a sense our contemporary, like Herman Melville and Henry James. As the late George F. Whicher wrote in 1947 in "Emily Dickinson among the Victorians": "Hers was an essentially modern spirit, learning, as we have not yet fully learned, to make the best of a world that has undergone an intellectual fragmentation bombing."

# Part Two. The Twentieth Century

*Each age, it is found, must write its own books; or rather, each generation for the next succeeding. The books of an older period will not fit this.*

Ralph Waldo Emerson, "The American Scholar"

*For myself, and I was not alone, all the conscious and recollected years of my life have been lived to this day [June 21, 1940] under the heavy threat of world catastrophe, and most of the energies of my mind and spirit have been spent in the effort to grasp the meaning of these threats, to trace to their sources and to understand the logic of this majestic and terrible failure of the life of man in the Western world.*

Katherine Anne Porter, *The Days Before*

# Chapter 6. General Characteristics

The nineteenth century, we may say, came to its end not in December, 1900, but in August, 1914, with the outbreak of the First World War. The Battle of Waterloo in 1815 had ended the long series of Napoleonic wars which—since in 1812 the United States was drawn into the conflict—might more properly be described as the *first* of the world wars. Except for the brief Franco-Prussian War and our own more disastrous Civil War there had been no major conflict for almost a century. The ninety-nine years that followed Waterloo were a time of comparative peace and prosperity.

With a sense of foreboding, the British foreign minister, Sir Edward Grey, remarked in August, 1914, as he witnessed the first London blackout: "The lights are going out all over Europe; they will not be rekindled in our time." An age of wars and revolutions of unprecedented magnitude had begun, and in April, 1917, peaceful, idealistic America was drawn out of its traditional isolation to fight a war on the other side of the Atlantic. The new century was to be an age of conflicting ideologies, of mass insanities, of unscrupulous dictators, of rapidly changing manners and moral codes, an age of anxiety, insecurity, and for millions, of stark tragedy.

Even before the end of the nineteenth century a shrewd observer might have seen that powerful forces were undermining the old order. It was, however, the First World War that broke the dam and released terrific forces that threatened to destroy much of what older Americans still cherished. The war had taken some four million young Americans from their homes. It was with a feeling of disillusionment that many of them returned from France.

The war seemed to them to have settled little of any consequence, and the terms of the Versailles Treaty convinced many of them that the United States should have kept to its traditional isolation from European affairs. They did not foresee that their own sons would be called upon to fight a Second World War. Woodrow Wilson knew better, but his words fell on insensitive ears.

The twentieth century brought with it tremendous forces making for change: a new science, a new technology, a new way of living, new ideas of many kinds, and new literary impulses and techniques. It followed that there would be marked changes in literary fashion and in critical standards. There was to be a second American renaissance comparable in importance to that which in 1837 Emerson had heralded in "The American Scholar." By 1920 we had in fact come to one of the sharp turning points in literary history.

There were new economists, like Thorstein Veblen and Charles A. Beard; and young writers were belatedly discovering Karl Marx, who was too often the only economist they knew anything about. There were scientists who taught that civilized man, like his remote ancestors, was essentially predatory, warlike, and promiscuous. There was a new psychology. Sigmund Freud had uncovered in the subconscious mind unsocial and irrational impulses, especially in matters pertaining to sex. Young novelists and playwrights thought that Freud had given them the key to the mysteries of human behavior. In 1931 George Santayana was to write in *The Genteel Tradition at Bay*: "So far, then, the gist of modern history would seem to be this: a many-sided insurrection of the unregenerate natural man, with all his physical powers and affinities, against the regimen of Christendom. He has convinced himself that his physical life is not as his ghostly mentors asserted, a life of sin; and why should it be a life of misery?"

The First World War served to reveal new depths of human depravity in a world that men had come to think of as civilized. After those four catastrophic years it was difficult to believe that mankind was steadily progressing toward higher and higher stages of civilization. In an influential book, *The Modern Temper* (1929), Joseph Wood Krutch pointed out that man no longer lived in an anthropocentric world of stable values. The scientists, he charged, had robbed man of his belief in the beneficence of the universe, and the psychologists had taken from him the sense of his own dignity. There appeared to be no longer any place in literature for heroes like Ulysses and William Tell or for great tragic figures like Agamemnon and King Lear.

When educated Americans were forced to reckon with the findings of the geologists, the anthropologists, and the higher critics of the Bible, devout Protestants, Catholics, and Jews alike found it increasingly difficult to regard the book of Genesis as an acceptable account of creation. Astronomers meanwhile were exploring a universe of unimaginable magnitude. The tiny planet on which we live was not the center of the universe as it had been described by Dante and Milton. Our sun was now seen as only one of millions of other star-suns in the huge galaxy known as the Milky Way; and there were billions of galaxies. In one of his finest poems, "The God of Galaxies," Krutch's friend Mark Van Doren wrote:

> The god of galaxies—how shall we praise him?
> For so we must, or wither. Yet what word
> Of words? And where to send it, on which night
> Of winter stars, of summer, or by autumn
> In the first evening of the Pleiades?
> The god of galaxies, of burning gases
> May have forgotten Leo and the Bull.

In the early nineteenth century when Emerson and Hawthorne were in college, Latin and Greek formed a large part of the curriculum. They were in fact the basis of a liberal education. At that time there were courses in rhetoric and composition, but almost no courses in the modern languages and none at all in either English or American literature. It was generally assumed that a gentleman would read for himself not only the romances of Scott and the poems of Byron but also the works of Shakespeare, Milton, Pope, and Addison. A student who in fact read any substantial portion of the great epics of Homer and Vergil, Plato's dialogues, the orations of Cicero and Demosthenes, and the histories of Livy and Herodotus acquired some knowledge of the world's great classics on which are based the literary traditions of the Western world. He also got a sense of the continuity of Western civilization.

Until well after the Civil War there was still, among educated men and women in this country, something that we may call a common literary mind. Longfellow and Poe, like Carlyle and Tennyson, could assume on the part of their readers some knowledge of the literature, mythology, and history of Greece, Rome, and Palestine. In the ancient classics the writer could find literary materials and artistic forms that could be adapted to whatever he wanted to write. He could enrich his style with images and allusions drawn from this common literary fund.

We in the last half of the twentieth century live under a different dispensation. In the college curriculum Latin and Greek have been displaced by the sciences, the social sciences, vocational studies, and by numerous courses in the modern languages and in English and American literature. The writer can no longer take it for granted that a college graduate will recognize an allusion to such literary and historical personages as Diomedes, Alcibiades, Tiresias, Janus, Cato, and Maecenas. Among the educated one often finds also an abysmal ignorance of the memorable characters and narratives of the

Old Testament. The writer of today cannot expect many of his readers to recognize a quotation from the Book of Job or to understand an allusion to Nathan the prophet or Naaman the leper. Except among English majors, a teacher is likely to encounter only ignorance when he mentions a character in *The Canterbury Tales, The Faerie Queene, The Rape of the Lock, Rob Roy,* or *Vanity Fair.* Few holders of college degrees can identify such memorable characters as Imogen, Parson Adams, Jeanie Deans, Uriah Heep, Becky Sharp, or Arthur Dimmesdale.

In his essay "Religion and Literature," T. S. Eliot wrote in 1935: "There never was a time, I believe, when those who read at all, read so many more books by living authors than books by dead authors; there never was a time so completely parochial, so cut off from the past." That is an accurate description of the situation as we know it today. Milton's once great reputation declined in the twentieth century in large part, I suspect, because men and women found it so difficult to read his poems. Eliot's pronouncement, however, makes one wonder whether he ever realized to what an impossible extent he and Ezra Pound expected their readers to recognize and understand quotations and allusions drawn from literary sources that are often more obscure than those one meets with in reading *Paradise Lost.*

In 1936 Willa Cather published a book of essays to which she gave the title *Not under Forty* because, as she explained, its contents would have "little interest for people under forty years of age." Looking backward at the age of sixty, she wrote: "The world broke in two in 1922 or thereabouts. . . ."

> Eighteen or twenty years ago there were graduated from our universities a company of unusually promising men, who were also extravagantly ambitious. The world was changing, and they meant to play a conspicuous part in this change: to make a new kind of thought and a new kind of expression; in language, color, form, sound. They were to bring about a renaissance within a decade or so. Failing in this, they made a career of destroying the past.

The destroyers of the past were also active in England. In 1922 Thomas Hardy published his *Late Lyrics and Earlier.* In his "Apology" for this volume he wrote:

> Whether owing to the barbarizing of taste in the younger minds by the dark madness of the late war, the unabashed cultivation of selfishness in all classes, the plethoric growth of knowledge simultaneously with the stunting of wisdom, "a degrading thirst after outrageous stimulation," or from any other cause, we seem threatened with a new Dark Age. . . . men's minds appear to be moving backwards rather than on.

In "The Second Coming" (1921) William Butler Yeats had written:

> Things fall apart; the centre cannot hold;
> Mere anarchy is loosed upon the world,
> The blood-dimmed tide is loosed, and everywhere
> The ceremony of innocence is drowned;
> The best lack all conviction, while the worst
> Are full of passionate intensity.

In the 1920's our young intellectuals were reading such writers as Zola, Proust, Nietzsche, Spengler, Mann, Ibsen, Dostoevski, Conrad, Masefield, Wells, Shaw, Yeats, and Joyce. They found it difficult to read sympathetically most of our nineteenth-century American writers. That earlier literature seemed to belong to an insulated, more innocent America, too unsophisticated and too complacent in its optimism, averting its eyes from unpleasant facts and cherishing all sorts of illusions about life. What was the importance of those antiquated writers, living in a provincial world, who had never read Karl Marx, Sigmund Freud, Bernard Shaw, or James Joyce? The young intellectuals were particularly severe upon the old New England poets. They found their attitude admirably expressed in George Santayana's *Character and Opinion in the United States* (1920):

> About the middle of the nineteenth century, in the quiet sunshine of provincial prosperity New England had an Indian summer of the mind; and an agreeably reflective literature showed how brilliant that russet and yellow season could be. . . . But it was all a harvest of leaves; these worthies had an expurgated and barren conception of life; theirs was the purity of sweet old age. . . . Their culture was half a pious survival, half an international acquirement; it was not the inevitable flowering of a fresh experience.

In an essay entitled "On Being Modern-Minded" Bertrand Russell wrote in 1950: "Our age is the most parochial since Homer. . . . We imagine ourselves at the apex of intelligence, and cannot believe that the quaint clothes and cumbrous phrases of former times can have invested people and thoughts that are still worthy of our attention." It was, Russell thought, "only since the 1914–18 war that it [had become] fashionable to ignore the past *en bloc*." The only way to interest the modern reader in a literary classic like *Hamlet*, he suggested, was to translate it "into the language of Marx or of Freud, or, better still, into a jargon inconsistently compounded of both."

In his *Twelve Great American Novels* (1967) Arthur Mizener commented on the difficulty professors of English have in persuading their modern-minded students to lay aside their prejudices against the unfashionable methods employed in many important American novels:

> How often readers are bored by Hawthorne because they find his novels static and posed—as indeed they are—when they have somehow got the notion that fluent action and a lively, informal style are essential to a good novel, how often they condemn Cooper because his novels have none of the minute analysis of feelings that they have somehow learned to think is the only virtue a novel can have. How often they confidently affirm that Faulkner is a bad novelist because his characters are nasty people who think all the time about incest—or that Henry James is because his characters are not.

In American literary history the year 1922 is clearly the turning point. It was the year of Sinclair Lewis's *Babbitt*, of Scott Fitzgerald's *Tales of the Jazz Age*, of James Joyce's *Ulysses*, and of T. S. Eliot's *The Waste Land*. In Nashville, Tennessee, a notable group of students and professors at Vanderbilt University published in 1922 the first number of the *Fugitive*. In 1922 Carl Van Doren brought out his *Contemporary American Novelists*, in which he tried to single out the most significant of living American writers of fiction. In 1922 Van Doren's older colleague at Columbia University, Brander Matthews, published *The Tocsin of Revolt*, in which he said that "a generation can never understand and appreciate the generation which preceded it or that which follows it."

In 1922 also the middle-aged leaders of the young intellectuals made clear their dissatisfaction with their own country in a symposium, *Civilization in the United States: An Inquiry*, by Thirty Americans. In his preface Harold Stearns, the editor, tried to sum up the ideas emphasized in the various essays. They seemed to him to boil down to a sharp dichotomy between what Americans professed to believe and what they really thought and did. The result was a kind of puritanical hypocrisy. Deems Taylor, for example, pointed out that Americans were spending millions on an art (music) in which they had failed to create anything of consequence. Van Wyck Brooks in "The Literary Life in America" contended that while the United States had never lacked talented young writers, they never seemed to develop into the important writers they might have become if society had only stimulated and nourished their talents. There was no chapter on religion. Those persons with whom Stearns discussed such a chapter felt that the country was under the domination of what they called "Protestant ecclesiasticism." They added that the subject did not interest them. In 1933 T. S. Eliot, who was not a contributor to the symposium, suggested that "the chief clue to the understanding of most contemporary Anglo-Saxon literature [was] to be found in the decay of Protestantism."

Most of the ideas advanced in the thirty essays were similar to the traditional complaints about American life that have been voiced by European critics for a century and a half. The Chicago novelist Henry B. Fuller suggested that the symposium should have been entitled "Thirty against America." The chief contributors, men like H. L. Mencken, Van Wyck Brooks, Deems Taylor, and J. E. Spingarn, lived in or not far from New York City. For the most part the contributors knew little about either the South or the West, and they knew little about labor or industry, economics or political science.

The new poetry made its way slowly. The diction and the subject matter of Sandburg and Frost were not to the taste of the editors of quality magazines. Many a young poet first saw his poems in print in the "little magazines," of which there were scores in every part of the country. There were many poetry societies, and their members were eager to see and hear the new poets. On the lecture platform Vachel Lindsay, Carl Sandburg, Robert Frost, and Amy Lowell were able to interest hundreds of college students in the strange new poetry. Before long the colleges and universities were offering courses in twentieth-century British and American poetry, and Louis Untermeyer and others were quick to provide the teachers with anthologies and handbooks.

The popular vogue of the new poetry was short-lived. Few bothered to read the poems of Wallace Stevens, Ezra Pound, or—until he published *The Waste Land* in 1922—T. S. Eliot. These and other poets seemed for the most part to be writing their poems for the few who understood their language; and highbrow critics looked contemptuously on such best-selling volumes of verse as Masters's *Spoon River Anthology* and Benét's *John Brown's Body*. The poets were losing their audience, and readers were becoming much more interested in the new fiction.

The new fiction found many more readers than the new poetry ever had, but Theodore Dreiser, the pioneer, who published *Sister Carrie* in 1900, was not widely read or acclaimed until he brought out *An American Tragedy* a quarter of a century later. The most influential champion of the new fiction was H. L. Mencken, who first in the *Smart Set* and later in the *American Mercury* promoted the reputations of Dreiser, Cabell, and many others. The "little magazines" played a part in the development of some of the younger writers of fiction. Eventually the *Saturday Evening Post*, which had a circulation of several million readers, printed some of the best short stories written by William Faulkner and Scott Fitzgerald. In 1930 when the Nobel Prize for literature was awarded to Sinclair Lewis, the new American fiction was being widely read in many European countries.

There were new publishing houses that were especially hospitable to the new writers. It was Harcourt, Brace and Company that published Sinclair Lewis's *Main Street, Babbitt,* and *Arrowsmith.* Alfred A. Knopf published some of the best books of the time, including the little-read poems of Wallace Stevens. It was, however, the old firm of Charles Scribner's Sons that brought out some of the best works of fiction written by Thomas Wolfe, Ernest Hemingway, and Scott Fitzgerald. Scribner's had in Maxwell Perkins an exceptionally able editor. In the 1920's it was evident that the young intellectuals were taking over not only publishing houses but also many of the better magazines and newspaper book pages.

In the twentieth century there were in the United States many more readers than in the nineteenth, but it had become more difficult for the serious writer to find those readers who could appreciate his work and would be willing to buy his books. There was no longer—if there ever had been—a large homogeneous reading public. Henry James, who was acutely conscious of his failure to find the many intelligent readers he wanted, wrote in 1898: "The public we somewhat loosely talk of for literature or for anything else is really as subdivided as a chessboard, with each little square confessing only to its own *kind* of accessibility." In his last years James found fewer and fewer of the many readers he had hoped for. Walt Whitman had discovered that the "divine average" that he had undertaken to celebrate could make little or nothing of his *Leaves of Grass.*

In the middle 1920's it was becoming evident that there were many discriminating lovers of good books who did not live in the vicinity of a good bookstore and were not being reached by advertisements printed in metropolitan newspapers. In 1926 Carl Van Doren organized the Literary Guild, and in the same year Henry Seidel Canby and his associates founded the Book-of-the-Month Club. Each of these organizations undertook to select for its subscribers the few best of hundreds of new books and to make them available at a substantial discount from the list price. The books selected were, especially in the beginning, much above the average in quality; but the founders soon discovered that if they were to stay in business, they must choose books that their subscribers would be willing to pay for. Many of the books recommended were merely popular fiction, and some masterpieces of poetry and fiction went unrecognized. The book clubs did not solve the problem, which for the young writer is still acute.

Literature in our time is not the possession of the whole people. With few exceptions our better American writers no longer speak both *for* and *to* the people of this country; and that is not a happy condition for the development of any serious writer. The ancient Greeks of whatever class knew and loved the poems of Homer and the plays of Sophocles and Aristophanes. In Shakespeare's London the groundlings as well as the nobles delighted in seeing *Henry IV, As You Like It,* and *Hamlet.*

Today, however, many of our ablest writers are alienated from the society in which they grew up and to which they must look for those who will buy their books. Paradoxically, it is from alienated writers that there come the loudest demands for governmental subsidies for artists and authors. Ezra Pound would if he could force the government to subsidize writers and artists even when what they produce is highly repugnant to those whose votes elect presidents, governors, and congressmen. Such a demand, as Jacques Barzun pointed out in the *Partisan Review* in 1952, "is unprecedented. . . . at no time within the 2,500 years of Western history has art been financed for the intrinsic reasons now proposed to our country." There are, however, many young American artists and writers who have received grants from universities, foundations, libraries, museums, philanthropists, and publishing houses; yet the writer of our time cannot expect to find a modern counterpart of a patron like Maecenas, to whom Horace and Vergil owed so much. As Katherine Anne Porter so well phrased it, "You cannot be a hostile critic of society and expect society to feed you regularly."

> *I think we English authors have much to learn from our fellow authors in America. . . . They have formed their style, unconsciously perhaps, more directly from the living speech that surrounds them; and at its best it has a directness, a vitality and a drive that give our more urbane manner an air of languor.*
>
> Somerset Maugham, *The Summing Up*

> *And yet, "Dust and ashes, dust and ashes" is the fundamental theme and final moral of practically every modern American novel of any distinction. High spirits and a heroic vitality are put into the expression of despair. The hopelessness is almost Rabelaisian.*
>
> Aldous Huxley, *Vulgarity in Literature*

## EUROPEAN RECOGNITION

*England.* Sydney Smith shocked his American admirers in January, 1820, when in the *Edinburgh Review* he asked the embarrassing question: "In the four quarters of the globe, Who reads an American book?" It was to be a hundred years before Americans succeeded in getting from England the kind of recognition they wanted for their literature. The official British view was that there was no such thing as an "American" literature. Yet many of the critics who held that general view had praise for individual American writers. For example, Harriet Martineau, who admired Emerson, wrote in her *Society in America* (1837): "If the American nation be judged by its literature, it may be pronounced to have no mind at all." In the middle 1880's Matthew Arnold wrote: "I see advertised *The Primer of American Literature.* Imagine the face of Philip or Alexander at hearing of a Primer of Macedonian Literature! . . . We are all contributors to one great literature—English literature." Yet Arnold had praise for the writings of Franklin, Hawthorne, and Emerson.

In the absence (until 1891) of an international copyright law British publishers could and did bring out inexpensive editions of Longfellow and other American writers intended primarily for middle-class readers. Among the intellectuals those critics most hospitable to American literature were likely to be liberals or journalists or Scotchmen. The situation at the end of the nineteenth century is thus summed up by Clarence Gohdes in his *American Literature in Nineteenth-Century England* (1944):

> Emerson was pretty generally regarded in the better critical circles as the outstanding writer of America, but Hawthorne was proclaimed the leading artist. . . . The century ended somewhat in doubt as to whether Poe or Whitman should be called the leading poet of the United States, and, likewise, there was a question whether Howells or James could be considered our greatest living novelist.

One result of the First World War was a recognition on the part of many Europeans that they knew all too little about the nation in the West which had emerged from its traditional isolation to become the decisive factor in the war. In the twentieth century British writers looked more often to America for serious literary criticism. For example, in the May, 1914, number of the *Poetry Review* Stephen Phillips stated his agreement with another English poet, Sir William Watson, that America "has become far more than England both the market and the assize of modern Anglo-American poetry. . . . The writer of modern verse must for the future look to America both for audience and criticism."

In 1922 Sinclair Lewis made a pronouncement that disturbed some English critics. "England," he said, "can no longer be the mother-country to American literature any more than she can be the mother-country to American politics or American life." Hugh Walpole, who had visited in the United States, defended Lewis and praised the new American literature. The younger American writers, said the English novelist, "have their lives before them, a new language, a new world to play with; Heavens, their luck!"

Walpole conducted his own private poll of the important living American writers. Among the novelists his first choice was Joseph Hergesheimer, the only one then widely read in England. The other five were Willa Cather, Sinclair Lewis, Sherwood Anderson, Floyd Dell, and F. Scott Fitzgerald. The six younger poets whom Walpole singled out were Vachel Lindsay, Carl Sandburg, Robert Frost, H.D. (Hilda Doolittle), Edgar Lee Masters, and Amy Lowell. For his six "modernist essayists and critics" Walpole chose Heywood Broun, Waldo Frank, Don Marquis, Burton Rascoe, Francis Hackett, and H. L. Mencken. Edwin Arlington Robinson and James Branch Cabell seemed to Walpole excellent writers but not a part of the modernist movement.

On April 14 of the following year Walpole wrote in an article in the *Independent* on "Contemporary American Fiction": "For myself—and all contemporary taste is absolutely personal—the younger leaders of the American novel are five—Joseph Hergesheimer, Sinclair Lewis, James Branch Cabell, Willa Cather, and Dorothy Canfield Fisher. There is also Theodore Dreiser and there is Sherwood Anderson." Walpole characterized Dreiser as "a novelist of the materialist school who has great native force but who has never learnt how to write."

In the *London Mercury*'s symposium on "Contemporary American Authors" (November, 1925 to July, 1926) the seven American writers singled out for discussion were Willa Cather, Theodore Dreiser, Robert Frost, Joseph Hergesheimer, Edwin Arlington Robinson, and Edith Wharton. One notes the absence of Sinclair Lewis, Ezra Pound, and T. S. Eliot. J. C. Squire, who edited the *London Mercury*, was no admirer of Eliot.

On December 15, 1920, D. H. Lawrence published in the *New Republic* an article entitled "America, Listen to Your Own." At that time Ezra Pound and T. S. Eliot were living in Europe and trying to create for themselves an eclectic and highly artificial tradition by the study of the literatures of many lands but not the literature of the United States. Lawrence congratulated America that it had no tradition. "A tradition, like a bald head," he said, "comes with years fast enough." "Happy is the nation which hasn't got a tradition and which lacks cultural monuments. How gay Greece must have been, while Egypt was sneering at her for an uneducated nobody. . . ." In 1923 Lawrence brought out his *Studies in Classic American Literature*, a book that was to have an important influence upon American criticism on Poe, Whitman, Melville, and Hawthorne.

On August 1, 1925, Virginia Woolf published in the *Saturday Review of Literature* a thoughtful article on "American Literature," in which she stated her conviction that "the English tradition is already unable to cope with this vast land."

> The English tradition is formed upon a little country; its centre is an old house with many rooms each crammed with objects and crowded with people who know each other intimately, whose manners, thoughts, and speech are ruled all the time, if unconsciously, by the spirit of the past. But in America there is baseball instead of society; instead of the old landscape which has moved men to emotion for endless summers and springs, a new land, its tin cans, its prairies, its cornfields flung disorderly about like a mosaic of incongruous pieces waiting order at the artist's hands; while the people are equally diversified into fragments of many nationalities.
>
> To describe, to unify, to make order out of all these several parts, a new art is needed and the control of a new tradition. That both are in process of birth the language itself gives the proof. For the Americans are doing what the Elizabethans did—they are coining new words. They are instinctively making the language adapt itself to their needs.

In 1879 the Macmillan Company added Henry James's *Hawthorne* to its notable English Men of Letters series. In the early twentieth century the series was expanded to include Emerson, Whittier, Prescott, Bryant, and Whitman. After the First World War the series was revived and three new titles were added: John Bailey's *Whitman* and John Freeman's *Melville*, both valuable critical studies, and Edward Shanks's *Poe*, which had little value of any kind.

Notable changes were made in the *Encyclopaedia Britannica* even before it became an American property in 1943. For the eleventh edition of 1911 George E. Woodberry wrote an article on American literature which in the *Bookman* for January, 1927, Bartlett Cormack described as "a kind of obituary in which he [Woodberry] said: 'There has been no product of ideas since Emerson.'" For the three new volumes added in 1921, William Lyon Phelps discussed the trend toward naturalism and expressed a low opinion of the novels of Theodore Dreiser. The thirteenth edition in 1926 contained an up-to-date general account by Henry Seidel Canby and other articles including one by Carl Van Doren on American fiction, another by Louis Untermeyer on poetry, and a discussion of the American language by H. L. Mencken.

In its issue of September 17, 1954, the *Literary Supplement of the London Times* (*TLS*) included a section entitled "American Writing To-day: Its Independence and Vigour." The section runs to one hundred pages, and along with book reviews and advertisements, it contains illuminating discussions of nearly every aspect of American literary activity. Among the essays are "The Living American Classics," "The Passing of English Influence," "The Southern Revival," "Negro Writing," and "Publishing Problems and Responsibilities."

The emphasis is naturally upon the twentieth century, but the earlier literature is competently treated in two essays. The authors are fully aware of the importance to Americans of Edward Taylor and Jonathan Edwards. The major writers are those whom a good American critic would have singled out, but the essayists have almost nothing to say of Emily Dickinson. In "Opinions at the Time" *TLS* reprints some of its earlier reviews of books by American writers.

In one of the few signed articles Edith Sitwell named as American poets "who have long been famous in England" T. S. Eliot, Ezra Pound, Marianne Moore, Robert Frost, Allen Tate, John Crowe Ransom, E. E. Cummings, H.D., and Wallace Stevens. She devoted most of her space to younger poets like Robert Lowell and Theodore Roethke. Lowell's "The Ghost" was, she said, "one of the most magnificent short poems of our time."

The author of "American Fiction since the First World War" noted that the critical estimates of literary historians too often lag far behind the verdicts of other critics. He had praise for Marcus Cunliffe's excellent Penguin *Literature of the United States*, also published in 1954. But of the nine authors whom Cunliffe had chosen as the best of our twentieth-century novelists, the *TLS* critics thought that James T. Farrell, Sherwood Anderson, John Dos Passos, John Steinbeck, Sinclair Lewis, and Thomas Wolfe had all in varying degrees lost ground since the Second World War. On the other hand, William Faulkner, Scott Fitzgerald, and Ernest Hemingway had emerged as major American novelists. Fitzgerald, he said, "is something more than a charming 'laureate of the Jazz Age' and Hemingway something more than an ominously anti-intellectual American tough." "It is pretty generally agreed," he said, "that Faulkner . . . is the greatest American novelist of the century." The essayist had praise for some of the younger writers of fiction, notably Robert Penn Warren, Katherine Anne Porter, James Gould Cozzens, John O'Hara, John P. Marquand, Glenway Wescott, Nathaniel West, and Caroline Gordon.

> *For the first time [after the First World War] we began to take for granted, as part of a larger culture, French literature from Stendhal and Flaubert to Proust and Valéry, whom we found to be as close to us as Yeats and Joyce in our own language.*
> Allen Tate and John Peale Bishop, "Introduction," *American Harvest*

*France.* Very early the French discovered certain American writers, most notably Cooper and Poe; and it was in French translations by Baudelaire and

Mallarmé that Spaniards, Portuguese, and Latin-Americans read the tales and poems of Poe. The First World War had the double effect of making the French much more aware of our literature and vastly increasing the influence of French writers upon our poets and novelists. Jean-Paul Sartre published in the *Atlantic Monthly* for August, 1946, an article entitled "American Novelists in French Eyes," in which he wrote:

> There is one American literature for Americans and another for the French. In France the general reader knows *Babbitt* and *Gone with the Wind*, but these books have had no influence on French literature. The greatest literary development in France between 1929 and 1939 was the discovery of Faulkner, Dos Passos, Hemingway, Caldwell, and Steinbeck.

None of the five novelists whom he named, said Sartre, enjoyed the popularity of Sinclair Lewis, but their influence was "infinitely more profound" than his. "We needed them," he continued, "and not your famous Dreiser." What it was in American fiction that aroused the enthusiasm of French novelists was "a veritable revolution in the art of telling a story." Before the twentieth century few of our authors except Poe, Whitman, and Henry James had made any notable contributions to literary theory or technique, and most of our writers had borrowed heavily from European models. Now at last we were repaying our literary debts.

*Clearing a stage,*
*Scattering the past about,*
*Comes the new age.*
*Bards make new poems,*
*Thinkers new schools,*
*Statesmen new systems,*
*Critics new rules.*
*All things begin again.*

Matthew Arnold, "Bacchanalia; or, The New Age"

*When we survey the various modern schools of criticism,*
*for example, we may be struck by the almost complete ab-*
*sence of what was for some 2000 years the only or the greatly*
*predominant view of literature, the ethical.*

Douglas Bush, "Literature: Lamp or Mirror,"
*Harvard Today,* Autumn, 1966

# Chapter 7. Critics Old-Style and New

## H. L. MENCKEN

Henry Louis Mencken (1880–1956) now seems more of a literary journalist than a critic of literature, and yet in the 1920's he had an enormous influence upon the young intellectuals, who were only too ready to laugh at the ideas, the customs, the books, and the people whom he ridiculed. Bright college students read his essays in the *Smart Set* and the *American Mercury.* They also revelled in his *Book of Prefaces* (1917) and the six series of *Prejudices,* which he published from 1919 to 1927. Young writers quickly learned to copy his pet phrases like "booboisie" and "Bible-belt," and to ridicule the old-fashioned ideas of their elders. Fred Lewis Pattee wrote in 1922: "H. L. Mencken at forty [he was forty-two] is training a surprisingly large group of youngsters, who should be the future makers of American criticism, into a kind of literary jazz band. Their writings confront one everywhere."

Mencken had a large part in the recasting of the American literary canon. The literary tradition so dear to the professors of English and the members of the American Academy of Arts and Letters, he said, was "not a tradition that would take in Poe, Hawthorne, Emerson, Whitman and Mark Twain, but a tradition that would pass over these men to embrace Cooper, Bryant, Donald G. Mitchell, N. P. Willis, J. G. Holland, Charles Dudley Warner, Mrs. Sigourney, and the Sweet Singer of Michigan [Julia A. Moore]." American literature, he said, "is chiefly remarkable, now as always, for its respectable mediocrity. Its typical great man, in our own time, has been Howells, as its typical great man a generation ago was Lowell, and two generations ago, Irving."

In making a point Mencken could be quite unscrupulous in his handling of facts. He could condemn important books—by Howells, for instance—without having read them. In "The Sahara of the Bozart" he wrote: "The entire South, for all its size and all its wealth and all the 'progress' it babbles of . . . is almost as sterile artistically, intellectually, culturally, as the Sahara Desert." "New England," he said, "has never shown the slightest sign of a genuine enthusiasm for ideas." Such blatant exaggeration was an effective means of arresting the attention of the younger generation, but it resulted in the creation of false notions of the American literary past. In "Puritanism as a Literary Force" Mencken anticipated Van Wyck Brooks, Louis Untermeyer, and Ludwig Lewisohn in attributing to the historical Puritans those aspects of American life that he found repugnant: Prohibition, censorship, herd morality, etc.

"A great literature," said Mencken, "is . . . chiefly the product of doubting and inquiring minds in revolt against the immovable certainties of the nation." In "The American Tradition" (*Prejudices, Fourth Series*, 1924) he said: "Go through the list of genuinely first-rate men: Poe, Hawthorne, Whitman, Mark Twain. One and all they stood outside the so-called tradition of their time; one and all, they remained outside the tradition that pedants try so vainly to impose upon a literature in active being today." "The artist among us," he continued, "is still a sort of pariah, beset by public contempt on the one hand and by academic enmity on the other. . . ." "Our literature," he said, ". . . is still oppressed by various heavy handicaps, chiefly resident in the failure of the new aristocracy of money to function as an aristocracy of taste." Again in "The National Letters" he lamented "the lack of a body of sophisticated and civilized public opinion, independent of plutocratic control and superior to the infallible philosophies of the mob—a body of opinion showing the eager curiosity, the educated skepticism, and the hospitality to ideas of a true aristocracy."

Mencken was on the whole a better critic of prose than of poetry. He fully appreciated the merits of Sinclair Lewis and Sherwood Anderson, but he had little use for either James or Howells. "Henry James," he wrote in the *Smart Set* in November, 1920, "would have been vastly improved as a novelist by a few whiffs from the Chicago stockyards." More seriously he added: "The West would have amused, intrigued and finally conquered him. He would have been a great artist in his own country." When he was only twenty years old, Mencken was certain that *Huckleberry Finn* was the greatest American novel. In February, 1913, he wrote in the *Smart Set*: "I believe that 'Huckle-berry Finn' is one of the great masterpieces of the world. . . . I believe that he [Mark Twain] ranks above Whitman and certainly not below Poe. I believe that he was the true father of the national literature, the first genuinely American artist of the blood royal."

Mencken, however, was badly off in his critical estimates of two of the best American poets of his time: "Frost? A standard New England poet, with a few changes in phraseology, and substitution of sour resignation for sweet resignation. Whittier without the whiskers. Robinson? Ditto, but with a polite bow. He has written sound poetry, but not much of it." In discussing contemporary American poetry in 1927 Mencken complained of its bloodlessness and of its "failure to produce anything that could stir the blood as true poetry does." The new poets were "too cerebral." They were attacking "the problems of a fine art with the methods of science." The poets had detached themselves from "the ordinary flow of American ideas." Poetry, he wrote, ought to reach "the generality of the literate," but apart from a few poems by Frost, Lindsay, Sandburg, Sara Teasdale, and Lizette Woodworth Reese, the contemporary poets seemed to be writing only for one another.

In 1927 Mencken wrote to James Tully:

> I am credited with discovering many writers who actually discovered themselves. Among those I whooped for in their earliest days are James Joyce, Ruth Suckow, James Stevens, Eugene O'Neill, and Dreiser. I also did a lot of writing about Joseph Conrad and Lord Dunsany when they were new to this country. But what I did for all these, and the rest likewise, was really very little. I was looking for good copy, not for orphans to rescue.

"He was the first editor to print James Joyce in America," said Ernest Boyd; "Havelock Ellis, Lord Dunsany, Pio Baroja, Ibsen, Hauptmann, Strindberg, Sudermann, Nietzsche and Shaw must be counted amongst the foreigners whom he introduced or helped to wider fame in this country." Among American writers Boyd named Theodore Dreiser, James Branch Cabell, Ring Lardner, Joseph Hergesheimer, Willa Cather, Eugene O'Neill, and Sherwood Anderson. He might have added still other names, like that of Julia Peterkin. Mencken had high praise for Cabell: "His one aim in life is to make himself a first-rate artist—and this aim, I am inclined to think, he has come nearer to realizing than any other American of his time."

Mencken was the ablest champion of Theodore Dreiser and one of his best critics. In the essay on Dreiser that he published in 1917 he took occasion to attack the professors of English, who he said were either ignoring living writers altogether or denouncing writers like Dreiser as un-Christian and un-

American. "College professors, alas," he wrote, "never learn anything." He continued: "The rancorous animosity that has pursued such men as Dreiser is certainly not wholly aesthetic, or even moral; it is, to a very large extent, racial."

Mencken was fully aware of Dreiser's shortcomings as an artist: his lack of humor, the "exasperating rolling up of irrelevant facts," "whole scenes spoiled by bad writing," and "no charms of style to mitigate the rigors of these vast steppes and pampas of narration." And yet, he concluded:

> One sees in the man all the special marks of the novelist: his capacity for photographic and relentless observation, his insatiable curiosity, his keen zest in life as a spectacle, his comprehension of and sympathy for the poor striving of humble folks, his endless mulling of insoluble problems, his recurrent Philistinism, his impatience of restraints, his fascinated suspicion of messiahs, his passion for physical beauty, his relish for the gaudy drama of big cities, his incurable Americanism. The panorama that he unrolls runs the whole scale of the colors; it is a series of extraordinarily vivid pictures.

When he reviewed *An American Tragedy* in the *American Mercury* for March, 1926, Mencken noted that all the old artistic faults were very evident, especially in the first volume. " 'An American Tragedy,' as a work of art, is a colossal botch, but as a human document it is searching and full of a solemn dignity, and at times it rises to the level of genuine tragedy. Especially the second volume."

## JOEL ELIAS SPINGARN

In 1909–1910 the Columbia University faculty gave a series of lectures on literature, which included Ashley H. Thorndike's admirable characterization of English literature but, surprisingly enough, no lecture on American literature. The series concluded in March, 1910, with a lecture on "'Literary Criticism" by the professor of comparative literature and a recognized authority on the history of criticism, Joel Elias Spingarn (1875–1939), who was to republish the lecture under the title of "Creative Criticism."

Spingarn's opening sentence no doubt met with Mencken's enthusiastic approval: " 'What droll creatures these college professors are whenever they talk about art,' wrote Flaubert in one of his letters, and voiced the world's opinion of academic criticism." In 1910 the ideas that Spingarn expounded in his lecture seemed almost revolutionary to a university audience (of whom

I was one). In his own words Professor Spingarn was attempting to clear the ground "of its dead lumber and weeds." We have done, he said, "with all the old rules," "with the *genres*, or literary kinds," "with the theory of style," "with the moral judgment of literature," "with technique as separate from art," "with the history and criticism of poetic themes," "with the 'evolution' of literature," and "finally, we have done with the old rupture between genius and taste"—which, he said, "means that fundamentally the creative and the critical instincts are one and the same." For many of these ideas Spingarn acknowledged his indebtedness to the Italian philosopher Benedetto Croce.

Spingarn was putting into the hands of the young intellectuals critical weapons with which they were to attack the professors of English and the American Academy of Arts and Letters. That was in 1910 when Spingarn was only thirty-five years old. A dozen years later when he published "The Younger Generation: A Manifesto," he wrote: "And now the day for revolt is over." In 1910, he explained, it had been "necessary to destroy the academic dry rot that was undermining the creative and intellectual spirit of the nation." He continued: "What shall we say of the fashionable theory of our day that all art and all wisdom are the products of physical youth, that nothing is good unless men now young have done it or like it, and that therefore the test of ideas is not truth or the test of art, excellence, but the only test of both is 'modernity'? . . . This is a form of disease. . . ." The young Davids were, he said, trying to destroy "that Goliath, the Past." And he emphasized what should have been an obvious truth: "For there is no past except the past that we love or hate. . . . the only past that does not live for us at all is the past we have forgotten and neither hate nor love. But if it lives for us it is no longer a past but a present. . . ." In 1922, however, the young Davids were more determined than ever to get rid of what seemed to them the "dead lumber and weeds" of the past.

## THE NEW HUMANISTS

In the 1920's when the young intellectuals and their allies were capturing the literary periodicals and the publishing houses, there were a few able conservative critics who protested against what seemed to them the false literary, social, and moral standards of the younger writers. For the most part, however, the conservative critics received not an intelligent hearing but misunderstanding and abuse from writers who wanted no part in the literary tradition which the conservatives were defending. "Like Whitman," said Norman Foerster in *American Criticism* (1928), "nearly all of them are in revolt against a past that they do not really know, often do not in the least care to know: their vital memories, for the most part, stop with Whitman himself, behind whom the past is a dim otherness and vast irrelevance."

Among the ablest and most vocal of the conservative critics were the New Humanists, who in 1930, under the editorship of Foerster, brought out the symposium, *Humanism and America*, in which several of the contributors launched a devastating attack upon certain contemporary journalistic critics and writers of fiction. Later in the same year C. Hartley Grattan brought out a rival symposium, *The Critique of Humanism*, in which the New Humanists were attacked as, in the words of Foerster, "academic, un-American, reactionary, and Puritanic." The popular vogue of the New Humanism soon passed, but its influence in academic circles was still very considerable.

The pioneers in the New Humanist movement were Irving Babbitt (1865–1933) and Paul Elmer More (1864–1937). Babbitt had a strong influence upon some able Harvard students; among them, Norman Foerster, Stuart P. Sherman, Walter Lippman, and T. S. Eliot. Babbitt was a moralist and a philosopher rather than an aesthetic critic. For him the great corrupting influence in nineteenth-century literature was Romanticism, especially as seen in the writings of Rousseau. Babbitt had little use for any of the literary rebels who were remaking the American literary tradition. His opinion of H. L. Mencken is reflected in the following sentence: "The best one would anticipate from a writer like Mr. Mencken, possessing an unusual verbal virtuosity and at the same time temperamentally irresponsible, is superior intellectual vaudeville." In *Manhattan Transfer* Babbitt thought John Dos Passos had "perpetrated a literary nightmare." After reading Dreiser's *An American Tragedy*, he felt that he had been "harrowed to no purpose." "It is hardly worth while," he said, "to struggle through eight hundred and more very pedestrian pages to be left at the end with a feeling of sheer oppression." Babbitt once remarked to one of his former students, G. R. Elliott: "Fighting a whole generation is not an easy task."

Paul Elmer More, the *bête noire* of the young intellectuals, was a better practicing critic than Babbitt. He had cause to complain, as he once did, that he was "one whose pathway through literature had been plentifully sprinkled with abuse." There were, however, among the younger critics at least two who rated More at his true worth: Edmund Wilson and Ludwig Lewisohn. In *Expression in America* (1932) Lewisohn wrote: "He is infinitely different from the caricature of a dull 'birch-man' so long imposed on large sections of the American public. He is, first of all, one of the soundest of American prose stylists."

More's critical standards were, as he well knew, not those of the younger generation. In the preface to his *Selected Shelburne Essays* (1935) he wrote:

> The one thing characteristic of modern criticism, as exemplified eminently by so influential a writer as I. A. Richards, is the complete absence of any search for the meaning of life, and in place of that an absorbing interest in what might be called the problem of aesthetic psychology,—which is indeed no more than a late-born offspring of the romantic heresy of art for art's sake. For this old-fashioned note I offer no apology; I am utterly convinced that literature divorced from life is an empty pursuit, and that an honest search for the meaning of life must lead to the simple faith of theism.

More was perhaps unwise—he was certainly untactful—when in his sixties he published "Modern Currents in American Literature," in the *Revue de Paris* and the *Forum* in December and January of 1927–1928. It reappeared in *The Demon of the Absolute* in 1928. More began by stating that he would not discuss "our most accomplished novelist, Edith Wharton, or . . . our eminent poets, Edwin Arlington Robinson and Robert Frost." Amy Lowell he thought of as "perhaps the leading spirit, as she was undoubtedly the most finished artist"; but still she seemed to him "a genius hag-ridden by theory." In James Branch Cabell's much-talked-of *Jurgen* More saw a "vein of unfulfilled genius"; but he thought "the erudition so lavishly displayed was more superficial than solid, the art more sophisticated than fine, and the superiorities of manner rather snobbish." More was a native of the Middle West, but he had no high opinion of the new novelists from that section.

> One of them, indeed, Sinclair Lewis, coming out of Sauk Center, Minnesota, has a degree from Yale University; but intellectually he is perhaps the crudest member of the group, cruder, for instance, than Theodore Dreiser . . . or Sherwood Anderson who apparently owes his acquaintance with the alphabet to the grace of God.

Dreiser when he tried to be literary, seemed to More "of the mongrel sort to be expected from a miscegenation of the gutter and the psychological laboratory." Dos Passos's *Manhattan Transfer* "with its spattered filth, might be described as an explosion in a cesspool." Gertrude Stein was "that adventuress into the lunar madnesses of literary cubism." No one of the books of these writers of fiction, he said, "despite their present fame, is likely to be remembered twenty years from now, or in fact has any claim to be called literature at all."

Paul Elmer More was a learned man, but for all his familiarity with the literatures of ancient and modern times, he had not grasped the elementary fact that the books written by a younger generation often cannot be accurately appraised by the standards of an older generation. Edmund Wilson, who knew and admired More, noted that although in later years he discussed Proust and Joyce, More did not like or approve of them. On a visit to Princeton, Wilson was dismayed to find that not only More but also Dean Christian Gauss and Frank Jewett Mather were "disposed to outlaw from literature the greatest literary artist then alive [James Joyce]." Wilson commented: "The same confounded old academic inertia! I thought; the same old proprietary interest in the classics, which made them unwilling to believe that anything new could have great value!" More, however, as Wilson noted, was an admirer of the essays of T. S. Eliot; but he "demurred over Eliot's poetry." When Wilson asked whether he didn't admire *The Waste Land*, More conceded: "Well, one can see that it's written by a man of parts."

## BRANDER MATTHEWS

In 1917 at the age of sixty-five Brander Matthews (1852–1929), essayist, critic, and professor of dramatic literature at Columbia University, wrote an essay entitled "The Tocsin of Revolt," which became the title essay in the book he published in 1922. I quote:

> When a man finds himself at last slowly climbing the slopes which lead to the lonely peak of three-score-and-ten he is likely to discover that his views and his aspirations are not in accord with those held by men still living leisurely in the foothills of youth. He sees that things are no longer what they were half-a-century earlier and that they are not now tending in the direction to which they then pointed. If he is wise, he warns himself against the danger of becoming a mere praiser of past times; and if he is very wise he makes every effort to understand and to appreciate the present and not to dread the future. He may even wonder whether he is not suffering from a premature hardening of the arteries of sympathy. He finds himself denounced as a reactionary; and he doubts whether he has the courage of his reactions.
>
> He cannot but be aware that his case has little novelty, since a generation can never understand and appreciate the generation which preceded it or that which follows it.

One would hardly guess from the tone of this passage that Matthews, now near the end of a distinguished career, was being attacked as a reactionary by youthful rebels. Brander Matthews was a philosopher and a gentleman.

In the essay he wrote: "The conflict between youth and age, between conservatism and radicalism, is unending, because it is eternally necessary to the vitality of the several arts, which need to be reinvigorated generation after generation."

In *Points of View* (1924) Stuart P. Sherman reprinted his review of *The Tocsin of Revolt* under the title "Brander Matthews and the Mohawks." The "Mohawks" were the youthful rebels who, said Sherman, were trying to blow up the National Institute of Arts and Letters, of which Matthews was a member. Young radicals like Randolph Bourne had labeled Matthews a reactionary because he seemed indifferent to the reforms which they were so hopefully advocating. Sherman was right in thinking that the "Mohawks" had no real case against Matthews, whom he addressed as follows: "You have given many younger men their 'start' [three of them were Stewart Edward White, Hatcher Hughes, and Elmer Rice], and have been the first to salute their maiden efforts; and yet you have not denounced your own masters, Arnold and Lowell. . . ."

Before he became a university professor at the age of forty, Brander Matthews had acquired some reputation as a minor man of letters by his poems, plays, short stories, and books about the theater. In his first year of teaching at Columbia University he offered courses in three subjects which at that time (1891–1892) were seldom taught in any American university: modern fiction, versification, and American literature. In 1896 he published a high school text, *An Introduction to the Study of American Literature*, of which a quarter of a million copies were sold in the next twenty-five years.

Professor Matthews had in some measure "the fourfold qualification of the genuine critic [which he found in the work of Andrew Lang]—insight, equipment, disinterestedness, and sympathy." In his autobiography, *These Many Years*, he took justifiable pride in recalling that he "had been fortunately able to follow the entire career of men of letters now [1917] recognized as masters." He singled out for special mention: Henry James, Howells, Mark Twain, Stevenson, Lang, Austin Dobson, Maupassant, Daudet, Zola, Brunetière, and Lemaître. In the London *Saturday Review* he had been "glad to acclaim the high quality of 'Huckleberry Finn' and of the 'Rise of Silas Lapham' when these two masterpieces originally appeared." Of two other great writers of fiction Matthews wrote:

> I sought out the dingy office in an obscure lane where I could procure the back numbers of the weekly *London*, and so possess myself of the successive stories which were to make up the "New Arabian Nights" of the then unknown Stevenson; and in like manner I haunted the early footsteps of Maupassant, turning over the smirched issues of the daily *Gil Blas* to spy out the brief tales which Maupassant warranted with

his own signature or with the pen-name he affected in that apprentice period, "Maufrigneuse."

Matthews, however, was no admirer of those irregular geniuses, Whitman, Melville, and Emily Dickinson.

Other elderly professors were not so tolerant of the youthful rebels as Brander Matthews. For example, there was Henry A. Beers of Yale, whose *Initial Studies in American Letters* (1893) I have briefly discussed on an earlier page. On February 3, 1923, Beers reviewed in the New York *Evening Post* Stuart Sherman's *Americans*. In thirty-six years Professor Beers had not changed his mind about *Leaves of Grass*. "If there are any worse bores than the mass of Whitman's so-called poems," he said, "it is the interpretation of them by the Whitmanites." He added:

> The present reviewer, who belongs exclusively to the nineteenth century, has not read the writings of Messrs. Lewisohn, Mencken, Cabell, Dreiser, Sandburg, *et al.*, and is therefore in no position to judge of the question at issue. There is a new reading public, a new set of novelists, poets, and critics in this country who strike no roots in the native soil, who are neither in the English nor in the older American tradition. They are not of colonial stock. They are Italians, Russians, Jews, Irish, Germans, Slavs, or descendants of such. Whatever literary antecedents this group of writers have are of Europe and of the Continent of Europe. They have no feeling of the American national past; they want no past anyway, only a present, and are particularly scornful of the New England tradition, of Puritanism, pilgrim fathers, Emerson, Longfellow, and the like.

Beers's review prompted Ludwig Lewisohn to write in his *Expression in America* (1932): "The epilogue of the polite mind and tradition in American letters was written, unconsciously enough, by Professor Henry Augustin Beers of Yale in the 'New York Evening Post' of February 3, 1923...."


## VAN WYCK BROOKS

The earlier phase of Van Wyck Brooks's (1886–1963) criticism is well represented in *America's Coming-of-Age* (1915), a little book that exerted a strong influence upon the young intellectuals of the time. Brooks did not question the greatness of Emerson, Hawthorne, Thoreau, or Poe—he had apparently not yet read Melville—but he had formed a low estimate of the old New England poets, those "kindly, grey-headed, or otherwise grizzled old men." Remembering the group portraits of these writers found in so many American homes, he said: "Nothing could make one feel so like a prodigal son" as to look at the picture of these "moralists . . . shot through with all manner of baccalaureate ideals." Brooks was particularly severe in his criticism of Longfellow and Lowell. "Longfellow," he said, "is to poetry, in large measure, what the barrel-organ is to music. . . ."

After Brooks had submitted the manuscript of his book to Charles Scribner's Sons, his friend Maxwell Perkins wrote him that "although strongly impressed by the cleverness and mental independence of the writer," the firm had rejected the manuscript. He added: "I gathered that 'you had swept these fellows into the dust-bin of the past with a contemptuousness of gesture which was at least pre-mature.'" The words quoted by Perkins are those of William Crary Brownell, who in 1909 had included Lowell in his *American Prose Masters*.

One of Brooks's ablest essays, "The Literary Life in America," first appeared in the symposium by Thirty Americans entitled *Civilization in America* (1922). Here Brooks stated the thesis that although in this country we have had no lack of gifted young writers, somehow they have not fulfilled their promise: "The blighted career, the arrested career, the diverted career are, with us, the rule. The chronic state of our literature is that of a youthful promise which is never fulfilled" because, he explained, our writers have been "insufficiently equipped, stimulated, nourished by the society into which [they were] born." Elsewhere Brooks had much to say about the "genteel tradition," the academic mind, and something called "Puritanism," which bore only a slight resemblance to the Puritanism of John Winthrop or John Milton. Brooks could not in 1922 find in American literature the "usable past" which the young writer needs to stimulate and direct his energies into the right channel.

While still in his earlier phase, Brooks vigorously maintained his thesis of youthful promise unfulfilled in *The Ordeal of Mark Twain* (1920) and *The Pilgrimage of Henry James* (1925). These books were not so much biographies as highly controversial special pleadings which made frequent use of Freudian psychology. Mark Twain, he thought, had the endowment that might have permitted him to become a great satirist like Cervantes or Swift; but his mother wanted to make him not an artist but a Christian of the Fundamentalist variety; his wife wanted to make him not a great writer but a gentleman; and so especially after he became the friend of H. H. Rogers and other wealthy businessmen, he said in effect: "Let some one else undertake the task." Brooks argued that Mark Twain's pessimism in his later years was the result of a failure to follow his native bent. As I have noted elsewhere, Bernard De Voto and other students of Mark Twain took vigorous exception to Brooks's thesis. *The Pilgrimage of Henry James* displeased those who—like Ezra Pound, T. S. Eliot, and some of the New Critics—cared little or nothing about literary nationalism, American democracy, or the social and economic reforms that Brooks advocated. Brooks in later life admitted to having made certain errors in his books on James and Mark Twain but not that his fundamental position was unsound.

After a breakdown that resulted in his living most of the time for four years in mental hospitals, Brooks in 1931 emerged with an entirely different attitude toward the older American literature. In *From the Shadow of the Mountain* (1961) he wrote: "My emotional tone had entirely changed from the days before my breakdown, when I had seen life so largely in negative terms, when I had been drawn to failures and misfits. . . ." In 1934 when he reprinted *America's Coming-of-Age* in *Three Essays on America*, he noted that he now saw that the "tone" of that book "was sometimes rash, even to the point of impudence." He added:

> A decade or two ago, we were all engaged in a game that might have been called bearding the prophets, all too ready to say, "Go up, thou baldhead," in the presence of the Elishas of the moment. We had had too much of the old New England poets. We were tired of hearing Longfellow called "the Just," and inscribed our shards against him, even to the number of six thousand, as the inconstant Athenians used to do.

He saw now that he had been guilty of "an oft-recurring mistake, that of attributing to one's own country the faults of human nature in general." Many another country can point to examples of youthful promise unfulfilled.

In 1932 Brooks published his *Life of Emerson*. He had finally discovered an American writer who had fulfilled the promise of his earlier years. Now in his second phase, Brooks was systematically preparing to write *The Flowering of New England* and the four other books which make up the series which he later named *Makers and Finders*. The five books run to 2,650 pages. During the nineteen years in which this project engaged most of his attention, Brooks read, according to his estimate, five thousand books. American literature seemed to him in 1931 "a No Man's Land" which "had never been properly mapped and [so] one had to know the whole of it before one could rightly forget any of its parts." Brooks wanted "to connect the literary present with the past, reviving the special kind of memory that fertilizes the living mind and gives it the sense of a base on which to build." The proper use of "tradition," he insisted, was "to fructify the present, to fertilize existing minds, and to stabilize our values."

*The Flowering of New England* (1936) and *New England: Indian Sum-*

*mer* (1940) were each a great popular success. They had little apparent influence, however, upon the younger writers of Brooks's own time who he had hoped would find in them a "usable past." The literary "tradition" that Ezra Pound, T. S. Eliot, and their disciples wanted was not an American literary tradition but an eclectic and artificial tradition extracted from the writings of European and Asiatic authors of all ages.

Many of the scholars who reviewed *The Flowering of New England* and its successors complained that these books were neither literary history nor literary criticism. If Brooks read the reviews in *American Literature* written by Kenneth B. Murdock, Robert E. Spiller, Arthur Hobson Quinn, and James D. Hart, he may well have felt that Edmund Wilson was right when he remarked to Brooks: "The professors certainly have it in for you." While in fact these scholars had considerable praise for certain features of *Makers and Finders*, they pointed out that Brooks had frequently discussed important writers without mentioning their books, that he had often given more space to minor writers than to the major, that his books lacked documentation, and that they contained errors of fact and judgment. Some of the unfavorable criticism was due to the failure of Brooks in the earlier volumes to make clear what kind of book he was writing. It was, he finally decided, a history not of American literature but of "the literary life in America."

Edmund Wilson praised the two New England books in the series as "one of the three or four prime light-diffusing works on the history of American society . . . that have appeared in our time." In 1953 one of the best literary critics among the professors, Norman Foerster, wrote: "*Makers and Finders* was no mean achievement. It showed great skill in the weaving of narrative and topical threads, in perception of the picturesque and idiosyncratic, in sympathy for men and places and times, in the creation of atmosphere and tone." Foerster added: "Brooks is not a thinker, or a moralist, or a literary critic, or a historian of literature; he is an artist."

In discussing Prescott's *The Reign of Ferdinand and Isabella* Brooks wrote a passage which, as James D. Hart has noted, suggests what Brooks actually accomplished in *The Flowering of New England* and its successors:

> A brilliant performance, as any child could see and no scholar was ever to deny. Its limitations were obvious enough. It was not a philosophical history. The author had no leading views, nor any profound feelings for human motives. There were depths upon depths behind and beneath the story that he never plumbed. But, as a work of art, a great historical narrative, grounded at every point in historical fact, and with all the glow and colour of Livy and Froissart, it was a magnificent success. . . . its pageantry of picturesque detail was calculated to feed as never before the starved imagination of the country.

In writing the final volume of the series, *The Confident Years: 1885–1915* (1952), Brooks found himself not in sympathy with certain writers and tendencies that he had to discuss. The earlier volumes of *Makers and Finders* had been both a critical and a popular success. In 1952, however, the New Critics and their academic admirers were in the driver's seat; and they had little interest in the American literary past. They were concerned primarily with aesthetic and not social problems. Brooks, on the other hand, was a social rather than an aesthetic critic, an optimist and a liberal like Vernon L. Parrington, whose first two volumes he had seen through the press for Harcourt, Brace and Company. They both saw Jeffersonian liberalism as central in the American tradition.

In a little book entitled *On Literature Today* (1941) Brooks revealed his great unhappiness about the state of literature and literary criticism in his own country. For him the "dominant mood in the history of literature" since the time of Homer had been the "mood of health, will, courage, faith in human nature." Yet the attitude of our contemporary writers was, he said, "cynical, bleak, hard-boiled, hard-bitten, and life for them [was] vain, dark and empty." Contemporary writing, he wrote elsewhere, was now "largely the creation of displaced persons, T. S. Eliot and Ezra Pound, James Joyce and Gertrude Stein, all of whom had left behind the countries of their origin and for whom human beings were more or less abstractions." Our writers had lost their sense of nationality along with their sense of the past. Literary critics were not interested in an author's experiences or his intentions, in the social effects of what he wrote, or in the climate of literary opinion in the author's own time. They preferred writers who were alienated from the society in which they had grown up. Poetry was a purely private affair intended for the aesthetic critic who would match his wits against the poet's in order to ferret out the author's secret meaning.

Brooks of course was unjust to the writers whom he so strongly condemned. He could not reconcile himself to the great shift in the Anglo-American literary tradition which had developed since 1900 and for which Brooks himself was partly responsible. But when one remembers the various unpredictable shifts in that literary tradition which have taken place since the time of Shakespeare, it is not inconceivable that Brooks may have been right when he predicted the time when John Donne would "return to the admired obscurity from which the twentieth century rescued him." It is not inconceivable either that the time may come when a new generation of unalienated American novelists and poets will find in the writings of Van Wyck Brooks a literary tradition which they can respect and use to their own advantage. At any rate *Makers and Finders*—like the histories of Prescott, Motley, Parkman, and Henry Adams—will continue to be read as literature.

# DONALD DAVIDSON

Donald Davidson (1893–1968), the ablest exponent of the thinking of intelligent southern conservatives, attained distinction as poet, essayist, historian, scholar, and teacher. He was a member of both the Fugitive and Agrarian groups. For Davidson, as he said at Mercer University in 1957, the Agrarian movement represented "the cause of civilized society, as we have known it in the Western World, against the new barbarism of science and technology controlled and directed by the modern power state." Industrial progress, he maintained, had brought about in the arts "a gradual corruption of integrity and good taste." Mass-production meant the sacrifice of quality to quantity.

Davidson's point of view was clearly and forcefully set forth in *The Attack on Leviathan* (1938). He found it "a strange disproportion that allowed a single city, in a far eastern corner of America, a practical monopoly in reporting the life of a continental area that it does not pretend to understand." "The South," he said—and he might well have added "the West"—"has never been able to understand how the North, in its astonishing quest for perfection, can junk an entire system of ideas almost overnight, and start on another one which is newer but no better than the first." The debunking "spokesmen of New York," said he, could find—to offer to "the most powerful nation on the globe, unravaged by war and anything but disheartened by circumstance"—nothing better than "a gospel of impotence and defeat" imported from Europe. In "Criticism Outside New York" (*Bookman*, May, 1931) Davidson wrote: "It is self-evident that New York sells its wares to the provinces without being very well acquainted with the various kinds of people that live, die, and occasionally read books in that vast region that lies outside of a circle described with a hundred mile radius from New York." The modern historians, as he pointed out in *The Attack on Leviathan*, had "found the life of the hinterland rich, abundant, diverse, where the [literary] critics [had] reported only barrenness." Davidson ridiculed "the labored attempts of Waldo Frank, Granville Hicks, Ludwig Lewisohn, and V. F. Calverton to camouflage the American tradition with their own peculiar obsessions about sex, Zionism, and the down-trodden proletariat."

In the years 1924–1930 Davidson, in addition to his duties as professor of English at Vanderbilt University, found time to edit the Nashville *Tennessean*'s book page, "The Spyglass" (later entitled "The Critic's Almanac"). Belatedly in 1963 the Vanderbilt University Press published a selection from

Davidson's reviews with editorial apparatus by John Tyree Fain. These reviews are in no way inferior to the best of those published in the metropolitan newspapers in the 1920's. Southerner though he was, Davidson had no hesitation in speaking his mind about writers from the South. In February, 1930, he wrote: "To the generation of rising young novelists, Mr. [James Branch] Cabell and his fellows bequeath fine words and a bucket of ashes."

In reviewing Julian Green's *The Dark Journey* on December 8, 1929, Davidson wrote: "It becomes doubtful whether, in any old and well-understood sense of the word, [our writers of today] can write tragedy at all, but they can and do produce painful literature." The "great writers of the past," he said, ". . . always had something to fall back on: Fate, the Gods, Divine Providence, a Moral Order. They had some sort of ethics underlying their tragedies." "But our writers," he continued, "have passed beyond good and evil, beyond the moral order, beyond even a sense of the dignity of man. They have no religion other than a vague religion of well-being, and so their Satan, their Evil Principle, their Hell is Pain."

In August, 1926, Davidson praised the editor of *Poetry* for "great names published and good causes sponsored"; but now, he thought, the magazine "should either be revitalized or it should be discontinued," for Harriet Monroe's great services as its editor lay in the past. In reviewing Miss Monroe's *Poets and Their Art* (1926) Davidson found the book "notable for its exclusions as well as its inclusions."

> Miss Monroe has space for the fifth-rate Marjorie Allan Seiffert and a pack of minor feminine singers, but nothing at all to say of Conrad Aiken, E. E. Cummings, John Crowe Ransom, Louis Untermeyer, John G. Neihardt, Robinson Jeffers, and William Ellery Leonard. Elinor Wylie gets only a narrow corner in Miss Monroe's gallery of women poets, and T. S. Eliot, whose "Waste Land" has had a greater influence, perhaps, than any other poem of the last five years, is strangely yoked in discussion with Lew Sarett, who has written some charming but mild lyrics about Indians.

In her book Miss Monroe had said of Carl Sandburg: "In my opinion, his finest lyrics rank, as artistic achievements, among the best in the language." Davidson held a different opinion. In reviewing *Good Morning, America,* which he said was not one of Sandburg's best books, he wrote: "One is led to think that Sandburg is, after all, a poetic-minded, notionate, delightful fellow who is nevertheless not quite a poet."

Davidson was probably less influenced by T. S. Eliot than any of his Vanderbilt associates. *The Waste Land* seemed to him "the triumph of defeatism and fastidiousness." He was fully aware of the "great distinction" of

Eliot's critical essays, but he noted that they were "built on the presumption that they are to be read by people of sound and extensive learning." He added:

> Furthermore, I am much intimidated by Mr. Eliot's impressive habit of referring to authors quite casually as with the presumption that any decent person knows them by heart, when in fact I do not know them at all or never heard of them. . . . If objection is to be made, it must be to Mr. Eliot's pontifical air. A chilly hauteur is part of his manner; one suspects it to be the psychological defense of a lonely heart. At any rate one feels icily repelled, put in one's proper uncouth place; it is the same as being viewed through a monocle.

In an article in the *Georgia Review* (Winter, 1966) Professor M. Thomas Inge reprinted Davidson's reviews of William Faulkner's first three novels—reviews that Mr. Fain had unaccountably omitted. They reveal Davidson as the most perceptive of Faulkner's critics before 1939 when Faulkner criticism really got under way with articles by Conrad Aiken and George Marion O'Donnell. Writing in the Nashville *Tennessean* for April 11, 1926, Davidson found *Soldiers' Pay* "a powerful book, done with careful artistry and with great warmth of feeling." It was, he thought, "superior to Dos Passos' 'Soldiers Three,' that much talked about war book, because it digs deeper into human nature." Faulkner, he said,

> reveals himself quite clearly . . . as a sensitive, observant person with a fine power of objectifying his own and other people's emotions, and of clarifying characters so that they possess the 'real life' within themselves which it is one of the functions of art to present. Furthermore, he is an artist in language, a sort of poet turned into prose; he does not write prose as Dreiser does, as if he were washing dishes, nor like Sinclair Lewis, who goes at words with a hammer and saw.

Three years later when on April 14, 1929, Davidson reviewed Faulkner's third novel *The Sound and the Fury*—still rated as one of his best—he said:

> Mr. Faulkner has already made his place as a novelist, though his work, for some strange reason, is not so well known as it should be. His two earlier novels . . . were clearly the product of a bold and original spirit, but they somehow escaped attention while we were all engaged with "An American Tragedy" and "Dark Laughter." . . . Let me at once have done with nice distinctions and say that as a stylist and as an acute observer of human behavior, I think that Mr. Faulkner is the equal of any except three or four American novelists who stand at the very top. His sole difficulty so far seems to be that he has not found a theme or a character that really comes up to the possibilities of his

style and his perception. For his style is a major style, not a trifling one; and his perception ought not to be lavished on weak or inconsequent persons.

In *Still Rebels, Still Yankees* (1957) Davidson was, in his own words, particularly concerned with "the extraordinary misjudgments that literary critics make when blinded by the vices of romantic progressivism and the false standards of social science." In "Why the Modern South Has a Great Literature" he attacked the methods of the economists and sociologists. That essay, written in 1950, the year in which William Faulkner journeyed to Stockholm to receive the Nobel Prize, throws light upon the development of the southern literary renaissance. As Davidson noted, the southern states—and especially Mississippi—had been denounced by northern critics and journalists as "ignorant," "reactionary," and "uncivilized." By every test employed by the economists and the sociologists Mississippi was indeed a "backward" state. It seemed to lack everything that made Massachusetts and Wisconsin great: "educational facilities, factories, libraries, hospitals, laboratories, art museums, theaters, labor unions, publishing houses, accumulations of wealth, high dams, electric power, agricultural machinery, birth control." Mississippi was among the poorest states in the Union. It had a very large percentage of tenant farmers and of persons unable to read or write. Nevertheless, as Davidson noted, if Mississippi were " 'indexed' according to the quality and consistency of its literary performance, it would indeed be very advanced," for it had produced such writers as Stark Young, William Alexander Percy, Eudora Welty, and William Faulkner. Taking Faulkner "at the current estimate of 1950," Davidson added: "To find a novelist comparable to Faulkner in all the Northeast they [the literary intellectuals of Harvard University] have to go to more backward times and read Henry James." The strange paradox that Davidson noted, applied to other southern states:

> We must then conclude that the way to produce a John Ransom, an Allen Tate, a Robert Penn Warren, a Julia Peterkin, a Stark Young, a Eudora Welty, a Thomas Wolfe, a Jesse Stuart, an Elizabeth Roberts, is to have them be born and grow up in a backward Southern community that loves everything that Massachusetts condemns and lacks nearly everything that Massachusetts deems admirable and necessary.

The South of 1920–1950 that produced the southern literary renaissance was, as Davidson emphasized,

> a traditional society which had arrived at a moment of self-consciousness favorable to the production of great literary works. A traditional society is a society that is stable, religious, more rural than urban, and politically conservative. Family, blood kinship, clanship,

folk-ways, custom, community, in such a society, supply the needs that in a non-traditional or progressive society are supplied at great cost by artificial devices like training schools and government agencies. A traditional society can absorb modern improvements up to a certain point without losing its character. If modernism enters to the point where the society is thrown a little out of balance but not yet completely off balance, the moment of self-consciousness arrives.

At such a moment "a writer awakes to realize what he and his people truly are, in comparison with what they are being urged to become." The literature of the twentieth-century South, as Davidson pointed out, "is not a literature of protest but a literature of acceptance"; and at its best, he said, it "displays a sense of form, a vitality, a grace, a power, and often a finality of treatment that are remarkably scarce in American literature elsewhere."

Among the northern writers Davidson noted "a lamentable conflict between head and heart. Out of the schism between head and heart," he continued, "arises the literature of realism, of protest, of social criticism." Rare indeed were the northern writers who, like Robert Frost, possessed that "knowledge carried to the heart" which the great writer must have. Davidson commented briefly on three northern writers of fiction who, he believed, were "injured by the fearful imbalance of Northern civilization":

> Sinclair Lewis has an excellent subject matter, but as to form he is still a cub reporter with a good memory, hacking out copy to catch the two o'clock edition. Dreiser impresses us with the mass of his enormous case histories, but they are written in laborious prose and have apparently been organized with a meat saw and a butcher knife. On the other hand, Thornton Wilder has a beautiful, though somewhat precious, prose style, but he has no subject matter for the prose to use. . . . the North shows a hodgepodge of experimentalists, propagandists, plausible but empty Book-of-the-Month Club specials, a vast number of scholars and critics, but very few writers of first rank who are not injured by the fearful imbalance of Northern civilization. . . . There are too many people looking over [the Northern writer's] shoulder as he writes—too many college professors, social welfare workers, atomic scientists, pressure groups, librarians, editors of slick magazines, impatient publishers, and seductive subsidizers.

*All that the critic can be expected to do is to study the masterpieces in a vain search for the secret of their lasting beauty. And for this task, so difficult and so delicate, none are so fit as those fellow-craftsmen who have the faculty of articulate expression.*

Brander Matthews, "Mr. Howells as a Critic," *Forum*

*May we not conclude, then, that Donne, Crashaw, Vaughan, Herbert and Lord Herbert, Marvell, King, Cowley at his best, are in the direct current of English poetry . . . ?*

T. S. Eliot, "The Metaphysical Poets"

# Chapter 8. *New Critics, Fugitives, and Expatriates*

In the 1920's the number of American writers and would-be writers who flocked to London and Paris exceeded anything known in the past. Before the devaluation of the dollar in 1933, living was much less expensive in most European countries than in the United States. There were of course other valid reasons why a writer might prefer to live in Europe. In Paris and London one could hear lively conversations on literature and the arts. In Paris one could get published—and inexpensively—poems and stories that would probably have been banned in New York or Boston. For a time Paris seemed the most important of American literary capitals, and French literature was more influential than that of England.

The expatriates were disillusioned about their own country. They felt that American democracy was a failure. They looked upon their countrymen back at home as uncultivated, puritanical, hypocritical, and moulded by the pressure of public opinion into a colorless uniformity. They particularly resented the Prohibition amendment to the U.S. Constitution. In Paris one could live as he pleased, and no one seemed to care. What had happened was that many of the expatriates had come to accept at face value traditional distorted European conceptions of life in the United States. Many of the young intellectuals living abroad felt no kinship with the literary tradition of their own country. They had no interest in American literary nationalism. The modern authors who interested them were Europeans. They read and talked about such writers as Sigmund Freud, Thomas Mann, Oswald Spengler, Marcel Proust, James Joyce, D. H. Lawrence, and William Butler Yeats.

Ezra Pound, T. S. Eliot, and John Crowe Ransom belonged to the same generation as Louis Untermeyer, Amy Lowell, Van Wyck Brooks, and H. L.

Mencken; but their attitude toward the literature of their own country was very different. Cleanth Brooks noted the difference in his *Modern Poetry and the Tradition* (1939):

> The history of modern American poetry as written by the Untermeyers and Monroes tends to something of the following form: The modern American poet has rid himself of clichés, worn-out literary materials, and the other stereotypes of Victorianism. Having sloughed off these dead conventions, he has proceeded (with the critic's hearty approval) to write of American scenes, American things, and the American people.

The work of the "modern" poets, said Brooks, "implies a critical revolution in the light of which the current conception of the history of English [and American] poetry must be revised." The "modern" poets were Pound, Eliot, Ransom, and their followers. They were literary critics as well as poets, and in both capacities they were the leaders in a new literary revolution which resulted in altering the canon of the great American writers as it was seen by Harriet Monroe, Mencken, Van Wyck Brooks, and Untermeyer.

The assets of the New Critics were intelligence, sensibility, a knowledge of craftsmanship, and complete confidence in the validity of their own methods. They complained that the professors of English were devoting their energies not to analyzing masterpieces and teaching their students how to read a poem but to the irrelevant study of social, historical, and biographical backgrounds of writers, most of whom had little or no intrinsic importance. I. A. Richards in fact had in his *Practical Criticism* (1929) demonstrated that most educated men and women did not know how to read a poem. In various textbooks Cleanth Brooks, Robert Penn Warren, and others undertook with some success to teach a generation of undergraduates how to analyze a poem, a play, a short story, or a novel.

In 1940 when the attack upon conservative English departments was at its height, two influential quarterlies, the *Southern Review* and the *Kenyon Review*, each printed one half of a lengthy symposium entitled "Literature and the Professors." John Crowe Ransom noted that in most colleges and universities there was a "lag between modern criticism and current methods of teaching literature." Cleanth Brooks denounced English departments for "the stupid, or trifling, or plainly muddle-headed books, articles, dissertations, and theses which [their] machinery commits [them] to turn out."

Eventually in most universities the New Critics compounded their quarrel with the professors. Many of them in fact became professors; among them, Austin Warren, R. P. Blackmur, Arthur Mizener, Francis Fergusson, Richard Chase, Yvor Winters, W. K. Wimsatt, Jr., and Harry Levin. In a judicious appraisal of the accomplishments of the New Critics, C. Hugh Holman wrote in 1955:

> The group has had a pervasive and revivifying influence on American criticism since the middle thirties. In fact, it has developed a theory of criticism, advanced a method of critical attack, invented a vocabulary (often to the exasperation of its readers), and called forth much of that body of excellent writing about literature which entitles us to look with pride upon the critical accomplishment of America in the last quarter of a century.

The New Critics glorified Dante, the French Symbolists, Dryden, Pope, Dr. Johnson, the later Elizabethan dramatists, and especially John Donne and the other Metaphysical Poets of the seventeenth century. Among the later writers who interested them were Hopkins, Joyce, Yeats, Proust, Rilke, and Kafka. The New Critics practically ignored Goethe, Tolstoy, Hugo, Robert Burns, Jane Austen, Dickens, Thackeray, George Eliot, and the Pre-Raphaelites. Among the very few nineteenth-century American writers who interested them were Hawthorne and Henry James. Their antipathy to most of the traditionally great Romantic and Victorian writers of England and America was so great that Howard Mumford Jones protested that the nineteenth century must not be regarded as merely "a regrettable hiatus between John Donne and John Crowe Ransom." The gravest charge brought against the New Criticism is, in the words of Robert E. Spiller, "that it has ignored altogether the relation of literature to life, the ways in which literature illuminates life and the insights and satisfactions it really gives to readers, and has reduced it [literary criticism] to an elaborate game of interest only to experts."

It was years before Eliot, who had once looked upon George Herbert as a "major" English poet, could see that Milton was a far greater poet. Even so, he regarded Milton as a bad model for the youthful poet, who could learn far more from a study of Dante than from Milton or Shakespeare. The New Critics had a special dislike for Shelley. Edmund Wilson wrote in *Axel's Castle* (1931): "It is as much as one's life is worth nowadays, among young people, to say an approving word for Shelley or a dubious one about Donne."

Professor Frederick A. Pottle, at Yale University, where there were many New Critics, applied to Shelley's poetry the touchstones of the New Criticism. The conclusion that he reached was that, by their own standards, Shelley was a much greater poet than the New Critics were willing to admit.* In one of his last essays Eliot, a better critic than any of his disciples, recognized Shelley as a "great poet."

---

* See "The Case of Shelley," *PMLA*, LXVII (1952), 509–608.

# THE FUGITIVES

It is not difficult to see why Pound and Eliot, both expatriates from a country for which they had little affection or admiration, displayed no enthusiasm for older American writers except Henry James, but it does seem odd that the southern poets who contributed to that regionalist symposium, *I'll Take My Stand* (1930), should be indifferent to nearly all earlier American writers, including the writers of their own section. The Fugitives were looking for a usable literary tradition, but they could not find it in the American past as interpreted for them by Van Wyck Brooks, Vernon L. Parrington, or the professors of English who contributed to *The Cambridge History of American Literature*.

The literary past that appealed to Allen Tate (1890–) was European rather than American. "For example," he wrote in the *Partisan Review* in 1939, "until the time of Pound and Eliot, there are no American poets whose styles have been useful in working towards a style that is suitable to my own kind of American experience. . . ." Like Eliot and Ransom, Tate saw in John Donne "the mainstream of English verse." Frost and Robinson, he conceded, were important but not very influential poets. "Mr. Frost," he said, "is . . . an end, not a beginning." Tate regarded Stephen Vincent Benét as only "an amiable and patriotic rhymester"; he disliked "the aggressive provincialism, which passes for American nationalism, of Mr. Carl Sandburg."

John Crowe Ransom (1888–), the oldest member and the recognized leader of the Vanderbilt University poets and critics, expounded his conception of both poetry and criticism in *The World's Body* (1938): "It is the age which among other things has recovered the admirable John Donne; that is the way to identify its literary taste. Therefore it is hardly the age of which it may be said that Miss [Edna St. Vincent] Millay is the voice." So great was Ransom's admiration for Donne's poetry that he once suggested that his "Valediction" is a better poem than Shakespeare's sonnet which begins:

> Not marble, nor the gilded monuments
> Of princes, shall outlive this powerful rime.

In "Poets Without Laurels" Ransom defended the "modern" poets, "those whom a small company of adept readers enjoys, perhaps enormously, and the general public detests; those in whose hands poetry as a living art has lost its public support." "The true poetry," he said, "has no great interest in improving or idealizing the world, which does well enough. It only seeks to realize the world, to see it better." The poetry of the right kind, he thought, was that being written by Eliot, Pound, Stevens, and Tate; it did not include the poems of Frost and Robinson. A dozen years later Ransom was to rank Frost and Robinson among the few major poets of the twentieth century.

## EZRA POUND

There are times when a youthful writer of genius can find little or no help in the literature of his own country. Then for his models and direction he must look to writers from other nations. Geoffrey Chaucer turned his back on the Anglo-Saxon poetic tradition and found his models, metrical forms, and inspiration in the literatures of France, Italy, and ancient Rome. Chaucer, however, was not an expatriate, but a thoroughly loyal Englishman.

Ezra Pound (1885–), like T. S. Eliot and Gertrude Stein, chose to live in Europe in those turbulent years when the United States was fast becoming not only the richest and most powerful of all nations but also a haven for such eminent artists and writers as Arturo Toscanini, Arnold Shoenberg, Pablo Casals, Thomas Mann, Aldous Huxley, and W. H. Auden. In this period when in Asia and Africa the great European empires were disintegrating, the United States became the chief defender of the political, social, economic, cultural, and religious values of Western civilization against attacks from both Fascists and Communists. In this period also our twentieth-century American writers came to have an enormous influence upon writers in Europe and Latin America.

In an essay entitled "Poetry and the Public World" (1939) Archibald Mac-Leish attempted to explain the indifference of poets like Pound to the imminent danger to this country posed by dictators like Mussolini, Hitler, and Stalin. "The poetry we call contemporary," he said, "was originally, and still remains, a poetry of revolt." "It is," he continued, "not formed by the human and political necessities of our own world but by the literary necessities of the world before the war [First World War]." For this reason, he concluded, "The responsible language of acceptance and belief is not possible to the poetry of literary revolt."

As a student at Hamilton College and later at the University of Pennsylvania Pound had a special interest in the romance languages; and for a time it seemed as though he was destined to become a professor in some American university. He went to Europe ostensibly in search of materials for a doctor's thesis, but he devoted his energies to writing poetry and promoting the new poetry. A skilled craftsman sensitive to new ideas, impulses, and techniques, he became the chief medium for the transmission of these influences to America. He learned from his study of many writers; among them, T. E. Hulme, William Butler Yeats, James Joyce, Browning, the Metaphysical Poets, the French Symbolists, the Goncourts, and Dante.

Pound and Eliot, like Ransom and Tate, found in the American literary tradition little that they could make use of; but they managed to create for themselves a highly eclectic and artificial literary tradition by piecing together materials culled from various European and Asiatic literatures. The process involved the rejection of major writers who seemed no longer of any use to serious young authors. In Pound's view Milton was "donkey-eared, asinine, disgusting"; he was "the worst sort of poison." Wordsworth was a "silly old sheep"; Vergil and Pindar had to be "chucked out." On the other hand, Landor was "perhaps the only complete and serious man of letters ever born in these [British] islands." The process that Pound had in mind he called "excernment," which he defined as "the general ordering and weeding out of what has actually been performed. The elimination of repetitions. . . . the ordering of knowledge so that the next man (or generation) can most readily find the live part of it, and waste the least possible time among obsolete issues."

The process that Pound called "excernment," or something very like it, takes place once or twice in nearly every century. In the preface to *Lyrical Ballads* Wordsworth in 1800 tried to weed out those eighteenth-century English poets whose conventional diction he had found no longer usable. Pound did more perhaps than any one else to provide the new poets with a language they could use; and poets as different as Carl Sandburg, Allen Tate, and the Imagists were indebted to him. He detested rhetoric, bombast, inversions, and generalities.

Pound and Eliot performed a useful service to younger poets who were trying to find the "live" part of the literary past; but they did an injustice to the many writers whose merits they did not appreciate. They failed to foresee the time, now arrived, when their own poetic diction would be no longer suited to the kind of poetry that younger poets wish to write. More than any other person Pound seems responsible for the divorce of poetry from life and the consequent loss to the poets of many potential readers. In 1967 James Dickey said in an address at the Library of Congress that "since the ascendency of Pound and Eliot . . . the poem has become a kind of high-cult *objet d'art*" and is unable to "speak to people deeply about matters of general concern." "Multiplicity of reference and 'richness of ambiguity,' " he said, "are no longer going to be the criteria by which the value of poetry is measured."

As poetry correspondent for such avant-garde magazines as the *Dial*, *Poetry*, and the *Little Review*, Pound promoted the reputations of Yeats, Eliot,

Frost, Joyce, and many other writers. Pound was probably at his best as a teacher. In fact he seemed to John Gould Fletcher "a queer combination of an international Bohemian and an American college professor out of a job." In a review of *The Letters of Ezra Pound* (1950) Katherine Anne Porter wrote:

> As critic he was at the very best in the teacher-pupil relationship, when he had a manuscript under his eye to pull apart and put together again, or in simply stating the deep changeless principles of the highest art, relating them to each other and to their time and society. As one of the great poets of the time, his advice was unfashionably good and right in these things, and they are not outdated, and they cannot be unless the standard is simply thrown out.

(I wish I were as certain as Miss Porter was that the "principles of the highest art" are "changeless" and "not outdated.") Pound was at his best when he helped Eliot to rework the original draft of *The Waste Land*. Eliot acknowledged the debt when he dedicated the poem: "For Ezra Pound, *il miglior fabbro*." In this instance at least Pound was "the better craftsman."

Ezra Pound was no literary nationalist. "Are you for American poetry or for poetry?" he wrote to Harriet Monroe on August 18, 1912; and he added: "The glory of any nation is to produce art that can be exported without disgrace to its origin." He ridiculed college courses in American literature. "You might as well," he said, "give courses in 'American chemistry,' neglecting all foreign discoveries." "No American poetry," he said, "is of any use for the palette." He had no higher opinion of American civilization. "Jefferson," he said, "was perhaps the last American official to have any general sense of civilization."

Of our major nineteenth-century writers Henry James was the only one of whom Pound wholly approved—and James was the only one of them who had chosen, like Pound and Eliot, to live in Europe while his own country was developing into a world power. Of James, Pound wrote: "He certainly has put America on the map. Given her a local habitation and a name." Emerson he once pronounced a "fraud"; Emily Dickinson was only "a little country blue-stocking." Whitman and Poe seemed to Pound the best of our older American writers. From London he wrote in 1909: "From this side of the Atlantic I am for the first time able to read Whitman. . . . I see him America's poet." Yet though he respected Whitman, he quarreled with him. At one time he thought he had found thirty well-written pages in *Leaves of Grass*. Twenty years later he said that he was no longer able to find them. Poe, he said, "is a good enough poet, and after Whitman the best America has produced (probably)"; but he added, "He is a dam bad model. . . . A dam'd bad rhetorician half the time."

Ezra Pound stayed away from his native land too long. Denouncing his own country became a habit with him. An alienated spirit, he had little comprehension of what was happening in the United States. During the Second World War while still retaining his American citizenship, he broadcast propaganda for the dictator of a nation at war with the United States. At the end of the war he was brought back to this country and indicted for treason. He was never brought to trial but was for years a prisoner at St. Elizabeth's Hospital in Washington. Through the influence of Archibald MacLeish, Robert Frost, and other writers he was finally released and permitted to return to Italy. The younger scholars and critics of our time, some of them busy denouncing the undeclared war in Vietnam, seem undisturbed by Pound's "treasonable" activities; but those who, with sons in the U.S. Army, Navy, and Air Force, listened in wartime to Pound's radio broadcasts from Italy cannot so easily forgive what in their ears sounded like treason to his country and theirs.

In 1948, while Pound was still a prisoner at St. Elizabeth's, a committee of distinguished writers awarded him the Bollingen Prize for his *Pisan Cantos*. Robert Hillyer and others immediately objected to the award, and there was a prolonged controversy. Karl Shapiro, the only member of the Library of Congress committee who voted against the award to Pound, defended his position: "I voted against Pound in the belief that the poet's political and moral philosophy ultimately vitiates the poetry and lowers its standard as literary work."

From the beginning there has been wide disagreement among critics about Pound's rank as a poet. Allen Tate, T. S. Eliot, Marcus Cunliffe, and many others have rated him as a major American poet. There is no doubt of Pound's superior craftsmanship, and yet one may well wonder whether in his poems he had much to say that will seem of importance to readers in the twenty-first century. It was his friend Eliot who wrote: "The 'greatness' of literature cannot be determined solely by literary standards, though we must remember that whether it is literature or not can be determined only by literary standards." Whatever rank the future literary historians of England and America may assign to Ezra Pound, there can be no question of the importance and the extent of his influence upon English and American poetry and literary criticism.

# T. S. ELIOT

Thomas Stearns Eliot (1888–1965), probably the most influential poet and critic writing in English in the twentieth century, was born in St. Louis, but his parents belonged to a well-known New England family, and insofar as in later life Eliot thought of himself as an American, it was as a New Englander. He was profoundly influenced by his years at Harvard University, where he took his B.A. degree in 1910 and his M.A. in 1911. In Eliot's time Harvard had a notable array of scholars and teachers, and many of the ablest were to be found in the departments of English and philosophy. Eliot had courses with some of the best.* It was Dean Le Baron Russell Briggs who introduced him to the poetry of John Donne. Eliot was fortunate in having a course in Elizabethan drama under George Pierce Baker, who was just beginning to teach playwriting in his 47 Workshop. Baker was a brilliant lecturer, and it was he who gave Eliot his first appreciation of the power and beauty of dramatists like Ben Jonson, Thomas Middleton, John Webster, and Cyril Tourneur. In *To Criticize the Critic* (1965) Eliot wrote: "It was from these minor dramatists that I, in my own poetic formation, had learned my lessons; it was by them, and not by Shakespeare, that my imagination had been stimulated, my sense of rhythm trained, and my emotions fed." Apparently Eliot did not register for the course in Shakespeare taught by the ablest of Harvard scholars, George Lyman Kittredge. He came under the influence of two exceptional men who taught in other departments: Irving Babbitt in French and George Santayana in philosophy. Many years later Eliot was to refer to the leader of the New Humanists as "My old teacher and master, Irving Babbitt, to whom I owe so much. . . ."

Few of the Harvard professors—and I think none of those who taught Eliot—had any keen interest in American literature. In *The Middle Span* (1945) Santayana wrote: "We poets at Harvard never read anything written in America except our own compositions." John Gould Fletcher, who spent four years (1903–1907) at Harvard, had, like Ezra Pound, to go to London to learn that Walt Whitman was a major American poet. There was in Eliot's time a course in American literature—it was in fact a half-course given only in alternate years—taught by Barrett Wendell, who was an Anglophile. Eliot may have read Wendell's *Literary History of America*, but he did not take his course nor the course in Emerson which Bliss Perry offered for the first time in 1909. In *Scenes and Portraits* (1954) Van Wyck Brooks, who was graduated from Harvard in 1907, summed up the Harvard influences which he thought had most deeply affected Eliot: "When one added these tastes to-

---

* In his *Notes on Some Figures Behind . . . T. S. Eliot* (1964) Herbert Howarth commented on some of Eliot's teachers and underrated some of the best, notably William Allan Neilson, William Henry Schofield, and Charles Townsend Copeland. I had courses with many of the professors who taught Eliot, but I had no personal acquaintance with the poet, who entered as a freshman in 1906, the year in which I enrolled in the graduate school.

gether, the royalism and the classicism, the Anglo-Catholicism, the cults of Donne and Dante, the Sanskrit, the Elizabethan dramatists and the French Symbolist poets, one arrived at T. S. Eliot, the quintessence of Harvard." This is the earlier Eliot who was interested in the literature of almost every country except that in which he was born and educated; it is the Eliot who once defined his position as that of "an Anglo-Catholic in religion, a classicist in literature, and a royalist in politics." Brooks was not quite fair to either Eliot or Harvard. If Harvard failed to teach its students to appreciate the literature of their own country, it did at least give many of them a lively sense of great literature as one of the supreme achievements of the human mind.

The city of Boston left its imprint upon some of Eliot's early poems including "The Love Song of J. Alfred Prufrock" and "The Portrait of a Lady." One wonders who were the ultra-refined Bostonians who led the poet in 1918 to write: "The society of Boston was and is quite uncivilized but refined beyond the point of civilization. . . ."

Like Ezra Pound, Eliot seemed destined for a professorship in an American university. He went abroad in 1914 looking for materials for a dissertation on F. H. Bradley. It was apparently the influence of Pound that saved him for poetry. On September 30, 1915, Pound wrote to Harriet Monroe: "He is the only American I know of who has made what I can call adequate preparation for writing. He has actually trained himself and modernized himself *on his own.*"

Eliot had found himself "alienated from the major English poets of the nineteenth century." He wrote in *On Poetry and Poets* (1957): "The kind of poetry that I needed, to teach me the use of my own voice, did not exist in English at all; it was only to be found in French." It was from French poets like Jules Laforgue, he said, "I learned that the sort of material that I had, the sort of experience that an adolescent has had, in an industrial city in America, could be the material for poetry. . . ."

In those early years there were few who cared for Eliot's poetry. About 1914 his friend Conrad Aiken (Harvard, 1911) took the manuscript of "The Love Song of J. Alfred Prufrock" to London, where it was "refused with outspoken horror by [Harold] Monro, for *Poetry and Drama*, and Austin Harrison, for the *English Review*, and then to be given an official stamp of delighted approval by Ezra Pound. . . ." It was Pound who sent the poem to Harriet Monroe in Chicago, but it took some persuasion on his part and that of John Gould Fletcher to induce her somewhat tardily to print the poem in *Poetry*. Miss Monroe, it should be remembered, belonged to an older generation; she was twenty-five years older than Pound and twenty-eight years older than Eliot.

Eliot's first and most notable success came in 1922 with the publication of "The Waste Land" in the first number of the *Criterion* in October and in this country in the *Dial* in November. The poem was hailed by young poets and critics as a magnificent specimen of "modern" poetry and a marvelous picture of a desolated postwar world. In the *Dial* for December, 1922, Edmund Wilson wrote: "Mr. Eliot is a poet—that is, he feels intensely and with distinction and speaks naturally in beautiful verse, so that, no matter in what walls he lives, he belongs to the divine company."

Academic critics in both England and America were slow to recognize Eliot as either a genuine poet or an important literary critic. One of his earliest English admirers, F. R. Leavis, who had read *The Sacred Wood* in 1920, published in the *Cambridge Review* in 1929 an article in praise of Eliot's literary criticism. The young editor of the *Review*, says Leavis, "very soon had cause to realize that he had committed a scandalous impropriety, and I myself was left in no doubt as to the unforgivableness of my offence." As late as 1943 Sir Arthur Quiller-Couch ("Q"), who had long held the chair of English literature at Cambridge University, wrote at the age of eighty that he wondered whether Eliot in all his life had ever composed three consecutive lines of *"poetry."* A younger British scholar, George Sampson, author of *The Concise Cambridge History of English Literature* (1941), complained that Eliot's verse was "the most bookish of its time." Eliot was, he said, "a poet with dust and ashes for his theme." Reluctantly, however, Sampson conceded that Eliot was "almost the only writer of his age who has made a constructive contribution to the literature of criticism." And yet, Sampson thought, "The critical studies of T. S. Eliot contain so many personal heresies that a Holy Office of Literature might suspect his orthodoxy."*

In *The Sacred Wood* (1920) Eliot wrote: "The important critic is the person who is absorbed in the present problems of art, and who wishes to bring the forces of the past to bear on the solution of those problems." The powerful effect of Eliot's early essays on younger writers was thus described by Conrad Aiken in the *Dial* for July, 1929:

> In The Sacred Wood and again in Homage to John Dryden, Mr Eliot provided his immediate generation with a group of literary essays which were an admirable corrective for many of the intellectual and aesthetic disorders of the time. They were compact, precise, astringent; they brought the past to bear on the present, the present into a visible relation with the past; in short they helped materially to restore, for a

* In other parts of this book I have noted the failure of such well-known American critics as Louis Untermeyer, Amy Lowell, and Paul Elmer More to see in *The Waste Land* a great poem. Asa Don Dickinson's "authorities" almost uniformly gave Eliot a low rating as poet, critic, and dramatist.

literary generation which had lost its bearings, a sense of tradition as a living and fruitful thing.

There were intelligent readers who were repelled by the lavish display of the poet's erudition in both the poems and the essays. Donald Davidson, poet, critic, and scholar, found himself "intimidated by Mr. Eliot's habit of referring to authors quite casually as with the presumption that any decent person knows them by heart, when in fact I do not know them at all or never heard of them." Eliot's "pontifical air" gave Davidson a feeling like "being viewed through a monocle."

Toward the end of his life Eliot reread his early essays and wrote in *To Criticize the Critic* (1965): "There are errors of judgment, and, what I regret more, there are errors in tone: the occasional note of arrogance, of vehemence or rudeness, the braggadocio of the mild-mannered man safely entrenched behind his typewriter." In his earlier years Eliot took "the extreme position that the *only* critics worth reading were the critics who practised, and practised well, the art of which they wrote." In "The Music of Poetry" (1942), Eliot noted that when a poet writes criticism, "He is not so much a judge as an advocate." Hence, he concluded, "We must return to the scholar for ascertainment of facts, and to the more detached critic for impartial judgment."

John Gould Fletcher, who knew Eliot in London, thought that some of his critical estimates were erratic. As he wrote in *Life Is My Song* (1937), "Ben Jonson he seemed to think equally as great as Shakespeare; Dryden he frankly preferred to Milton; and among the moderns, he tended to rate Pound far above Yeats." Eliot, however, finally conceded that Milton, though a bad model, was a great poet; and George Herbert, he realized, was not the major poet that he had once considered him.

Here of course we are concerned primarily with Eliot as a critic of American literature, a subject that did not as a rule deeply interest him. In his early years there were, he said, "no older poets in the United States who were of any use in helping me to create a style." The only older American writer who aroused his admiration was that accomplished craftsman and expatriate, Henry James. Writing in the *Little Review* for August, 1918, Eliot propounded the dubious theory that James was "positively a continuator of the New England genius." Of the New England writers of the American renaissance Eliot wrote:

> None of these men [Emerson, Thoreau, Hawthorne, and Lowell], with the exception of Hawthorne, is individually very important; they all can, and perhaps ought to be made to look very foolish; but there is a "something" there, a dignity, about Emerson, for example, which persists. . . . Omitting such men as Bryant and Whittier as absolutely

plebeian, we can still perceive the halo of dignity around the men I have named, and also Longfellow, Margaret Fuller and her crew, Bancroft and Motley, the faces of (later) [Charles Eliot] Norton and [Francis James] Child pleasantly shaded by the Harvard elms. . . .

On April 23 of the following year when Eliot in the *Athenaeum* reviewed Volume 2 of *The Cambridge History of American Literature*, he said—ignoring Thoreau as well as Whittier and the Cambridge poets—that the only important writers discussed in the book were Poe, Whitman, and Hawthorne. In a passage that I have quoted earlier he continued:

> Hawthorne, Poe and Whitman are all pathetic figures; they were none of them so great as they might have been. . . . [They lived and wrote in a] starved environment. . . . Their world was thin; it was not corrupt enough. Worst of all it was secondhand; it was not original and a self-dependent—it was a shadow. Poe and Whitman, like bulbs in a glass bottle, could only exhaust what was in them.

No wonder that Eliot seemed to John Gould Fletcher "a person who had cut himself off completely from all his American roots, and left them altogether behind. There was nothing in either his speech, his dress, or his demeanor that proclaimed the former middle-westerner. . . ." Conrad Aiken remembers that both Eliot and Pound disapproved of his publishing the *Selected Poems of Emily Dickinson* in 1924:

> [Pound and Eliot] were very much annoyed with me for bringing out Dickinson. They did their damnedest to stop me from doing it. I think they thought this was really cutting the ground from under their feet— I mean, to have a great poet looking over their shoulders suddenly, a little embarrassing. So they pooh-poohed it and said no, no, it's just a little bluestocking, a little country bluestocking.

In later life Eliot was less unsympathetic in his comments on the older American writers. In an address at Washington University in St. Louis in 1953 he named Poe, Whitman, and (surprisingly) Mark Twain as the greatest of American writers. He had recently read *Huckleberry Finn*, apparently for the first time, and had discovered that it was a literary masterpiece.

When Eliot gave up the editorship of the *Criterion* in 1942, he remarked: "Twenty years largely wasted." Perhaps, like many of his admirers, he wished that he had devoted much more of his time and energies to the creation of poems like *The Waste Land* or *The Four Quartets*. Nevertheless, some of his essays are literary masterpieces, and we must be grateful for them. Their influence upon poets, critics, and teachers has been enormous. By employing Eliot's methods scholars and critics have been able to understand and appreciate better the work of American writers who did not interest him.

# Chapter 9. *Literary Prizes, Critical Polls, and Individual Estimates*

> *Time for the wearisome old debate:*
> *Why did it win the Pulitzer Prize?*
> > Franklin P. Adams, "Ballade of the Annual Query"

## THE PULITZER PRIZES

The government of the United States has not done much for our writers except to invite a few of them to appear at the White House or address the Congress. It has on rare occasions appointed a man of letters, like Lowell or Hawthorne, as our diplomatic representative in some European country. There are in America, however, as in Europe, many private organizations that distribute medals and other awards to writers whom they wish to honor. The monetary value of these prizes is usually small, but the prestige they carry is sometimes reflected in the author's royalty checks, for they influence the sale of his books. In our time a large proportion of such awards has gone to the poets, who must be content to receive honors rather than the large royalties that go more often to playwrights and writers of fiction.

The selection of a writer to be honored poses difficult critical problems: How are the judges to be chosen? What criteria shall they employ? What are the limitations placed on their freedom to choose? As we shall soon see, the critical problems have not been solved by the authorities that select the winners of the Pulitzer and the Nobel prizes in the field of literature.

Joseph Pulitzer (1847–1911), one of the most successful of American journalists, stipulated that a portion of the interest on the endowment he had given to the Columbia University School of Journalism should be devoted to prizes for excellence in the fields of journalism and literature. Five of the prizes were to be awarded each year for the best works in poetry, fiction, drama, history, and biography.

Among American poets who have won the Pulitzer Prize for Poetry are Edwin Arlington Robinson, Robert Frost, Conrad Aiken, W. H. Auden, and Archibald MacLeish. The poetry prize, however, was never awarded to any one of the distinguished poets of the Fugitive group—John Crowe Ransom, Donald Davidson, or Allen Tate—until it was awarded in 1958 to Robert Penn Warren, who had won the Pulitzer Prize for Fiction in 1947. The poetry prize was never given to Wallace Stevens, Ezra Pound, or T. S. Eliot, who was eligible until he became a British subject in 1927, five years after he had published *The Waste Land.*

Joseph Pulitzer stipulated that the fiction prize should be given "For the original American novel published during the year which shall best present the wholesome atmosphere of American life and the highest standard of American manners and manhood." With such restrictions upon their freedom of choice, it is understandable that the judges passed over the controversial *Jurgen* of James Branch Cabell and even Willa Cather's *My Ántonia*. Sinclair Lewis's *Main Street* created something like a sensation—especially in the small towns—but the Pulitzer judges in 1921 gave the prize to Edith Wharton's *The Age of Innocence,* which after all is probably the better novel of the two. In 1922 the prize went not to Lewis's *Babbitt* but to Booth Tarkington's *Alice Adams*. In 1926 the judges finally decided to award the prize to Lewis for his *Arrowsmith*. He flabbergasted them by rejecting the prize. He said: "Between the Pulitzer Prizes, the American Academy of Arts and Letters and its training-school, the National Institute of Arts and Letters, amateur boards of censorship, and the inquisition of earnest literary ladies, every compulsion is put upon writers to become safe, polite, obedient, and sterile." Lewis was too good a journalist not to know that if he rejected the prize, his publishers would sell more copies of *Arrowsmith* than they would have sold if he had accepted it.

As a matter of fact, as early as 1929, when the judges awarded the fiction prize to Julia Peterkin's *Scarlet Sister Mary,* they were disregarding Pulitzer's outmoded conception of the function of a novel. Sister Mary had no less than seven illegitimate children. In 1931 the Advisory Board announced that thereafter the fiction prize would be given "for the best novel published during the year by an American writer."

The fiction prize has been given to a number of our best novelists, but in most cases the award has come late. As David Dempsey pointed out in "The Literary Prize Game" (*Horizon,* July, 1963), "Measured from *The Sun Also Rises,* published in 1926, it took the Pulitzer Advisory Board twenty-seven years to discover Hemingway. Ellen Glasgow won with her twenty-third [and last] novel, Upton Sinclair with his forty-seventh." In discussing "The Pulitzer Prizes" (*Atlantic Monthly,* July, 1957) Arthur Mizener wrote: "If you measure from Faulkner's first indubitably great novel, *The Sound and the Fury* (1929), it was twenty-six years before [the judges] discovered him." Six years after being awarded the Nobel Prize, Faulkner won the Pulitzer Prize in 1955 with

*A Fable*, two years after Hemingway had won it with *The Old Man and the Sea*.

In retrospect it is difficult to understand why men as intelligent as the Pulitzer judges could pass over some of the finest American novels published in the 1920's and award the fiction prize to such mediocre novels as Margaret Wilson's *The Able McLaughlins*, Edna Ferber's *So Big*, and Louis Bromfield's *Early Autumn*. Among the novels of that decade that failed to win the Pulitzer Prize were Dreiser's *An American Tragedy*; Ellen Glasgow's *Barren Ground* and *They Stooped to Folly*; Willa Cather's *A Lost Lady*, *The Professor's House*, and *Death Comes for the Archbishop*; Wolfe's *Look Homeward, Angel*; Faulkner's *Sartoris* and *The Sound and the Fury*; and Hemingway's *A Farewell to Arms*.

In 1940 the fiction prize was given to Steinbeck's *The Grapes of Wrath*, a book of considerable literary merit; but, it is said, the Columbia University authorities were unhappy over the award. There was no Pulitzer Prize for fiction in 1941 because, according to the New York *Times*, President Nicholas Murray Butler had forced the advisory board to overrule the decision of the judges who had chosen *For Whom the Bell Tolls*. Hemingway's novel was nevertheless both a popular and a critical success.

In *The Pulitzer Prize Novels* (1966), Professor W. J. Stuckey concluded that "the Pulitzer authorities have consistently passed over the best and most significant novels of our time." He continued:

> Before 1952 not one of the major American novelists of this century received a Pulitzer prize, although all were eligible more than once. Dreiser, Anderson, Dos Passos, Fitzgerald, Hemingway, and Faulkner head the list of those whose books were repeatedly ignored by the Pulitzer prize givers. Since 1952 Hemingway and Faulkner have received prizes but only after having established popular and widespread critical acceptance. Their prize-winning books, moreover, were clearly inferior to their earlier, more controversial work. It is quite evident that the Pulitzer authorities have made a practice of getting belatedly onto the band wagon.

In 1933, when the Pulitzer judges passed over Ellen Glasgow's *The Sheltered Life* (which she knew was one of her best books) to award the prize to T. S. Stribling's pedestrian *The Store*, she wrote to Lewis Gannett:

> Although I am still imperfectly reconciled to a world in which the noisy, the timely, and the second best almost invariably win in the race, I have learned, after thirty years of watching, that the race itself is far from important. Nothing really matters but to preserve, at whatever cost, one's own sense of artistic integrity.

In 1947 when a reporter informed Robert Penn Warren that his *All the King's Men* had won the Pulitzer Prize in fiction and asked: "How do you feel, Mr. Warren?" "I feel," replied the novelist, "guilty about all the writers better than I am who have never received the Pulitzer Prize."

> *When one reflects that the Nobel Prize was given to such third-raters as Benavente, Heidenstam, Gjellerup and Spitteler, with Conrad passed over, one begins to grasp the depth and density of the ignorance prevailing in the world, even among the relatively enlightened.*
>
> H. L. Mencken, *A Mencken Chrestomathy*

## THE NOBEL PRIZE FOR LITERATURE

The Nobel Prize for Literature carries far more prestige and a greater cash value than any of the Pulitzer prizes. It is one of the prizes established by a bequest of the Swedish inventor, Alfred Nobel (1833–1896), and it was first awarded in 1901. The literary prize has been awarded to some of the most distinguished writers of the twentieth century; among them, Anatole France, Kipling, Yeats, and T. S. Eliot. Yet one can compile a long list of distinguished European writers who have not won the Nobel Prize: Tolstoy, Ibsen, Hardy, Conrad, Zola, Proust, Valéry, Rilke, and Joyce.

As we have seen, the selection of an American novelist to receive the Pulitzer Prize poses a difficult critical problem. The selection of a Nobel Prize winner involves the further difficulty of weighing the merits of writers who are not comparable: poets, novelists, dramatists, biographers, historians, etc., most of them not living in Sweden and not writing in any of the Scandinavian languages. Doubtless also political and personal prejudices have affected the judgment of members of the Swedish Academy. It appears that Tolstoy would have been awarded the prize but for the determined opposition of the academy's long-time secretary, the poet Carl Wirsén, who disliked the Russian novelist's later books. In 1958 the academy voted to award the prize to the Russian poet Boris Pasternak for his novel, *Doctor Zhivago*, which had not been published in the Soviet Union; but the Russian authorities brought such pressure to bear upon Pasternak that he had to decline the prize.

Not until 1930 was the Nobel Prize awarded to an American writer. By that time the new American literature of the 1920's had made a strong impression upon many European intellectuals. The choice in 1930 was apparently between Theodore Dreiser and Sinclair Lewis, who won by only a single vote. It had been decided in advance to give the prize to an American writer. In a study of the reception of American literature in Sweden, Carl Anderson suggested that one reason why the prize was given to Lewis was that his unfavorable picture of American life bore a strong resemblance to that in the writings of the Norwegian novelist, Knut Hamsun, who received the award in 1920. The Nobel Prize was awarded to Lewis "for his vigorous and graphic art of description and his ability to create, with wit and humor, new types of people." Alfred Nobel had stipulated that the literary prize should be awarded to "the person who shall have produced in the field of literature the most outstanding work of an idealistic tendency." He might have been summarizing the stipulations that Joseph Pulitzer would lay down for the prize that Sinclair Lewis would decline in 1926. Far from declining the Nobel Prize, however, Lewis had for several years been urging his publishers to see that he got it.

The award to Lewis displeased a number of American writers. In his life of Lewis, Mark Shorer notes that Hemingway, "writing to a friend, called the award a filthy business whose only merit was that it eliminated the Dreiser menace." Dreiser for his part, says Shorer, "sulked in his tent." A good many academic critics felt that Lewis did not deserve the high honor; among them, Irving Babbitt, Fred Lewis Pattee, and Henry Van Dyke. Lewis was angered by Van Dyke's public statement that he was unworthy of the award, and in his acceptance speech in Stockholm he denounced professors of English for their indifference to literature written by living men and women. In *The Literature of the American People* (1951) George F. Whicher wrote: "Though by 1930 he [Lewis] had conclusively demonstrated the barrenness of his gift for novel writing, he was in that year awarded a Nobel Prize for literature, being the first American author to be so honored. His selection remains one of time's little ironies."

In 1936 the Nobel Prize was awarded to Eugene O'Neill "for the power, honesty and deep-felt emotions of his dramatic works, which embody an original concept of tragedy." The award came at a time when O'Neill's standing with other American writers was low. On November 21, 1936, Bernard De Voto published in the *Saturday Review of Literature* an editorial article entitled "Minority Report," in which he said:

> The Nobel Prize, although it was once awarded to Rabindranath Tagore, is supposed to recognize only the highest distinction in literature, and Mr. O'Neill falls short of that. He falls short of it both absolutely and relatively. Whatever his international importance, he can hardly be called an artist of the first rank; he is hardly even one of the first-rate figures of his own generation in America.

In the December 5 number of the *Saturday Review* Dorothy Canfield Fisher, Howard Mumford Jones, Elmer Davis, and others expressed their full approval of De Voto's article. Davis suggested that the awards to Lewis and O'Neill had been given to them "not as literary artists, in the sense in which literary artists have been defined in Europe from Homer's day to Proust's, but as specimens of the Noble Savage."

As we look back now from the perspective of 1971, the least defensible award to an American writer came in 1938 when the prize went to Pearl Buck, whose novel with a Chinese setting, *The Good Earth*, had won the Pulitzer Prize in 1932. Did the Swedish Academy think that Mrs. Buck was a better writer than Edith Wharton, Willa Cather, or Ellen Glasgow—to name only a few writers of fiction among American women? There was general approval of the selection of T. S. Eliot in 1948, of William Faulkner in 1949 (the award was not made until the following year), and of Ernest Hemingway in 1954. In 1962 the prize went to John Steinbeck; and, in the words of Warren French, "Steinbeck's reception of the award brought forth a spate of new criticisms, mostly expressing surprise or dismay at the award."

The student of American literature cannot help remembering the names of certain distinguished American writers who never won the Nobel Prize: Mark Twain, Henry James, William Dean Howells, Edwin Arlington Robinson, Robert Frost, Wallace Stevens, Carl Sandburg, and Scott Fitzgerald. Some of these were no doubt in Hemingway's mind when he wrote in accepting the Nobel Prize: "No writer who knows the great writers who did not receive the prize can accept it other than with humility."

*A new book is the property, the prey of ephemeral criticism, which it darts triumphantly upon; there is a raw thin air about it, not filled up by any recorded opinion; and curiosity, impertinence, and vanity rush eagerly into the vacuum.*
William Hazlitt, "On Reading Old Books"

*One of my fantasies is to think of the literary scene as a stock exchange of writers. A characteristic in this country is the marked fluctuation of authors' reputations. If a writer gets a great deal of praise, it doesn't take a keen-eyed prophet to tell that within five years his stock will have sunk below par. And if any author of talent is completely neglected as Fitzgerald was for fifteen years, then you can bet with a good chance of winning your money that his stock will jump up to*

> 500 or 600 on the exchange. After a while you become cynical
> about the prevailing quotations. You judge a writer by what
> he is worth and you risk your status on the bet that some day
> his stock will be back at par.
>
> Malcolm Cowley quoted in Harvey Breit,
> *The Writer Observed*

## CRITICAL POLLS AND INDIVIDUAL ESTIMATES: AUTHORS

In the late nineteenth century the avowed purpose of the editors of the *Critic* in polling its readers was to select those writers and artists worthiest to constitute a non-existent American academy of arts and letters. After the founding of the academy a new generation of magazine editors continued to initiate polls because they knew that their readers would be interested in the results.

By 1920 a new generation of writers was attracting wide attention. There were new poets, novelists, and playwrights and also a new generation of literary journalists eager to promote their fame. The young intellectuals were taking over the book review sections of the metropolitan newspapers. They were also taking over some of the older publishing houses and literary magazines and were establishing new magazines and new publishing houses. They were also vigorously attacking the traditional canon of the great American writers. Their motto might well have been "Pereant isti qui ante nos nostra dixerunt."

Vanity Fair, Bookman, *and* Literary Digest *(1922)*. The year 1922, as I have indicated earlier, marked a turning point in our literary history. In that year, within a period of four months, no less than three influential magazines announced the results of their critical polls. In April when *Vanity Fair* published its findings under the caption "The New Order of Critical Values," the editors explained:

> A great Transvaluation of Values, to use the Nietzschean phrase, has
> recently taken place in America. A new set of Critics has arisen to take
> the place of the old; in Poetry, Mr. [Louis] Untermeyer's gang of pi-
> rates has scuttled Stedman's Anthology; in ideas, The New Republic
> and The Freeman have eclipsed The Atlantic Monthly of W. D.
> Howells....

In July when the *Literary Digest* brought out the results of its poll, it printed the following paragraph from a communication sent to the editors by H. L. Mencken:

We are in the midst of a shifting of standards. The dominant critical opinion of the United States, once strongly Puritan, has become very anti-Puritan, and it has, to some extent, carried the more enlightened sort of public opinion with it. The change is visible in the collapse of the reputation of Howells. But I doubt that it has materially modified the position of Emerson, Hawthorne and Poe, it has unquestionably helped Whitman and Mark Twain.

In May of the same year the *Bookman* published the results of its poll under the title "Spring Elections on Mount Olympus." The editor commented on the results of the *Vanity Fair* poll: "They [the ten judges] are lukewarm toward the Victorian poets and novelists and skeptical of all the moderns except Sherwood Anderson. . . . their stern judgment of the American poets amounts almost to hostility."

In each of the first two polls the judges were given a long and miscellaneous list of names of well-known persons whom they were asked to rank on a scale running from +25 to −25. The nine judges of the *Bookman* gave Longfellow only +.6 of a point; they gave Henry James +9 and Walt Whitman +17.1. The ten judges of *Vanity Fair* gave Whitman +15.8. On both magazine polls the judges rated William Butler Yeats a better poet than Alfred Tennyson. The *Bookman* gave Tennyson only +2 points; *Vanity Fair* gave him +6.3. Yeats's score was +9 in *Vanity Fair* and +12.3 in the *Bookman*. Nietzsche's vogue among American intellectuals was near its peak in 1922; the *Bookman* gave him +13.2 points and *Vanity Fair*, +19. On each poll Shakespeare scored exactly +22.4 points. The *Bookman* judges gave Milton +19.4 points, but the more radical judges of *Vanity Fair* gave him only +7.1; Burton Rascoe gave him −15. *Vanity Fair* gave Ezra Pound +4.1 points and Edwin Arlington Robinson +3.5. The *Bookman* gave Theodore Dreiser +9.2 points; Sherwood Anderson, +7.7; and James Branch Cabell, +6.7. I give below the scores of the nine American writers who were included in both polls:

|  | Vanity Fair | Bookman |
|---|---|---|
| Sinclair Lewis | + .7 | + 5.3 |
| Amy Lowell | + .7 | − .3 |
| H. L. Mencken | + 8.5 | + 8.7 |
| Paul Elmer More | − 8.5 | − 9.9 |
| George Jean Nathan | + 5.3 | + 5.3 |
| Eugene O'Neill | + 7.8 | + 8.4 |
| Louis Untermeyer | + 4.0 | + 4.7 |
| Edith Wharton | + 5.5 | +10.0 |
| Walt Whitman | +15.8 | +17.1 |

The majority of the judges selected by both the *Bookman* and *Vanity Fair* were literary journalists. *Vanity Fair*'s panel of ten consisted of Heywood Broun, Henry McBride, H. L. Mencken, George Jean Nathan, Burton Rascoe, Paul Rosenfeld, Gilbert Seldes, Deems Taylor, Edmund Wilson, and Willard Huntington Wright. *The Bookman's* jury of nine consisted of Ernest Boyd, Henry Seidel Canby, Floyd Dell, John Farrar, Llewellyn Jones, Ludwig Lewisohn, John Macy, Louis Untermeyer, and Carl Van Doren.

On neither poll did the judges take their task very seriously. Their reactions were obviously emotional rather than intellectual. Mencken, for example, gave o to Milton, Petrarch, Marcus Aurelius, Picasso, Racine, Raphael, Sir Walter Scott, Sophocles, Shelley, and Tennyson. He gave Whitman +20 and Tolstoy −20. He gave +10 to both Sinclair Lewis and Eugene O'Neill and, surprisingly, +25 to Plato. Burton Rascoe gave −25 to Ruskin, Scott, and Henry Van Dyke; to Milton he gave −15. John Macy gave +1 to no less than eleven authors: Sherwood Anderson, Theodore Dreiser, Floyd Dell, Scott Fitzgerald, James Joyce, Ring Lardner, Longfellow, O'Neill, Sinclair Lewis, Sandburg, and Mencken. Van Doren gave o to Tennyson, Browning, Longfellow, and Paul Elmer More. To Kipling he gave −10, but to Lewis he gave +10 and to Cabell +18. He gave +25 to Shakespeare and +22 to both Bernard Shaw and Tolstoy.

The *Literary Digest*'s poll, published on July 22, 1922, under the title "America's Literary Stars," included only living writers. The *Digest* had asked fifty-six magazine editors and literary advisers to publishing houses (only thirty-three complied): "Whom would you name, offhand, as the five leading American literary stars that have risen above the horizon in the past ten years?" The sixteen writers who were ranked highest, with the number of votes each received, were:

1. Joseph Hergesheimer, 22
2. Eugene O'Neill, 14
3. Sherwood Anderson, 13
4. Willa Cather, 12
5. Robert Frost and James Branch Cabell, 8
6. Edgar Lee Masters, 7
7. Sinclair Lewis and Edna St. Vincent Millay, 6
8. Carl Sandburg, Hendrik Van Loon, and Edwin Arlington Robinson, 5
9. Amy Lowell and Scott Fitzgerald, 4
10. Don Marquis and John Dos Passos, 3

It is difficult nowadays to realize that intelligent critics could rate Masters as a poet higher than Robinson or regard Hergesheimer as a better novelist than Willa Cather. The modern reader looks in vain for the names of such poets as Eliot, Pound, and Stevens. We do not find these names in the lists sent in by four of the most intelligent critics on the *Digest* panel. Van Wyck Brooks named Sherwood Anderson, Willa Cather, Conrad Aiken, Edwin Arlington Robinson, and Randolph Bourne. Henry Seidel Canby, who named seven writers, listed Robert Frost, Vachel Lindsay, Edgar Lee Masters, Joseph Hergesheimer, James Branch Cabell, Amy Lowell, and Willa Cather. Ludwig Lewisohn's five were in order of importance: H. L. Mencken, Joseph Hergesheimer, Sherwood Anderson, Eugene O'Neill, and William Ellery Leonard. On Carl Van Doren's list were the names of Sherwood Anderson, Robert Frost, Joseph Hergesheimer, Edna St. Vincent Millay, and Carl Sandburg. Presumably Van Doren omitted his favorite Cabell on the ground that he had "risen above the horizon" more than ten years earlier.

*Booksellers' Poll* ( 1921 ). On September 24, 1921, the *Publishers' Weekly* printed the results of its poll under the title "Leading Names in Contemporary American Literature: The Result of a Ballot among the Booksellers." The literary taste of the two hundred booksellers who were polled was more old-fashioned than that of those who participated in the three magazine polls of 1922. The booksellers were no doubt impressed by the sensational success in 1920 of *Main Street*, but they rated Henry Van Dyke and Winston Churchill as better writers than Sinclair Lewis. They still thought highly of the novels they had read in their youth by writers as unfashionable in the 1920's as Thomas Nelson Page and Margaret Deland.

The booksellers were instructed not to rate books merely by their salability, but how was a busy bookseller, with the best will in the world, to find time to read books written by the forty writers who made the final list—not to mention others who had some claim to his consideration? He was in the business of selling books, and, like his customers, he was influenced by reviews and advertisements in the metropolitan newspapers. Moreover, so many persons came into his bookstore asking for books by Joseph C. Lincoln, Kathleen Norris, Zane Grey, and Mary Roberts Rinehart that he felt they ought to be on the final list.

The books most in demand in the bookstores were fiction, and in the final list of forty writers there are just six poets and only one dramatist, O'Neill. It is at first surprising that the booksellers should give Edith Wharton a slight preference over Joseph Hergesheimer, but then one remembers that in 1921 *The Age of Innocence* was a best seller and a Pulitzer Prize novel. But why, one wonders, did not more booksellers see that Willa Cather was a better writer than Gertrude Atherton? The booksellers no doubt knew that in 1921 the vogue of the new poetry was on the wane. They did not include among the final forty the names of Ezra Pound, T. S. Eliot, Edna St. Vincent Millay, or Sara Teasdale; and they ranked Amy Lowell (7 points) and Edgar Lee Masters (8) as better poets than Frost (13), Robinson (16), Lindsay (21), and Sandburg (39).

| | |
|---|---|
| 1. Booth Tarkington | 21. Vachel Lindsay |
| 2. Edith Wharton | 22. Mary Roberts Rinehart |
| 3. Joseph Hergesheimer | 23. Irving Bacheller |
| 4. Henry Van Dyke | 24. H. L. Mencken |
| 5. Gertrude Atherton | 25. Agnes Repplier |
| 6. Winston Churchill | 26. Eugene O'Neill |
| 7. Amy Lowell | 27. Irvin S. Cobb |
| 8. Edgar Lee Masters | 28. William Roscoe Thayer |
| 9. James Branch Cabell | 29. Frederick O'Brien |
| 10. Sinclair Lewis | 30. Zane Grey |
| 11. Joseph Lincoln | 31. Woodrow Wilson |
| 12. Owen Wister | 32. Stewart Edward White |
| 13. Robert Frost | 33. Kathleen Norris |
| 14. Theodore Dreiser | 34. Gene Stratton Porter |
| 15. Dorothy Canfield Fisher | 35. Thomas Nelson Page |
| 16. Edwin Arlington Robinson | 36. Alice Brown |
| 17. Christopher Morley | 37. Brander Matthews |
| 18. Margaret Deland | 38. Mary Watts |
| 19. Zona Gale | 39. Carl Sandburg |
| 20. Willa Cather | 40. Kate Douglas Wiggin |

Booth Tarkington, whose name led all the rest in the Booksellers' Poll, was still in 1921—the year he published *Alice Adams*—a very popular novelist. He was not, however, as we shall see later, the favorite of any one of the nine judges on the *Bookman*'s second poll in 1927. On July 23, 1922, the New York *Times* included Tarkington's name as the very last in its composite list of the "Twelve Greatest [Living] American Men." On the same day the *Times* published an editorial entitled "Greatness in Literature," in which it commented: "Mr. TARKINGTON is perhaps the best of our male novelists—the existence of Mrs. WHARTON necessitates the sexual qualification—but his pre-eminence is not exactly that of Everest among the Himalayas." Tarkington was not greatly impressed even though he was the only writer among the twelve named by the *Times*. " 'Yes, I got in as last on the *Times* list,' he commented: 'What darned silliness! You *can* demonstrate who are the 10 *fattest* people in a country and who are the 27 tallest . . . but you can't say who are the greatest with any more authority than you can say who are the 13 damnedest fools.' "

*Book Collectors' Polls* (*1936, 1948*). In its autumn issue for 1936 the *Colophon: A Quarterly for Booklovers* announced the results of a poll it had taken of its readers, who had been asked to name the twenty living American writers most likely to be regarded as classics in A.D. 2000. Twelve years later a similar poll was taken by the *Colophon*'s successor, the *New Colophon: A Book Collectors' Quarterly*. The results of the second poll were announced in the January, 1949, issue. Between 1936 and 1948 came the Second World War, and in the latter year certain writers were obviously losing ground. Cabell, who was 10th in 1936, was not among the top twenty in 1948. Edna St. Vincent Millay had sunk from 4th place to 10th. In the same period, however, Eliot's standing rose from 20th to 7th; Van Wyck Brooks's from 28th to 13th; and Thornton Wilder's from 29th to 11th. Mencken rose from 12th place to 8th; Hemingway from 13th to 4th; and Sandburg from 17th to 5th. In 1948 John Steinbeck was ranked 6th, but in 1936 no one seems to have mentioned him. Wallace Stevens apparently got few or no votes in either 1936 or 1948. In the 1936 poll, the *Colophon* stated, Scott Fitzgerald, Joseph Hergesheimer, and William McFee got only six votes "between them." The passing of a dozen years brought little change in the relative standings of Eugene O'Neill, Sinclair Lewis, Robert Frost, Hervey Allen, H. L. Mencken, and George Santayana. The following writers who had figured in the 1936 poll were no longer living in 1948: Stephen Vincent Benét, Willa Cather, Theodore Dreiser, Ellen Glasgow, Booth Tarkington, Edith Wharton, and Thomas Wolfe.

| *Colophon* (1936) | points | *New Colophon* (1948) | points |
|---|---|---|---|
| 1. Sinclair Lewis | 332 | 1. Eugene O'Neill | 346 |
| 2. Willa Cather | 304 | 2. Sinclair Lewis | 344 |
| 3. Eugene O'Neill | 292 | 3. Robert Frost | 329 |
| 4. Edna St. Vincent Millay | 205 | 4. Ernest Hemingway | 293 |
| 5. Robert Frost | 180 | 5. Carl Sandburg | 275 |
| 6. Theodore Dreiser | 149 | 6. John Steinbeck | 249 |
| 7. James Truslow Adams | 115 | 7. T. S. Eliot | 152 |
| 8. George Santayana | 113 | 8. H. L. Mencken | 150 |
| 9. Stephen Vincent Benét | 91 | 9. George Santayana | 145 |
| 10. James Branch Cabell | 90 | 10. Edna St. Vincent Millay | 136 |
| 11. Thomas Wolfe | | 11. Thornton Wilder | |
| 12. H. L. Mencken | | 12. Hervey Allen | |
| 13. Ernest Hemingway | | 13. Van Wyck Brooks | |
| 14. Hervey Allen | | 14. William Faulkner | |
| 15. John Dos Passos | | 15. Albert Einstein | |
| 16. Edith Wharton | | 16. Thomas Mann | |
| 17. Carl Sandburg | | 17. John Dos Passos | |

*The Limited Editions Club Awards (1954).* The literary taste of the book collectors, like that of the booksellers, was more old-fashioned than that of literary critics like Carl Van Doren and Edmund Wilson. In 1954 the Limited Editions Club in New York awarded silver medals to ten living American authors who had published books adjudged "the most likely to endure as the classics of our time": Van Wyck Brooks, Rachel Carson, Bernard De Voto, William Faulkner, Robert Frost, Ernest Hemingway, H. L. Mencken, Samuel Eliot Morison, Carl Sandburg, and John Steinbeck. The literary student of today may well question the inclusion of half the names on this list. In particular, he will note that Edmund Wilson is now considered a better literary critic than Bernard De Voto, and he will wonder why the Limited Editions Club overlooked so fine a poet as Wallace Stevens.

Various critics have had the temerity to climb out on a long limb, as Bernard De Voto once phrased it, and attempt to single out our greatest writers. In October, 1932, Henry Hazlitt, then literary editor of the New York *Nation*, published an article in the *Forum* entitled "Our Greatest Authors: How Great Are They?" "Not more than three or four of our current writers—at most—," he said, "seem likely to achieve a place as great as that already held by a dozen American writers of the past." Hazlitt's first choice was George Santayana; his second, T. S. Eliot. The contest for other high places, he said, was among Dreiser, Lewis, O'Neill, Frost, and Robinson Jeffers. He failed to mention Hemingway, Faulkner, Scott Fitzgerald, Wolfe, Stevens, or any of the better-known women poets and novelists.

On some twentieth-century polls Santayana had been ignored or given a lower rating than he deserves, but has any one besides Hazlitt pronounced him the greatest American writer of this century? O'Neill and Frost still hold their own, but nowadays Wallace Stevens and Edwin Arlington Robinson are held in higher critical esteem than Robinson Jeffers. Scott Fitzgerald is now regarded as a major novelist of the twentieth century while Lewis's claim is perhaps no better than that of Thomas Wolfe, Edith Wharton, Willa Cather, or Ellen Glasgow.

With Hazlitt's mediocre record as a literary prophet one may compare that of the *Dial* under the editorship of Scofield Thayer and Marianne Moore in the years 1920–1929. Notable recipients of the *Dial* award were Sherwood Anderson, Van Wyck Brooks, Kenneth Burke, E. E. Cummings (he was a *Dial* discovery), T. S. Eliot, Marianne Moore, Ezra Pound, and William Carlos Williams. In 1929, the year the *Dial* expired, the editors considered giving the award to Wallace Stevens but gave it to Burke instead.

*Edmund Wilson, "The All-Star Literary Vaudeville" (1926).* A remarkable appraisal of the better-known American writers of the early 1920's appeared in the *New Republic* for June 30, 1926, under the title "The All-Star Literary Vaudeville." The unsigned article was written by the youthful Edmund Wilson (1895–), who began it by remarking that he really felt "only the mildest interest in most of the literary goods which now find so wide a market." The new generation of writers had won their battle for an audience, and now he found it difficult to distinguish "the reviews from the advertising: both tend to convey the impression that masterpieces are being manufactured as regularly and as durably as new models of motor-cars." The American novelists, Wilson noted, were considered "our principal glory"; and yet, he added: "I must confess that I cannot read our novelists." Not one of them belonged in the same class as Henry James, Marcel Proust, and James Joyce. "Dreiser rightly commands our respect; but he writes so badly that it is almost impossible to read him, and, for that reason, I have difficulty in believing in his literary permanence." Sinclair Lewis, said Wilson, possesses "a vigorous satiric humor," but his novels "have beauty neither of style nor of form and they tell us nothing new about life." "Willa Cather is a good craftsman but she is usually dull. In spite of a few distinguished stories, she suffers from an anaemia of the imagination . . . and is given to terrible lapses into feminine melodrama." James Branch Cabell, "though a man of real parts," seemed to Wilson sentimental and "intolerably insipid"; and "the whole Poictesme business" bored the critic "beyond description." "Joseph Hergesheimer, though he can tell a story, writes nearly as badly in a fancy way as Dreiser does in a crude one: the judgment of him that I most agree with is the remark attributed to Max Beerbohm, 'Poor Mr. Hergesheimer, he wants so much to be an artist.' " Wilson was more hopeful about two younger novelists, John Dos Passos and Scott Fitzgerald; but the best work in American fiction, he thought, was to be found in short stories, especially those of

Sherwood Anderson, Ring Lardner, Gertrude Stein, and Ernest Hemingway. All of these employed "the same simple colloquial language based directly on the vocabulary and rhythm of American speech; and, if there can be said to be an American school of writing . . . these writers would seem to represent it." All of them, he suggested, were indebted to Mark Twain's masterpiece, *Huckleberry Finn.*

Coming to the literary critics, Wilson had praise for Van Wyck Brooks and Paul Rosenfeld. H. L. Mencken, whom "the youngest literary generation" had now thrown overboard, was "perhaps a prophet rather than a critic." Wilson was tired of Mencken's continual repetition of his limited stock of ideas, but at the same time he insisted that Mencken was "ordinarily underrated as a writer of English prose." Wilson had unexpected words of praise for the most unpopular of the literary critics:

> The much abused Paul Elmer More remains our only professional critic whose learning is really great and whose efforts are ambitious. His prose is quite graceless and charmless, but always accurate and clear; his point of view, though a product of Puritan rationalism, is definitely formulated and possesses the force of deep and serious conviction; and, though hopelessly deficient in artistic sensibility, he has become, in so far as it is possible to be without it, a real master of ideas.

"As for poetry," Wilson continued, "the new movement of twelve years ago seemed at the time to assume impressive proportions. But who can believe in its heroes now?" Carl Sandburg, he said, was a better poet than Edgar Lee Masters or Vachel Lindsay, but Wilson was "disappointed . . . to discover how meager appear his emotions and how obvious his ideas." "The work of Amy Lowell," he said, "is like a great empty cloisonné jar; that of [John Gould] Fletcher a great wall of hard descriptive prose mistaken for poetry." Wilson had reservations, too, about Conrad Aiken, Marianne Moore, H.D., and William Carlos Williams. He thought somewhat more highly of Wallace Stevens, who had "a fascinating nonsense gift of words . . . and [was] a charming decorative artist." E. E. Cummings had a remarkable lyric gift but was a poor artist. For Ezra Pound, Wilson had praise as "a champion and pioneer," but Pound's many fine passages seemed "only fragments in the patternless mosaic of a monument to poetic bankruptcy."

Wilson's most surprising failure to appreciate one of his really great contemporaries is seen in his summary disposal of Robert Frost, who, he said, "has a thin but authentic vein of poetic sensibility; but he is excessively dull and writes abominable verse. In my opinion, he is the most generally overrated of this group of poets." Wilson noted that the younger poets were now having great difficulty in getting their poems published. The magazines, "which, having brought out two or three crops of poets, seem content to close the canon, and have no place for the new poetry of unknown men—even if so obviously gifted as Allen Tate or Phelps Putnam—who cannot be found in Mr. Untermeyer's anthologies or among the charter contributors to *The Dial.*" Wilson suggested that the women poets—Lizette Woodworth Reese, Edna St. Vincent Millay, Sara Teasdale, and Elinor Wylie—"though less pretentious," were "more rewarding than the men: their emotion is more genuine and their literary instinct surer."

Wilson left to the last the two poets whom he admired most: T. S. Eliot and Edwin Arlington Robinson. Wilson had written one of the best critical explications of *The Waste Land*; and now though he deplored "the mood of extreme fatigue and despondency which seems lately to have been drying up both his poetry and his criticism," he added: "Both as poet and as critic, he deserves the position of influence which he now occupies." Robinson seemed to Wilson to have, like Eliot, "the authentic lyric gift and the artist's mastery of it." He was in Wilson's opinion "the last and, artistically (leaving the happiest flashes of Emerson aside), the most important of the New England poets."

Wilson ended on the hopeful note that perhaps one might find among his contemporaries the peers of Emerson, Whitman, Poe, Thoreau, and Melville. He added a very unconventional estimate of certain unfashionable older American writers:

> And when we look back on the literary era which preceded the recent renascence, we are surprised, after all that has been written about its paleness, its tameness and its sterility, to realize the high standard of excellence to which its best writers attained. When we consider Henry James, Stephen Crane, and such lesser novelists as Cable and Howells, with such critics as Babbitt, Brownell and Paul Elmer More, who belong essentially to the same era, we are struck with certain superiorities over the race of writers of today. These men, in general, with less liberal ideas, possessed a sounder culture than we; and though less lively, were better craftsmen. They were professional men of letters and they had thoroughly learned their trade.

That is the kind of judicial appraisal one might have expected to come twenty years later from a competent academic literary historian rather than from a young metropolitan literary journalist who held left-wing political opinions. In 1926 when Wilson published "The All-Star Literary Vaudeville," he was at the age of thirty-one not far from the beginning of a distinguished career. Thirty years later when he reprinted the essay in *A Literary Chronicle, 1920–1950*, he modified only slightly a few of his earlier estimates. In 1955 Robert E. Spiller was to write in *The Cycle of American Literature*: "To Wilson must be credited the most impressive body of literary criticism produced by any one writer of this generation."

*Malcolm Cowley* (ed.), After the Genteel Tradition, 1910–1930 (*1937*). This symposium, which bore the descriptive subtitle *American Writers since 1910*, contains essays of varying degrees of merit by different hands. The fourteen essays are: (1) "Theodore Dreiser," by John Chamberlain; (2) "Upton Sinclair," by Robert Cantwell; (3) "Willa Cather," by Lionel Trilling; (4) "Van Wyck Brooks," by Bernard Smith; (5) "Carl Sandburg," by Newton Arvin; (6) "Sherwood Anderson," by Robert Morss Lovett; (7) "H. L. Mencken," by Louis Kronenberger; (8) "Sinclair Lewis," by Robert Cantwell; (9) "Eugene O'Neill," by Lionel Trilling; (10) "The James Branch Cabell Period," by Peter Monro Jack; (11) "Two Poets: Jeffers and Millay," by Hildegarde Flanner; (12) "Dos Passos: Poet against the World," by Malcolm Cowley; (13) "Homage to Hemingway," by John Peale Bishop; and (14) "Thomas Wolfe," by Hamilton Basso.

The book is dedicated to Van Wyck Brooks, "who will not agree with some of our ideas, but who nevertheless helped us to reach them." Cowley's foreword, "The Revolt against Gentility," is built around Sinclair Lewis's Stockholm address, and the reader feels that the authors discussed in the book are chiefly those whom Lewis had singled out for praise. The New Critics and the New Humanists are conspicuously absent both as authors and as essayists. There is a chapter on Carl Sandburg and another that deals with both Robinson Jeffers and Edna St. Vincent Millay, but there are no chapters on Robert Frost, Edwin Arlington Robinson, Wallace Stevens, T. S. Eliot, Ezra Pound, Conrad Aiken, E. E. Cummings, Sara Teasdale, Amy Lowell or any one of the Fugitive poets. The symposium includes essays on eight novelists, one of whom is Upton Sinclair, but there is none on Scott Fitzgerald, Ellen Glasgow, or William Faulkner. By 1937 Cowley had already reviewed two of Faulkner's books, but it was to be nine years before he would bring out *The Portable Faulkner*, a book that would contribute notably to the Faulkner revival.

In his "Postscript: Twenty Years of American Literature" Cowley made a large claim for the writers of the 1920's who, he thought, "naturalized the profession of letters in a country that had come to think of it as a foreign or female accomplishment. They found an audience for serious books and, in spite of their personal failures, they created a new literary tradition." And yet Cowley felt that "hardly any of these writers chose and carried out the work they might have completed." He pointed to Dreiser and Upton Sinclair, "whose blunders are so enormous" and to Lewis "with his continual nasal jokes that end by being more tiresome than the business men they are intended to hit off, and Hergesheimer with his rhythms tortured to hide a simple meaning, and Cabell with his adjectives that ring false, and O'Neill with his bad and tasteless style."

One thinks of Carl Sandburg traveling round the country with his guitar, a great poet hired as an entertainer for business men's luncheon clubs; one thinks of Van Wyck Brooks retiring from the field of contemporary letters and writing historical portraits completely insulated from the life that used to inspire him to hope or anger. And one cannot help feeling that the talent of all these writers was somehow being diverted and dispersed at the very moment when that work was being praised most extravagantly.

Perhaps Cowley when he came to write his "Postscript" felt doubts about the greatness of some of the fourteen authors discussed in his book. Perhaps also he had come to feel that he had left out certain writers who were more important than some whom he had included. In the "Postscript" he referred to Eliot as "the most influential poet of the decade," but he had no word of praise for Eliot's critical essays. Cowley obviously was not ready to accept Eliot's contention that the true Anglo-American literary tradition stemmed from John Donne and other seventeenth-century English poets.

In the 1964 edition of *After the Genteel Tradition* Cowley added an essay on Edwin Arlington Robinson that he had written in 1948. He noted that "among our poets of stature he is the one who paid the highest price in his life for having rejected optimism and ideality." Cowley thought of including Robert Frost, but "his work," he said, "stands somewhat apart from the movement we were trying to revalue." Cowley noted that there were important younger writers like Hemingway and Dos Passos who did not fit into the pattern he had adopted. Cowley thus explained why he left out Conrad Aiken, Amy Lowell, John Gould Fletcher, Ezra Pound, and T. S. Eliot: "They too were in revolt against the genteel tradition, but only in so far as it interfered with the writing of honest and experimental poems. Most of them lived abroad. At first they had little interest in social questions, they were trying to establish literature as an independent country, with a history and geography of its own."

*Where are the novels of yesteryear? In what dim limbo of deserted circulating libraries do they now repose unmolested, with the dust thickening upon their heads?*
                    Brander Matthews, *These Many Years*

*My task which I am trying to achieve is, by the power of the written word, to make you hear, to make you feel—it is, before all, to make you see. That—and no more, and it is everything. If I succeed, you shall find there according to your deserts: encouragement, consolation, fear, charm—all you demand and, perhaps, also that glimpse of truth for which you have forgotten to ask.*
                    Joseph Conrad, "Preface," *The Nigger of the Narcissus*

## CRITICAL POLLS AND INDIVIDUAL ESTIMATES: FICTION

*Bookman's Second Poll: "The All American Fiction Nine" (1927).* In June, 1927, the *Bookman* printed the results of a poll which was undertaken to identify "the greatest living American writers." The results were announced under the caption "The All American Fiction Nine" in spite of the fact that two of the nine authors chosen were not novelists but poets. The nine judges with their selections were: Bruce Bliven: Theodore Dreiser; Witter Bynner: Edna St. Vincent Millay; Dorothy Canfield: Robert Frost; R. L. Duffus: Sinclair Lewis; John H. McGinnis: Theodore Dreiser or James Branch Cabell; Emily Post: Sherwood Anderson; Frances Newman: James Branch Cabell; Helen Woodward: W. E. Woodward; and Stark Young: Sherwood Anderson.

McGinnis felt that whether one picked Dreiser or Cabell depended upon one's critical criteria. He did not indicate his own preference. Helen Woodward, for reasons of her own, selected her husband. Hergesheimer and Tarkington, who stood highest on earlier polls, were not mentioned on this one. That was perhaps to be expected, but it seems strange that there were no votes for Willa Cather, Edith Wharton, Ellen Glasgow, Edwin Arlington Robinson, Scott Fitzgerald, Carl Sandburg, or T. S. Eliot, who did not become a British subject until 1927.

*A Psychologists' Poll (1929).* Two young psychologists from universities in the Middle West, who apparently regarded earlier polls as without any scientific basis, undertook one of their own. John M. Stalnaker and Fred Eggan published their findings in the *English Journal* for April, 1929, under the title "American Novelists Ranked: A Psychological Study." Stalnaker and Eggan asked sixty-five "outstanding critics" to rank seventy-two American novelists by arranging them in ten groups according to their "general literary merit." Of the sixty-five critics who were asked to take part in the poll only thirty-one sent in usable replies. Zona Gale's reply came in too late to be used. John Macy, who declined to take part in the poll, wrote: "It is impossible to rank novelists or other people who think. Psychologists can be ranked with fair accuracy as sub-morons." Undeterred by so discouraging a reply, Stalnaker and Eggan used these two sentences as epigraph for their article.

After studying the returns, the psychologists classified the novelists in five rather than in ten groups. Within each of the five groups the names of the novelists are arranged in no fixed order, and the number of authors included varies from group to group. Stalnaker and Eggan regarded Hemingway (whose *A Farewell to Arms* appeared in 1929) as only a writer of short stories. Nevertheless nine of the "outstanding critics" gave him so high a rating that he won a place in the third group.

### The Critics

| | |
|---|---|
| Thomas Beer | Don Marquis |
| Ernest Boyd | K. B. Murdock |
| Percy Boynton | George Jean Nathan |
| Herschel Brickell | V. L. Parrington |
| Van Wyck Brooks | Fred Lewis Pattee |
| Fanny Butcher | Louise Pound |
| Henry Seidel Canby | Burton Rascoe |
| Elmer Davis | Upton Sinclair |
| Zona Gale | Vincent Starrett |
| Isaac Goldberg | William K. Stewart |
| E. Haldeman-Julius | Lewis [sic] Untermeyer |
| Archibald Henderson | Dorothy Van Doren |
| Llewellyn Jones | Mark Van Doren |
| Joseph Wood Krutch | Hendrick Van Loon |
| Henry Goddard Leach | William Allen White |
| Robert Morss Lovett | Stanley Williams |

### The Novelists

Group 1
Willa Cather . . . . . 30*
Edith Wharton . . . . 30

Group 2
Theodore Dreiser . . . 31
James Branch Cabell . . 29

* Number of critics who ranked each artist.

| | | | |
|---|---|---|---|
| Sherwood Anderson | . . 30 | Edna Ferber . . . . . | 29 |
| Sinclair Lewis . . . . | 31 | DuBose Heyward . . . | 21 |
| | | Hamlin Garland . . . . | 26 |

**Group 3**

| | | | |
|---|---|---|---|
| Thornton Wilder . . . | 24 | **Group 5** | |
| Glenway Wescott . . . | 22 | F. Scott Fitzgerald . . . | 28 |
| Joseph Hergesheimer . . | 30 | Mary Austin . . . . . | 26 |
| Zona Gale . . . . . . | 29 | John Dos Passos . . . . | 28 |
| Booth Tarkington . . . | 29 | John Erskine . . . . . | 28 |
| Ellen Glasgow . . . . | 29 | Anne Parrish . . . . . | 21 |
| Ernest Hemingway . . . | ? | Robert Nathan . . . . | 24 |
| | | Dorothy Canfield Fisher . | 29 |

**Group 4**

| | | | |
|---|---|---|---|
| Elizabeth Madox Roberts . | 20 | Mary Johnston . . . . | 26 |
| Ruth Suckow . . . . . | 27 | Thomas Boyd . . . . . | 19 |
| William McFee . . . . | 27 | Christopher Morley . . . | 27 |
| Robert Herrick . . . . | 28 | James Boyd . . . . . | 18 |
| Thomas Beer . . . . . | 26 | Upton Sinclair . . . . . | 28 |
| Elinor Wylie . . . . . | 28 | Carl Van Vechten . . . . | 28 |
| Louis Bromfield . . . . | 27 | Floyd Dell . . . . . . | 29 |

The pollsters' method of procedure is not altogether clear to me, and I see little that is scientific about it. For each novelist they give the number of judges who ranked him, but they do not give the individual rankings of any of the judges. They thus explain why it was that they placed Willa Cather and Edith Wharton in group one. Willa Cather was placed in the highest group by twenty judges and in groups three, four, and five by one each. Sixteen judges placed Mrs. Wharton in the highest of the ten groups; ten placed her in the second group; and four in the third group.

There was evidently no unanimity of opinion among the thirty-one judges as to the merits of the seventy-two writers included in the poll. Nevertheless the results do reflect changes in the reputations of certain novelists in the seven years since the 1922 polls. The two top novelists in 1929—if the psychologists were right—were both women. Willa Cather had been fourth on the *Literary Digest*'s poll in 1922, but no woman novelist was the favorite of any one of the nine critics who in 1927 had taken part in the *Bookman*'s second poll. Booth Tarkington and Joseph Hergesheimer, who had enjoyed great popularity in 1922, were in 1929 demoted to the third group while Floyd Dell, Dorothy Canfield Fisher, Upton Sinclair, and Mary Johnston were now relegated to the fifth and lowest category. Also in the fifth group were John Dos Passos and F. Scott Fitzgerald, each of whom would eventually attain a much higher rating. Also on their way up were two novelists in the third group: Thornton Wilder and Ellen Glasgow. The list of critics assembled by the psychologists is a distinguished one, but few if any of them voted to include William Faulkner, who in 1929 published two of his greatest novels, *Sartoris* and *The Sound and the Fury*.

*William Lyon Phelps Lists the Best American Novels (1930).* William Lyon Phelps (1865–1943) gave at Yale University in the 1890's what was one of the first college courses in contemporary fiction ever offered in this country. In his books he discussed a wide variety of writers, including many of his own contemporaries. He was (after Brander Matthews) one of the very first academic critics to rank Mark Twain as a great writer. His literary taste, however, was essentially conservative. He praised the great Russian novelists, but he underrated many of the best French writers of fiction.

A popular feature in *Scribner's Magazine* was Phelps's miscellany, "As I Like It." In October, 1930, he printed a list of what he regarded as the one hundred best novels. The thirteen American titles chosen were: Nathaniel Hawthorne, *The Scarlet Letter*, and *The House of the Seven Gables*; Harriet Beecher Stowe, *Uncle Tom's Cabin*; Henry James, *The American*, and *The Portrait of a Lady*; William Dean Howells, *A Modern Instance*; Mark Twain, *The Adventures of Tom Sawyer*, and *The Adventures of Huckleberry Finn*; Stephen Crane, *The Red Badge of Courage*; Jack London, *The Call of the Wild*; Edith Wharton, *The Age of Innocence*; Sinclair Lewis, *Dodsworth*; and Thornton Wilder, *The Bridge of San Luis Rey*.

As a modern reader looks over this list, he wonders why Phelps did not make a place for any novels written by Sherwood Anderson, James Branch Cabell, Willa Cather, Theodore Dreiser, John Dos Passos, Scott Fitzgerald, Ellen Glasgow, Ernest Hemingway, Thomas Wolfe, or William Faulkner. It should be remembered, however, that Wolfe's first novel, *Look Homeward, Angel*, had appeared only the year before Phelps published his list. Hemingway's *A Farewell to Arms* was also published in 1929. Two of Faulkner's best novels were published in 1929 and 1930: *The Sound and the Fury* and *As I Lay Dying*. Phelps in 1930 was sixty-five years old; and even if he read these four novels, he would have found it difficult to appreciate them. Perhaps the circumstance that Lewis and Wilder were Yale men had something to do with his inclusion of *Dodsworth* and *The Bridge of San Luis Rey*.

If Professor Phelps were living today, he would, I think, readily admit his failure to mention some of the best works of fiction written during his lifetime; and he would not be greatly surprised at his failure to include anything written by Hemingway, Faulkner, and Wolfe. In July, 1907, he had written in the *North American Review*: "The only real test of the value of a book is Time. Who now reads Cowley? Time has laughed at so many contemporary judgments that it would be foolhardy to make positive assertions about literary stock quotations one hundred years from now. Still, guesses are not prohibited."

*Carl Van Doren's* Contemporary American Novelists *(1922)*. Carl Van Doren, as I have noted on another page, was one of the four editors of *The Cambridge History of American Literature* (1917–1921). In 1921 he published *The American Novel* and followed it up the next year with *Contemporary American Novelists 1900–1920*. The major portion of the latter book is given to ten novelists, each of whom is discussed in a separate chapter: Hamlin Garland, Winston Churchill, Robert Herrick, Upton Sinclair, Theodore Dreiser, Booth Tarkington, Edith Wharton, James Branch Cabell, Willa Cather, and Joseph Hergesheimer. In 1940, when Van Doren brought out a revised edition of *The American Novel*, he expressed somewhat different opinions of some of the ten novelists who had seemed to him so important in 1922. In reviewing the book in *American Literature* for November, 1940, Fred B. Millett commented on some of the more conspicuous changes in Van Doren's critical estimates:

> The passage of two decades has wrought striking changes in Mr. Van Doren's hierarchy of novelists, and of the ten, the only ones to receive more extended treatment in the new edition are Dreiser, Wharton, Cather, and Cabell. The rest receive abbreviated comments in the chapters devoted to general movements and trends. Of the minor figures treated in the earlier book, Ernest Poole has disappeared entirely, and Floyd Dell, whose *Moon-Calf* was once thought "very beautiful," is now mentioned only incidentally. Perhaps Mr. Van Doren's sharpest alteration of opinion concerns Hergesheimer. *Cytherea*, hailed as a "masterpiece" in 1922, is now considered "a confusion of unhappy passion and unconvincing symbolism," and *Linda Condon* is no longer "nearly the most beautiful American novel since Hawthorne and Henry James."

Professor Millett might have noted that Van Doren was inclined to rate Sinclair Lewis as the best novelist of his generation and had suggested that *Babbitt* would live long after Detroit was dust. In 1932 Van Doren concluded a book-length study of James Branch Cabell with this extravagant estimate: "There seems to be no longer a reason for not associating him with the only comparable romancers, Hawthorne and Melville."

With his exceptional knowledge of American literary history, Carl Van Doren can hardly have been greatly surprised to discover in 1940 that his rankings of contemporary writers in that year were quite different from what they had been in 1922 when he wrote in the preface to his *Contemporary American Novelists*:

> Only in writing of dead authors can the critic feel that any considerable portion of his task is done when he has arranged them in what he thinks their proper categories and their true perspective. In the case of living authors he has regularly to remember that he works with shifting materials, with figures whose dimensions and importance may be changed by growth, with persons who may desert old paths for new, reveal unsuspected attributes, increase or fade with the mere revolutions of time.

If Van Doren overrated some of his contemporaries—he was not alone in this—it may have been in part because he knew some of them so intimately. In the preface to the revised edition of *The American Novel* he wrote: "Much of what I have written about recent novelists comes from what they themselves have told me." Most of the men and women who were teaching American literature in the colleges and universities found it difficult enough in those years, with the scanty materials available to them, to make adequate preparation to teach the standard nineteenth-century authors. They often did not bother to discuss the living writers and too often, alas, failed to read them.

Critics and literary historians in discussing the novelists of their own time have had to choose from the many a few who seem to them the best; and they are fortunate if a decade afterwards they do not regret their failure to include at least one writer whose reputation has risen in the meantime. For his *American Fiction, 1920–1940* (1941) Joseph Warren Beach chose eight novelists: Erskine Caldwell, John Dos Passos, James T. Farrell, William Faulkner, John P. Marquand, Ernest Hemingway, John Steinbeck, and Thomas Wolfe. In 1968 the reader may well wonder why Beach did not make places for Scott Fitzgerald, Edith Wharton, Willa Cather, or Ellen Glasgow. In "Our Novelists' Shifting Reputations," published in the *English Journal* for January, 1951, Granville Hicks noted that in the ten years that had elapsed since the publication of Beach's book Steinbeck had lost ground but not nearly so much as Caldwell. A new edition of *American Fiction*, said Hicks, should probably include Robert Penn Warren. In *The Great Tradition* Hicks had made public his own low estimates of Scott Fitzgerald, Edith Wharton, Willa Cather, and Ellen Glasgow; and he did not suggest that Beach had underestimated them.

In *Cavalcade of the American Novel* (1952) Edward Wagenknecht gave six of his twenty-three chapters to Edith Wharton, Ellen Glasgow, Willa Cather, James Branch Cabell, Sinclair Lewis, and Ernest Hemingway. Herbert Brown, who reviewed the book in *American Literature* for May, 1953, noted that "the formidable figures of F. Scott Fitzgerald and James T. Farrell fail to appear" and "so significant a contemporary as William Faulkner is compelled to share a chapter with Wolfe, Steinbeck, Marquand, Caldwell, and a handful of historical novelists."

In a review of Percy H. Boynton's *America in Contemporary Fiction* (*American Literature*, March, 1941) DeLancey Ferguson pointed to one of the difficulties confronted by the historian of contemporary literature: "The trouble with any sort of contemporary literature is that it refuses to stay put. Today's writers fade out tomorrow, or come in retrospect to mean different things as lines of descent and relationship are clarified by time. *Main Street, Cytherea*, or *Jurgen* is already seen to be more important as a revelation of the tastes of the decade than as literature." With Carl Van Doren as well as Professor Boynton in mind, Ferguson continued: "But if a critic has once committed himself to a full-length study of a contemporary, he finds it difficult to make the radical adjustments of perspective which are necessary after the lapse of a decade or two." In Boynton's book, he said: "The revisions are superficial; the deeper insight into the literature of that post-war decade has not been achieved. By this time anyone ought to realize that much of the characteristic writing of twenty years ago was a throwback to the 1890's, alike in its revolt against the village and in the preciosity of such an author as James Branch Cabell."

"SRL *Poll on Novels and Novelists*" (*1944*). On August 5, 1944, the *Saturday Review of Literature* celebrated its twentieth anniversary with a special number entitled "Literature between Two Wars." One of its features was a poll which the editors had taken of an unspecified number of the four thousand contributors whose names were printed in this issue. They were asked "to nominate the leading American novelist and the leading novel of the last twenty years." The ten best novelists were judged to be: (1) Ernest Hemingway; (2) Willa Cather; (3) John Dos Passos; (4) Sinclair Lewis; (5) Thomas Wolfe; (6) Ellen Glasgow; (7) Theodore Dreiser; and (8) Kenneth Roberts, William Faulkner, and Marjorie Kinnan Rawlings. Hemingway received twice as many votes as Willa Cather, but the contributors divided their votes for the best novel between his two best with the result that *Arrowsmith* got a few more votes than *A Farewell to Arms*. The results were: (1) Lewis, *Arrowsmith*; (2) Hemingway, *A Farewell to Arms*; (3) Dos Passos, *U.S.A.*; (4) Steinbeck, *The Grapes of Wrath*; and (5) Hemingway, *For Whom the Bell Tolls.*

The editors of *The Saturday Review* [the report concluded] did not contribute to the poll, but in the estimation of at least one of them [Henry Seidel Canby?], the votes for the first four of the outstanding novelists might have read, Ernest Hemingway, Sinclair Lewis, John

Steinbeck, and Ellen Glasgow. The novels might have been "Arrowsmith," "For Whom the Bell Tolls," "The Grapes of Wrath," and "Barren Ground."

Only two of the five novels were judged worthy of the Pulitzer Prize for Fiction: *Arrowsmith* and *The Grapes of Wrath*. Pearl S. Buck's *The Good Earth*, which had won the Pulitzer Prize in 1932—she received the Nobel Prize in 1938—did not make the *SRL* list. Neither did Willa Cather's *Death Comes for the Archbishop* nor Ellen Glasgow's *Barren Ground* nor *The Sheltered Life*. Faulkner was ranked among the ten best novelists, but not one of his novels made the list. The name of Scott Fitzgerald does not appear. In wartime who cared to read of the doings of the idle rich? The Fitzgerald revival would come in the 1950's. The romantic novels of Joseph Hergesheimer and James Branch Cabell, so overrated in the 1920's, were also out of fashion.

*SRL* in its anniversary issue included an essay by William Rose Benét, "Poetry's Last Twenty Years," which indicates that the associate editor held no high opinion of expatriate American poets: "Eliot . . . whose witty and skeptical 'Prufrock' had preceded his 'Wasteland,' titillated the jaded appetite of critics. In my opinion, some of his earlier poems still remain his best, despite the power he has since shown in poetic drama, notably 'Murder in the Cathedral.' Mysticism ate him up, as it has done many a good man of verse." There is no mention of the memorable *Four Quartets*, which had been published in 1943.

Of Ezra Pound, living in Italy and now broadcasting propaganda for Mussolini, Benét wrote:

> Ezra Pound after shrugging off the First World War as conflict for
>             an old bitch gone in the teeth,
>             for a botched civilization
> became a permanent exile and slowly but surely assassinated himself.
> We draw a veil.

Did Benét know, I wonder, that Pound had once written that he thought he would be justified if he were to kill Canby and the editor of the *Atlantic Monthly*?

*A Graduate Students' Poll (1958).* In the spring of 1958, while I was a visiting professor at Columbia University, I took a poll of English 224, one of my courses in American literature. (A member of the class, John Burke, compiled the results for me.) The sixteen students who took part were mature men and women ranging in age from twenty-five to thirty-five, and most of them were teaching or soon to be teaching in colleges in the New York area. They chose as the great American writers:

| | | | |
|---|---|---|---|
| Mark Twain | | Walt Whitman | 11 |
| Eugene O'Neill | 14 | Emily Dickinson | |
| Herman Melville | | Nathaniel Hawthorne | |
| Henry David Thoreau | | Robert Frost | 10 |
| T. S. Eliot | | Edgar Allan Poe | |
| Stephen Crane | 13 | F. Scott Fitzgerald | 9 |
| Henry James | | Ralph Waldo Emerson | |
| William Faulkner | | Thomas Wolfe | |
| Ernest Hemingway | 12 | Ezra Pound | 6 |

There were no votes for Cooper, Howells, Henry Adams, or Edith Wharton. Emerson and Poe are on the list, but they were not among the favorite authors of my students.

The results of the balloting for the greatest American novels were:

| | |
|---|---|
| Hawthorne, *The Scarlet Letter* | |
| Melville, *Moby Dick* | 15 |
| Mark Twain, *Huckleberry Finn* | 13 |
| Stephen Crane, *The Red Badge of Courage* | 9 |
| Scott Fitzgerald, *The Great Gatsby* | 6 |
| Henry James, *The Ambassadors* | |
| Ernest Hemingway, *For Whom the Bell Tolls* | 4 |

A difference of opinion as to the writer's best novel may explain not only the small number of votes given to *The Ambassadors* and *For Whom the Bell Tolls* but also the failure of any Faulkner novel to make the second list. The students did not choose any novel by Cooper, Howells, Dreiser, Lewis, Dos Passos, Farrell, Steinbeck, Wolfe, Edith Wharton, Willa Cather, or Ellen Glasgow.

Book Week, *"American Fiction: The Postwar Years, 1945–65"* (*1965*). In its issue for September 26, 1965, *Book Week* published the results of a poll of "200 prominent authors, critics and editors." The editors of *Book Week* were hoping to find out (1) which of the numerous American writers of fiction had created "the most substantial body of work during the period" and (2) which of some ten thousand books of fiction seemed "most likely to survive as monuments to these restless 20 years." The results are listed below. For the first of these, the authors, critics, and editors were asked: "Which authors have written the most distinguished fiction during the period 1945–65?" Each of those polled was asked to name no more than ten writers of fiction. "The principal criterion for selection," it was stated, "should be quality, not quantity, of performance." For the second table the authors, critics, and editors were asked: "Which works of fiction written between 1945 and 1965 are the most memorable and likely to endure?"

### The Twenty Best Writers of Fiction

1. Saul Bellow
2. Vladimir Nabokov
3. William Faulkner
4. Bernard Malamud
5. J. D. Salinger
6. Ralph Ellison
7. Norman Mailer
8. Ernest Hemingway
9. Flannery O'Connor
10. Robert Penn Warren
11. John Updike
12. William Styron
13. John Cheever
14. Eudora Welty
15. J. F. Powers
16. John Hawkes
17. John O'Hara
18. Nelson Algren
19. Katherine Anne Porter
20. John Barth

### The Twenty Best Works of Fiction

1. Ralph Ellison, *Invisible Man*
2. Vladimir Nabokov, *Lolita*
3. J. D. Salinger, *Catcher in the Rye*
4. Saul Bellow, *Herzog*
5. Saul Bellow, *Seize the Day*
6. Saul Bellow, *The Adventures of Augie March*
7. Norman Mailer, *The Naked and the Dead*
8. Robert Penn Warren, *All the King's Men*
9. Bernard Malamud, *The Assistant*
10. Ernest Hemingway, *The Old Man and the Sea*
11. Joseph Heller, *Catch-22*
12. William Styron, *Lie Down in Darkness*
13. Flannery O'Connor, *A Good Man is Hard to Find*
14. Vladimir Nabokov, *Pale Fire*
15. Saul Bellow, *Henderson the Rain King*
16. Nelson Algren, *The Man with the Golden Arm*
17. William Burroughs, *Naked Lunch*
18. John Barth, *The Sot-weed Factor*
19. James Gould Cozzens, *Guard of Honor*
20. Philip Roth, *Goodbye, Columbus*

The editors of *Book Week* stated that nine other writers "frequently mentioned were (in order) Mary McCarthy, Philip Roth, James Gould Cozzens,

John Steinbeck, James Purdy, James Baldwin, James Jones, Wright Morris, and Carson McCullers."

After seeing the results of the poll, Katherine Anne Porter wrote:

> It is rather a strange list of writers supposed to represent American literature that omits the names of Peter Taylor, William Humphrey, George Garrett, Walter Clemons, Andrew Lytle, James Agee, Truman Capote, Glenway Wescott, Caroline Gordon, Allen Tate, each a first-rate artist in exactly his own style and character, living in his own mysterious gift, on his own ancestral ground, speaking his mother tongue; if you ignore these writers, it is somewhat like leaving out the spinal column when making a man.

Although the poll suggests that Ralph Ellison's *Invisible Man* is the best book of fiction written during the period, it would seem that the two best novelists are Saul Bellow, who placed no less than four of his books on the final list, and Vladimir Nabokov, who placed two. Katherine Anne Porter was ranked 19th on the list of twenty best writers of fiction, but *The Ship of Fools* was not included in the list of the twenty best works of fiction. James Gould Cozzens's *Guard of Honor* is 19th among the best works of fiction, but its author's name does not appear in the list of the best writers of fiction. In 1967, however, Arthur Mizener gave *Guard of Honor* a chapter in his *Twelve Great American Novels.**

The great novelists of the older generation had written most of their best books before 1945. Steinbeck's name appears only among the runners-up. Faulkner, whom Mizener rated as "unquestionably the greatest American novelist of the twentieth century," is third on the list of twenty best writers of fiction, but not one of his later books was deemed worthy of a place among the twenty best works of fiction.

The majority of the critics whose comments on the final lists were printed in *Book Week* thought that American fiction in the postwar years was notably inferior to that written in the great period between the two world wars. "Not a very good period," wrote Mary McCarthy. John W. Aldridge could find no major novelist to succeed the giants of the earlier period. R. W. B. Lewis wrote: "The present generation of writers of fiction has not fulfilled

* The novels discussed in Mizener's book—he does not claim that these are the greatest—are: James Fenimore Cooper, *The Deerslayer* (1841); Nathaniel Hawthorne, *The Scarlet Letter* (1850); Herman Melville, *Moby-Dick* (1851); Mark Twain, *Huckleberry Finn* (1884); Henry James, *The Ambassadors* (1903); Edith Wharton, *The Age of Innocence* (1920); John Dos Passos, *The Big Money* (1936); F. Scott Fitzgerald, *Tender Is the Night* (1934); Ernest Hemingway, *The Sun Also Rises* (1926); William Faulkner, *The Sound and the Fury* (1929); James Gould Cozzens, *Guard of Honor* (1948); Robert Penn Warren, *All the King's Men* (1946).

the large expectations aroused in the early fifties." Gilbert Highet summed up his reaction: "Many readable routine books; some eccentric and experimental; none permanent." Leon Edel, the biographer of Henry James, wrote: "There are a lot of promising younger men but somehow they do not usually fulfill their promise." "Fantasy-pornography, I fear," he continued, "is killing taste, feeling for style, the sense of what is and what is not relevant to story-telling. No one seems to think of 'beauty' any more."

The years from 1945 to 1965 seemed to Malcolm Cowley "a rich period in American fiction," and Albert Guérard thought there were "a larger number of first-rate novelists than at any time in the past." Gore Vidal climbed out on a still longer limb when he termed the times "easily the richest period in the history of the American novel."

Vivian Mercier wrote: "Too many respectable American novels have been the victims of ballyhoo, not only on the part of their publishers' advertisements but also on that of serious critics who ought to know better." "No novel, however great," wrote Dawn Powell, "can endure when publishers remainder them or scrap them if it [sic] sells less than 5,000 copies. Immortality depends on promotion, not on literary genius." Albert Guerard, however, thought that "the colleges, with their healthy interest in very recent writers and their utter unconcern with the 'best seller,' might help to get the best novels into the hands of those who would enjoy them."

As I study the results of this inconclusive poll, I feel certain that we do not in fact know who are our greatest living novelists, and I doubt whether we can ever identify them by polling any number of editors, critics, and authors. I do not have complete confidence in the ability of our professors of English to select the greatest contemporary novels and put them in the hands of college students, but I hope they keep on trying.

In *American Literary Scholarship* for 1969 James H. Justus provided this summary:

> At the end of the decade, scholarship patterns show that [Norman] Mailer, [Flannery] O'Connor, and [Saul] Bellow are the favorite contemporary novelists. Steady interest continues in [Vladimir] Nabokov, [Robert Penn] Warren, and [William] Styron; work in [Bernard] Malamud registers a slight gain, and the [J. D.] Salinger industry is bankrupt. The most remarkable changes are in the widespread recognition of I. B. Singer and the sudden interest in Thomas Berger. The first promises to remain substantial because that recognition is so belated; time must determine whether the second can be sustained.

*Stand still, true poet that you are!*
 *I know you; let me try and draw you,*
*Some night you'll fail us; when afar*
 *You rise, remember one man saw you,*
*Knew you, and named a star!*

Robert Browning, "Popularity"


*No poetic reputation ever remains exactly in the same place:*
*it is a stock market in constant fluctuation. There are the*
*very great names which only fluctuate, so to speak, within a*
*narrow range of points: whether Milton is up to 104 today,*
*and down to 97–1/4 to-morrow, does not matter. There are*
*other reputations like that of Donne, or Tennyson, which*
*vary much more widely, so that one has to judge their value*
*by an average taken over a long time.*

T. S. Eliot, "What Is Minor Poetry?" in *Poetry and Poets*

## CRITICAL ESTIMATES: POETS

*Amy Lowell,* A Critical Fable *(1922).* Amy Lowell (1874–1925) probably did more than any other person to win converts to the new poetry. In her *Tendencies in Modern American Poetry* (1917) she discussed in this order the six living poets who seemed to her the best: Edwin Arlington Robinson, Robert Frost, Edgar Lee Masters, Carl Sandburg, H.D. (Hilda Doolittle), and John Gould Fletcher. Conrad Aiken in *Scepticisms* (1919), noting that the two Imagist poets were placed last, accused Miss Lowell of playing up the group to which she belonged as representing the climax of the new poetry movement.

In 1922, the year of numerous critical polls, Miss Lowell published—at first anonymously—*A Critical Fable,* a poem modeled upon her kinsman's *A Fable for Critics.* In her poem James Russell Lowell appears as interlocutor. When she tells him that nowadays Poe and Whitman are considered the two greatest American poets, he exclaims: "In the name of the Furies, what's come to the nation?" Somewhat later Miss Lowell was to rank Emily Dickinson as third among the greatest American poets. In *A Critical Fable* she was still of the opinion that Robinson, Frost, Masters, Sandburg, H.D., and Fletcher were the best living American poets; but among the twenty-one poets mentioned she gave high ratings to Sara Teasdale, Vachel Lindsay, Edna St. Vincent Millay, Alfred Kreymborg, Conrad Aiken, and Wallace Stevens. She was afterward to regret that she had not included Elinor Wylie.

When her interlocutor asks: "Is there more?" Miss Lowell responds: "A few odds and ends, but not much you need heed." Among the "odds and ends," it soon appears, are Ezra Pound and T. S. Eliot, "Each of whom has more brains than heart." Pound, with whom Miss Lowell had quarreled, is dubbed "a victim / Of expatriation." Eliot, she said, "has raised pedantry to a pitch." Of his poetry she wrote:

> The poems are expert even up to a vice,
> But they're chilly and dead like corpses on ice.

Presumably Miss Lowell had not yet read *The Waste Land*—also published in 1922. On November 1 of that year, however, after she had read the poem she wrote to Gilbert Seldes: "I do not think that Eliot was intended by nature to be a poet. . . ." On March 4, 1925—the year in which she died—she wrote to Archibald MacLeish that she could not agree with him "that the coming generation is made up of Eliot and Cummings and their followers." She continued:

> I think they are a passing phase. There is no hope for Cummings unless he stops revolting against Cambridge and his Unitarian minister father and tries to do something, and stops trying not to do anything; and I have no hope at all for Eliot unless he can overcome his mental anaemia, but as it seems to be a real disease with him, I do not think there is much likelihood of its cure.*

Amy Lowell was sadly out in her critical estimate of Eliot, but instinctively she must have felt that any critical rating of her own poems based upon the principles that Eliot was elaborating in his essays was bound to be low. Posterity has not dealt kindly with her poems. They are often pronounced too intellectual and, cruelest of all charges, she is said to have had every quality that makes a poet except the "divine fire."

*John Crowe Ransom, "The Poetry of 1900–1950" (1951).* Amy Lowell would have been acutely unhappy if she could have known that within a few years after she had published *A Critical Fable* the doctrines of Eliot and the New Critics would be accepted in most critical circles and in departments of English in American universities. The New Critics would maintain that the genuine Anglo-American poetic tradition stems from John Donne and the other Metaphysical poets of the seventeenth century. They would denigrate most of the nineteenth-century poets of both England and America. Most of the New Critics, indeed, would have little use for any older American writers except Henry James, Melville, and Hawthorne.

---

* In "A Bookshelf of Modern Poets" which Amy Lowell compiled for Doubleday, Page and Company, she listed fifty books of poetry but nothing by Ezra Pound, T. S. Eliot, E. E. Cummings, Archibald MacLeish, Elinor Wylie, or John Crowe Ransom. [From an anonymous undated newspaper clipping.]

By 1951 when Ransom published "The Poetry of 1900–1950" in the *Kenyon Review* (Summer) and in *ELH* (June), he had become more tolerant of those English and American poets who were not in his sense of the word "modern." He was fully aware that he was climbing "out on a long limb" when he named "the poets of 1900–1950 who seem as of this moment to have established themselves, and to have good prospect of surviving in our literature for a few half-centuries." In Ransom's opinion the major poets of the period were Thomas Hardy, William Butler Yeats, Edwin Arlington Robinson, Robert Frost, and T. S. Eliot. Apparently he regarded Hardy as the greatest of the five. Ransom ranked as minor poets Robert Bridges, Walter de la Mare, John Masefield, Vachel Lindsay, William Carlos Williams, Ezra Pound, Marianne Moore, E. E. Cummings, Hart Crane, and Allen Tate. He added: "It will be noticed that there are fine poets junior to those who fail to make my list. I do not feel able to rank them." Ransom named four poets "of whom I cannot tell whether they belong with the Minor Poets . . . or with the Major Poets. . .": A. E. Housman, Wallace Stevens, W. H. Auden, and Dylan Thomas. Among the older poets whom Ransom did not mention were Robinson Jeffers, Archibald MacLeish, John Gould Fletcher, Carl Sandburg, Edgar Lee Masters, Conrad Aiken, Donald Davidson, Amy Lowell, Elinor Wylie, Edna St. Vincent Millay, and Sara Teasdale.

*Randall Jarrell, "Fifty Years of American Poetry" (1962).* In the fall of 1962 Randall Jarrell (1914–1965) gave a lecture at a poetry festival sponsored by the Library of Congress. In the spring of the next year he printed it in the *Prairie Schooner* under the title "Fifty Years of American Poetry." Jarrell was a poet, a critic, a teacher of English, and a graduate of Vanderbilt University. Looking back to the nineteenth century, he noted that Melville, Emerson, and Thoreau had written "good poems," but he considered Walt Whitman and Emily Dickinson the two greatest. The best of the twentieth-century poets were, he thought, Robert Frost, Wallace Stevens, and T. S. Eliot. Edwin Arlington Robinson, he said, "wrote a great deal of poetry and only a few good poems, and yet there is a somber distinction and honesty about him—he is a poet you respect." Wallace Stevens, he wrote, "has an extraordinarily original imagination, one that has created for us—so to speak—many new tastes and colors and sounds, many real, half-real, and non-existent beings." Jarrell had high praise for Allen Tate, William Carlos Williams, and John Crowe Ransom, whose poems, he said, were "not poems of the largest scope or the greatest intensity, but they [were] some of the most original poems ever written." Ezra Pound, he thought, was the great educator for other poets and critics, but, he added, "It is surprising that a poet of Pound's extraordinary talents should have written so few good poems all his own." Marianne Moore and

Elizabeth Bishop seemed to Jarrell "the best woman poets since Emily Dickinson." Carl Sandburg, he said, was "a colorful, appealing, and very American writer"; but his poems were only "improvisations whose wording is approximate: they do not have the exactness, the guaranteeing sharpness and strangeness, of a real style." Of Conrad Aiken he said that he had written "poems that come as close to being good poems, without quite being so, as any I know."

In spite of all his reservations about individual poets, Jarrell believed that "the generation of American poets that included Frost, Stevens, Eliot, Pound, Williams, Marianne Moore, Ransom"—all "American classics"—had established "once and for all the style and tone of American poetry." Moreover, the American poetry of this half-century was, he thought, "the best and most influential in the English language."

As one examines the various books and articles that deal with the poetry of the twentieth century, one comes to feel that the only kind of poetry that ever gets adequate recognition is the kind that the current critical apparatus is prepared to deal with. In a lecture published by the Library of Congress in *American Poetry at Mid-Century* (1958) a poet and critic of distinction, John Hall Wheelock, noted that in the preceding forty years "the dominant influences [appeared] to have been Yeats, Eliot, Auden, and Frost, in that order." "Very real today," he added, "is the influence of Wallace Stevens, of Dylan Thomas and, to a lesser degree, of Marianne Moore." Wheelock had praise for two lyric poets whose work did not conform to the notions of Pound, Eliot, and the New Critics. He said:

> The resistance to feeling directly expressed in the first-person-singular lyric, and with a fine Sapphic disregard for "the objective correlative," has in our day, been so strong as virtually to eliminate from serious critical consideration the work of such poets as Edna St. Vincent Millay and Sara Teasdale. The beautiful and tragically austere later work of Sara Teasdale, in particular, appears to be unknown to contemporary critics. That later work, in its force, intensity and profundity of feeling, and absence of rhetoric, will, surely, more and more reveal her as one of the purest and finest lyric poets we have. The fact that both women wrote love-poems, a genre which runs counter to the taste of the age and has been little practiced by poets of the period, may partially account for the decline in their reputations among the literati.

Wheelock might well have added that the current critical apparatus does not furnish the right approach to his own poems, some of which I believe to be among the best of their kind written in our time.

In an essay on "Poetry and Tradition" (in *Still Rebels, Still Yankees,* 1957) another poet and critic of distinction, Donald Davidson, issued a warning to poets and critics alike:

The publishers of books . . . no longer welcome the poets to their lists. The admission of modern poetry to the textbooks of school and college classes may be, in a sense, as much an entombment as a triumph. This is for poetry a kind of death-in-life, to exist only on the printed page, not on the lips of men, not to be carried by their voices and therefore almost never in their memories, rarely in their hearts.

. . . . . . . . . . . . . . . . . . . . . . . .

A poetry that puts itself in a position not to be recited, not to be sung, hardly ever to be read aloud from the page where it stands, and almost never to be memorized, is nearing the danger edge of absurdity.

Nearly a century ago Matthew Arnold wrote in his introduction to Ward's *English Poets*: "The future of poetry is immense, because in poetry, where it is worthy of its high destinies, our race, as time goes on, will find an ever surer and surer stay." Time has only shown how bad a prophet Arnold was. The poets today are not, as Shelley thought, "the unacknowledged legislators of the world." What members of Congress, one wonders, have ever read any of the poems of Ezra Pound or John Crowe Ransom? In Russia thousands of eager listeners have gathered to hear a Russian poet read his new poems; but one cannot imagine ten thousand persons crowding into Yankee Stadium to hear Robert Lowell or Richard Wilbur read his own poems or anybody else's for that matter. With rare exceptions our poets today have no audience except a few other poets and professors of English willing to try to make sense of their obscure verses.

Narrative and dramatic poetry are almost obsolete forms, and the lyric too often belies its name. In the poet's verses the lay listener hears something that resembles too closely the discords he dislikes in contemporary music. Too much of life and thought find no expression in modern poetry. The poet is forbidden to be passionate; he must not write poems of love or hate. Poetry must no longer in the words of Keats "soothe the cares and lift the thoughts of man." It would seem that, as Edmund Wilson suggested some years ago, verse is "a dying technique." As George R. Stewart has suggested, the novelists have taken over much of the function of poetry: there are in the novels of Wolfe and Faulkner memorable passages of prose poetry. Older readers if they do not care for the poems, say, of Frost, Robinson, Aiken, and Wheelock, may turn back to the great poems of Shakespeare, Milton, or some of the unfashionable poets of the late unlamented nineteenth century.

*If the making of an anthology could be put in the hands of an ideal anthologist of infallible taste, how happy we should all be! At least theoretically. As a matter of fact we must usually put up with a taste that is anything but infallible, as I am uneasily aware.*

Bliss Carmen "Preface," *The Oxford Book of American Verse*

*The manipulation of the stock of an author, alive or dead, while it may lead to an artificial bull market in which many people load up with the handsomely engraved share certificates, is sure to be followed by a distaste for the commodity, decline in earnings, and a selling campaign which leaves the holders of the securities weary and disgusted. This has happened in the case of Stevenson.*

Robert Morss Lovett, review of George S. Hellman's *The True Stevenson, New Republic,* March 10, 1926.

# Chapter *10. Anthologists and Literary Historians*

## ANTHOLOGISTS

The nineteenth century had a few widely-read anthologies like those of Cheever, Griswold, and Stedman; but the twentieth century has had many more, and they are of many different kinds. For the general reader there are anthologies in hard covers and in paperbacks. There are numerous anthologies intended for students in school and college: collections of poems, essays, plays, and short stories dealing with the newer or the older writers or both. There are series of annual anthologies featuring the "best" of the year in poetry, drama, and fiction.

It is an age of anthologies. Nowadays few persons buy a volume of short stories and fewer still a volume of poems by a contemporary poet. Who in our time except a reader with special interests has bought a volume of poems by Wallace Stevens, John Crowe Ransom, or Robert Lowell? One result of this situation is that the popular anthologist finds himself in a position to build up or to diminish a writer's reputation. The academic anthologist, as we have seen, is only too likely to find that new and original writers are not congenial to his conservative taste. On the other hand, when a poet or a writer of fiction edits an anthology, he is all too often a partisan with no tolerance for writers whose aims and methods are different from his own.

For these and other reasons anthologies are not always reliable indexes to the current rating of American writers. If an anthology is to sell, then the editor, the publisher, and their advisers must consider the state of the market and include what the public is willing to pay for or what teachers of English will accept in a text designed for students. The result is too often a compromise between what the editor really likes and what he must include if his book is to bring him any royalties. Compilers of anthologies of contemporary literature have frequently found it difficult or impossible to secure permission to reprint materials still in copyright; and even when the compiler receives permission to reprint certain materials, he may find the cost prohibitive.

Anyone studying the reputation of Emily Dickinson who should examine the various anthologies designed for college students might easily form a wrong conclusion as to the literary taste and judgment of the editors. For example, in 1929 Arthur Hobson Quinn could not induce the publishers of her poems to permit him to reprint more than eight of her poems. In 1936, when many of her poems were soon to go out of copyright, Little, Brown and Company refused to permit me to reprint more than five of the more than five hundred Emily Dickinson poems then in print. In the same year, however, for reasons unknown to me, the publishers permitted Harry Hayden Clark to reprint in his *Major American Poets* no fewer than forty of her poems.

Sometimes it is the author rather than the publisher who refuses permission to reprint the particular selections that the editor wants. Even such an editor can sympathize with a poet who, like Carl Sandburg, was irritated or bored by the inevitable request for permission to reprint "Fog" and "Chicago" —as if they were clearly superior to every other poem he had written. But what will the teacher, the student, and the general reader think if the compiler leaves them out?

*Louis Untermeyer.* If an anthology is popular enough to go into many editions, like those of Griswold in the nineteenth century or of Louis Untermeyer (1885–) in the twentieth, it may serve as an index to changes in literary fashion. In 1919 Untermeyer brought out the first of the many editions of his *Modern American Poetry.* Of the poets whom he included in the fifth edition in 1936, twenty were absent from the sixth edition in 1942. In 1937 Robert Hillyer had written in *A Letter to Robert Frost*:

> Taste changes. Candid Louis Untermeyer
> Consigns his past editions to the fire;
> His new anthology, refined and thrifty,
> Builds up some poets and dismisses fifty,
> And every poet spared, as is but human,
> Remarks upon his critical acumen.

In 1919 Untermeyer brought out a collection of his various critical articles and book reviews under the title *The New Era in American Poetry*. In 1923, with some changes and additions, the book reappeared as *American Poetry since 1900*. At that time Untermeyer held a low opinion of the older poets of New England; and, like Mencken and Van Wyck Brooks, he blamed their shortcomings upon "a peculiar hypocrisy that was rooted in the old puritanism." As I have noted on an earlier page, he condemned Stedman's *An American Anthology* (1900) as a "gargantuan collection of mediocrity and moralizing." In its nearly nine hundred pages, he thought, one might find "perhaps sixty pages of genuine poetry and no more than ten pages of genuine American poetry."

In *American Poetry since 1900* Untermeyer ranked Robert Frost and Edwin Arlington Robinson as the "twin summits of our poetry—eminences to which no American poets, since Poe and Whitman, have ever attained." He gave five pages to Wallace Stevens, but he made it clear that he cared little for Stevens's poetry and believed Harriet Monroe mistaken in ranking Stevens in 1919 as "the peer of any poet now living and of many a famous one now dead and enshrined." The 1919 edition of Untermeyer's book had contained only a passing reference to T. S. Eliot as "one of the ablest of the insurgents." In 1923 he discussed *The Waste Land*, which had appeared in the preceding year; but it seemed to Untermeyer little better than Eliot's earlier poems, which he considered no better than "extraordinarily clever—and eminently uncomfortable—verse." *The Waste Land* seemed to him "a set of separate poems upon which a scheme of unification [had] been arbitrarily—and unsuccessfully—imposed as an afterthought. . . . this is poetry not actuated by life but by literature." There were "moments of imaginative vigor" in *The Waste Land*, but still it seemed to Untermeyer "a pompous parade of erudition, a lengthy extension of the earlier disillusion, a kaleidoscopic movement in which the bright-colored pieces fail to atone for the absence of an integrated design." In his autobiography, *From Another World* (1939) Untermeyer noted that he had finally come to admire Eliot's "combination of flat statement and rich rhetoric, of power and triviality." Yet, he maintained, Eliot is "not a major poet" but "a minor poet in the grand manner."

In his old age Conrad Aiken, who was one of Eliot's champions, told some friends in Savannah that it was "important to fight Louis Untermeyer. . . . because his taste was so bad and his influence so enormous, this had to be kicked out. We didn't succeed and he managed to outlast us."

In 1931 Untermeyer published a new anthology, *American Poetry from the Beginning to Whitman*. The foreword reveals the anthologist as conscious of changes in his own taste. The book, he said, was "a set of reap-

praisals, unpartisan examinations, even, at times, of reversed judgments."
In 1931 it was, he said, no longer the fashion to ridicule the old New England
poets. Longfellow now seemed to him a really good poet. The outstanding
figures among our nineteenth-century poets were, Untermeyer felt, Emerson,
Longfellow, Whitman, Poe, and, surprisingly enough, Bryant. Untermeyer
added that "he would call attention to the almost unknown but significant
work" of Carlos Wilcox, Edward Coote Pinkney, William Ellery Channing
the younger, George Hill, Jones Very, Thomas Holley Chivers, and Herman
Melville (as a prose poet). Untermeyer also included the Virginian John
Cotton's fine elegy, "Bacon's Epitaph Made by His Man"—overlooked by
many anthologists—and pronounced it "our first indubitable poem." Perhaps
Robert Frost, to whom Untermeyer dedicated his anthology, had suggested
a reconsideration of the work of the old New England poets and possibly the
inclusion of some dimly remembered figures found in Griswold's *The Poets
and Poetry of America* and in Stedman's *American Anthology*.

The Oxford Book of American Verse *(1927, 1950)*. The marked changes
in literary taste that came about in the twenties and thirties are very evident
when we compare the two editions of *The Oxford Book of American Verse*.
The 1927 edition was prepared by the Canadian-American poet Bliss Carman
(1861–1929), who in the 1890's had collaborated with Richard Hovey in
*Songs from Vagabondia*. Professor F. O. Matthiessen (1902–1950), who compiled the 1950 edition, taught his first class in the year that Carman's edition
was published. Even in 1927 Carman's literary taste—he was then sixty-six
years old—must have seemed a little old-fashioned to many readers of the
new poetry. He included only one poem by Sandburg, one by Pound, and
none at all by Eliot. Carman, however, had been an early admirer of Emily
Dickinson, and he reprinted 27 of her poems; Matthiessen included 58.

Matthiessen in his more than eleven hundred pages reprinted 571 selections from 51 poets. He had an aversion to "the kind of rhetoric that over-
flowed into poetry from the oratory of the day." Holmes, Whittier, and Lowell
were "the worst offenders." Holmes emerged with only two poems and Lowell
with only extracts from *A Fable for Critics* and *The Biglow Papers*. Longfellow and Emerson fared better. The forgotten Jones Very had eleven of
his poems included. Henry Timrod and not Sidney Lanier seemed to Matthiessen the best of the southern poets. The two "central figures" in our twentieth-century poetry, he thought, were Robert Frost and T. S. Eliot. "The two
great pivotal figures in our nineteenth century," he said, "were Poe and
Whitman." In his *American Renaissance* (1941) Matthiessen had treated with
great distinction five major writers whose best books, he thought, were written in the years 1850–1855: Emerson, Hawthorne, Thoreau, Melville, and

Whitman. He did not include Poe, who had died in 1849; but he contributed a chapter on Poe to *The Literary History of the United States* (1948).

*Conrad Aiken.* Two anthologies edited by American poets much younger than Bliss Carman appeared in 1929 and 1933: Conrad Aiken's (1889–) *American Poetry, 1671–1928* and Mark Van Doren's (1894–) *American Poets, 1630–1930.* Aiken's anthology, which in a revised edition was in 1944 added to the Modern Library, was the more revolutionary of the two. The time had come, said the editor in his introduction, for "a firm revision of our critical attitude" toward American literature. An editor's tests, he said, should be based on aesthetic and not historical considerations; and this involved getting rid of "excess baggage" in the shape of the sentimental, the oratorical, and the "politically tendentious." To the five so-called "major" New England poets he gave only twenty-five pages. He granted about the same space to Anne Bradstreet and Philip Freneau and likewise to T. S. Eliot and Wallace Stevens. He played up Poe, Whitman, and Emily Dickinson as probably the greatest of the American poets. He apparently thought that Trumbull Stickney and Thomas Holley Chivers were better poets than any of the old New England poets except Emerson. From Bryant he reprinted four poems; from Whittier, three; from Holmes, only "The Last Leaf"; from Lowell, three; and from Longfellow, five. In the 1944 edition, the twentieth-century poets who got most space were Eliot, Pound, Stevens, Robinson, and Frost; but in this edition Aiken included an abnormally large number of minor twentieth-century poets who now rarely appear in any anthology. Among these are Cale Young Rice, George Cabot Lodge, Shaemus O'Sheel, Marsden Hartley, John Wheelwright, and Oscar Williams. He included also three whose critical essays now seem far better than their verses: Edmund Wilson, Malcolm Cowley, and R. P. Blackmur.

In the introduction to his revised edition Aiken commented upon the changes brought about by the passing of time:

> Perspective changes; the critic's eye changes; poetry changes too. . . . One's own view of the mass and current [of his day], meanwhile, has been imperceptibly changing with the changing times; the shadows and lights fall now in other places; what seemed formerly only a tendency, and of the vaguest and most tentative at that, now reveals itself as a quite definite and accomplished direction; what formerly seemed to be a direction has now become vestigial, stopped off; one of Nature's little experiments which, alas, has failed.

*Mark Van Doren.* Mark Van Doren's (1894–) *American Poets* (1933), the work of a poet who was also professor of English at Columbia University, still seems to me over the more than thirty years since it first appeared, one of the best of its kind. In his preface Van Doren commented on certain poets whom he included:

There is so much of Emerson here for instance because I like him so much; at his best I think him the peer of almost any English poet. So with Emily Dickinson; and so, though to a lesser degree, with Whitman, whose message—which he depended on—has lost much of its interest, while his art, whenever it appears at all, appears now the more clearly because it can be seen in its simplicity. Among the other standard poets of the century I have found Bryant and Whittier still clear and sure, though scarcely strong; and I have taken pains to show how melodious a virtuoso Longfellow could be in those relatively few poems in which he somehow refrained from relaxing into the sentiment so natural to him. Holmes and Lowell boiled down, I thought, to very little, though in the case of Holmes that little still seems to me perfect of its kind. For the rest, Thoreau struck me as singularly good after fifteen years during which I had not reread his verse, and I hope I have not done him too much justice by including so many of his somewhat singular but certainly very accurate exercises in the metaphysical mode. Chivers is here, not merely because he is being discussed and rediscovered these days, but because there was a strength in his wildness, a method in his experiment, which I could not put out of mind. So Boker's sonnets seemed to me too vigorous to leave in their obscurity.

Van Doren's representation of his own contemporaries seems to me admirable except that, as he stated in his preface, he could not get permission from publishers to include enough poems by Wallace Stevens, T. S. Eliot, and Archibald MacLeish. He did include, however, a few poets who rarely find a place in any anthology nowadays: James Rorty, George E. Woodberry, and Maxwell Bodenheim.

*Oscar Williams.* In his widely-circulated *Little Treasury of American Verse* (1949) Oscar Williams (1900–) gave scant representation to any American poet of the nineteenth century. Said he: "The last fifty years have seen the publication of much more poetry of a much higher standard than all that was written in the preceding two hundred years." No responsible literary historian could possibly agree with such an extravagant estimate. In a review of Williams's anthology in the winter, 1949, number of the *Hudson Review* the late Donald A. Stauffer said:

Mr. Williams is severe on the nineteenth century, so that Longfellow gets fewer pages than Frankenberg, Lowell (James Russell) less than Coman Leavenworth, and Whittier less than a third as much as Eberhart. Was the nineteenth century as bad as all that? Or are our current standards of taste—*l'art pour l'art*, irrationality, allusion, compression, mystery, expressionism, suggestion—somewhat limited? . . . It is a grave charge to dismiss the New England School as "sentimental and largely meretricious" and to suggest that omitting them entirely might have been an even more courageous effort to raise the standard of taste and to educate the young "through serious poetry."

"Such an attitude," Stauffer concluded, "intimates again, what the world is always too willing to believe, that truth and beauty have been discovered in our own day for the first time."

In *Poetry and the Age* (1953) Randall Jarrell paid his respects to Williams's anthology. It had, he said, "a dust-jacket that crams down the gullets of the hungry sheep this 'authoritative collection of the best poems written during the last fifty years.'" Jarrell noted the "extremely poor job Mr. Williams [had] done with Auden, Bridges, Hardy, Housman, Pound, MacNeice, Graves, Moore, and others." He pointed out that the book contained not a single poem by Robert Lowell. Still, Jarrell admitted, the anthology did contain many good poems. He added: "Also the book has the merit of containing a considerably larger selection of Oscar Williams's poetry than I have ever seen in any other anthology. There are nine of his poems—and five of Hardy's. It takes a lot of courage to like your own poetry almost twice as well as Hardy's."

*George W. Arms.* One able scholar who could not possibly agree with Oscar Williams's conclusions, George W. Arms (1912–) of the University of New Mexico, wondered just how the schoolroom poets of New England would fare if their work were tested by the contemporary touchstones of "complexities, ironies, ambiguities," "designs of self-containment," "structural intensity," "controlling image," "tension," etc. And so in 1953 Professor Arms made the experiment in *The Fields Were Green*. He reprinted what he thought could thus be salvaged from the collected poems of Bryant, Longfellow, Holmes, Lowell, and Whittier. He noted in the beginning that in the way of our appreciation of the older poets there stand certain barriers which belong more to fashion than to critical standards: "a literary rather than a colloquial diction, the use of poetical-picturesque subject matter, and an effect of relaxation." Another difficulty is our habit of regarding them as either major poets or no poets at all. They are all, Arms insisted, minor poets, and they are perhaps no better than four other minor poets of the nineteenth century: Frederick Goddard Tuckerman, Jones Very, Henry David Thoreau, and Sidney Lanier. The major American poets in Arms's estimation were

Emerson, Poe, Melville, Whitman, and Emily Dickinson. In his view Lowell came off worse than the other four poets. He quoted Thackeray as saying: "Why a man who can delight the world with such creations as *Hosea Biglow* should insist upon writing second-rate serious verse I cannot see." Arms reprinted Lowell's long humorous poem, "Fitz Adam's Story," which had been overlooked or undervalued by earlier anthologists.

Arms considered Longfellow the best of the five poets. He noted that the better nineteenth-century critics from Margaret Fuller to Edmund Clarence Stedman had all had their reservations about Longfellow's rank as a poet. Yet Longfellow, Arms insisted, had "craftsmanship," "integration of form and content," and "harmony of 'tone and idea.'" He added that many of his shorter poems could be improved merely by the omission or the rearranging of certain stanzas.

Even if Longfellow is only a minor poet, can we afford to neglect a writer of his historical importance? In a review of the late Newton Arvin's *Longfellow: His Life and Work* (1963), Edward Wagenknecht in *American Literature* for November, 1963, denounced

> the lazy tendencies now in vogue to narrow down the teaching and study of American literature to a little handful of writers who happen to be currently popular. (If you make up your mind beforehand that the others are not worth reading, then you don't have to read them, and this leaves much more time for golf.) And if teachers would only take [Arvin's] strictures to heart, perhaps we might get some courses in American literature again instead of getting only courses in Emerson, Thoreau, Hawthorne, Melville, Whitman, Mark Twain, and Henry James.

> *All must be told with just selection, emphasis, perspective; with that historical imagination and sympathy that does not judge the past by the canons of the present, nor read into it the ideas of the present. Above all the historian must have a passion for truth above that for any party or idea.*
>     Frederick J. Turner, "The Significance of History"

> *There was a time when the literary historian was monarch of all he surveyed. He was the one kind of literary scholar that could claim respectability in the company of*

*scientists and he had a stranglehold on the English curriculum in the university. But times have changed and he is now a very humble companion of the critic, both new and old, in the halls of academe and in the world of art.*

Robert E. Spiller, "Is Literary History Obsolete?"

## LITERARY HISTORIANS

In the 1920's there emerged a new generation of scholars who undertook the difficult and unfashionable task of rewriting our literary history. Their activity had its chief focus in the Modern Language Association. In 1928 the American Literature Group of the association brought out *The Reinterpretation of American Literature*, in which they stated their aims and suggested the methods they proposed to employ. In 1929, with the cooperation of the Duke University Press, they launched their own organ, the quarterly journal, *American Literature*, which bore the descriptive subtitle *A Journal of Literary History, Criticism, and Bibliography*. Since that time members of the association have compiled invaluable checklists of magazine articles, manuscripts in American libraries, doctoral dissertations, and other studies including Clarence Gohdes's invaluable guides and the annual *American Literary Scholarship*, edited first by James Woodress and subsequently by J. Albert Robbins. The remarkable development of American literary scholarship took place during the very decades when our twentieth-century writers were publishing their best books of poetry, fiction, drama, and literary criticism. The same years saw the rise of the United States both to its present position of world power and to a position of literary leadership in the Western world.

In the 1920's the canon of the great American writers was being radically revised by poets, novelists, and literary journalists who often did not bother to read or reread the older writers whom they so freely condemned. The younger scholars were rediscovering Herman Melville and Emily Dickinson. They were also beginning to apply their methods to the study of living writers like James Joyce and T. S. Eliot.

There were, however, older scholars who cared little or nothing for Melville or Emily Dickinson and found themselves indifferent or hostile to Eliot, Joyce, Faulkner, and Hemingway. Some of them made the mistake of trying to assess the newer writers whose books they could not discuss with the sympathy and understanding they gave to authors enshrined in the New England literary canon.

*Fred Lewis Pattee.* Fred Lewis Pattee (1863–1950) was a native of Vermont and a graduate of Dartmouth College, where he heard Charles F. Richardson lecturing on living writers from the proofsheets of the second volume of his *American Literature.* Richardson's admiration for Philip Freneau made a lasting impression on young Pattee, who in 1902–1907 brought out a good three-volume edition of Freneau's poems. Pattee wanted to become a creative writer, and eventually he did publish several volumes of verse and prose fiction; but he got no encouragement or helpful advice from his Dartmouth professors.

Beginning in 1894 Pattee taught for more than thirty years at Pennsylvania State College (now University), and after his retirement in 1928 he began a new career at Rollins College. He was, I believe, the first man to be given the title of professor of American Literature. In that neglected field he was one of the most influential pioneers. He was also a competent scholar and a fine teacher, witty, companionable, and able to communicate his own enthusiasm to his students. He was a frequent contributor to the *American Mercury.* He was also one of the members of the original board of editors of *American Literature,* and his wise and witty comments on manuscripts submitted to that journal were a joy to read.

In 1896, after several other publishers had declined the manuscript, Silver, Burdett and Company published Pattee's *A History of American Literature.* In his posthumously published autobiography, *Penn State Yankee* (1953), he noted that many academic critics and literary journalists had protested that there was no such thing as "American literature," or else they maintained that if there was, it was all too recent for the literary historian to treat it objectively.

In the 1890's, as Pattee noted, such courses as were given in the literature of this country were generally limited to the authors whom he called the "Big Ten": Irving, Cooper, Bryant, Emerson, Hawthorne, Longfellow, Whittier, Holmes, Lowell, and Poe. Occasionally Thoreau or Mrs. Stowe might be included but not Whitman or Melville.

Pattee, however, was greatly interested in the living writers who were creating a new literature different from that of the American renaissance. In 1915 he published the best of all his books, *A History of American Literature since 1870.* The book covers only the seventies and eighties, a period that seemed to him at once the greatest and the most neglected in our literary history. In his preface he wrote: "The field is a new one: no other book and no chapter of a book has ever attempted to handle it as a unit. It is an important one: it is our first really national period, all-American, autochthonic." Pattee had embarked on a fascinating study but a difficult one, for the basic factual materials he needed were almost "non-existent." For such materials he had to appeal to the authors themselves. The letters he received from Hamlin Garland, Mary Wilkins Freeman, Helen Hunt Jackson, George W. Cable, and others were invaluable.

Unlike the New England literary historians who preceded him, Pattee did not overrate the writers of that section. One of his best chapters is devoted to "Recorders of the New England Decline." He treated with obvious sympathy and understanding the southern and western humorists and writers of fiction. An admirer of Taine, he was particularly interested in the various aspects of American life portrayed by writers of fiction. He was on the whole a better critic of fiction than of poetry; he considered Sidney Lanier only "a poet of magnificent fragments." He did, however, include in the book a spirited defense of Walt Whitman. Pattee's enthusiasm sometimes led him to overrate a living author whom he liked. H. L. Mencken, who praised Pattee's book, wrote to him: "You were far too gentle with Garland. He needs the ax." Pattee's most conspicuous failure is seen in the two paragraphs that he gave to the poems of Emily Dickinson. "They are," he said, "mere conceits, vague jottings of a brooding mind; they are crudely wrought, and, like their author's letters . . . they are valueless and for the most part lifeless. . . . They should have been allowed to perish as their author intended."

In his *Tradition and Jazz* (1925) Pattee included a witty and illuminating essay entitled "The Aftermath of Veritism: A Letter from the Sabine Farm to Hamlin Garland." The young radical from the Middle Border who had published *Crumbling Idols* in 1894 was in the 1920's and 1930's out of sympathy with the new generation of novelists in both England and America. In *Afternoon Neighbors* (1934) Garland noted that ten years earlier he had printed in the New York *Times* a piece entitled "Heroes and Heroines of Modern Fiction," in which he denounced the "female libertine [who was] in the process of being glorified," and "the whole school of 'free-lovers' and 'shock-mongers.'" In his open letter Pattee reminded Garland that "these 'young radicals' of to-day are precisely what your generation has made them." "These sex-obsessed youngsters who so fill you with 'weariness and disgust' —what were they reading in the days that for them were formative? They were reading many things, but surely in the list are 'Maggie,' which you and Howells so heroically rescued from the scrap-heap, and 'Rose of Dutchers Coolly,' which bore your name as author." Pattee reminded Garland that the *Critic* had complained: "Mr. Garland's word 'sex-maniac' is bad enough; but the continual dwelling on (we had almost said gloating over) the thing is far worse."

Garland for his part in *Roadside Meetings* (1930) republished some words that he had printed in *Crumbling Idols* in 1894: "Rebellious youth breaks away from the grim hand of the past and toils, in his own way, till (grown old) *he, too, becomes oppressor in his turn. . . .*" Rather sorrowfully Garland added his own confession: "As I write these words, in 1930, it is only fair to underscore the line in which I foretold, at thirty-four, that I, in my turn, would surely come to be conservative, a barrier to be overleaped. I commend this cautious forecast to those of our present-day writers who feel that in them the ages have culminated and that nothing superior can conceivably arise."

While Pattee was making merry over Garland's failure to remember what so often happens to young radicals as they grow old, he seemed unaware of what was happening to his own literary taste and judgment. In *Tradition and Jazz* there is an essay, "The *Ars Poetica* and Scofflaw Poetry" (which I had earlier published in the *Southwest Review*), in which Pattee wrote: "The new group [of poets] that a decade ago I viewed with such extravagant hope seems on the whole a failure. It has talked itself to death; it has touched the fatal pitch of realism and has befouled its wings." Pattee liked the younger prose writers no better than the poets. "The Cabells and the Andersons and the Dreisers and the Menckens," he said, "rule the moment by their clatter and their cocksureness, but their day is brief." Pattee should have remembered what he had said in his open letter to Hamlin Garland: "On being sixty is a serious theme, Brother Hamlin. We who were born in the sixties are getting rude shocks these rough latter days. . . . But what good to rage about it? Let the heathen rage—the thirty authors of 'Civilization in America.' "

Determined to complete his mature survey of our literature, Pattee in 1930 published *The New American Literature, 1890–1930*. Like his other books, this one is highly readable, but he should have left the task to younger scholars who could treat sympathetically the writers whom he could not stomach. He liked Robert Frost, but T. S. Eliot seemed to him only the "leading eccentric of the period." He had little or no sympathy for Dreiser or Henry Adams or "such writers as Ernest Hemingway who have violated every canon of the old handbooks and even the elementary rules of grammar." Eugene O'Neill is not mentioned even in a footnote.

Once again Pattee revealed his inability to appreciate the poems of Emily Dickinson. "Already," he wrote, "it is seen that the enduring part of her poetry is embedded in much that is childish, much that must be dismissed as jingling nonsense." In a chapter entitled "Revaluations" Pattee finally did something like justice to Stephen Crane. He was not able, however, to agree with those critics who were downgrading the old New England poets. In reviewing Carl Van Doren's *American Literature: An Introduction* (1933) in *American Literature* in January, 1934, he wrote: "It is time to cease damning Puritanism and defining literary greatness in terms of rebellion. Melville, I prophesy, will wane back to the fifth magnitude to which his own generation adjudged him, and Longfellow and Whittier and Bryant are not always to be condemned as mere 'pictures of whiskers on the walls of school-rooms.' "

An able younger scholar who specialized in contemporary American literature, Fred B. Millett, in reviewing Pattee's last book in *American Literature* for November, 1931, noted the great difficulties encountered by the historian who undertakes to classify and rank the authors of his own time:

> The literary historian faces no task more exacting than that of writing the history of contemporary literature, since it presents constantly the most acute problems of selection, organization, proportion, and evaluation. For historians of earlier periods, most of these problems have in large measure already been solved. Time, the whirligig of taste, and the industry of earlier workers have already determined, not only what writers are worth consideration but also what patterns may be imposed most easily on the literary phenomena in question. Without the support of traditional approval or disapproval, the historian of contemporary literature must hazard an individual evaluation of a host of writers with whom he may or may not find himself in sympathy.

Reluctantly one concludes that the mature literary historian who undertakes to rank the authors of his own time is only too likely to come up with critical estimates either already out of date or destined quickly to be outmoded. By the time the scholar feels that he is equipped for the difficult task and knows enough about the field, his own literary taste and judgment may be too old-fashioned for the task he has undertaken.

*Arthur Hobson Quinn.* How is the academic literary historian to rank the writers of his own or a still younger generation? "One of the most embarrassing moments of my life," wrote Arthur Hobson Quinn (1875–1960) in 1925, "presented itself through a question put to me by Hopkinson Smith. 'You read a lot of these American writers, don't you?' he inquired. 'Yes,' I replied, 'it is my business.' 'Well,' he continued, 'perhaps you can tell me something, then. How much of my stuff is going to last?' How I answered him, I cannot remember. I hope I was sincere." One cannot doubt that Quinn's answer had the merit of sincerity, but few would now agree with the estimate that he gave in an article entitled "Passing of a Literary Era" (*Saturday Review of Literature*, March 21, 1925). He was discussing those southern local colorists that he had come to love in his youth: Thomas Nelson Page, Joel Chandler Harris, James Lane Allen, George W. Cable, and F. Hopkinson Smith.

> Just what is to remain among the work of these five writers as a permanent contribution to our literature in the placid days after "Main Street" and "The Triumph of the Egg" are forgotten? I am most sure of the early work of all of them. With Cable it is "Old Creole Days," "Madame Delphine," and "The Grandissimes." With Page it is "In Ole Virginia" and "The Old Gentleman of the Black Stock." With Smith, it

is "Colonel Carter" and "The Romance of an Old Fashioned Gentle-man." With Allen it is "The Kentucky Cardinal," "Aftermath," and "The Choir Invisible." With Harris, it is, of course, the Uncle Remus stories and "Free Joe."

. . . . . . . . . . . . . . . . . . . . . . . .

It was a brave world these men painted for us, shot through with loyalty and patriotism, with sacrifice for the sake of honor, with a pride of race that passed from memory to memory. When this life faded out of America it left a void that has not been filled, but the Providence that watches over a people's literature decreed that before it disap-peared it should be interpreted by those who wrought with skill and with sincerity.

Quite obviously Quinn had not revised his youthful estimates of Hopkinson Smith and his southern contemporaries. For the critic of our time who has studied the lessons set by those masters, Henry James, I. A. Richards, and T. S. Eliot, these old-fashioned local colorists now represent only an eddy on the margin of the mainstream of American fiction.

Quinn's reluctance to revise his youthful ratings is obvious in his *American Fiction* (1936), which has good chapters on Willa Cather, Edith Wharton, and Ellen Glasgow but contains unsympathetic discussions of the work of Theodore Dreiser, Sinclair Lewis, and Sherwood Anderson. Quinn gave more space to S. Weir Mitchell and F. Marion Crawford than other historians of our fiction have felt they deserve; and he underrated Stephen Crane and Herman Melville. Only in *Moby-Dick*, he thought, did Melville rise to "sustained greatness in fiction"; and, Quinn added: "One has to wade through much that is forbidding; the confused introductory chapters and the tiresome lectures on the structure and classification of whales illustrate again Melville's besetting weaknesses, his lack of a sense of proportion and his inability to distinguish fact from fiction."

On the other hand, Quinn's treatment of the work of Poe in *American Fiction* and in his fine biography of the poet is much less open to objections from the contemporary critic. Quinn's special field was the drama, and his books show no lack of sympathy for Eugene O'Neill and other twentieth-century playwrights. In the cooperative *Literature of the American People* (1951) Quinn wisely left to two able younger scholars, Clarence Gohdes and George F. Whicher, the task of appraising those writers who emerged after the Civil War.

Quinn and Pattee were by no means the only academic literary historians to misjudge or overlook writers who now seem among the best. In 1919, for example, Percy H. Boynton of the University of Chicago published *A His-*

*tory of American Literature,* in which, so his index indicates, there is no mention of Herman Melville, Emily Dickinson, Stephen Crane, Theodore Dreiser, Ezra Pound, or T. S. Eliot. A few years later, however, Boynton was to discover these and other writers and to speak or write of some of them with some enthusiasm.

The Cambridge History of American Literature. *The Cambridge History of American Literature* was published in four volumes in the years 1917–1921. Of the four editors three—William Peterfield Trent, John Erskine, and Carl Van Doren—were members of the English staff at Columbia University; the fourth, Stuart P. Sherman, was professor of English at the University of Illinois. In the preface to Volume 1 the editors emphasized their historical point of view: "To write the intellectual history of America from the modern aesthetic standpoint is to miss precisely what makes it significant among modern literatures, namely, that for two centuries the main energy of Americans went into exploration, settlement, labour for subsistence, religion, and statecraft."

A great difficulty faced by the editors was the scarcity of competent specialists available for the various subjects to be included. For some important topics the editors turned to men who taught American history. Among the contributors one notes widely varying conceptions of literary history and criticism. There is, incidentally, no chapter on American literary criticism. Stuart Sherman's chapter on Mark Twain and Joseph Warren Beach's on Henry James are critical essays, but John Erskine's chapter on Hawthorne is practically limited to a discussion of the novelist as a critic of Transcendentalist ideas. Killis Campbell's chapter on Poe and Emory Holloway's on Whitman are good factual studies and are mainly biographical. There is almost no indication of the approaching denigration of the schoolroom poets of New England; each of them is given a separate chapter. Emily Dickinson is discussed only briefly in the chapter on "The Later Poets." The second volume (1918) included Carl Van Doren's excellent appraisal of Melville which in expanded form appeared in *The American Novel* in 1921.

The extensive bibliographies in *The Cambridge History* were of great value to the rapidly increasing number of students interested in American literature. The new generation of American poets and writers of fiction, however, did not find in *The Cambridge History* the "usable past" which Van Wyck Brooks and others felt was so urgently needed; and the younger writers with their newer critical standards found the traditional canon of the great American writers unacceptable. For example, Conrad Aiken on March 22, 1924, published in the London *Nation & Athenaeum* a review of the

1922 one-volume abridgment of *The Cambridge History*. "What we come to," he said, "is the fact that the short *History* lights in America an almost total lack of critical standards."

What strikes one, in this series of essays by different hands, is the uniformity and persistence with which American critics—most of them professors—weigh their subjects in the scales of moral and social *usefulness*. That explains the interloping presence here of Edwards, Franklin, and Lincoln—who have little importance in letters—and Beecher, Brooks, Whitney, and Ticknor—who have none. One is a little dismayed at the singleness with which all these critics expect a man of letters to be, first and last, a social and spiritual *leader*. . . . The aesthetic question is seldom raised; the responsibility is declined. . . . Emerson's "ideas" are discussed—but not his prose or verse. Poe's bad habits are represented, his social and ethical deficiency marked with a red lantern, but his genius is left unmarked, unanalyzed, and unplaced. We are given no reason to suppose that Bryant was less important than Poe. . . . it nowhere says that Bryant is thoroughly commonplace and dull. Nowhere is it said that Longfellow was a tenth-rate sentimentalist, a manufacturer of blancmange, who wrote two or three good poems; that Whittier was a jingling moralist; or that Howells was an honest novelist of manners with an appallingly undistinguished style. . . . Henry Adams is looked at askance because of his *"sense of futility."*

Surely not every one would have agreed with Aiken in denying any literary importance to Edwards, Franklin, and Lincoln. Aiken lamented "the glaring omission of Emily Dickinson—a poet who rivals any American poet in importance, and who is unquestionably the finest woman poet who has used the English language." Aiken did not realize that while Emily Dickinson was not discussed in the one-volume abridgment, she had been discussed in Volume 3 of the complete edition. Norman Foerster, in a chapter dealing with a dozen minor poets contemporary with her, had said: "Despite her defective sense of form . . . she [has] acquired a permanent following of discriminating readers through her extraordinary insight into the life of the mind and the soul." "Her place in American literature," he had concluded, "will be inconspicuous but secure."

T. S. Eliot was living in London when the second volume of *The Cambridge History* came out in 1918. He was not yet a British subject, but the review he published in the London *Athenaeum* for April 25, 1919, suggests that he was justifying himself for something like expatriation from a country where literary greatness was so difficult to achieve. One is reminded of Henry James, who in his *Hawthorne* in 1879 had enumerated "the items of high civilization" absent from American life. Ignoring Longfellow, Lowell, Holmes, Whittier, and even Thoreau, Eliot said: "The three important men in this book are Poe, Whitman, and Hawthorne." He added:

> Hawthorne, Poe and Whitman are all pathetic figures; they are none of them so great as they might have been. . . . [They lived and wrote in a] starved environment. . . . Their world was thin; it was not corrupt enough. Worst of all it was secondhand; it was not original and self-dependent—it was a shadow. Poe and Whitman, like bulbs in a glass bottle, could only exhaust what was in them.

If the editors of *The Cambridge History* had undertaken their task ten or fifteen years later than they did, the results would no doubt have been quite different. Professor Trent, born in 1862, was perhaps too old to modify materially his critical estimates. Stuart P. Sherman, however, was in 1924 to leave the University of Illinois to edit the "Books" section of the New York *Herald-Tribune*. There his reviews of the new books soon convinced Irving Babbitt and Paul Elmer More that their favorite disciple had betrayed the New Humanist movement.

In 1910 John Erskine had included in his *Leading American Novelists* the six writers of fiction whom, he said, "time has sifted . . . for special remembrance": Charles Brockden Brown, Fenimore Cooper, William Gilmore Simms, Nathaniel Hawthorne, Harriet Beecher Stowe, and Bret Harte. Why, the modern reader may well wonder, are there no chapters on Herman Melville, Mark Twain, Henry James, William Dean Howells, Sarah Orne Jewett, Frank Norris, or Stephen Crane? In 1925 Erskine was to scandalize some staid professors of English and the ancient classics by publishing *The Private Life of Helen of Troy*.

Carl Van Doren (1885–1950), the youngest of the four editors, soon gave up teaching. As one of the editors of the *Nation* and later of the *Century* and as founder of the Literary Guild in 1926 he gave notable encouragement to various writers of his own generation. As I have pointed out elsewhere, Van Doren had an important part in the radical revision of the American literary canon that took place in the 1920's and 1930's.

*Vernon L. Parrington.* In 1927, when Vernon Louis Parrington (1871–1929) brought out the first two volumes of his *Main Currents in American Thought*, he was so little known that his name did not appear in *Who's Who in America*. The impact of the book was immediate and profound. It won for its author the Pulitzer Prize not in literature but in history. The Great Depression and the New Deal made Parrington's liberal point of view seem much more timely than that of any one of his predecessors. Some of the young intellectuals found in *Main Currents* the "usable past" that they could not find in *The Cambridge History*. Even yet his book appears to be the most influential study of American literature that has been made; and this is true in spite of the fact that, as Parrington insisted, *Main Currents* is not a history of American literature, "that difficult task for which no scholar is as yet equipped." The book is primarily a study of American liberal thought as revealed by various writers whose intrinsic literary importance varies greatly.

Parrington was a professor of English, but his point of view was not academic. In 1918 he replied to a questionnaire sent to members of his class (1893) at Harvard that he was "up to [his] ears in the economic interpretation of American history, getting the last lingering Harvard prejudices out of [his] system." He had read Karl Marx, but one gathers that he was more deeply influenced by Taine, Charles A. Beard, and his colleague at the State University of Washington, J. Allen Smith. In the foreword to Volume 1 Parrington wrote: "The point of view from which I have endeavored to evaluate the materials, is liberal rather than conservative, Jeffersonian rather than Federalistic; and"—he was honest enough to add—"very likely I have found what I went forth to find, as others have discovered what they were seeking." Parrington's point of view and his critical method enabled him to throw new light upon the literature of the seventeenth and eighteenth centuries. He had no use for the genteel tradition, and he found the old New England poets too didactic, too sentimental, and too feeble. On the other hand, the effect of Parrington's book was to assign a new importance to Cooper, Thoreau, Melville, Whitman, and Howells. He regarded Whitman as the greatest of American writers. Volume 2 of *Main Currents* included a section entitled "The Mind of the Old South," in which the liberal historian displayed unexpected sympathy and understanding for such neglected figures as Beverley Tucker, John Pendleton Kennedy, William Gilmore Simms, Hugh Swinton Legaré, and John C. Calhoun.

Although Parrington was not greatly concerned with aesthetic judgments, many of his critical estimates still seem valid. It is obvious, however, as one reads the unfinished third volume, that he overrated some of his own contemporaries, like Sinclair Lewis, Sherwood Anderson, and James Branch Cabell. Who nowadays could agree with his estimate of Cabell? "A self-reliant intellectual, rich in the spoils of all literature, one of the great masters of English prose, the supreme comic spirit thus far granted us, he stands apart from the throng of lesser American novelists, as Mark Twain stood apart, individual and incomparable." Yet Parrington could put his finger on the weaknesses of the popular Joseph Hergesheimer, whom he found "a dabbler in psychology," with "always a hint of artistic insincerity." "His gorgeous prose style," he added, "is spotty and streaked by amazing crudeness."

Later critics have made much of Parrington's unfortunate comments on Poe and Henry James. Of Poe, whom he regarded as "the first of our artists and the first of our critics," he said that he had "no philosophy and no progress and no causes." "The problem of Poe," he concluded, "fascinating as it is, lies quite outside the main current of American thought, and it may be left with the psychologist and the belletrist with whom it belongs." Henry James seemed to Parrington not a realist but "the last flower of the Genteel Tradition." James, he said, "suffered the common fate of the *déraciné*; wandering between worlds, he found a home nowhere. It is not well for the artist to turn cosmopolitan, for the flavor of the fruit comes from the soil and sunshine of his native fields." James, he continued, "was concerned only with *nuances*. He lived in a world of fine gradations and imperceptible shades. Like modern scholarship he came to deal more and more with less and less." Modern scholarship has its shortcomings no doubt, but one gratefully remembers that it has shown how mistaken Parrington was in his estimates of two of our greatest writers.

*The Marxists.* The Great Depression turned the minds of rebellious young intellectuals toward economic and political problems. Some of them concluded prematurely that American democracy was a failure and fancied that salvation was to be found in Russian communism. In Russia of course the official view was that it was the duty of artists and writers to promote the Communist revolution. That also was the view of V. F. Calverton and Granville Hicks, who undertook the task of reinterpreting our literary history as the result of the economic conflict of classes.

In *The Liberation of American Literature* (1932) Victor Francis Calverton (1900–1940) held that American literature needed to be freed from servile imitation of European models and obedience to the dictates of the petty bourgeoisie, whose ethics made for "reticences and pruderies." The freedom that Calverton advocated had begun to come with the advent of Theodore Dreiser, Jack London, Upton Sinclair, and Michael Gold. For Calverton, Whitman was the greatest American writer, but he would have been still greater, said Calverton, if he had only espoused the ideals of a collectivist economy. Surprisingly enough, Calverton hailed Mark Twain as "the first American prose writer of any importance." The book is marred by many errors of fact as well as of judgment. Henry James is not even mentioned.

In 1933 Granville Hicks (1901– ), who was then a member of the English department at the Rensselaer Polytechnic Institute, brought out *The Great*

*Tradition*, a history of American literature since 1865. For Professor Hicks "the great tradition" was the critical and revolutionary spirit which, he felt, "moves in the noblest creations of all American writers," especially Emerson, Thoreau, Whitman, and Howells. These four along with Melville and Hawthorne, he thought, were our greatest writers. Hicks, as one might have expected, had no high opinion of Poe, Lowell, Henry James, Mark Twain, Emily Dickinson, or Stephen Crane. His verdict on Mark Twain was: "He was, and knew he was, merely an entertainer." Henry James, who was not able "to understand his own country," belonged to the class "that refused to justify existence in terms of anything it did." "For James," he said, "art was not a form of action but a form of enjoyment, and the artist was not a participant but an observer."

The best American writers of fiction in the twentieth century were, in Hicks's opinion, Dreiser, Lewis, Anderson, and Dos Passos. James Branch Cabell seemed to him "doubly a fraud, for neither his romanticism nor his pessimism is genuine." Quite mistakenly Hicks looked upon Ellen Glasgow as "one more apologist for a way of life that is rapidly vanishing." He admired Willa Cather's expert craftsmanship, but even "with her mastery of rhythm and her gift for imagery at their peak, she has become dull and empty except for those who find religiosity a satisfactory substitute for imaginative power."

When Hicks could forget the thesis which he was riding so hard, he could be a sound critic. Of Sarah Orne Jewett he said: "For a moment, as we yield to her art, we feel that here is a master, though a master of a tiny realm." He recognized the power to be found in the poems of Emily Dickinson, but they seemed to him too "fragile and remote." Hicks's verdict upon Edwin Arlington Robinson was that "much of his poetry is cold and remote, and some of it has no significance at all for Robinson's America." Hicks recognized Robert Frost as an important poet, but he added: "For all his common sense and originality, he has chosen to identify himself with a moribund tradition." Hicks held a still lower opinion of the writings of T. S. Eliot, especially after he got religion and joined the Anglican Church. Truly, as Edmund Wilson wrote in an essay entitled "Marxism and Literature," "The leftist critic is always trying to measure works of literature by tests which have no validity in that field."

The Stalin-Hitler Pact of 1939, which was soon to result in the partition of Poland, disillusioned Granville Hicks, and he resigned from the Communist party.

The Marxist critics saw plainly enough some of the shortcomings of democratic societies, but they refused to see what state control would do to poets and novelists who had no interest in promoting a Communist revolution. Marx and Engels had some appreciation of great literature and music, but the Communist rulers in Eastern Europe seem to value literature and the other arts merely as forms of propaganda. In the classless society of the future, according to Marx and Engels, the government would shrink to almost nothing. In such a society, if it ever came into being, what would be the function of the writer whose business had been to promote the Communist revolution? What would be left to the Communist poet but to write hymns and odes to the Communist saints, Marx, Engels, and Lenin? It would never do of course to celebrate the achievements of those discredited leaders, Trotsky, Stalin, Molotov, Bulganin, and Khrushchev.

*Ludwig Lewisohn.* In the preface to his *Expression in America* (1932), later entitled *The Story of American Literature*, Ludwig Lewisohn (1882–1955) wrote: "I use the organon or method of knowledge associated with the venerated name of Sigmund Freud." He was in effect trying to write a history of American literature from a point of view quite unhistorical. The "historical estimate," said Lewisohn, "is an academic delusion." Philip Freneau, he declared, was "excellent . . . only in comparison with his dreadful contemporaries." Lewisohn had had sound academic training, and he could write better than most of our literary historians. When his judgment was not distorted by prejudice, he could write excellent criticism; but his prejudices were many and unyielding, especially those involving race, religion, sex, and censorship. He could see Puritanism only as a repressive force. Imaginative literature, he thought, had had no place in the New England colonies.

Lewisohn had praise for Poe as an "artist," but, he added, "As a critic he does not exist." Whitman was for him the greatest of the American poets; but without offering any evidence for an opinion not shared by the better Whitman authorities—he asserted: "He was a homosexual of the most pronounced and aggressive type." The "undersexed" Emerson was the only one of the New England group who had "a self-sustaining and permanent existence." Longfellow, Whittier, Holmes, and Lowell were "underbrush about this single soaring tree." Thoreau, however, was a minor classic. "He was intellectually one of the bravest men that ever lived, and also a clammy prig. He was a prose-stylist of singular and signal excellence and left no complete book behind him." Dr. Holmes, Lewisohn saw as "a snob, though a not unamiable one." Lowell, he thought, had "no critical method," and so "his formal criticism is justly forgotten." In the Harvard commemoration ode Lowell "mistook excitement for inspiration." For Lewisohn, Whittier was "a far more respectable and memorable figure than Longfellow." "The thing to establish in America," he said, "is not that Longfellow was a very small poet, but that he did not partake of the poetic character at all." Hawthorne he recognized as a classic, but he thought the Melville revival had proceeded much too far. *Mardi* and *Pierre* he considered "sheer phantasmagories, clinical material rather than achieved literature." The fine things in *Moby-Dick* constituted only "one-fourth of the long book." "Of the rest what is not sound and fury is inchoate and dull. . . . No, Melville is not even a minor master. His works constitute rather one of the important curiosities of literature." Mark Twain, who had no sense of form, was the "eternal adolescent" and hence paradoxically the creator of "the finest picaresque novel composed for centuries."

Lewisohn noted that in 1932 Howells was almost unread and that Henry James had only "a small circle of readers among the elderly and determinedly refined. But," Lewisohn boldly predicted, "I am persuaded that the revolutions of time and taste will, in their strangely cyclic course, restore both to an honorable place in the history of American civilization. . . ." This was in spite of the fact that "Howells, like his age, was acutely and negatively sex-conscious." Lewisohn did not care for James's later phase, but in spite of his faults James was "as stylist, master of form, creator of a body of memorable work . . . probably the most eminent man of letters America has yet to show." James's friend Edith Wharton, Lewisohn said, belonged with the "snobs and players of a social game." He added his own opinion: "One cannot be an artist and a lady." Had he forgotten Jane Austen, Willa Cather, and Ellen Glasgow? He apparently did not remember what he had written about a lady from Maine: "If ever there came into being a library of American literature devoted to creative expression and not to document, a slender volume would assuredly be dedicated to Sarah Orne Jewett." Lewisohn in discussing a lady from Amherst, Massachusetts, called Emily Dickinson "a great poet," but he did not approve of the "cult and tradition" which had grown up around her. He hailed *The Education of Henry Adams* as "not only a great but a crucial book, a classic of both American literature and American life." He saw George Santayana, neglected and undervalued by most of our earlier literary historians, as "a great writer and within his self-appointed limits a great sage."

Lewisohn was no great admirer of the poets and novelists of the twentieth century. Robert Frost, he admitted, was "no minor poet," but Ezra Pound was only a "strange curiosity of literature" who had nothing to say and whose work smelled "ferociously of the lamp." Eliot seemed to Lewisohn not much better than Pound: "The future will doubtless assign him a definite place among the minor poets and characteristic phenomena of the post-war period." He considered Hemingway's style "strong and sound and refreshing" even in his earlier books. He found Faulkner's books "needlessly intricate and essentially confused," and he was repelled by Faulkner's picture of man as "a vile animal crawling about a heap of ordure." Still, he admitted, "The dreadful Mississippians in his pages are set forth with ferocity and therefore with sharp vividness."

*Expression in America* contains some excellent literary criticism, but it is not what it seemed to many who read it in 1932. In that year Carl Van Doren wrote in the *Nation* for April 13: "The book, incidentally a superb history of American literature, is primarily a moral epic of America."

The Literary History of the United States *(1948)*. Published in three stout volumes in 1948, *The Literary History* was the most ambitious large-scale co-operative history to appear since the publication (in 1917–1921) of *The Cambridge History*. The editorial board was made up of seven distinguished scholars: Robert E. Spiller, Willard Thorp, Thomas H. Johnson, Henry Seidel Canby, Howard Mumford Jones, Dixon Wecter, and Stanley T. Williams. The third volume contained an indispensable bibliography which listed the many important scholarly and critical books and articles which had been published since 1921. In 1391 pages of text the seven editors and the forty-five other contributors discussed a total of no less than two hundred and six American authors. Aesthetic considerations and cultural movements figure more conspicuously in the *LHUS* than in the *CHAL*. There are many fine chapters on a great variety of topics. Among the best chapters are those that deal with publishing, copyright laws, booksellers, and periodicals; and there are excellent chapters on the interrelations of American and European literatures.

It is easy now to criticize the proportions of the book. Why, one wonders, when separate chapters were given to Edwards, Franklin, Irving, and Cooper, was it deemed necessary to lump together in a single chapter of less than forty pages the three Cambridge poets, Longfellow, Lowell, and Holmes? Their historical importance (and this book is a literary history and not a collection of critical essays) would have justified fuller treatment. And again, when a separate chapter was devoted to Henry Adams, why was Emily Dickinson not given a chapter by herself but paired with that very different poet, Sidney Lanier? The implication is that in 1948 the editors saw Emily Dickinson as only a minor poet. Jones Very is barely mentioned, and Frederick Goddard Tuckerman gets only part of a single paragraph. Among the twentieth-century writers Theodore Dreiser was given a chapter to himself, but that honor was not accorded to Sinclair Lewis, Thomas Wolfe, Scott Fitzgerald, Ernest Hemingway, William Faulkner, Edith Wharton, Willa Cather, or Ellen Glasgow. Of the twentieth-century poets only Edwin Arlington Robinson was given a separate chapter. Why not Robert Frost or T. S. Eliot, whose writings are discussed in four different parts of the book? Wallace Stevens gets less than two pages; E. E. Cummings, only a single paragraph.*

In an article entitled "Literary Economics and Literary History" (*English Institute Annual 1949* [1950]) the late William Charvat wrote:

> Nothing better demonstrates the dilemma of literary history than its uncertainty about what to do with popular writers in general and with the fireside poets—Bryant, Longfellow, Whittier, Lowell, Holmes —in particular. In every new history the space devoted to them shrinks. The shrinkage may be justified on critical but hardly on historical grounds, for the importance of these poets in their own century cannot decrease. We err, as historians, in allowing the taste of the modern reader to nullify the taste of the nineteenth-century reader. It is as if the political historian were to ignore the administration of Grant because it was not in accord with the social principles of Franklin D. Roosevelt.

In the *Hudson Review* (Summer, 1949) a specialist in the history of literary criticism, René Wellek, reviewed the *LHUS* under the caption "The Impasse of Literary History." The editors, he maintained, had no clear conception of either "literature" or "history." He could find in the book "no definite method, no focus of interest, no coherent critical standards." As examples of mistaken estimates Wellek pointed to the low ratings of Katherine Anne Porter and Robert Penn Warren. He objected to the praise of Carl Sandburg's *The People, Yes* as "one of the great American books."

With few exceptions the fifty-odd contributors were (or had been) professors of English. Some reviewers, however, were puzzled by the conspicuous absence of such distinguished specialists as Ralph Leslie Rusk, Arthur Hobson Quinn, Norman Foerster, Clarence Gohdes, James D. Hart, and DeLancey Ferguson. They noted also that among the contributors were younger scholars who had published nothing that appeared to justify their inclusion. One looks in vain also for the names of such well-known literary critics as Van Wyck Brooks, Mark Van Doren, Cleanth Brooks, Allen Tate, Edmund Wilson, Conrad Aiken, and T. S. Eliot. Some of the contributors had praise for Eliot and for a few of the New Critics; but, one infers, the editors had little sympathy with the methods or the aims of the New Critics. For their part, the New Critics had little interest in American literary history or indeed in most of the two hundred and six authors discussed in the *LHUS*.†

* In the July, 1949, number of the *South Atlantic Quarterly* I pointed out the shortcomings of the *LHUS* in its treatment of the writers of the southern states.
† Some time in the 1950's I heard one of the editors of *LHUS* remark: "When we were graduate students, the great enemies of scholarship in our field were the philologists; now, damn it, it's the New Critics!"

Yet if some younger readers of the *LHUS* felt that the rankings of important writers were already out of date, there were in 1948 a few older scholars who shared the feelings of Professor Rusk, who wrote in *American Literature* in January, 1950:

> And what a document for future historians, this snapshot of literary reputations old and new at the high noon of the twentieth century! Poe's antiquarian of nine centuries hence may look into it to discover that in our day T. S. Eliot was still stubbornly praised as a great poet, though he was plainly only a very clever, pedantic, and, as it happened, influential one; or that Melville, the high priest of a revived Calvinism from which both heaven and the grace of God had at last been pretty much omitted, was revered not only as a powerful artist, which he sometimes was, but as a deep philosopher. And yet, if Pundit, the antiquarian, looks carefully, he will see signs that these opinions suited to dwellers in a waste land and in an age of despair were already weakening.

In the one-volume edition of the *LHUS*, published in 1953, the editors added a "Postscript at Mid-Century," in which they recognized the now dominant position held by Eliot as both poet and critic, but they still seemed not quite ready to rank as a major American writer any one of the following: Frost, Stevens, Fitzgerald, Hemingway, and Faulkner.

In *The Cycle of American Literature* (1955), which is in large measure based upon the *LHUS*, Professor Spiller stated: "The first task of the new American literary historian was to discover which were or are the major American authors, and not to be misled by the fact that some of them denied their country and became expatriates, others lashed out against it with satire or overt denunciation, or escaped from it into dreams and fantasies." The twentieth-century writers whom Spiller now ranked as major figures were Adams, Dreiser, Robinson, Frost, O'Neill, Hemingway, and Faulkner. Of Scott Fitzgerald, Spiller remarked that only in *The Great Gatsby* did he manage "to say what he had to say in a tightly wrought artistic form." Wallace Stevens was mentioned only along with Archibald MacLeish, Hart Crane, Marianne Moore, and William Carlos Williams as among "Eliot's associates and followers in the classical movement" who were "far more American than he because they remained at home or returned."

That was in 1955. In 1968 the Jackson Bryer poll made it clear that Fitzgerald and Stevens are now regarded by the academic critics as major American writers. In 1955, however, a jury made up of academic critics would hardly have ranked either Fitzgerald or Stevens as a major American writer.

*The Literary Historian in a Changing Age.* In 1948 the editors of *The Literary History of the United States* began their preface by saying: "Each generation should produce at least one literary history of the United States, for each generation must define the past in its own terms." That was over twenty years ago, and perhaps the time has come when American scholars should once again undertake a large-scale cooperative history of American literature. There is no lack now of competent specialists, and the scholars of today have had excellent training in critical methods. They have available in our American libraries a great wealth of published materials in books, magazines, and guides of various kinds. There is also something like a consensus among older scholars as to just who are our important major and minor American writers.

And yet the future literary historian should remind himself that in this country disturbing shifts in literary taste and fashion come quickly and are not predictable. The historian cannot be sure that his appraisals will not become obsolete within a decade. As I shall point out in my conclusion, there are now plentiful signs that we are soon likely to see something like a thorough revision of the American literary canon. We are entering a new literary era, and its nature is obscure. In the words of Matthew Arnold, we seem to be

> Wandering between two worlds, one dead
> The other powerless to be born.

The future literary historian will be fortunate if for a decade the scholars accept his book as standard. He will be lucky if living poets and novelists do not brand his book as obsolete at the time of its publication.

The primary function of the literary historian is to provide student, teacher, and critic with useful and accurate factual information about important writers and the conditions under which they managed to write their books. For most of this factual information the historian is indebted to the many scholars who have provided him with a wealth of printed materials that he cannot afford to ignore even though he may find most of them either trivial or irrelevant. The American studies programs in our universities, useful though they certainly are, have not taught us how to synthesize aesthetic criticism with literary and cultural history; and the New Critics failed to develop a method that could promise to give us better literary histories than those we now have. There is, however, as G. R. Thompson pointed out in *American Literary Scholarship* for 1969, a "worldwide intellectual movement toward a firmer critical theory and toward a critical literary history as yet but incompletely noticed in America."

The literary historian of the future cannot, like some of his predecessors, think of literary history as primarily a scientific discipline. The choices that historian and anthologist are compelled to make are essentially critical in nature. New literary histories and anthologies are necessarily critical revaluations. The author must decide just which writers deserve inclusion in his book and what space and emphasis he shall give them. He should not shirk his responsibility as a critic by merely repeating the critical estimates of his predecessors. Scholarship, no matter how exact and extensive, is not a substitute for a catholic literary taste and sound critical standards.

There are no "definitive" literary histories. The individual historian cannot escape his own limitations. He is handicapped by his personal prejudices and prepossessions, by the defects in his training, by the deficiencies in his literary taste and in his critical judgment. It is difficult for him to escape the limitations of the generation of scholars to which he belongs.

The uses of the past are many and various, and each new generation of scholars has a different way of looking at those writers in whom it is interested. Every new literary history is already a little outmoded by the time it is published. The literary historian must expect younger scholars to disagree with some of his critical estimates, but they will, he can hope, find the factual matter in his book both accurate and useful. The historian must not confuse the student and the literary critic by repeating such exploded conjectures as that of Lewis Mumford, who in his life of Melville contended that in "Ethan Brand" Hawthorne had modeled his leading figure upon Melville and that the publication of the story caused a coolness between the two friends. As Randall Stewart pointed out, "Ethan Brand" was written and published before Hawthorne ever saw Melville.

If the literary historian does not learn from the failings of his predecessors, he is destined to repeat the mistakes of the past. In 1900 Barrett Wendell ignored Emily Dickinson, barely mentioned Melville, and failed to recognize Whitman as a great poet. In 1917 when the editors of the CHAL brought out their first volume, they did not foresee the revolt of the young intellectuals, who had little regard for the old New England poets. By 1921 when the last two volumes of CHAL appeared, many of its critical ratings were already outmoded. The new generation of poets and novelists could not find in its pages a "usable past." Again, by the time the three volumes of the LHUS came out in 1948, it was clearly evident that the New Critics, who were not numbered among the contributors to the LHUS, were rapidly winning control of English departments in many American colleges and universities. Judged by their critical tests, the LHUS not only contained outmoded critical ratings but also included too many authors who had no right to be there.

The literary historian must not permit his own advanced social and political opinions to prevent him from dealing justly with conservative authors like Paul Elmer More or Donald Davidson. He must not permit his personal feelings about expatriates to bias his treatment of T. S. Eliot or Ezra Pound. He should be able dispassionately to discuss the works of those authors (and they are not a few) whose private lives seem to him shockingly immoral. The historian must not, like the Marxist critics, treat poetry and fiction as without value when they do not advocate changes in the social order. The historian should free himself from such prejudices as that which led Ludwig Lewisohn to believe that no "lady" could possibly write enduring literature. Finally, the historian should remember that a fact is always a fact while the future rankings of American authors will be determined largely by changes in critical standards and literary taste.

There are two categories of writers who, it seems to me, have not in our day received from either literary historians or critics the full recognition they deserve. One type of author has a great many readers; the other, comparatively few.

Literary historians have been so preoccupied with classifying and ranking our poets, playwrights, and novelists that they seem not to realize that in many instances the sciences and the social sciences have taken over functions formerly reserved to belles-lettres. The physician, the psychologist, the philosopher, the physicist, the sociologist, and the economist find fewer readers than the successful novelist; but each of them has special qualifications for understanding the human environment and interpreting the human experience that the average novelist conspicuously lacks. Some of them, moreover, have superior literary talents.

Many of the modern poets have been more deeply concerned with technical problems and aesthetic effects than with exploring the meaning of life. This abrogation of the great poet's traditional function is no doubt one reason why today poets have no such wide circle of readers as those who eagerly awaited new volumes by Longfellow and Tennyson. In the nineteenth century readers looked upon the major poets as prophets; but in our time no critic, analyzing poems that demand elaborate explication, would maintain that the poets are, in Shelley's words, "the unacknowledged legislators of the world." W. H. Auden is not the only major poet of our time who has found that writing poetry is less profitable than lecturing or writing about his own poems. One is tempted sometimes to agree with Thomas Love Peacock, Lord Macaulay, and George Santayana that—so Macaulay phrased it in his essay on Milton—"as civilization advances, poetry almost necessarily declines."

Our modern novelists have found many more readers than any poet of the twentieth century; but too many of them have been content merely to mirror a world of disorder and violence, and some of them have filled their books with such despicable characters as to suggest that the unfortunate novelist has known no other kind. That is not the type of fiction that a century ago in England and America men and women looked for in new novels by George Eliot and Hawthorne.

Justice Oliver Wendell Holmes was, like his father, elected to the Hall of Fame for Great Americans, but his election came because he was a great jurist, not because he was a distinguished man of letters. And yet Justice Holmes was master of a racy prose style hardly inferior to that employed by his father in *The Autocrat of the Breakfast-Table*. Unfortunately the justice wrote primarily for members of his own profession and not for the *Atlantic Monthly*'s wider circle of readers. Literary historians have too often neglected or underrated such accomplished prose writers as William James and George Santayana because they could find no suitable category for them. They have made us fully aware of the literary merits of Prescott, Motley, Parkman, and Henry Adams; but they have had little to say about Alfred T. Mahan and such later historians as Carl Becker, Allan Nevins, and Samuel Eliot Morison. The literary historians have not always fully appreciated the literary power of members of their own guild; yet who among those now living can write like Vernon L. Parrington or Van Wyck Brooks? Our literary historians have made much of Jonathan Edwards, the Mathers, and other Colonial ministers; but they have had little to say about Henry Ward Beecher and Lyman Abbott or such eloquent later ministers as the late Harry Emerson Fosdick. The literary historians have made much of the writings of Franklin, Jefferson, and Lincoln, but they have almost ignored Woodrow Wilson. In their preoccupation with such major poets as T. S. Eliot and Robert Frost the critics and literary historians alike seem to have forgotten such gifted humorous poets as Richard Armour and Morris Bishop, and strangely enough, they have shown only a casual interest in Eliot's fine humorous poems about cats.

In *From the Shadow of the Mountain* (1961) Van Wyck Brooks stated his belief that "the best writers are now the writers of natural history who are ignored commonly in critical circles." The authors that Brooks had in mind were not writers of scientific fiction or the journalistic popularizers of scientific discoveries but such respected scientists as William Beebe and Rachel Carson and competent amateurs like Joseph Wood Krutch. It may be worth our while to remember that back in the nineteenth century the literary historians regarded Henry David Thoreau as little more than an eccentric amateur naturalist. It remained for the twentieth century to discover that he was in fact a major American writer. Is literary history in danger of repeating that mistake?

Many of our literary critics and historians have been so attracted to sophisticated, alienated, and obscure writers that they have neglected widely-read poets and novelists who were able to speak both *for* and *to* their countrymen. They have magnified obscure poets like Jones Very and Gerard Manley Hopkins and have not done full justice to those favorites of middle-class readers, Longfellow and Tennyson. Critics and historians alike have preferred to write about novelists like Henry James, who was caviar to the general public, and poets like T. S. Eliot, whose poems demand elaborate explication. Eliot himself had much to say about the merits of minor seventeenth-century English poets and playwrights like George Herbert and Cyril Tourneur but not much in praise of the greatest of them all, Shakespeare and Milton.

Critical suspicion of the popular author for many years kept the literary historians from seeing that Mark Twain was a major American writer, and I think it still stands in the way of full recognition of the merits of William Gilmore Simms and Harriet Beecher Stowe. Neither Simms nor Mrs. Stowe was an accomplished stylist or a finished artist. Their books betray plentiful signs of carelessness and haste; but, like Scott, Dickens, and Dumas, they had the true instinct for narrative, a sense of the dramatic, and the ability to depict unforgettable scenes and to create memorable characters.

Critical suspicion of the popular author has led literary historians to underestimate the merits of a number of widely-read writers in the twentieth century. In his discussion of "Van Wyck Brooks's Second Phase" Edmund Wilson wrote in 1940:

> Van Wyck Brooks has now suffered the fate of many a good writer before him. Beginning as an opposition critic, read by a minority of the public, he has lived to become a popular author, read by immense numbers of people and awarded a Pulitzer prize—with the result that the ordinary reviewers are praising him indiscriminately and the highbrows are trying to drop him. One has seen the same sort of thing happen with Eugene O'Neill, with Miss Millay, with Hemingway, with Thornton Wilder—and always to the obscuration of their actual merits and defects.

Wilson might well have expanded his list to include the names of Stephen Vincent Benét, James Branch Cabell, Robert Frost, Vachel Lindsay, Carl Sandburg, Owen Wister, and Booth Tarkington. The poets approved by the New Critics and their successors are not poets who can sing, like Burns, Shelley, or Edna St. Vincent Millay. Sandburg and Benét might have fared better with the critics if they had been less consciously American and had filled their poems with phrases and allusions drawn from esoteric sources in many literatures. Booth Tarkington was an expert craftsman. He displayed great skill in his handling of description, dialogue, and narrative; and he always had a good story to tell. In the 1920's, however, he lost favor with the intellectuals because, like the earlier Howells, he had chosen to write chiefly about the pleasanter aspects of American life. Owen Wister's reputation has suffered from a critical confusion of his best-seller, *The Virginian*, with dime novels that have their background in the cattle country. That romance, however, contains some memorable scenes and also a thoughtful interpretation of the course of western history. His *Lady Baltimore*, which gives evidence of his study of the novels of his friend Henry James, is a carefully-planned and well-written picture of life in Charleston which did much to promote better understanding of southern life among northern readers.

Literary historians have for the most part ignored the most amazing best-seller of the twentieth century, *Gone with the Wind* (1936), as though it were nothing but a subliterary melodramatic romance. Margaret Mitchell's book is in fact better than that. It is not to be ruled out as a conventional romance of the Civil War, a Georgia local-color story, or a glorification of the antebellum southern plantation. Except in the motion picture version the chief characters do not belong to great planter families and do not live in southern "mansions." Miss Mitchell's style can hardly be called distinguished; but, unlike many modern novelists, she had an instinct for narrative and she had a great story to tell. The book contains some moving and unforgettable scenes. The novel expressed the postwar mood of thousands of American and European readers who had lived through the First World War. In reading the story of Melanie Wilkes and Scarlett O'Hara they experienced the katharsis of reliving vicariously some of their own tragic experiences.

As a work of art *Gone with the Wind* has serious flaws, and they are spelled out in detail in the spring, 1970, number of the *Southern Literary Journal* in an article by Professor Floyd Watkins of Emory University in Atlanta, Georgia. "Great literature," Watkins admits, "can occasionally be popular and certainly popular literature can occasionally be great. But with a few notable exceptions such as the Bible but not *Gone with the Wind*, greatness and popularity are more likely to be contradictory than congenial." As Watkins sees the novel, it "consists of melodrama, sentimentality, perfect characters, evil and good in black and white, anti-Negro racism . . . , artificial dialogue, exaggerated Negro dialect," etc. The novel is "false to historical fact and also false to the human heart." "It created a myth which seems to ease the hunger of all extravagantly Southern and little romantic souls."

The indictment that Watkins has brought against Margaret Mitchell's romance could with a few minor alterations be brought against Shakespeare's *Henry V* and *Richard III*, against Scott's *Ivanhoe*, Cooper's *The Last of the Mohicans*, Simms's *The Partisan*, and Dumas's *The Three Musketeers*. None of these historical novels or plays gives an accurate picture of the past, and there is slovenly writing in most of them. In "A Gossip on Romance" Robert Louis Stevenson pointed out a not untypical bit of slovenly writing in the midst of one of the finest scenes in *Guy Mannering*. Nevertheless, he wrote: "Walter Scott is out and away the king of the romantics."

Professor Watkins's bias, and that of other academic critics, is indicated in his opening paragraph: "The practices of the best modern novelists present meditation above all other things. Story in the sense of a straightforward narrative may matter little or none." In another chapter I have quoted Watkins's opinion that "the discipline of modern methods of criticism and the art of Thomas Wolfe's books seem to move at cross purposes." Margaret Mitchell's romance is not one of the great American books, but it has merits that "the discipline of modern methods of criticism" tends to belittle or ignore.

*Part Three. Current Views of the American Literary Canon*

*When I first thought of this address, I had prepared a copi-*
*ous list of titles to present your highness, as an undisputed*
*argument for what I affirm [that our age is not "altogether*
*unlearned, and devoid of writers in any kind"]. The originals*
*were posted fresh upon all gates and corners of streets; but,*
*returning in a very few hours to take a review, they were all*
*torn down, and fresh ones in their places. I inquired after*
*them among readers and booksellers; but I inquired in vain;*
*the memorial of them was lost among men; their places were*
*no more to be found; and I was laughed to scorn for a clown*
*and a pedant, without all taste and refinement. . . .*

> Jonathan Swift, A *Tale of a Tub* (1704),
> "The Epistle Dedicatory to His Royal
> Highness Prince Posterity"

# Chapter 11. The Major American Writers

## THE NINETEENTH CENTURY

*Carl Van Doren, "Toward a New Canon" (1932).* "The canon of American literature refuses to stay fixed." So wrote Carl Van Doren in the *Nation* on April 13, 1932. What had happened, he asked, to the old American literary canon?

> Emerson and Hawthorne and Thoreau, risen dramatically above Bry-
> ant, Longfellow, Whittier, Holmes, and Lowell, stand in the rarer
> company of Poe and Whitman. Irving and Howells have shrunk and
> faded. Cooper has scarcely held his own. Mark Twain seems a great
> man of letters as well as a great man. Henry James seems a brilliant
> artist whatever nation he belongs to. Herman Melville has thrust him-
> self by main strength, and Emily Dickinson has gently slipped, into
> the canon.

Why, Van Doren wondered, had it taken so long to make these alterations in the canon of the great American writers?

> There is no use trying to calculate how much the rank of some of
> these older classics was due to the vested interest of publishers who
> had issued collected editions, or of teachers in schools and colleges
> who knew how to "teach" Longfellow but not Emily Dickinson, How-
> ells but not Dreiser, Irving but not Mencken. Vested interests were not
> all. A good many men and women taught to read in the nineteenth

century could not endure to read about the twentieth when they saw it bared in literature. Patriotism and propriety had a hand. So, of course, had the natural inertia with which each age resists the age that follows it.

Van Doren thought that years would have to pass before the traditional canon was thoroughly revised and, he added, before Americans would be ready "to distinguish between their major and their minor prophets." In a prophetic mood he continued:

> Not much help can be expected from the American Academy or from the universities. They will do no more than wait till the work has been done by actual workers. Then they will hold on to the revised canon with stubborn opposition to any further changes which some later age may have to insist upon.

In 1935 when Van Doren published a little book entitled *American Literature: An Introduction,* a somewhat unsympathetic reviewer who belonged to an older generation, Professor Fred Lewis Pattee, thus indicated the nature of the new canon as Van Doren now saw it:

> Van Doren's little volume excludes Bryant, Longfellow, Whittier, Holmes, Lowell, Stowe, Harte, and the like, and fills one fourth of his space with Emily Dickinson, Henry Adams, Mencken, Cabell, Dreiser, Lewis. Paine, Poe, Melville, Thoreau, Whitman, Mark Twain, and Emerson (who was feared by his own generation as a heretic)—these are the American writers worth a modern critic's ink.

*Dumas Malone, "Who Are the American Immortals?" (1937).* In April, 1937, a distinguished historian, Dumas Malone (1892–), published in *Harper's Magazine* an article entitled "Who Are the American Immortals?" As editor-in-chief of *The Dictionary of American Biography* Malone had had a large share of the responsibility for the selection of those Americans no longer living who were to be included in the *Dictionary* and of indicating to contributing specialists the limited space allotted to each biographical sketch. Malone was fully aware of the "fundamental difficulty" inherent in the selection of the greatest Americans. There is, he said, "no acceptable criterion of greatness."

The first five names on Malone's list were in order: (1) Washington, (2) Lincoln, (3) Jefferson, (4) Franklin, and—to the surprise of many readers in 1937—(5) Woodrow Wilson. The first four had been ranked at the top in 1900 by the college of electors who placed them in the Hall of Fame for Great Americans. Each of Malone's top five was a writer of some importance, but not one of them—not even Franklin—owed his selection primarily to what he had written.

> Of the men of letters [Malone explained] I speak with diffidence and with no pretense of finality. Fashions change more rapidly in literature than in politics. It has been incumbent upon me to consider the historical importance rather than the present–day popularity of authors; but, like everybody else, I am affected by contemporary taste, which militates against the claims of old favorites like Longfellow and Whittier. Before writing this article I again consulted some of the literary historians and I have deferred largely to their judgment. However, they did not entirely agree with one another and no one of them will agree fully with me.

The eight men of letters on Malone's list were: (1) Emerson, (2) Hawthorne, (3) Mark Twain, (4) Whitman, (5) Poe, (6) Henry James, (7) Thoreau, (8) Cooper.

> About the continuing importance of Emerson [Malone said] my advisers pretty generally agreed, but they differed widely about Thoreau. Hawthorne seems to be holding his ground rather well, Mark Twain and Whitman to be gaining, and Poe to be slipping somewhat. Henry James and Cooper are preferred to Washington Irving and James Russell Lowell.

In 1937 some one among Malone's advisers should have told him that Melville and Emily Dickinson were being ranked as major writers by competent critics and also that in 1937, the year of the Howells centenary, his reputation was clearly on the rise.

On April 3, 1937, Bernard De Voto (1897–1955), the new editor of the *Saturday Review of Literature*, printed in that magazine an editorial entitled "At the Cannon's Mouth," in which he said that Dumas Malone had climbed "out on a long limb" and had failed to rank the great American writers in their proper order. Malone's rankings were, he thought, pretty much those in vogue when *The Cambridge History of American Literature* (1917–1921) appeared "except that Mark Twain has too high a place and Melville's name does not appear." Hawthorne, to whom Malone had given second place, was probably ranked too high "for today's opinion." Henry James and Thoreau, he said, "are certainly ranked too low." Fenimore Cooper seemed to De Voto "hardly more than a text-book figure." De Voto seemed unaware of the keen new interest among scholars in Cooper as a critic of American life. He was clearly mistaken in thinking that Poe was "important chiefly as a vested interest of professional scholars." De Voto was, he said, sure only that the three greatest American writers were Emerson, Thoreau, and Mark Twain, but he did not know in what order their names should appear. (Apparently De Voto had forgotten that he had criticized Malone for giving third place to Mark Twain.) For the next five places De Voto's selections were Hawthorne, Henry James, Melville, Whitman, and James Russell Lowell. He had some praise for Howells and for Emily Dickinson ("a good bet for the long pull"), but he did not add them to his list of immortals. Aware that he, too, had climbed "out on a long limb," De Voto concluded: "The list is for today only and has no necessary relation to opinions its compiler held last year. Public notice: He will not debate it on this page or by letter."

Five years earlier Carl Van Doren had done a better job of ranking the major nineteenth-century writers than either Malone or De Voto. Van Doren, however, it should be remembered, was not only a shrewd critic but a literary historian with a scholar's training at Columbia University. He had tried his hand with some success at writing both verse and prose. As a magazine editor and as founder of the Literary Guild he had come to know many contemporary writers and had heard them discuss their aims and methods.

Malone did not include in his list the names of Bryant, Longfellow, Whittier, Holmes, or Lowell. De Voto, who included Lowell, defended his choice by asserting: "A strong case can be made out for the first American critic of importance [why not Poe?] and the writer of 'The Biglow Papers.'" Such a verdict would have surprised no one had it been made in the 1890's. In October, 1891, shortly before Lowell's death, the *Review of Reviews* had hailed him as "the most eminent American who has lived in the last decade of the century." In "A Calendar of Great Americans" in *Mere Literature and Other Essays* (1896), Woodrow Wilson wrote: "Among men of letters Lowell is doubtless most typically American, though [George William] Curtis must find an eligible place on the list." Lowell, Wilson conceded, "was self-conscious . . . [and] a trifle too 'smart' . . . [but he] was so versatile, so urbane, of so large a spirit, and so admirable in the scope of his sympathies, that he must certainly go on the calendar." Wilson, who did not include on his list any one of the nine or ten nineteenth-century writers now rated as major, was a better judge of statesmen than of literary men and women.

The most surprising item in Malone's list of the forty American immortals is the name of Woodrow Wilson, who a few years earlier had been so unmercifully maligned and ridiculed by H. L. Mencken, John Dos Passos, and many others. On *Vanity Fair*'s poll in April, 1922, Wilson was given —2.9 points on a scale ranging from +25 to —25. A month later the *Bookman*'s panel of judges gave him —7.2. H. L. Mencken, Willard Huntington Wright, Ernest Boyd, Floyd Dell, and John Macy each gave Wilson —25. Carl Van Doren gave him —10, and Gilbert Seldes, Burton Rascoe, and Louis Untermeyer gave him o. That was in 1922. As we look back nearly half a century later, one feels keenly the naiveté and lack of intelligence in political matters of so many of our novelists, poets, playwrights, and in particular our literary critics.

*Ernest Hemingway*, The Green Hills of Africa (*1935*). Hemingway (1898–1961) thought it was a mistake for a novelist to write literary criticism. He did, however, go so far as to name a number of writers whom he admired. He had praise for the great French and Russian novelists: Stendhal, Dumas, Flaubert, Maupassant, Tolstoy, Turgenev, and Dostoevski; and he liked Thomas Mann. Among the English and Irish writers he admired Fielding, Marryat, Emily Bronte, Kipling, W. H. Hudson, George Moore, and James Joyce. The writers whom he admired most were those whose books had aided him in his search for a technique suited to the expression of his own vision of life. He was especially indebted to Sherwood Anderson, Ezra Pound, and Gertrude Stein, who had given him helpful advice. The list of important writers of fiction whom Hemingway did not name is a long one: Scott, Jane Austen, Dickens, Thackeray, George Eliot, Meredith, Stevenson, Hardy, Hugo, Balzac, George Sand, Zola, Irving, Cooper, Hawthorne, Howells, Harte, Cable, Edith Wharton, Willa Cather, and Ellen Glasgow.

Hemingway's low opinion of nineteenth-century American writers is best expressed in *The Green Hills of Africa* (1935). Poe, he said, "is a skilful writer. It is skilful, marvellously constructed, and it is dead." Hemingway did not relish the rhetoric in Melville's *Moby-Dick*. There were good things in the book, he admitted. "But the people who praise it, praise it for the rhetoric which is not important. They put a mystery in which is not there." Hemingway admitted that Thoreau was "supposed to be really good," but he added that he had not yet been able to read him. Thoreau's New England contemporaries seemed to Hemingway "very good men with the small, dried, and excellent wisdom of Unitarians; men of letters; Quakers with a sense of humor." Of "Emerson, Hawthorne, Whittier and Company" Hemingway remarked that "they had minds, yes. Nice, dry, clean minds."

"The good writers," said Hemingway, "are Henry James, Stephen Crane, and Mark Twain." "All modern American literature," he said, "comes from one book by Mark Twain called *Huckleberry Finn.* . . . All American writing comes from that. There was nothing before. There has been nothing as good since."

In an essay on "Mark Twain and the Art of Writing" (*Harper's*, October, 1920) Brander Matthews noted Clemens's dislike of Scott, Cooper, and other well-known writers of fiction and commented: "Here we come face to face with one of Mark's most obvious limitations as a critic of literature—he is

implacable in applying the standards of today to the fiction of yesterday."
Brander Matthews was writing about his friend and contemporary; but he
accurately described the attitudes of Ernest Hemingway, William Faulkner,
Nelson Algren, John O'Hara, and some other twentieth-century writers of
fiction.

*Academic Estimates.* In the summer of 1951 two distinguished scholars,
Randall Stewart of Brown University and Stanley T. Williams of Yale,
planned a book which in 1956 the Modern Language Association published
under the title *Eight American Authors: A Review of Research and Criticism.**
The eight authors included, with the names of the scholars who wrote the
various chapters, are in order: Poe (Jay B. Hubbell), Emerson (Floyd Stovall), Hawthorne (Walter Blair), Thoreau (Lewis Leary), Melville (Stanley
T. Williams), Whitman (Willard Thorp), Mark Twain (Harry Hayden
Clark), and Henry James (Robert E. Spiller). As to the basis of selection
the editor, Professor Stovall, stated in his preface: "They were chosen both
for their intrinsic worth and for the significance of the biographical and critical writing that has been done on them and their work." Howells and Emily
Dickinson were both considered and rejected, Howells apparently because
the scholars consulted were not sure that he was a major American writer.
The case of Emily Dickinson was somewhat different. In the 1950's while
many scholars regarded her as a major American writer, there was in those
years no scholarly edition of either her poems or her letters, and there could
be no full and accurate biography until the Dickinson family were willing
for accredited scholars to examine their carefully hoarded manuscripts.

There was never then any more than there is now any absolute agreement
among scholars as to which of our earlier authors belong in the canon of the
great American writers. In 1955, a year before the publication of *Eight
American Authors,* Professor C. Hugh Holman wrote in an essay on American literary criticism since 1930:

> There is a . . . tendency, as the contemporary critic looks back, to
> re-evaluate the writers of the nineteenth century. The great trans-
> cendentalists of New England have given place before an intensive
> interest in Herman Melville and Nathaniel Hawthorne. Jonathan Ed-
> wards has begun to challenge Benjamin Franklin's eighteenth century
> supremacy. Henry James has gained an unquestioned ascendency over
> William Dean Howells. Whitman has been partially eclipsed by inter-
> est in figures like Emily Dickinson and Stephen Crane, while the re-

* The revised edition of *Eight American Authors,* edited by James Woodress and
published in 1971 by W. W. Norton and Company, contains new information about the
reputations of these major American writers.

vival of interest in Poe, particularly as a critic, is rapidly restoring him to a prominent position as the artist of the nineteenth century in America.

Eight years later (September 1, 1963) Alexander Cowie wrote in the New York *Times Review of Books*:

> Emerson is down; Hawthorne is up. Whitman is down; Melville is up. Howells is written off; Mark Twain is "active" but is read less for his humor than for tokens of pessimism, disturbed conscience, signs of "psychic wound." Poe, always lurking in a shadowed niche, has moved a little more clearly into view. Thus does the age reshuffle the position of the gods in America's literary pantheon. They will be reshuffled again—be sure of that.*

Five years later Hyatt H. Waggoner was to note that Emerson's stock was rising while Hawthorne's was falling. Nevertheless the ten American writers to whom I have given separate chapters seem to be holding their own. Howells's claim to major status is less secure than that of his friends Mark Twain and Henry James.

How the twenty-first century will rank the ten no one can tell. It is well to remember, however, that in its selection of the major writers of the nineteenth century, the twentieth has singled out those writers who seem in some way alienated from the society in which they lived. This is especially the case with Poe, Melville, Thoreau, and Henry James. These men, however, did not see themselves as alienated or wish to be alienated; and none of them was so completely alienated as Ezra Pound or T. S. Eliot.

In recent years the emphasis in college courses has been upon the major writers and their masterworks, and as a result there are textbooks in which the term "major" is stretched to include far too many writers who in my restricted sense of the word are definitely minor. For example, the 1945 edition of *Major American Writers*, edited by Howard Mumford Jones and Ernest E. Leisy, contained selections from no less than thirty-five "major" authors. *The Mentor Book of Major American Poets* (1962), edited by Oscar Williams and Edwin Honig, included selections from no less than twenty poets. I do not believe that we have as many as twenty major American poets; and I do not believe that in my sense of the word Edward Taylor, Longfellow, and Stephen Crane (who is perhaps a major American writer of fiction) are major poets. In 1962 also appeared *Major Writers of America*, under the general editorship of the late Perry Miller. The two volumes included no less than thirty-eight "major" American writers. Among the fifteen

---

* When I asked Professor Cowie why he had not mentioned Emily Dickinson, who is one of his favorite poets, he replied: "I think that for the moment I simply forgot her."

authors in Volume 1, I find the names of William Bradford, Edward Taylor, Irving, Cooper, Bryant, Longfellow, and Lowell. Since the editors relaxed their standards enough to admit three of the schoolroom poets, one wonders on what basis they chose to exclude Whittier and Holmes. And, above all, why did they choose to leave out Howells, Bret Harte, Cable, Francis Parkman, and Sarah Orne Jewett—to name no others—who by aesthetic standards are greater writers than William Bradford and Edward Taylor. One can understand why the editors would like to acquaint their students with these writers, but why confuse the students by labeling minor authors as "major"?

As these anthologies suggest, there is now in academic circles a new interest in our minor writers. For the Colonial period there is keen interest in Edward Taylor and Jonathan Edwards. There is a disposition to rank Longfellow as the best of the schoolroom poets. Lanier, who in 1900 seemed to some critics almost a major poet, was down-graded in the 1920's and 1930's, but there are indications that his stock is slowly rising. Of the other minor poets there is considerable interest in Jones Very, Frederick Goddard Tuckerman, Henry Timrod, and George Henry Boker. They now seem better poets than Bayard Taylor, Richard Henry Stoddard, and Edmund Clarence Stedman. In *American Literary Scholarship* for 1969 J. V. Ridgely wrote: "The relatively elevated reputations of Irving, Cooper, Howells, and Crane have not been successfully challenged; no other aspirant among nineteenth-century fiction writers has yet made it to this modest mountaintop." He added, however, that Simms and Mrs. Stowe were "on the verge of achieving 'major minor' status."

> *I hung my verses in the wind*
> *Time and tide their faults may find,*
> *All were winnowed through and through*
> *Five lines lasted sound and true.*
>
> . . . . . . . . . .
>
> *Have you eyes to find the five*
> *Which five hundred did survive?*
> Ralph Waldo Emerson, "The Test"

> *There are many qualities and causes that give permanency*
> *to a book, but universal vogue during the author's lifetime is*
> *not one of them.*
> Woodrow Wilson, "An Author's Company" in
> *Mere Literature and Other Essays*

# THE TWENTIETH CENTURY

If it is difficult to get a consensus among critics as to who the great nineteenth-century writers are, it is almost impossible to get them to agree on which of the writers of the present century should be admitted to the canon of the great American writers. The various polls and critical ratings that I have noticed show continual changes in the status of the later writers on every level whether their merits are appraised by booksellers, book collectors, literary journalists, or academic specialists. It was many years before T. S. Eliot was generally ranked as a major writer, and it was still longer before William Faulkner was widely regarded as a great novelist. During the Depression era the immensely popular Joseph Hergesheimer lost ground, and so did Edith Wharton and Scott Fitzgerald; but there has been a Fitzgerald revival and Mrs. Wharton is now more highly regarded than she was a decade or two ago. There are no signs, however, of a Hergesheimer revival.

*Academic Appraisals.* The 1920's and 1930's were a great period in American literary history; but its poets, novelists, and playwrights are little read outside of college classes. Their reputations are now largely in the keeping of academic specialists, who are often better scholars than literary critics.

In 1962 at a conference on Editions of American writers, the Committee on Priorities of the Modern Language Association headed by Henry Nash Smith named Hawthorne, Poe, Whitman, Mark Twain, Melville, Emerson, Thoreau, and Henry James as major American writers of the nineteenth century. With less unanimity they agreed that Eliot, Faulkner, Frost, Hemingway, O'Neill, and Wallace Stevens might justly be called major writers of the twentieth century. All fourteen they considered worth full and fine editions. Emily Dickinson was not named because in 1962 there were excellent editions of both her letters and her poems.

The committees of the Modern Language Association, however, are not in agreement as to the greatest American writers of this century. In December, 1959, the association initiated the policy of electing creative writers as Honorary Fellows of the Association. Thus far (through 1968) the following American authors have been honored: W. H. Auden, T. S. Eliot, Robert Lowell, Archibald MacLeish, Marianne Moore, Katherine Anne Porter, John Crowe Ransom, John Steinbeck, Thornton Wilder, and William Carlos Williams. These are all writers of some importance, but one wonders at finding none of the following names on the list: Donald Davidson, James Dickey, John Dos Passos, William Faulkner, Ernest Hemingway, Ezra Pound, Carl

Sandburg, Wallace Stevens, Allen Tate, Robert Penn Warren, Eudora Welty, John Hall Wheelock, and Edmund Wilson.

In the annual review of criticism and research, *American Literary Scholarship*, edited first by James Woodress and currently by J. Albert Robbins, there is in each volume a chapter entitled "Fiction: 1900 to the 1930's." In the 1965 volume (published in 1967), C. Hugh Holman wrote: "Ten major figures of the period now appear to be, in order of their appearance on the literary scene, Henry James, Edith Wharton, Ellen Glasgow, Theodore Dreiser, Willa Cather, John Dos Passos, Sinclair Lewis, F. Scott Fitzgerald, Ernest Hemingway, William Faulkner, Thomas Wolfe, and John Steinbeck." Holman did not indicate which of these twentieth-century writers of fiction he would rank, along with Henry James, in the rarer company of Poe, Hawthorne, and Mark Twain. Under the caption of "Lesser Writers" Holman discussed Sherwood Anderson, Katherine Anne Porter, and Jack London. He added: "James T. Farrell, whose contribution to the American novel has been great, has fallen of late on bad critical days." In the 1965 volume of *American Literary Scholarship* Faulkner is (with the exception of Henry James) the only one of Holman's "major figures" who was given a separate chapter. In *ALS* for 1969 William White wrote:

> Hemingway and Fitzgerald enthusiasts and specialists . . . are almost being drowned in a sea of academic ink. Much of the writing, if not most of it, is of a fairly high quality, though some of the work is in the area of esoterica, a little of it is pedantic, and some scholarly mountains bring forth professional mice. Those who have followed Hemingway's reputation from the time, even before his death in 1961, when many wondered how long he would survive on the American literary scene, cannot but be surprised—and some of us pleased—at the high position he now occupies. The same thing may be said of Fitzgerald, whose climb upward has been longer and slower.

As one looks through the annual volumes of *ALS* for 1963–1969, it becomes evident that the poets who interested the academic critics were Frost, Robinson, Pound, Hart Crane, and Cummings. (Eliot, classified as an English poet, was not included.) In the 1965 volume Ann Stanford remarked: "By far the bulk of criticism for 1965 is on Pound. . . . Even Allen Tate, critical of Pound's ideas and the lack of order in his poetry, finds that Pound has done more than any other man to rejuvenate the language." Rated as minor poets only are Conrad Aiken, Carl Sandburg, Archibald MacLeish, John Gould Fletcher, and Vachel Lindsay. In the 1966 volume Gorham Munson wrote: "It is doubtful if anything written in 1966 will raise the drooping reputations of Sandburg, Jeffers, and Masters or revive the dead reputation of [Edwin] Markham." In 1966, however, William Carlos Williams and Wallace Stevens were referred to as "towering figures." The 1967 volume of *ALS* indicates that the scholars' interest in Pound and Stevens is still running strong; that "Frost's reputation is permanently fixed on a high level" but that the reputations of Sandburg and Edna St. Vincent Millay have sunk to a new low; and that the "place in literary history" now held by Hemingway and Fitzgerald "is so secure that editors, bibliographers, critics, and scholars treat what they have written with the greatest respect."

The academic anthologists are not in agreement as to who are the major American writers of the twentieth century. In the 1945 edition of their *Major American Writers* Howard Mumford Jones and Ernest Leisy included selections from Robinson, Frost, Sandburg, MacLeish, Norris, Lewis, Hemingway, Mencken, and Ellen Glasgow. There were no selections from Eliot, Pound, Stevens, Faulkner, Fitzgerald, or Willa Cather. Three important anthologies appeared in 1962. In *Twelve American Writers* William M. Gibson and George Arms included only Eliot, Frost, and Faulkner. In their *Major Writers of America* Perry Miller and his associates included Dreiser, O'Neill, Frost, Anderson, Fitzgerald, Hemingway, Eliot, and Faulkner. Only two of the eight authors were poets, but in *The Mentor Book of Major American Poets* Oscar Williams and Edwin Honig included no less than thirteen modern "major" American poets: Robinson, Frost, Lindsay, Stevens, William Carlos Williams, Pound, Marianne Moore, Ransom, Edna St. Vincent Millay, MacLeish, Cummings, Auden, and Hart Crane. In 1966 appeared an anthology entitled *Masters of American Literature*, edited by Leon Edel, Thomas H. Johnson, Sherman Paul, and Claude M. Simpson. Here "the principal figures in American literature" are Edward Taylor, Jonathan Edwards, Benjamin Franklin, Poe, Emerson, Thoreau, Hawthorne, Melville, Whitman, Emily Dickinson, Mark Twain, Henry Adams, Henry James, Stephen Crane, O'Neill, Frost, Eliot, and Faulkner. The list does not include the names of Howells, Hemingway, Fitzgerald, Stevens, or any one of the important poets and novelists of the twentieth century who happened to be women. "The most significant American poets before Pound and Eliot" included in Francis Murphy's *Major American Poets to 1914* ( 1966 ) are Anne Bradstreet, Edward Taylor, Philip Freneau, Bryant, Emerson, Longfellow, Whittier, Poe, Jones Very, Thoreau, Whitman, Melville, Timrod, Lowell, Frederick Goddard Tuckerman, Emily Dickinson, Lanier, Robinson, and Frost. The only one of the old New England poets excluded is Holmes.

*Jackson Bryer, ed.,* Fifteen Modern American Authors *(1969).* In 1951 when Randall Stewart and Stanley T. Williams outlined their plan for *Eight American Authors*, it was fairly obvious what nineteenth-century writers should be included. In the late 1960's, however, when Professor Jackson Bryer of the University of Maryland made plans for a sequel that would include ten twentieth-century American writers, he felt strongly the need for something like a consensus among the specialists who would make use of the book. Accordingly he asked 182 scholars to name the ten authors whom they would like to see included. He received 138 replies. Bryer had asked the specialists to select the ten American writers from the long list in the 1964 "American Bibliography" in *PMLA*. Since T. S. Eliot's name appears only in the section devoted to English authors, many of the specialists appear to have forgotten him, for he got only 29 votes. W. H. Auden, who is an American citizen, got no votes. This was obviously due in large part to the circumstance that the MLA bibliographers inconsistently list him along with Eliot in the section devoted to English authors. As a result *Fifteen Modern American Authors* contains no bibliographical essay on one of the best poets of our time.

When Professor Bryer studied the returns, he decided (rightly, I think) that, with the consent of his publishers, the Duke University Press, it would be better to raise the number of authors included from ten to fifteen rather than to leave out writers so important as Thomas Wolfe, Willa Cather, Hart Crane, and T. S. Eliot. Acting on his own judgment, Bryer passed over numbers 15–18 in order to include John Steinbeck, whose rank was 19th on the poll. No doubt there are some scholars who will question the ranking of Steinbeck above Dos Passos, Sinclair Lewis, E. E. Cummings, and William Carlos Williams. Lewis's historical importance is great, and Williams's stock appears to be rising.

Not many will be surprised to find that the names of Hemingway, Faulkner, and Frost top the list on the Jackson Bryer poll. A decade ago, however, far fewer academic critics would have ranked Fitzgerald, Stevens, or O'Neill among the highest seven. A non-academic jury might, I think, have given more than 8 votes to Robert Lowell, Katherine Anne Porter, and Theodore Roethke; more than 7 votes to Ellen Glasgow; and more than 4 votes to Allen Tate and James Thurber.

Some of the scholars who make use of Professor Bryer's book will no doubt wonder whether we have in the twentieth century as many as fifteen major American writers worthy to stand in the company of the major writers represented in *Eight American Authors*. Nevertheless most of the scholars would, I think, agree that at least eight of our twentieth-century writers may now be definitely regarded as major: Eliot, Faulkner, Fitzgerald, Frost, Hemingway, O'Neill, Robinson, and Stevens. Perhaps the eight can hold their own until the twenty-first century decides which of the numerous runners-up belong in their company.

The accompanying list gives the names of all writers who received as many as 4 votes on the Jackson Bryer poll. One may wonder why some of those authors who got less than that number fared so badly on the poll. James Gould Cozzens, Jack London, Flannery O'Connor, and John O'Hara each got 3 votes. There were only 2 votes for Maxwell Anderson, Stephen Vincent Benét, Donald Davidson, Ralph Ellison, James T. Farrell, Carson McCullers, Mary McCarthy, Henry Miller, William Vaughn Moody, George Santayana, and Richard Wright. Santayana surely deserved more than 2 votes. Each of the following writers received only a single vote: Irving Babbitt, John Peale Bishop, Erskine Caldwell, Joseph Hergesheimer, Edna St. Vincent Millay, William Styron, Richard Wilbur, and Stark Young. No votes were cast for Pearl Buck, Amy Lowell, Paul Elmer More, O. Henry, Jesse Stuart, Booth Tarkington, Sara Teasdale, Yvor Winters, or Elinor Wylie.

It should be remembered that the scholars who told Professor Bryer what authors they wished to see included in his book were not attempting to rank American writers in their order of merit. The authors for whom they voted were obviously writers for whom they had a high regard, writers whom they would like to teach, and writers whose historical importance (as in the case of Dreiser) is so great that they had to be included. No doubt scholars who regard James Dickey and Eudora Welty as important writers remembered that for younger authors the materials for a good bibliographical essay are still somewhat scanty.

*Ballot Results (Writers receiving four or more votes)*

182 Ballots sent: 138 Votes cast

| name | votes | name | votes |
|------|-------|------|-------|
| Ernest Hemingway | 127 | William Carlos Williams | 24 |
| William Faulkner | 125 | John Steinbeck | 23 |
| Robert Frost | 108 | Saul Bellow | 19 |
| F. Scott Fitzgerald | 101 | Robert Penn Warren | 18 |
| Wallace Stevens | 87 | Edith Wharton | 18 |
| Theodore Dreiser | 84 | John Crowe Ransom | 12 |
| Eugene O'Neill | 83 | Tennessee Williams | 12 |
| Ezra Pound | 76 | Edmund Wilson | 12 |
| E. A. Robinson | 46 | Arthur Miller | 10 |
| Sherwood Anderson | 43 | James Branch Cabell | 9 |
| Thomas Wolfe | 34 | Marianne Moore | 9 |
| Willa Cather | 32 | Robert Lowell | 8 |
| Hart Crane | 31 | Katherine Anne Porter | 8 |
| T. S. Eliot | 29 | Theodore Roethke | 8 |
| John Dos Passos | 26 | Ellen Glasgow | 7 |
| Sinclair Lewis | 26 | H. L. Mencken | 7 |
| E. E. Cummings | 24 | Robinson Jeffers | 6 |

| Bernard Malamud | 6 | Thornton Wilder | 5 |
| Carl Sandburg | 6 | Vladimir Nabokov | 4 |
| Eudora Welty | 6 | J. D. Salinger | 4 |
| Nathanael West | 6 | Allen Tate | 4 |
| Norman Mailer | 5 | James Thurber | 4 |
| Gertrude Stein | 5 | | |

*Some Reappraisals.* As to how the twenty-first century will rank these American writers one can only speculate. It is fair to assume, however, that its critical standards will not be those in vogue today, and consequently some of the writers who are now ranked as major will be down-graded. There are current critical estimates that seem to me nothing short of extravagant. While the reputation of Hemingway seems to be declining and that of Eliot certainly not rising, some other writers are riding high. "Fitzgerald is fast approaching a kind of literary sainthood where everything he wrote is considered sacred because he wrote it." So wrote Richard Lehan in *American Literature* for March, 1968. Wallace Stevens is riding high, too.

No American writer of the twentieth century is now so highly praised as Faulkner. Randall Stewart, as I have noted, found Faulkner in 1957 the only twentieth-century American writer worthy of a place beside Hawthorne, Melville, and Henry James. In *The Half-World of American Culture* (1965) Carl Bode wrote: "Frost has been the greatest American poet to appear in this century. The greatest novelist has been William Faulkner." In his *Three Modes of Modern Southern Fiction* (1966) C. Hugh Holman referred to Faulkner's *The Sound and the Fury, As I Lay Dying, Light In August,* and *Absalom, Absalom!* as "novels of firm integrity and great strength. They appear to me," he said, "to be not only unsurpassed in Faulkner's total career but also to constitute one of the major creations of the American imagination."

Occasionally one finds a modern critic expressing reservations about Faulkner. In his *Re-Appraisals* (1966) Martin Green treated both Faulkner and Hemingway as only minor American writers. Yet in the same year Michael Millgate in *The Achievement of William Faulkner* climbed out on a long limb and concluded that "it is alongside Dickens, the greatest of the English novelists, that Faulkner must ultimately be ranked." A reader who doubts whether Dickens is a greater novelist than Fielding, Scott, Thackeray, George Eliot, and Hardy may well wonder whether Faulkner ever wrote a novel quite so memorable as *The Scarlet Letter, Huckleberry Finn,* or *The Portrait of a Lady.* (One is glad, however, to be assured that in Oxford, Mississippi, the author of *Sanctuary* has been forgiven.)

In the autumn, 1957, number of the *American Scholar* Walter F. Taylor published an article entitled "Reappraisals: William Faulkner: The Faulkner

Fable," in which he noted that the "special techniques of modern criticism" are likely to afford "only partial and fragmented views." Faulkner criticism, he said, "in its concern with structure and symbol" had "neglected value and meaning." Contrary to the general opinion, he said, *A Fable*, is not "a Christian allegory."

> In overwhelming degree, Faulkner's view is that man is not really man but subman, a creature subrational, disgusting, bestial, filthy and devoted to boundless and incalculable folly. This—the hopeless bestiality of man, reiterated as it is in a hundred incidents . . . is the actual, underlying theme of *A Fable*.
>
> An accurate appraisal, a reasonable judgment [Taylor concluded], will be anything but easy. For any critic, Faulkner is the most deceptive of subjects, not because of any willful dishonesty on his part, or any lack of aesthetic integrity, but because of his intellectual abundance, his astounding and apparently quite sincere sophistries, his self-contradictions, his symptoms of inner stress and still unreconciled conflicts. . . . [The critic must remember] that the marsh lights of Faulkner's idealism flicker often enough above a veritable inferno of the violent, the destructive and the daemonic.

In the spring of 1967 the *Mississippi Quarterly* published a symposium entitled "Re-Evaluation of Southern Novelists." The editor of the symposium, John O. Eidson, wrote: "Continual re-evaluation of recognized writers, both major and minor, is a necessity—all the way from re-classifying the classics to the classification of some who have never been classified at all." Professor Eidson noted that anthologists often failed to see the necessity for reevaluating the authors whose work they were reprinting. He gave two examples from nineteenth-century English literature: "One [anthologist] was solemnly assuring Alfred Tennyson [the Poet Laureate] as late as 1853 that he had 'enough intrinsic merit, probably, to assure him a permanent place in the third or fourth rank of contemporary English poets.' And to the end of the nineteenth century American gift-books were assuring Felicia Hemans that she was the greatest poet that ever lived."

The late Edd Winfield Parks, who contributed to the symposium an excellent study of James Branch Cabell, concluded: "I believe that the best of Cabell will survive, for I believe that the writer who best represents a particular literary movement at a given period, the man pre-eminent even in a narrow field, will continue to have something vital to say to perceptive readers. In the philosophical romance in this century, Cabell is the best we have had." The need for a reappraisal of Cabell was obvious, for his romances had long been out of fashion. It was back in the 1920's that Burton Rascoe asserted that "not Ecclesiastes, 'The Golden Ass,' 'Gulliver's Travels,' or the works of

Rabelais have a surer chance of immortality than Mr. Cabell's 'Jurgen.'"
Truly, as Hazlitt said in his essay "On Criticism," "The characters of prophet
and critic are not always united."

Professor Floyd C. Watkins, who contributed the essay on Thomas Wolfe,
found the task of reevaluation much more difficult. He concluded that "a
new and fair evaluation is impossible. One can at best," he said, "hope to find
new grounds for old opinions" about a novelist so uneven as Wolfe. A great
difficulty was, he found, "that the discipline of modern methods of criticism
and the art of Thomas Wolfe's books seem to move at cross purposes." In
1969 C. Hugh Holman concluded his essay on Wolfe in *Fifteen Modern
American Authors*:

> Wolfe still poses for the critic the persistent questions of autobiogra-
> phy and form, of impassioned rhetoric, and of the present-day validity
> of the aesthetic assumptions of nineteenth-century Romantics. His
> work stands vast, flawed, imperfect, and in its own way magnificent;
> and it flings down a challenge to the serious critic that has largely been
> ignored.

The reputations of minor writers are, like those of the major, subject to
wide fluctuation with the passing of time. And in the case of authors who are
not widely read today the responsibility of the literary historian is very great.
If he lacks taste and judgment and sympathy with the aims and methods of
authors old and new, he will only confuse the whole problem. But reevaluation is his obligation. In his *Renaissance in the South* (1963) John M.
Bradbury wrote:

> I have made a number of virtual rediscoveries, authors whose enduring
> qualities have been buried in the avalanche of more recent writing,
> their graves all but unmarked through critical neglect. At the same
> time, I have felt it time to shuffle up and down a few established repu-
> tations. Popular novelists like Ben Lucian Burman, Jesse Stuart, and
> Erskine Caldwell I have thus relegated to the pulpy limbo where I am
> convinced they belong. Isa Glenn, Frances Newman, Anne Winslow,
> Edwin Granberry, and others I have restored to positions of honor
> which I feel they deserve. These are to me acts of simple justice which
> I trust the future will confirm.

Our twentieth-century literature has abundant vitality and it is notable
for its technical virtuosity, but what do our poets and novelists have to offer
to Europeans that they cannot find in the work of their own writers? Are we
in any position to justify the literary leadership forced upon us by two world
wars that left so much of Europe in a state of exhaustion?

Although we have all too often underrated some of our greatest writers, we have at the same time continued to exaggerate the merits of our literature in comparison with the literatures of Europe and Latin America. In reviewing the *Hawthorne Centenary Essays* in *American Literature* in March, 1965, Irving Howe charged that the book continued "that massive overestimation of American literature which, in the last forty years, the equally massive expansion of American literary studies seems to have made inescapable." Perhaps the situation is not so bad as Howe thought, but it seems to me that our literary critics, academic and journalistic alike, know less than their predecessors knew about the great writers of earlier ages. It is too easy for the critic to assert that John O'Hara or Mary McCarthy is a greater novelist than Jane Austen or Henry Fielding, for few of those who read what the critic is saying will have read *Pride and Prejudice* or *Tom Jones*.

In the more than two centuries which have elapsed since the birth of Goethe in 1749, the population of the world has increased enormously and important writers have been born in many countries, but not one of them seems to belong in the rare company of the world's greatest. Few competent critics would claim as much for any American authors as Burton Rascoe did in 1932 when he included in his *Titans of Literature* no less than three American writers: Poe, Whitman, and Mark Twain. Little England of the Renaissance held a mere fraction of the population of the twentieth-century English-speaking world, and most of its inhabitants could not read or write. Yet we cannot match Frost and Eliot, Hemingway and Faulkner, or Yeats and Joyce against Spenser, Bacon, Shakespeare, Ben Jonson, Donne, and the other great poets and dramatists of that unique age. Our "major" American writers, from Emerson and Hawthorne down to Faulkner and Frost, seem only minor when we place them by the side of Chaucer or Milton. Perhaps Lionel Trilling was thinking of Van Wyck Brooks's essay, "The Literary Life in America," when he wrote in *After the Genteel Tradition* (1937):

> A history of American literature must be, in Whitman's phrase, a series of "vivas for those who have failed." In our literature there are perhaps fewer completely satisfying books and certainly fewer integrated careers than there are interesting canons of work and significant life stories. Something in American life seems to prevent the perfection of success while it produces a fascinating kind of search or struggle, usually unavailing, which we may observe again and again in the collected works and in the biographies of our writers.

Would any reputable critic go so far as to predict that in the twenty-second century *Ulysses* or *The Waste Land*, *A Farewell to Arms* or *The Sound and the Fury* will be ranked along with the *Aeneid*, the *Divine Comedy*, or *Paradise Lost*? Perhaps Walt Whitman was right when in old age he hazarded the prediction that in the future the average excellence of our writing would be higher but that there would be fewer masterpieces.

In 1926 Rudyard Kipling said in a speech that "'quite a dozen writers [had] achieved immortality in the past 2,500 years." The New York *Times* asked a jury of fifteen authors drawn from seven countries to select the world's twelve greatest writers. When on July 25, 1926, the *Times* announced the results of its poll, it was noted that no American author was included among the twelve. Shakespeare topped the list with 12 votes out of a possible 15. The other eleven authors chosen were: Homer and Dante, 11 votes; Vergil, 9; Balzac, Cervantes, and Goethe, 7; Molière, 6; Plato, 5; Dickens and Voltaire, 4; and Milton, 3. Jacques Bainville named no less than seven French authors among his twelve! There was no single Oriental author on the list.

In 1969 we in America still have no Homer, no Shakespeare, no Molière, and no Goethe; but ours is a time of changed literary fashions and critical standards. One may now question whether Dickens, Balzac, or even Voltaire is a greater writer than a dozen others that failed to make the New York *Times* list: Chaucer, Spenser, Wordsworth, Dostoevski, Tolstoy, Ibsen, Camoens, Aeschylus, Sophocles; and among American writers: Hawthorne, Emerson, Poe, Melville, Whitman, Mark Twain, Emily Dickinson, and Henry James.

*We do not so abound in masterpieces that we can afford to neglect the finest of the few we have.*
                    William Dean Howells, *The Henry James Yearbook*

# Chapter *12*. American Books


## THE BEST BOOKS


*Henry W. Lanier, " 'Million' Books and 'Best' Books . . ." (1926).* The editor of the *Golden Book Magazine*, Henry W. Lanier, a son of the poet, took a poll of "some thousands" of the men and women who taught American fiction in high school and college. He got about four hundred replies. What he asked them was:

> If some condescending international critic were to intimate that the United States had not yet produced *anything* really worthy of a place beside the acknowledged masterpieces of fiction,—which ten works by American writers could be selected that would best represent our bid for a permanent place in this section of the world's literature?

The results of the poll were announced in the *Golden Book Magazine* for September, 1926, under the title " 'Million' Books and 'Best' Books: A Glance Towards the Top of the Fiction America Has Produced in Three Hundred Years."


### [i]

1. Poe's *Tales*
2. Hawthorne, *The Scarlet Letter*
3. Mark Twain, *The Adventures of Huckleberry Finn*
4. Cooper, *The Last of the Mohicans*
5. Joel Chandler Harris, *Uncle Remus*
6. Melville, *Moby-Dick*

### [ii]

7. Howells, *The Rise of Silas Lapham*
8. Edith Wharton, *Ethan Frome*
9. Bret Harte, *Tales*
10. Mrs. Stowe, *Uncle Tom's Cabin*

11. Henry James, *The Portrait of a Lady*
12. Stephen Crane, *The Red Badge of Courage*
13. Irving, *The Sketch Book*
14. Owen Wister, *The Virginian*
15. Willa Cather, *My Ántonia*
16. Lew Wallace, *Ben-Hur*
17. Cable, *Old Creole Days*
18. Hawthorne, *The House of the Seven Gables*
19. Henry James, *Daisy Miller*
20. Jack London, *The Call of the Wild*
21. O. Henry, *The Four Million*
22. Irving, "Rip Van Winkle"
23. Mark Twain, *The Adventures of Tom Sawyer*
24. Irving, "The Legend of Sleepy Hollow"
25. S. Weir Mitchell, *Hugh Wynne*

The editor noted that the four hundred teachers who sent in replies were practically unanimous in placing Poe's *Tales* and Hawthorne's *The Scarlet Letter* at the top of the list. He added that he found "little difference of judgment" in the rating of Nos. 3–6. It was in the second group (Nos. 7–10) that the "expected differences of opinion became much in evidence." He noted, for example, that *The Rise of Silas Lapham* received less than half as many votes as *Moby-Dick*. In the third section the editor found abundant evidence of the conservative taste of the men and women who were teaching American literature.

If we compare the results of the *Golden Book Magazine*'s poll with that taken by the *Critic* in 1893, a third of a century earlier, we note important changes in the ranking of certain writers. Hawthorne, Howells, Mrs. Stowe, and Lew Wallace were on the *Critic*'s list of authors of the ten best American books; but Mark Twain was only fifteenth among the runners-up while Poe, Melville, and Henry James were nowhere to be seen. On the 1926 list one finds two books by each of the following: Hawthorne, Mark Twain, and Henry James. New names on the *Golden Book Magazine* poll were those of Fenimore Cooper and Joel Chandler Harris. On neither list does one find a book by Sarah Orne Jewett, Charles Brockden Brown, or William Gilmore Simms.* The editor concluded his observations: "It seems beyond question that . . .

* Irving's *The Sketch Book* might have been ranked higher than thirteenth but for the fact that a good many teachers voted not for the book but for one of the two best-known tales included in it, "Rip Van Winkle" and "The Legend of Sleepy Hollow."

these are the books that Americans are being taught to consider the highest achievement of our native fiction-writers thus far."

It is when we look at the *Golden Book Magazine*'s rating of contemporary American writers of fiction that we realize how conservative the literary taste of the English teachers was. Among the twenty-five books on the list one looks in vain for a single title by novelists who in 1927 were so widely read as Theodore Dreiser, James Branch Cabell, Ellen Glasgow, and Sinclair Lewis. The American literary canon was being expanded to include twentieth-century poets and novelists, but it would seem that most of the teachers of English did not care for the "new school."

S R L, *"An American Canon" (1927)*. On October 17, 1927, the *Saturday Review of Literature* printed a leading article entitled "An American Canon." The unsigned article was presumably written by the editor, Henry Seidel Canby. The idea of compiling the American list of books was suggested by a passage in Ernest Barker's recently published *National Character* (1927), in which the distinguished English historian had selected what he considered "the dozen books, or poems, or passages of literature most likely to be chosen, by common consent, as those which have established themselves definitely as a national possession or influence." "The canon of such a list," said Barker, "will be neither artistic excellence nor fidelity in the expression of the national genius (though some element of both . . . is obviously necessary . . .): what matters most is rather the range and vogue of acceptance, and the degree of the effect produced on social thought and imagination."

> First in such a list would come the Authorized Version of the Bible. . . . The *Pilgrim's Progress* might come next; and after it the tragedies and histories of Shakespeare. . . . Milton might be counted fourth . . . and after the poems of Milton we might reckon some of the earlier sonnets and some of the odes of Wordsworth. Then, in a place by themselves, there might come the great hymns of the Wesleys, and Watts, and Cowper; and after them . . . the social poems of Burns. The *Pickwick Papers* of Dickens might be given the next place; and Defoe's *Robinson Crusoe* . . . would have to be included. At the end of the list . . . choice becomes difficult. But there is Gray's *Elegy [Written] in a Country Churchyard* (if one small perfect poem can be set by the side of its more massive companions); there is Boswell's *Life of Johnson*; and who would exclude Sir Walter Scott or forget the *Heart of Midlothian*? The list is full; and how much is left outside . . . .

The editor of the *Saturday Review of Literature* quoted most of the passage I have reprinted and noted that Barker's "canon for the English is a canon for Americans also. These are all our books. . . ." The editor's American canon, which follows, is in effect "an addition to the English canon."

Such a list would begin with the "Autobiography of Benjamin Franklin," and would contain "The Declaration of Independence." "Rip Van Winkle" and "The Legend of Sleepy Hollow" would belong in the canon. Hawthorne's "Scarlet Letter" and the Leatherstocking Tales of Cooper must certainly follow. Thoreau's "Walden," which is New England incarnate, and Melville's "Moby Dick," one of the greatest of American books, we probably must omit from the canon. They have not, and probably will not, become national influences. But Emerson's essays and lectures have colored the whole stream of American thinking and must go on. Likewise that immortal book of boys, "Huckleberry Finn," which is also a saga of the frontier. Bret Harte is too fragile. "Uncle Tom's Cabin" is doubtful. . . . Poe belongs in the canon though with a national influence not comparable to that of Emerson or Burns. Whitman, the most American of them all in his democratic ideals, we must exclude. He is a great name with the intellectuals, a great influence, but by his comrades, the American democracy, he was and is unread. Instead of his vigor we must insert a weaker man and a lesser, if more skilful, poet, Longfellow. His melodious didacticism has been as influential in its way as "Pilgrim's Progress," and is admirably adapted to youth and to the moral and esthetic instinct in youthful stages. The fashion now is to decry him, yet if his excellence is not deep it is certainly wide. He must go in the American canon.

The editor of the *Saturday Review* named only a single twentieth-century American author:

If there is a later addition it must be Sinclair Lewis. His books, like Bunyan's, Dickens's, Shakespeare's, have given names to the language. They are not yet time-tested but it seems probable that "Babbitt" at least will stay among the few books of which all reading Americans will be conscious and which most Americans will read.

The editor concluded:

The American canon does not compare in the importance of individual books with the English list, although Emerson, Hawthorne, Twain ( in one book ), and perhaps Poe could be shifted [to the English canon] without too much incongruity.

*Asa Don Dickinson, "The Best Books of Our Time"* [1901–1945]. In 1928 Dickinson (1876–1960), who was the librarian of the University of Pennsylvania, published *The Best Books of Our Time 1901–1925*. In 1937 and 1948 he brought out two supplementary volumes which covered the decades 1926–1935 and 1936–1945. The subtitle of the earliest volume suggests the plight in which librarians and booksellers found themselves when confronted with the rapidly increasing number of books published each year: "A Clue to the Literary Labyrinth for Home Library Builders Booksellers and Librarians Consisting of a List of the One Thousand Best Books Selected by the Best Authorities Accompanied by Critical Descriptions . . . ."

Dickinson's plan was to utilize lists of best books put out by libraries and library associations and similar lists to be found in literary histories, critical essays, and the annual lists of best books published in magazines and newspapers. The compiler tried to be objective, and he was in general judicious and sparing in his own comments on authors and books. In many instances, like the compilers of the annual *Book Review Digest*, he quoted from his "authorities." He selected his quotations with considerable skill, and they are by no means all favorable.

It was natural and proper for an intelligent librarian to turn to the recognized "authorities." "In the multitude of counsellors there is safety," wrote the author of Proverbs (11:14), and Dickinson quoted the passage with obvious approval. He could not know that Edmund Wilson, Donald Davidson, or the editors of the *Dial* could have done a better job of naming the best books of the age than any of his "authorities." Nevertheless, Dickinson's lists of "best books" are probably a more reliable index to the changing literary taste of cultivated American readers in the years from 1901 to 1945 than any of the numerous critical polls that have been initiated since the turn of the century.

As one looks at the various tables in Dickinson's first volume, it becomes evident that the most popular writers of the first quarter of the twentieth century belonged to the older generation. In one of his tables he listed authors according to the number of "endorsements" they and their books received from his "authorities." Perhaps it should not surprise us to find that of the highest ten only three were American authors.

| | | | | | |
|---|---|---|---|---|---|
| 1. | John Galsworthy | 197 | 6. | Joseph Conrad | 110 |
| 2. | H. G. Wells | 172 | 7. | Booth Tarkington | 103 |
| 3. | Arnold Bennett | 137 | 8. | Rudyard Kipling | 79 |
| 4. | Bernard Shaw | 123 | 9. | W. H. Hudson | 78 |
| 5. | Edith Wharton | 118 | 10. | Joseph Hergesheimer | 74 |

Of the next fifteen authors nine (if we count Henry James as an American) belong to the United States.

| | | | | | |
|---|---|---|---|---|---|
| 11. Eugene O'Neill | 67 | | 19. Henry James | 58 |
| 12. Hugh Walpole | 66 | | 20. Gamaliel Bradford | 57 |
| 13. G. K. Chesterton | 66 | | 21. William J. Locke | 55 |
| 14. Stewart Edward White | 65 | | 22. James Branch Cabell | 54 |
| 15. Willa Cather | 64 | | 23. John Millington Synge | 53 |
| 16. James Barrie | 63 | | 24. May Sinclair | 51 |
| 17. Jack London | 61 | | 25. Theodore Dreiser | 49 |
| 18. Winston Churchill | 60 | | | |

By 1925, the last year covered in Dickinson's first book, the new generation of American writers and literary journalists had got possession of many influential magazines, book pages, and publishing houses; and their books and articles were being widely circulated. It is evident, however, that some of Dickinson's "authorities" held no high opinion of younger writers, like Sinclair Lewis, who received only 38 "endorsements"; H. L. Mencken, who got 26; Henry Adams and Robert Frost, who each received 23; and Van Wyck Brooks, who got no more than 9. The great Irish poet, William Butler Yeats, got only 18.

Dickinson listed no writer who got less than 4 "endorsements." That was the number given to Emily Dickinson, to Ezra Pound, and to Harold Bell Wright. The Emily Dickinson revival was just beginning in 1925. Mr. Dickinson notes that Harold Bell Wright in the years 1895–1926 was the "third most popular American fictionist" and "the first in popularity in the years from 1909 to 1921." The librarian and his "authorities," however, were not impressed by Wright's popularity. Dickinson evidently held no high opinion of Ezra Pound's verses, which he described as "largely in the cubist, imagistic, or vorticist styles." He did note, however: "Carl Sandburg thinks he has done more to 'make new impulses in poetry' than any other writer in the English language."

In one of his tables Dickinson listed the books which received the largest number of "endorsements":

1. Arnold Bennett, *The Old Wives Tale*          25
2. John Galsworthy, *The Forsyte Saga*          23
3. Rudyard Kipling, *Kim*          23
4. John Masefield, *Narrative Poems*          23
5. Edith Wharton, *The House of Mirth*          23
6. Romain Rolland, *Jean-Christophe*          21
7. Joseph Hergesheimer, *Java Head*          20
8. Booth Tarkington, *Penrod*          20
9. Edgar Lee Masters, *Spoon River Anthology*          20
10. Jack London, *Call of the Wild*          19
11. H. G. Wells, *The Outline of History*          19

Willa Cather's *My Ántonia* was given 17 "endorsements." Lewis's *Babbitt* got 16 and *Main Street* 15. Sherwood Anderson's *Winesburg, Ohio* was on 13 lists, but Cabell's controversial *Jurgen* got only 8 "endorsements." D. H. Lawrence's *Sons and Lovers* got 9 and Marcel Proust's *Remembrance of Things Past*, 7. I find no mention of James Joyce's *Ulysses*. There were 18 "endorsements" for Robert Frost's *Selected Poems* and 12 for Carl Sandburg's *Chicago Poems*, two more than were given to Thomas Hardy's *Collected Poems*. If T. S. Eliot's *The Waste Land* got any "endorsements," the number must have been less than four. Of the first six names on this list only one, Edith Wharton, is that of an American author.

In his second volume, Dickinson, now librarian at Brooklyn College, listed four hundred "best books" of the decade 1926–1935. In his preface he explained that by "best" he meant *selected by a consensus of expert opinion as most worthy the attention of intelligent American readers.* To this in his third volume he added the words: *with at least a high school education or its equivalent.*

The second volume included the early years of the Great Depression and the Roosevelt New Deal, but these events seem to have had little immediate effect upon the ranking of books and authors. There is evident, however, one notable change: the favorite writers are now nearly all Americans.

The "new poetry" is well represented in Dickinson's table, "The Best Poetry of the Decade":

|  |  | points |
|---|---|---|
| 1. | Stephen Vincent Benét, *John Brown's Body* | 216 |
| 2. | Edna St. Vincent Millay, *Fatal Interview* | 170 |
| 3. | Robert Frost, *Collected Poems* | 170 |
| 4. | Edwin Arlington Robinson, *Tristram* | 159 |
| 5. | Archibald MacLeish, *Conquistador* | 147 |
| 6. | Edna St. Vincent Millay, *Wine from These Grapes* | 138 |
| 7. | Edwin Arlington Robinson, *Collected Poems* | 136 |
| 8. | Carl Sandburg, *American Songbag* | 128 |
| 9. | Elinor Wylie, *Collected Poems* | 116 |
| 10. | William Butler Yeats, *Collected Poems* | 116 |
| 11. | Dorothy Parker, *Death and Taxes* | 100 |
| 12. | Robert Frost, *West Running Brook* | 90 |
| 13. | Sara Teasdale, *Dark of the Moon* | 88 |

None of Ezra Pound's books is on the list. T. S. Eliot, who was not represented in Dickinson's earlier volume, appeared in the second with two titles.

His *Selected Essays, 1917–1932* (1932) which scored 95 points out of a possible maximum of 380, was 7th in Dickinson's list of the nine "best" books of essays, but it was not listed among the "Fifteen Best Books about Literature" nor among the "Ten Best English Books of the Decade." Eliot had become a British subject in 1927. Dickinson's comment seems a little ambiguous: "Probably no judgments of greater authority [than Eliot's] have been handed down during this generation." Eliot's play, *Murder in the Cathedral*, won only 84 points, a bare four above the minimum—and it was not listed among the "Best Plays of the Decade."

New names predominate in Dickinson's "Best American Fiction of the Decade 1926–1935." The twenty books that received the greatest number of points are:

1. Pearl Buck, *[The] Good Earth* — 330
2. Willa Cather, *Death Comes for the Archbishop* — 306
3. Thornton Wilder, *The Bridge of San Luis Rey* — 247
4. Ernest Hemingway, *A Farewell to Arms* — 209
5. Ellen Glasgow, *The Romantic Comedians* — 192
6. Willa Cather, *Shadows on the Rock* — 190
7. Elizabeth Madox Roberts, *The Time of Man* — 184
8. Margaret Ayer Barnes, *Years of Grace* — 180
9. Thomas Wolfe, *Of Time and the River* — 180
10. Sinclair Lewis, *Dodsworth* — 162
11. Ernest Hemingway, *Men without Women* — 162
12. Edna Ferber, *Show Boat* — 162
13. Stark Young, *So Red the Rose* — 161
14. Thornton Wilder, *The Woman of Andros* — 160
15. Ellen Glasgow, *The Sheltered Life* — 158
16. Ellen Glasgow, *Vein of Iron* — 156
17. De la Roche, *Jalna* — 153
18. Julia Peterkin, *Scarlet Sister Mary* — 153
19. Elizabeth Madox Roberts, *The Great Meadow* — 150
20. Mary Ellen Chase, *Mary Peters* — 150

Among the other twenty books in the table are two by Sinclair Lewis: *It Can't Happen Here*, 132 points, and *Work of Art*, 127; Thornton Wilder's *Heaven's My Destination*, 132; John Dos Passos's *1919*, 116; and Ellen Glasgow's *They Stooped to Folly*, 114. Those once-popular novelists, James Branch Cabell and Joseph Hergesheimer, are not represented.

Mrs. Buck's *The Good Earth* (1931), which topped the list, was in 1931 and 1932 the best-selling novel in the United States. Mrs. Buck was awarded the Pulitzer Prize for Fiction in 1932, and in 1938 she won the Nobel Prize.

It was to be many years before Ernest Hemingway would win either a Pulitzer or a Nobel prize, but Dickinson's "authorities" obviously regarded *A Farewell to Arms* as an exceptionally important book. It was twelfth among the "Fifty Best Books" of the decade and fourth in the "Best American Fiction of the Decade." Dickinson's brief description of the story suggests that he did not relish the Hemingway manner: "A story of tragic love against the lurid background of the World War. Modernly frank in expression; laconic; boringly realistic in dialogue. The hard-boiled crust is thin in places and sometimes breaks to reveal depths of shame-faced tenderness."

William Faulkner made his first appearance in Dickinson's second volume with *Sanctuary* (1930), which had already been added to the Modern Library. The book won only 84 points, four above the required minimum. Dickinson's summary follows: "Like Dostoievsky, Faulkner is obsessed with the degenerate, the vicious, the abnormal members of the human race. He belongs to 'the School of Cruelty.' This story is concerned chiefly with a rape and a lynching." Dickinson, like most of his "authorities," was too much repelled by Faulkner's subject matter to note his superior craftsmanship and his highly flexible and expressive style.

Among the "Fifteen Best Books about Literature," Parrington's *Main Currents in American Thought* was first with 170 points; Ludwig Lewisohn's *Expression in America* was second with 137; and Edmund Wilson's *Axel's Castle* was sixth with 110. Among the fifteen T. S. Eliot, Ezra Pound, and the New Critics are unrepresented.

Dickinson's third volume, which covers the decade 1936–1945, was not published until 1948, but while the effect of the Depression is evident in some instances, I see little to indicate that the Second World War had yet greatly affected American poetry or fiction.

I list the highest twenty-two of the forty titles in the table of the "Best American Fiction":

|  |  | points |
|---|---|---|
| 1. | Ernest Hemingway, *For Whom the Bell Tolls* | 680 |
| 2. | John Steinbeck, *The Grapes of Wrath* | 589 |
| 3. | John Hersey, *[A] Bell for Adano* | 472 |
| 4. | Lillian Smith, *Strange Fruit* | 368 |
| 5. | Kenneth Roberts, *Northwest Passage* | 323 |
| 6. | Margaret Mitchell, *Gone with the Wind* | 312 |
| 7. | Marjorie Kinnan Rawlings, *The Yearling* | 306 |
| 8. | Betty Smith, *A Tree Grows in Brooklyn* | 297 |
| 9. | Katherine Anne Porter, *The Leaning Tower* | 288 |
| 10. | John P. Marquand, *The Late George Apley* | 272 |
| 11. | John P. Marquand, *So Little Time* | 264 |

| | | | |
|---|---|---|---|
| 12. John P. Marquand, *H. M. Pulham, Esq.* | | | 260 |
| 13. H. P. Brown, *Walk in the Sun* | | | 253 |
| 14. Sinclair Lewis, *Cass Timberlane* | | | 252 |
| 15. Richard Wright, *Native Son* | | | 250 |
| 16. John Steinbeck, *Of Mice and Men* | | | 246 |
| 17. Ellen Glasgow, *In This Our Life* | | | 220 |
| 18. Willa Cather, *Sapphira and the Slave Girl* | | | 210 |
| 19. Kenneth Roberts, *Oliver Wiswell* | | | 210 |
| 20. George Santayana, *The Last Puritan* | | | 200 |
| 21. Thomas Wolfe, *You Can't Go Home Again* | | | 200 |
| 22. George R. Stewart, *Storm* | | | 200 |

Pearl Buck's *Dragon Seed* rated no higher than 31st with 147 points, but that was three points higher than the rating given to Dos Passos's *The Big Money* and Scott Fitzgerald's *The Crack-Up*. Hemingway's *For Whom the Bell Tolls* was rated the best of the "Fifty Best Books" for the decade 1936–1945. It was also tops in the lists of the "Twenty Best Novels" and the "Twenty Best American Books." It was given 680 points, the maximum possible. "This book's 'score,'" as Dickinson noted, "is the highest on record." It did not, however, win the Pulitzer Prize for its author. *The Grapes of Wrath* (1939), which scored 589 points, the second highest on record, won the Pulitzer prize for John Steinbeck in 1940. That novel had a strong appeal for many readers in the Depression era, during which Scott Fitzgerald's stock declined.

In Dickinson's list of the fourteen "Best Books on Literature and Language" the three highest scores went to Van Wyck Brooks. *New England Indian Summer* won 560 points; *The Flowering of New England*, 510; and *The World of Washington Irving*, 471. In Dickinson's second volume Brooks's *Emerson and Others* had won only 128 points and his life of Emerson only 105. In Dickinson's first volume *The Ordeal of Mark Twain* was given just 5 "endorsements" and *America's Coming-of-Age* only 4.

Dickinson's list of the 16 "Best Books of Poetry" follows:

| | | | points |
|---|---|---|---|
| 1. Frost | *Collected Poems* | 1939 | 327 |
| 2. Auden | *Collected Works* | 1945 | 199 |
| 3. Sandburg | *The People, Yes* | 1936 | 176 |
| 4. Jeffers | *Selected Poems* | 1938 | 171 |
| 5. Miller, A. D. | *White Cliffs* | 1941 | 170 |
| 6. Benét, S. V. | *Western Star* | 1943 | 165 |
| 7. Van Doren, M. | *Collected Poems* | 1939 | 161 |
| 8. Benét, W. R. | *Dust Which Is God* | 1941 | 160 |
| 9. Millay | *Conversation at Midnight* | 1937 | 153 |
| 10. Housman | *Collected Poems* | 1940 | 150 |

| 11. Frost | *Witness Tree* | 1942 | 137 |
| 12. Davenport, R. | *My Country* | 1944 | 127 |
| 13. Millay | *Collected Sonnets* | 1941 | 120 |
| 14. Eliot | *Collected Poems* | 1936 | 120 |
| 15. Cummings | *Collected Poems* | 1938 | 117 |
| 16. Shapiro | *Essay on Rime* | 1945 | 108 |

The list includes Eliot but not Pound, who is listed only in Dickinson's first volume, published in 1928. Eliot was not rated in that volume even though *The Waste Land*, which created a sensation in certain literary circles, had been published in 1922. In his third volume Dickinson wrote: "His *Waste Land* (1922), wail of the 'lost generation,' stands as an important landmark in American literature."

In an appendix to his third volume Dickinson listed as "The Runners-Up" 600 books of the decade which were "praised by many critics, though none of their scores (53 to 99) were large enough to win them places among the four hundred best." It is astonishing that Dickinson's "authorities" should fail to give the minimum of 100 points to such books as these:

| | points |
|---|---|
| W. H. Auden, *On This Island* | 68 |
| John Peale Bishop, *Selected Poems* | 60 |
| Willa Cather, *Not under Forty* | 80 |
| Emily Dickinson, *Bolts of Melody* | 96 |
| John Dos Passos, *Adventures of a Young Man* | 76 |
| T. S. Eliot, *Family Reunion* | 57 |
| James T. Farrell, *World I Never Made* | 96 |
| Robinson Jeffers, *Such Counsels You Gave Me* | 85 |
| James Joyce, *Collected Poems* | 85 |
| Carson McCullers, *The Heart Is a Lonely Hunter* | 80 |
| Edna St. Vincent Millay, *Collected Lyrics* | 66 |
| Katherine Anne Porter, *Pale Horse, Pale Rider* | 85 |
| Edwin Arlington Robinson, *Collected Poems* | 68 |
| John Steinbeck, *In Dubious Battle* | 80 |
| Wallace Stevens, *Man with the Blue Guitar* | 85 |
| Allen Tate, *Selected Poems* | 68 |
| Sara Teasdale, *Collected Poems* | 68 |
| James Thurber, *My World—and Welcome to It* | 84 |
| Robert Penn Warren, *At Heaven's Gate* | 77 |
| Eudora Welty, *Curtain of Green* | 60 |
| John Hall Wheelock, *Poems* | 64 |
| Thornton Wilder, *The Skin of Our Teeth* | 84 |
| Edmund Wilson, *The Triple Thinkers* | 90 |
| William Butler Yeats, *Last Poems and Plays* | 81 |

Dickinson might have added titles by some important writers not listed even among the runners-up: Ezra Pound, John Crowe Ransom, Donald Davidson, Kenneth Burke—but why go on?

Among the runners-up I find no mention of a book which obviously disturbed the compiler when he read it: Henri Peyre's *Writers and Their Critics* (1944). In his preface Dickinson noted that Professor Peyre had demonstrated that "in every age and country they [the critics] have failed to recognize budding genius." Dickinson's first reaction was: "This direful truth would seem to cut the ground from under a book of this kind." Yet, he insisted, he had been right in appealing to "a *consensus* of the best opinion obtainable." And, indeed, what else could an intelligent librarian have done? No librarian can wait for posterity to select the few best books from the hundreds pouring from the presses every year. But what can he or any one else do about the many books that get printed but are rarely reviewed and never advertised in the metropolitan newspapers?

*UNESCO Poll* (1949). As a rule the ablest professors of English are not eager to take part in any attempt to rank writers as though they were big-league baseball players whose batting averages can be accurately determined. In 1949, however, the professors felt that they could not refuse a request for a list of the twenty best American books which came from one branch of UNESCO (United Nations Educational, Scientific, and Cultural Organization). These books, it was hoped, would be speedily translated into many foreign languages. That hope, however, was not realized; and the results of the poll attracted little attention.

The officers of the Modern Language Association approved the request and asked the American Literature Section to select the books. The task was delegated to a committee consisting of three members of the English staff of Duke University: Lewis Leary, Jay B. Hubbell, and Clarence Gohdes, chairman. The committee decided that the best results would be obtained if the scholars to be polled were outstanding specialists in American literature. Among the twenty-six who had a part in the poll (two others failed to send in their selections) were the six editors of *American Literature*, the four editors and three associate editors of *The Literary History of the United States* (1948), and "a representative selection of professors of American literature in various universities and colleges." Three of the judges—though they too had been teachers of English—were primarily men of letters: Van Wyck Brooks, who had been for two years instructor in English at Stanford University; Mark Van Doren, who was professor of English at Columbia University; and Henry Seidel Canby, who taught for several years at Yale but was in 1949 editor of the *Saturday Review of Literature*.

Newton Arvin (Smith College)
Walter Blair (University of Chicago)
Sculley Bradley (University of Pennsylvania)
Van Wyck Brooks
Herbert R. Brown (Bowdoin College)
Henry Seidel Canby (*Saturday Review of Literature*)
Harry Hayden Clark (University of Wisconsin)
Norman Foerster (State University of Iowa)
Clarence Gohdes (Duke University)
Theodore Hornberger (University of Minnesota)
Jay B. Hubbell (Duke University)
Howard Mumford Jones (Harvard University)
Lewis Leary (Duke University)
F. O. Matthiessen (Harvard University)
Gregory Paine (University of North Carolina)
Fred Lewis Pattee (Rollins College)
Henry Pochmann (University of Wisconsin)
Arthur Hobson Quinn (University of Pennsylvania)
Lyon N. Richardson (Western Reserve University)
Ralph Leslie Rusk (Columbia University)
Henry Nash Smith (University of Minnesota)
Robert E. Spiller (University of Pennsylvania)
Willard Thorp (Princeton University)
Mark Van Doren (Columbia University)
George F. Whicher (Amherst College)
Stanley T. Williams (Yale University)

COMBINED RESULTS OF POLL OF 26 SPECIALISTS
IN AMERICAN LITERATURE

| Authors | Comparative Weight in poll | Titles most frequently suggested |
|---|---|---|
| Hawthorne | 164 | *The Scarlet Letter* |
| Poe | 163 | *Collected Tales* (18); *Collected Poems* (15) |
| Melville | 143 | *Moby-Dick* |
| Henry James | 143 | *The Portrait of a Lady* |
| Mark Twain | 141 | *Huckleberry Finn* |
| Emerson | 140 | *Selected Essays* (9); *Selected Essays and Poems* (7) |
| Thoreau | 125 | *Walden* |
| Whitman | 120 | *Leaves of Grass* |

| | | |
|---|---|---|
| Frost | 109 | *Collected Poems* (12); *Selected Poems* (8) |
| Franklin | { 103 | *Autobiography* |
| Cooper | { 103 | *The Last of the Mohicans* |
| Irving | 92 | *The Sketch Book* |
| Willa Cather | 85 | *Death Comes for the Archbishop* (12); *My Ántonia* (8) |
| Emily Dickinson | 81 | *Selected Poems* (9); *Collected Poems* (8) |
| O'Neill | 77 | *Selected Plays* |
| Howells | 75 | *The Rise of Silas Lapham* |
| Dreiser | 70 | *An American Tragedy* |
| Lewis | 65 | *Babbitt* (6); *Arrowsmith* (5) |
| Henry Adams | 64 | *The Education of Henry Adams* |
| Robinson | 58 | *Collected Poems* (8); *Selected Poems* (5) |

RUNNERS-UP

| | | |
|---|---|---|
| T. S. Eliot | 54 | *Collected Poems* |
| Crane | 46 | *The Red Badge of Courage* |
| Longfellow | 45 | *Selected Poems* |
| Hemingway | 44 | *A Farewell to Arms* |
| Edith Wharton | 33 | *The Age of Innocence* (4); *Ethan Frome* (3) |

As we look back to 1949 two decades later, we miss the names of such important critics as John Crowe Ransom, Allen Tate, Cleanth Brooks, Austin Warren, Carl Van Doren, and Edmund Wilson. All of these except Wilson at one time or another held long-term academic appointments. The New Critics are conspicuous by their absence.

The judges were asked to name twenty American works "which you would select as the best representatives of the literary art of our country," giving assurance in the list of "some variety of authors, genres, and periods." The specialists were asked to nominate twenty books, each of which was weighted five points, and to add others if they wished. These latter were each weighted three points. Two titles or collections are given when one title or collection was not overwhelmingly the favorite. The numbers in the table indicate comparative frequency of mention.

The committee's instructions were interpreted by the specialists in various ways. Newton Arvin commented: "One can make out a very short list of books one feels to be on the highest level of all, but there are not twenty of these; there are not even ten. And what one does after listing these few is simply to go on with a sampling of very good and representative books. . . ." Arvin included in his list only one book of poems, *Leaves of Grass*, for poetry, he said, is "untranslatable." Only Rusk listed more than one book by a single author: two by Poe and three by Emerson. The other judges did not follow his example, but Norman Foerster did note that if one were to select the ten greatest English plays, they would all be by Shakespeare. Foerster noted that he had seriously considered but finally rejected *Babbitt, An American Tragedy, U.S.A.,* and *Look Homeward, Angel.* Rusk, who gave twentieth place to *A Farewell to Arms,* commented: "Another time I might substitute other titles for two or three of these. I hardly know what to take as the basis of choice. Of course everybody else will include T. S. Eliot [they didn't] and, in another mood, I might too. I am most dubious about Robert Frost [who is eighteenth on Rusk's list]."

Henry Pochmann left out such well-known contemporary poets as Eliot, Jeffers, and MacLeish because, as he explained, "I believe the older, more-established people represent the mainstream of American literary tradition better." A number of scholars listed books of obvious historical importance but hardly to be classed among "the best representatives of the literary art of this country." These included books by Edward Bellamy, William Bradford, Hector St. John Crèvecoeur, John Dewey, Lincoln Steffens, and John Woolman.

The average age of the specialists was nearer sixty than fifty, and it is evident that the older professors were less hospitable than the younger to the twentieth-century writers. Fred Lewis Pattee, who was born in 1863, was the only specialist who voted for Whittier, and Arthur Hobson Quinn, who was born in 1875, cast the only vote for Bryant. On Pattee's list were books by Mrs. Stowe, Lowell, Jack London, and surprisingly H. L. Mencken. On Quinn's list were books by Lowell, William Vaughn Moody, Holmes, George Henry Boker, and S. Weir Mitchell. Quinn, however, made places for such contemporary dramatists as Eugene O'Neill, Maxwell Anderson, Sidney Howard, and Philip Barry.

A jury made up of younger scholars would not, I think, have listed among the top twenty any books by Irving or Cooper and perhaps none by Lewis or Dreiser; but a younger jury would have included in the top twenty books by T. S. Eliot, Ernest Hemingway, William Faulkner, Stephen Crane, and perhaps Sherwood Anderson, Thomas Wolfe, Scott Fitzgerald, and Wallace Stevens. The votes of two of the youngest specialists seem to me significant. Lewis Leary was the only one who voted for Fitzgerald (*The Great Gatsby*), and Henry Nash Smith cast the only vote for Stevens (*Harmonium*).

Three writers whose reputations were at a low ebb in 1949—George W. Cable, Sidney Lanier, and Hamlin Garland—won only three points each and only as alternates. There were no votes for Conrad Aiken, W. H. Auden, Van Wyck Brooks, Pearl Buck, E. E. Cummings, James T. Farrell, John Gould Fletcher, Joseph Hergesheimer, Vachel Lindsay, Amy Lowell, Edna St. Vincent Millay, Paul Elmer More, John Crowe Ransom, George Santayana, Sara Teasdale, William Carlos Williams, or Elinor Wylie. There were no votes for Ezra Pound, who in 1949 was at St. Elizabeth's in Washington under indictment for treason.

In addition to the five runners-up listed in the committee's report there were other writers whose books won more than ten points: the authors of *The Federalist*, 28; Carl Sandburg, 25; Mrs. Stowe and Sherwood Anderson, 23; Sarah Orne Jewett and Ellen Glasgow, 20; Crèvecoeur, Dos Passos, William James, Lincoln, and Thomas Wolfe, 18; Stephen Vincent Benét, Jonathan Edwards, and James Russell Lowell, 15; and William Faulkner and John Steinbeck, 11.

Fifty-six years earlier the *Critic* had polled its readers to select the ten best American books. On its list there were books by Bryant, Longfellow, Lowell, Holmes, Whittier, and Lew Wallace—none of whom made the UNESCO list. On the UNESCO list there were books by Mark Twain, who was 15th on the *Critic*'s list; by Whitman, who was 20th; by Thoreau, who was 30th; and also books by Melville and Poe, who were nowhere even among the runners-up in the *Critic*'s poll in 1893. On the *Critic*'s list eight of the ten leading authors were New Englanders. On the UNESCO list eight of the twenty best books were also the work of New England authors.

The judges in 1949 were not asked to rank American authors but to choose the twenty best books; otherwise Franklin, who was not a man of letters, probably would not appear among the first twenty. The results do suggest that the judges regarded Hawthorne and Poe as the two greatest American writers, and yet there were among the twenty-six scholars more than one who would have protested strongly against giving either Hawthorne or Poe priority over Emerson, Thoreau, Whitman, Melville, Emily Dickinson, or Henry James.

*It will perhaps suffice to mention the names of Darwin, Marx, Nietzsche, Bergson, Croce, Freud, Einstein, and Kierkegard to suggest the multifarious and unreconcilable doctrines, all making claim to authority, which contributed a colorful confusion to the hodgepodge of the national mind.*
George F. Whicher, *The Literature of the American People*

# THE MOST INFLUENTIAL BOOKS

*Cowley and Smith* (*eds.*), Books That Changed Our Minds (*1939*). In the late 1930's Malcolm Cowley and Bernard Smith undertook a study that resulted in a series of articles in the *New Republic* and in 1939 a book entitled *Books That Changed Our Minds*. The twelve books finally selected were discussed in chapters bearing these titles:

1. Sigmund Freud and *The Interpretation of Dreams*
2. *The Education of Henry Adams*
3. Frederick J. Turner's *The Frontier in American History*
4. William Graham Sumner's *Folkways*
5. Thorstein Veblen and *Business Enterprise*
6. John Dewey and his *Studies in Logical Theory*
7. Franz Boas and *The Mind of Primitive Man*
8. Charles A. Beard's *The Economic Interpretation of the Constitution*
9. I. A. Richards's *The Principles of Literary Criticism*
10. V. L. Parrington's *Main Currents in American Thought*
11. V. I. Lenin's *The State and Revolution*
12. Oswald Spengler's *The Decline of the West*

As we look at the Cowley-Smith list, we cannot help wondering why in 1939, when Adolf Hitler was about to plunge the world into a Second World War, they left out his *Mein Kampf*. Karl Marx's *Das Kapital* has been far more influential than any book by Lenin, Trotsky, or Stalin. In certain instances the editors seem to me not to have chosen the author's most influential book. Better choices for Veblen and Dewey would have been *The Theory of the Leisure Class* and *School and Society*, which had a profound influence upon American public schools. Richards's *Practical Criticism* (1929) probably had a wider influence than *The Principles of Literary Criticism* (1924). The most glaring defect on the part of the compilers was their failure —in an age when science exerted a far greater influence than poetry, drama, or fiction—to include works by Albert Einstein and other eminent scientists.

On March 23, 1935, the *Publishers' Weekly* had printed a composite list of the twenty-five most influential books published since 1885, selected by Charles A. Beard, John Dewey, and Edward Weeks. The three judges were unanimous in their choice of Edward Bellamy's *Looking Backward*, Sir James G. Frazer's *The Golden Bough*, Karl Marx's *Das Kapital*, and Oswald Spengler's *The Decline of the West*. Cowley and Smith included only the last of the four. Two of the *Publishers' Weekly*'s judges named *The Theory of the Leisure Class, The Education of Henry Adams,* William James's *The Principles of Psychology,* Alfred T. Mahan's *The Influence of Sea Power upon History,* and Sinclair Lewis's *Main Street.* The third judge selected *Babbitt.*

Cowley and Smith professed to be interested primarily in influences that affected American literature, and these for the most part came from the Old World. Yet among the twelve books on the list all but four are by American writers. The list includes no books by Henrik Ibsen, Emile Zola, Marcel Proust, William Butler Yeats, James Joyce, John Masefield, H. G. Wells, Bernard Shaw, Thomas Hardy, Friedrich Nietzsche, or any of the great Russian novelists. Among influential American writers not represented are H. L. Mencken and Van Wyck Brooks. The list includes no book by T. S. Eliot, whose poems and essays had by 1939 done more than other books to change the current of American criticism and the technique of American poetry. Katherine Anne Porter in *The Days Before* (1952) asserted that "a whole generation of writers" learned their trade not in school or college but from their study of five writers—none of them on the Cowley-Smith list: Henry James, James Joyce, William Butler Yeats, T. S. Eliot, and Ezra Pound. "The beginning artist," she concluded, "is educated by whoever helps him to learn how to work his own vein, who helps him to fix his own standards, and who gives him courage. I believe I can speak for a whole generation of writers who acknowledge that these five men were in just this way, the great educators of their time."

What method of procedure does one follow when he attempts to select the most influential books? The scientist would ask: Where are your "controls"? and the critic's answer would be embarrassingly vague. Furthermore, the influences that Cowley and Smith had in mind came to the attention of the young writers in the main not through books but in such magazines as *Poetry,* the *Dial,* the *New Republic,* the *Smart Set,* the *American Mercury,* the *Fugitive,* the *Hound and Horn,* the *Little Review,* and other "little magazines," some of them printed in Europe. In many instances no doubt the new influences came through conversations with other writers. That was especially true of young writers who, like Malcolm Cowley, had lived abroad and learned through conversations with Gertrude Stein, Ezra Pound, T. S. Eliot, and other writers. In America many college students who wanted to be writers had the opportunity to hear lectures or readings by such well-known American poets as Carl Sandburg, Robert Frost, Vachel Lindsay, and Amy Lowell. In many colleges and universities there were instructors who introduced their students to important new poets, dramatists, and novelists.

*Eric F. Goldman, "Books That Changed America" (1953).* This article from the pen of an able Princeton historian appeared in the *Saturday Review of Literature* on July 4, 1953. From his list Professor Goldman ruled out such books as the King James Bible and the plays of Shakespeare, which successive generations have in various ways interpreted for their own needs. What the historian looked for was books which had had "a substantial role in changing America during a particular period." These were books which, appearing "at some critical juncture, caught a latent trend and by catching it with just the right nuance, whirled it ahead." He chose:

( 1 ) Thomas Paine, *Common Sense;*
( 2 ) *The Federalist;*
( 3 ) Harriet Beecher Stowe, *Uncle Tom's Cabin;*
( 4 ) Herbert Spencer, *The Study of Sociology;*
( 5 ) Henry George, *Progress and Poverty;*
( 6 ) Charles Sheldon, *In His Steps;*
( 7 ) Sigmund Freud, *The Interpretation of Dreams;*
( 8 ) Charles A. Beard, *An Economic Interpretation of the Constitution;*
( 9 ) J. Maynard Keynes, *The Economic Consequences of the Peace;*
( 10 ) John Dewey, *Human Nature and Conduct;*
( 11 ) Sinclair Lewis, *Babbitt;*
( 12 ) Lincoln Steffens, *Autobiography;* and
( 13 ) Wendell Willkie, *One World.*

If Goldman were revising his list at the present time, it is not unlikely that he would question the inclusion of numbers 6, 11, 12, 13, and perhaps 9. The lowering of the Iron Curtain seemed to end the hopes of Wendell Willkie and American liberals for friendly relations with the Communist bloc. Even in the late 1940's Asa Don Dickinson's "authorities" had given *One World* only 253 points out of a possible total of 680. Keynes's book in 1920 exerted a profound influence upon American economists, but did it really do much, as Goldman suggested, "to buttress an America that wanted to have done with Wilsonian internationalism"? I think that American soldiers returning disillusioned from the trenches in France in 1919 had much more to do with the change in the American attitude than *The Economic Consequences of the Peace* or the speeches in the Senate of Henry Cabot Lodge. The change had occurred before Keynes's book was published in this country in 1920. In part at least Steffens's *Autobiography* was required reading for many undergraduates, but it does not follow that the book had any great influence upon their actions after college. There is no doubt that Sinclair Lewis's *Main Street* and *Babbitt* were very influential, but so were the novels of Ernest Hemingway and (for a time) of James Branch Cabell. H. L. Mencken and Van Wyck Brooks probably should be somewhere on the list. The only scientific book in Goldman's list is Freud's *The Interpretation of Dreams*. Did not *The Origin of Species* have a tremendous and immediate impact upon American thinking

—more in fact than any one of Herbert Spencer's books? And surely Albert Einstein, who spent his last years at the Princeton Institute for Advanced Study, belongs in any list of writings that changed America and the rest of the civilized world.

*Robert B. Downs,* Books That Changed the World *(1956).* This book is the work of an able American librarian, and it was published by the American Library Association. Downs had no intention of compiling a list of "best books" or "great books." "The making of such lists is," as he said, "a favorite pastime of literary critics, authors, editors, educators, and librarians." His aim was rather "to discover those books which have exerted the most profound influence on history, economics, culture, civilization, and scientific thought." His "number one criterion" was that "the book must have had a great and continuing impact on human thought and action, not for a single nation, but for a major segment of the world." For practical reasons he decided to omit all books written before the Renaissance and the invention of printing. For practical reasons also he included only "books in science and the social sciences," omitting such important fields as religion, philosophy, and literature. Regretfully he left out "the great literary monuments—fiction, drama, poetry, essays—that have moved and inspired the world." Their influence, he concluded, is "virtually immeasurable."

### The World of Man

1. Niccolò Machiavelli, *The Prince*
2. Thomas Paine, *Common Sense*
3. Adam Smith, *Wealth of Nations*
4. Thomas Malthus, *Essay on the Principle of Population*
5. Henry David Thoreau, "Civil Disobedience"
6. Harriet Beecher Stowe, *Uncle Tom's Cabin*
7. Karl Marx, *Das Kapital*
8. Alfred T. Mahan, *The Influence of Sea Power upon History*
9. Sir Halford J. Mackinder, *The Geographical Pivot of History*
10. Adolph Hitler, *Mein Kampf*

### The World of Science

11. Nicolaus Copernicus, *De Revolutionibus Orbium Coelestium*
12. William Harvey, *De Motu Cordis*
13. Sir Isaac Newton, *Principia Mathematica*
14. Charles Darwin, *Origin of Species*
15. Sigmund Freud, *The Interpretation of Dreams*
16. Albert Einstein, *Relativity, The Special and General Theories*

Downs's definition of a "book" was elastic enough to permit him to include the two essays by Thoreau and Einstein. One wonders why he did not leave out *Common Sense* and substitute for it the Declaration of Independence or the U.S. Constitution. Their influence has been great and continuing. *Common Sense* was important in the early days of the American Revolution, but its influence has been slight ever since 1794, when Paine published *The Age of Reason*. During the nineteenth century he was known chiefly as, in the words of Theodore Roosevelt, a "filthy little atheist." *Common Sense* clearly belongs in Goldman's list but not, I think, in Downs's.

It would appear that it is almost as difficult to select the most influential books as it is to name those that eventually will be recognized as literary masterpieces. Downs, however, it seems to me, performed his task more successfully than Goldman, Cowley and Smith, or the English author, Horace Shipp, who in 1945 published *Books That Moved the World*. His list: (1) The Bible; (2) Plato, *The Republic*; (3) St. Augustine, *The City of God*; (4) *The Koran*; (5) Dante, *The Divine Comedy*; (6) Shakespeare, *Plays*; (7) Bunyan, *The Pilgrim's Progress*; (8) Milton, *Areopagitica*; (9) Darwin, *The Origin of Species*; and (10) Marx, *Das Kapital*. It seems almost incredible that Shipp could find room in his list for no single book written in France, Germany, Spain, Russia, China, India, or the United States. His list does not include the *Iliad* or the *Odyssey*, the *Aeneid, Don Quixote*, or *Faust*. The oddest thing is his inclusion, not of the obvious choice, *Paradise Lost*, but of Milton's *Areopagitica*. That prose classic is probably the best of Milton's tracts, but it has had little if any influence upon world opinion. An accomplished Milton scholar, William Haller, who edited *Tracts on Liberty in the Puritan Revolution*, found no evidence that the other seventeenth-century writers who discussed liberty of the press ever read the *Areopagitica*.

The secret (if there is one) of the success of the most influential books, Downs suggests, is that the times were ready for them. "In some other historical epoch," he said, "the work would either not have been produced at all, or if it had appeared would have attracted little attention." Downs noted that many of the books on his list are "badly written books, lacking in literary style." He noted also that some of them (but not the scientific books) were the work of agitators and radicals like Karl Marx and Thomas Paine or even fanatics like Adolf Hitler. Badly written in some respects *Uncle Tom's Cabin* and *Mein Kampf* may be, but these books had the power to communicate to many readers the passionate convictions of those who wrote them.

In 1961, feeling that he had left out too many of the most influential books, Downs published *Molders of the Modern Mind: 111 Books That Shaped Western Civilization*. He explained its "central idea" by quoting from Walt Whitman's *Democratic Vistas*: "It is strictly true that a few first-class poets, philosophs, and authors have substantially settled and given status to the entire religion, education, law, sociology, etc., of the hitherto civilized world, by tinging and often creating the atmospheres out of which they have arisen." Although the emphasis is still upon the sciences and the social sciences, Downs made room for more books of belles-lettres, and especially American literature.

Thomas Jefferson's *A Summary View of the Rights of British America* (1774)
Thomas Paine's *Common Sense* (1776)
*The Federalist* (1788)
Benjamin Franklin's *Autobiography* (1791)
Noah Webster's *An American Dictionary of the English Language* (1828)
William Holmes McGuffey's *Eclectic Readers* (1836–1837)
Ralph Waldo Emerson's *Essays* (1841–1844)
Henry David Thoreau's *Resistance to Civil Government* (1849)
Harriet Beecher Stowe's *Uncle Tom's Cabin* (1852)
Abraham Lincoln and Stephen A. Douglas, *Political Debates* (1860)
Horatio Alger, Jr., *Ragged Dick* (1867)
Walt Whitman's *Democratic Vistas* (1871)
Henry George's *Progress and Poverty* (1879)
Edward Bellamy's *Looking Backward, 2000–1887* (1888)
Alfred T. Mahan's *The Influence of Sea Power upon History, 1660–1783* (1890)
Frederick Jackson Turner's *The Significance of the Frontier in American History* (1893)
Thorstein Veblen's *The Theory of the Leisure Class* (1899)
John Dewey's *School and Society* (1899)
Woodrow Wilson's *The New Freedom* (1913)

*Robert B. Downs*, Books That Changed America *(1970)*. In the introduction to his third attempt to single out the most influential books Downs admitted that "a unanimous verdict is exceedingly difficult to achieve on any given work. Inevitably," he continued, "selection is highly personal and subjective." Nevertheless, he thought that all of the twenty-five books he had chosen "would rank high in a vote by any knowledgeable and impartial jury." What he looked for among the more than eighty books that he had seriously considered was books which had played "key roles in shaping the American world of today."

### The Twenty-five Books

Thomas Paine, *Common Sense*
Meriwether Lewis and William Clark, *History of the Expedition*
Joseph Smith, *The Book of Mormon*

William Beaumont, *Experiments and Observations on the Gastric Juice and the Physiology of Digestion*
Alexis de Tocqueville, *Democracy in America*
Horace Mann, *Annual Reports*
Oliver Wendell Holmes, *The Contagiousness of Puerperal Fever*
Henry David Thoreau, *Resistance to Civil Government*
Harriet Beecher Stowe, *Uncle Tom's Cabin*
Edward Bellamy, *Looking Backward, 2000–1887*
Alfred T. Mahan, *The Influence of Sea Power upon History, 1660–1783*
Frederick Jackson Turner, *The Significance of the Frontier in American History*
Lincoln Steffens, *The Shame of the Cities*
Upton Sinclair, *The Jungle*
Abraham Flexner, *Medical Education in the United States and Canada*
Jane Addams, *Twenty Years at Hull-House*
Frederick Winslow Taylor, *The Principles of Scientific Management*
Charles A. Beard, *An Economic Interpretation of the Constitution of the United States*
Henry Louis Mencken, *Prejudices*
Benjamin N. Cardozo, *The Nature of the Judicial Process*
Robert S. and Helen Merrell Lynd, *Middletown*
W. J. Cash, *The Mind of the South*
Gunnar Myrdal, *An American Dilemma*
John Kenneth Galbraith, *The Affluent Society*
Rachel Carson, *Silent Spring*

The list includes three novels but no drama and no book of poems. The emphasis is, as Downs noted, upon the social sciences and not on science or the humanities. Among the runners-up are Dana's *Two Years before the Mast*, *Huckleberry Finn*, and *Moby-Dick*. There are many unexplained differences between the books included in *The Books That Changed America* and the American books listed in *The Molders of the Modern Mind*. One wonders why Downs dropped Whitman's *Democratic Vistas*, Emerson's *Essays*, and Veblen's *The Theory of the Leisure Class*. One wonders also just why Downs in his attempt to single out the most influential American books included *The Book of Mormon*, and *The Mind of the South*. *The Influence of Sea Power upon Naval History* was no doubt a very influential book, but it exerted a greater and more immediate influence upon Japan, England, and Germany than upon the United States. Thoreau's "Resistance to Civil Government" (better known as "Civil Disobedience") exerted a decisive influence upon Gandhi, but its influence in this country was, I think, very little except perhaps belatedly in the case of Martin Luther King, Jr. Of the twenty-five books chosen by Downs all but two were written by Americans.

*Rochelle Girson, "Mutations in the Body Politic" (1964).* In 1964 the *Saturday Review* (formerly the *Saturday Review of Literature*) polled twenty-seven "historians, economists, political analysts, educators, social scientists, and philosophers" to ascertain "what books published during the preceding four decades [had] most significantly altered the direction of our society" and also "which [might] have a substantial impact on public thought and action in the years ahead." The results of the poll were reported in the August 29, 1964, number.

## THE PANEL

| | |
|---|---|
| Samuel Flagg Bemis | J. Ben Lieberman |
| Sir Denis Brogan | Walter Lippmann |
| Geoffrey Bruun | Ashley Montague |
| Arthur E. Burns | Hans J. Morgenthau |
| Stuart Chase | Allan Nevins |
| Margaret L. Coit | J. H. Plumb |
| William O. Douglas | Harry Howe Ransom |
| Dwight L. Dumond | Lillian Smith |
| Horace L. Friess | Richard P. Stebbins |
| August Heckscher | Henry P. Van Dusen |
| Richard D. Heffner | Mark S. Watson |
| Robert L. Heilbroner | Louis J. Walinsky |
| Sidney Hook | Paul Woodring |
| Arthur Larson | |

## THE MOST INFLUENTIAL BOOKS

John Maynard Keynes, *The General Theory of Employment, Interest and Money*, 12 votes
Gunnar Myrdal, *An American Dilemma*, 11
Adolf Hitler, *Mein Kampf*, 8
Norbert Wiener, *Cybernetics*, 7
David Riesman, *The Lonely Crowd*, 7
Alfred Kinsey and Others, *Sexual Behavior in the Human Male* and *Sexual Behavior in the Human Female*, 7
John Steinbeck, *The Grapes of Wrath*, 6
Benjamin Spock, *The Common Sense Book of Baby and Child Care*, 5
John Kenneth Galbraith, *The Affluent Society*, 4
Adolph A. Berle, Jr., *The Modern Corporation and Private Property*, 4
Reinhold Niebuhr, *The Nature and Destiny of Man*, 4
Rachel Carson, *Silent Spring*, 4
Arnold J. Toynbee, *A Study of History*, 4

Girson concluded his article by suggesting that these thirteen are the books which "have prodded, inspired, or frightened us into altering our thought patterns and folkways during the past forty years." Perhaps, but the total number of books mentioned was 163, and Keynes's book, which heads the list, got only 12 votes from the twenty-seven specialists. Eleven other books each got 3 votes and nineteen each got only 2.

The problem of singling out the most influential books is not less difficult than the problem of choosing the best books. What kind of readers are we to judge by? Shall we employ pollsters to interrogate the intelligent and influential few who are moved by writers like Thoreau, Mahan, and Veblen or the many thousands who read such books as *Ben-Hur*, *Main Street*, and *Gone with the Wind*?

The readers of our time do not constitute a homogeneous reading public like those English and American book-lovers who in the 1850's eagerly awaited new books by Longfellow, Tennyson, Hawthorne, and Thackeray. In spite of the vast numbers of books that are published and read in our time Americans are less influenced by books than was the case in the 1850's when thousands were reading *The Scarlet Letter* and *Uncle Tom's Cabin* and the intelligent few were being moved by *Moby-Dick*, *Walden*, and *Leaves of Grass*.

There are of course contemporary books that do move their readers to thought and action. Two recent examples are Ralph Nader's *Unsafe at Any Speed* and Rachel Carson's *Silent Spring*. But nowadays books have powerful rivals in motion pictures, radio, and television. No book published in the 1940's moved British and American listeners like the speeches of Winston Churchill. Nowadays we do not have to read books to learn about the progress of the war in Vietnam or riots in the streets and demonstrations on college campuses. We see them on television and we expect our newsmen to give us an explanation of these events.

The reader whose primary interest is in the literary quality of American books will be disappointed to find that in all the lists discussed in this chapter only two of our literary classics won places in the highest group: Thoreau's "Resistance to Civil Government" and Steinbeck's *The Grapes of Wrath*. Why, one wonders, did the judges not give higher ratings to the poems and essays of Emerson, the short stories of Poe, and Mark Twain's masterpiece, *Huckleberry Finn*? In the *Saturday Review*'s 1964 poll *The Grapes of Wrath* won a place among the top thirteen with only 5 votes from the twenty-seven judges. Four works of fiction got as many as 3 votes, but none of the four was the work of an American author. Three novels got as many as 2 votes: J. D. Salinger's *Catcher in the Rye* and Hemingway's *The Sun Also Rises* and *For Whom the Bell Tolls*. Important books which got only a single vote were O'Neill's *Mourning Becomes Electra* and *The Iceman Cometh*, Richard Wright's *Native Son* and *Uncle Tom's Children*, Faulkner's *Intruder in the Dust*, Fitzgerald's *The*

*Great Gatsby,* and Joyce's *Ulysses.* The only book of poems to receive a single vote was Robert Frost's *Complete Poems,* chosen by Allan Nevins. Nothing by T. S. Eliot got a single vote.

Perhaps a main reason why so much of the best of our contemporary literature fails to move the American people to thought and action is its negative and unrepresentative character. What result can an American writer expect when what he writes is the kind of thing suggested by Harriet R. Holman in *John Fox and Tom Page* (1970)? "New fashions in thought and in literature have accustomed readers to expect to find any 'serious' writing predicated upon the assumption that man is a tragic or ridiculous figure living in a faceless urban society and always the victim of forces—biological, social, economic, psychological, ethnic, any kind—forces beyond his power to manipulate."

The reader whose interest is primarily in the literary qualities of American books should remember that if we are considering the *literary* influence of books, no intelligent judge can afford to overlook Poe, Whitman, and Henry James in the nineteenth century or Faulkner, Hemingway, and Eliot in the twentieth. In this century writers for whose books the great mass of readers cares little or nothing, like James Joyce and Ezra Pound, have had an important influence upon many a writer who is better and more favorably known to the general public than either Joyce or Pound.

*Part Four. Conclusion / Afterword*

*The delight men take in books will continue, their ever-changing tastes dictating popularity for some, neglect for others. What a new year or a new era will select is not to be foretold, either by what has been or by what is, for like the muffled forces of history, the shape of taste is various and changing, conditioned by events and conditioning them, never the same and never to be plotted in advance.*

James D. Hart, *The Popular Book*


*The "greatness" of literature cannot be determined solely by literary standards, though we must remember that whether it is literature or not can be determined only by literary standards.*

T. S. Eliot, "Religion and Literature"


# Conclusion

In my opening chapter I quoted from an essay entitled "Critical Certainties," in which E. E. Kellett complained that the greatest difficulty in the way of confident and sound criticism lies in "the constant shifting in the standards of taste." That was in 1928. In the following year the British scholar amplified his thesis in a book entitled *The Whirligig of Taste*. He could find, he concluded, "no permanent or established principles in criticism."

> The verdict of posterity, of which we hear so much, is a pure phantom, invented by unsuccessful authors to console themselves for contemporary neglect. . . . To which of the thousand generations of posterity is a Euripides or a Tennyson to appeal? . . . [posterity's] verdict is like that "judgment of history" to which statesmen profess to look forward for their vindication. There is no such thing as "history": there are only historians, and each decides according to his own bias.

Kellett obviously believed that the verdicts of literary historians are no more accurate or unbiased than the critical appraisals of those who write our political, economic, and social histories. "The moral," he said, "is obvious. He [the critic] must deal less freely than is his wont in triumphant certainties and 'absolute shalls.'"

For the critic or the literary historian who may be formulating his own estimate of an older author like Milton or Donne or a contemporary writer like Robert Lowell or Eudora Welty it is disconcerting to be told that there are "no permanent or established principles in criticism" and no such thing as literary history but only literary historians each of whom "decides according to his own bias."

Kellett was perhaps unduly pessimistic; and yet in the twentieth century, as in the nineteenth, most of our best writers had long years to wait before many critics or literary historians could see them as major American writers. Only after they were dead did that honor come to Poe, Melville, Thoreau, and Whitman. In the twentieth century also most of our better writers waited long before being recognized as the peers of their great predecessors. Literary criticism is still not a science, and we are no wiser than our fathers and our grandfathers. In the twentieth century many of our most influential critics have been as wrong about their contemporaries as their predecessors were when they so confidently made public their inability to appreciate the greatness of *Moby-Dick* and *Leaves of Grass*. The nineteenth-century critics were not less intelligent than those men and women who in the twentieth century displayed their inability to see anything great in the poems of Robert Frost and T. S. Eliot and the novels of William Faulkner and Ernest Hemingway.

Edwin Arlington Robinson told two friends of mine that for fifteen years he felt that he was writing for about fifteen readers. The general public was unaware of Robinson's existence until the president of the United States publicly praised his poems. It so happened that Theodore Roosevelt's son Kermit had a teacher at Groton who had discovered Robinson's poetry. For about twenty years Robert Frost sent his poems to the four most prominent American quality magazines; they rejected almost every poem that he sent them. He was thirty-nine years old when his first book was published. His first recognition came not in his own country but in England. When his second book of poems, *North of Boston*, was republished in New York in 1915, Amy Lowell and Louis Untermeyer began praising him as one of the best living American poets. Yet even after he had published three of his best books, his royalties, as he told me in 1923, amounted to only about a thousand dollars a year. No wonder that he spent so many years in teaching or lecturing. The poems of Wallace Stevens won high praise from Harriet Monroe and Edmund Wilson long before he was recognized as a major figure in the 1950's. His poems seemed of little importance to those influential promoters of the new poetry, Amy Lowell and Louis Untermeyer.

Conrad Aiken took some poems of his friend T. S. Eliot to London, where he found that English publishers and magazine editors did not care for them. Ezra Pound and John Gould Fletcher persuaded Harriet Monroe to print some of them in *Poetry: A Magazine of Verse*. In 1922 *The Waste Land* attracted wide attention, much of it unfavorable, but the poem quickly became a rallying point for youthful poets and future New Critics. And yet H. L.

318

Mencken, Van Wyck Brooks, Louis Untermeyer, and Amy Lowell could not see Eliot as a major American writer. It was not until after the Second World War that Eliot was widely recognized in this country as at once a great poet and the most important literary critic of his time.

The American writers of fiction found many more readers than the poets, but in the eyes of many "critical authorities" Dreiser, Hemingway, Sherwood Anderson, Dos Passos, Fitzgerald, Faulkner, Edith Wharton, Willa Cather, and Ellen Glasgow rated no better than Joseph Hergesheimer, Gertrude Atherton, and Erskine Caldwell. Readers looking for the "ideal" and the sentimental found only "dust and ashes" in such books as *An American Tragedy*, *A Farewell to Arms*, *The Great Gatsby*, and *The Sound and the Fury*. Dreiser had to wait a quarter of a century before he received any real public recognition as a writer of importance. Scott Fitzgerald's stories were widely read, but after the advent of the Great Depression few critics thought his books would be long remembered.

In the years 1929–1932 when William Faulkner was bringing out his best books, most critics were either puzzled, angered, or disgusted by what they found in them. Northern readers misconstrued his attitude toward the South, and southern readers found it difficult to forgive him for a book like *Sanctuary* or a story like "A Rose for Emily." Too many of Faulkner's characters resembled the Yahoos of *Gulliver's Travels*. In 1945 all of Faulkner's seventeen books were out of print. In 1946 Malcolm Cowley brought out *The Portable Faulkner*, and from that time on the greatness of the Mississippi novelist was increasingly recognized. Seventeen years before *The Portable Faulkner* appeared Donald Davidson, reviewing *The Sound and the Fury* in 1929, had pointed out that Faulkner was "an acute observer of human behavior," had praised his style as "a major style, not a trifling one," and had stated his belief that Faulkner was "the equal of any except three or four American novelists who stand at the very top." We are fortunate that each one of our major American writers has found a few discerning critics who recognized his genius long before the general public was aware of his significance.

## THE POET-CRITICS

In 1845 James Russell Lowell, noting that American literature was handicapped by the lack of carefully-thought-out critical standards, wrote in his essay on Edgar Allan Poe: "But, before we have an American literature, we must have an American criticism." In the early twentieth century Irving

Babbitt and Paul Elmer More were again and again to express a similar opinion. No doubt our literature has suffered from its lack of carefully-thought-out critical standards, but the history of literature and literary criticism gives little support to the position taken by Lowell, Babbitt, and More. What is new in art comes chiefly from the practitioners. It is the artists who develop new techniques and give us new critical standards. The Greek dramatists wrote their masterpieces before Aristotle undertook to formulate the principles that underlie the tragedies of Aeschylus, Sophocles, and Euripides.

The youthful literary genius develops his critical standards while actually writing or trying to make up his mind as to the kind of poetry or fiction he wants to write. He sees the literature of the past chiefly in terms of what can be of use to him. A minor poet may be of greater service than an unfashionable major poet. The youthful Coleridge was indebted to the sonnets of the forgotten William Lisle Bowles. A century later T. S. Eliot owed much to the poems of Jules Laforgue. For Eliot and Pound, John Donne was for long a greater poet than John Milton, whose style seemed to them a bad model for poets in the twentieth century. In the 1920's the new poets found it difficult if not impossible to do justice to Longfellow and Tennyson.

Most of the great critics of the nineteenth century were poets or writers of fiction. The number includes Coleridge, Arnold, Poe, Lowell, Howells, and Henry James. In the twentieth century a very large proportion of our best critics also have been poets: Eliot, Pound, Aiken, Ransom, Davidson, Tate. These and other creative writers of the early twentieth century were often the discoverers of new talents.

In his youth, so Eliot wrote in 1923, he had been "inclined to take the extreme position that the only critics worth reading were the critics who practised, and practised well, the art of which they wrote." In 1942 a wiser Eliot noted in "The Music of Poetry" that when the poet writes criticism he is "not so much a judge as an advocate." The poet, he added, "at the back of his mind, if not as his ostensible purpose, is always trying to defend the kind of poetry he is writing, or to formulate the kind that he wants to write." Hence, Eliot concluded: "We must return to the scholar for ascertainment of facts, and to the more detached critic for impartial judgment."

The failures of the creative writers when they practice criticism of their contemporaries are conspicuous. Poe was a first-rate critic when he was writing about Hawthorne and Dickens but not when he wrote about Emerson or Carlyle or the numerous women writers of his time. Emerson was quick to see the merits of Carlyle, Whitman, and Thoreau; but he failed dismally to recognize in his friend and neighbor Hawthorne a great writer of fiction. Henry James was an admirable critic of Hawthorne, but when he wrote about Poe, Whitman, and Thoreau, he showed little understanding or appreciation. Whitman was at times a great poet, but when he was asked to name the great English and American poets, he came up with nothing better than the conventional Victorian estimate. In the twentieth century Ezra Pound and T. S. Eliot played an important part in discovering and promoting new poets, and they had a profound influence upon the New Critics who were to apply their methods to American writers who had little importance for either Eliot or Pound. The two poets fully recognized the greatness of Hawthorne and Henry James, but they greatly underrated such major American writers as Emerson, Thoreau, Melville, Whitman, Emily Dickinson, and Mark Twain.

In 1954 William Faulkner named as the best American novelists of his time: Thomas Wolfe, Ernest Hemingway, John Dos Passos, Erskine Caldwell, and himself. He rated Wolfe first and himself second. He placed Hemingway last of the five, as he said to Harvey Breit, "because he stayed within what he knew. He did it fine, but he did not try for the impossible." (Had Faulkner forgotten Hemingway's comments on the "Fifth Dimension"?) Today one wonders why Faulkner did not name Dreiser, Lewis, Fitzgerald, or his old friend Sherwood Anderson instead of Erskine Caldwell; and why did he not extend his list to include Willa Cather, Edith Wharton, or Ellen Glasgow?

The creative writer may be right about his contemporaries and wrong about his predecessors. Nelson Algren, for example, said to Harvey Breit: "I think there's nobody better than Faulkner and Hemingway. They're in another league over and above Washington Irving, Henry James or Hawthorne who anyway are the dullest writers that ever walked in shoe leather."

It was not Algren, however, but John O'Hara who proclaimed Hemingway the greatest writer born since Shakespeare died in 1616. If such a notion seems incredible, consider the verdict of a well-known novelist who was also professor of English at the University of Chicago: "It would not be too strong to call it mere garbage." Robert Herrick was talking about Hemingway's A Farewell to Arms.

## ACADEMIC CRITICS

Until long after the turn of the century there were few literary critics in the faculties of American colleges and universities. The professor of English was far more likely to be a philologist than a literary critic. If he had not received his graduate training in Germany, he had at least studied under scholars familiar with German scholarship. What most concerned him was matters of fact: sources, influences, analogues, textual problems, the economic and social backgrounds of authors, and biographical details. The professor of English rarely reviewed books, and the periodicals to which he contributed were the scholarly journals, which ignored living writers.

As a rule to which there were few notable exceptions, the professors of English had little interest in American literature or in the contemporary literature of any country.* As late as 1920 American literature was just beginning to be a respectable subject for scholarly investigation and only then for writers who had been dead for a quarter of a century. Until after the First World War the professors had only a minor part in determining the status of American writers living or dead. The actual work of revising the American literary canon was done—often in spite of the opposition of academic critics— by young intellectuals led by such critics and propagandists as H. L. Mencken, Louis Untermeyer, Van Wyck Brooks, Amy Lowell, and Conrad Aiken.†

The situation in the 1960's is vastly different from what it was half a century ago. The reputations of our older American writers and of nearly all our twentieth-century poets are now in the keeping not of the poet-critics but of the professors of English, who are far more numerous than they were in the 1920's. It is the professors who select the authors whose books are to be studied; they prepare the handbooks; they write the literary histories; and they edit most of the anthologies.

The academic critics have come in for more than their share of the creative writer's traditional antipathy to literary critics as a class. For example, Archibald McLeish wrote in 1940: "It is not for nothing that the modern scholar invented the Ph.D. thesis as his principal contribution to literary form. The Ph.D. thesis is the perfect image of his world." In 1952 Delmore Schwartz warned the readers of the *Partisan Review* that the New Critics were intrenching themselves in the English departments of the universities: "As the New Criticism naturally tends to attach literature to the university, so only a critical non-conformist intelligentsia, inside and outside the university, can right the balance and keep serious literature from becoming merely a set of courses in the departments of English and comparative literature."

It is a captive audience that the professors have in their classrooms, and too often it is the only audience that the poets have. A heavy responsibility rests upon the professors of English, and I wonder how many of them are

* Two notable exceptions to my generalization were Brander Matthews of Columbia University and Bliss Perry of Harvard. I was fortunate enough to have courses with both of them. Another was John Livingston Lowes of Harvard whose *Convention and Revolt in Poetry* (1919) placed the new poetry in the proper historical perspective.

† In *South and Southwest* (1965) I have treated this subject at length in an essay entitled "The Creative Writer and the University, with Special Reference to the 1920's."

aware of the dangers inherent in this unprecedented situation. As a rule, neither the professors nor their students read books primarily for the delight that one finds in great poetry, drama, and fiction. Students read to find materials to be used in reports, term papers, theses, and dissertations. Professors read chiefly for professional reasons, and what they read includes only a small segment of the world's great literature.

In his chosen field the American professor of English is a competent scholar, but his graduate training has seldom given him the ability to discriminate between the best and the second-best. If he is in his forties or fifties, his literary taste is probably a little old-fashioned. He is still teaching his students that the last word in critical standards is to be found in the essays of Henry James, T. S. Eliot, and John Crowe Ransom. The professor of English is accordingly rarely among the first to salute an original poet or novelist. Much of what he reads, as I have suggested, he reads for professional reasons, not for his own enjoyment. When he reads a poem, he is looking for recurrent themes, images, phrases, myths, Freudian influences, etc. Much of what the productive scholar reads is not literature but special studies by other scholars, biographies, articles in scholarly journals, literary criticism written by amateurs, public documents, letters, old magazines and newspapers, and the work of minor writers.

The academic critic is in danger of finding himself in a predicament not unlike that in which Ellen Glasgow found herself after "reading so widely in the writings of science that it required total immersion in the centuries of sound English prose to restore [her] natural ear for rhythm and [her] instinct for style." In *A Common Measure*, from which I am quoting, Miss Glasgow noted that for her, books had been "one of the vital elements of experience, not a thing apart, not a collection of classified facts." She had "never approached literature by way of college courses in English, arranged neatly with dates of birth and death in a lank row of epitaphs."

In the last quarter of a century the number of college students who have taken courses in English and American literature runs up into the millions. And yet I wonder how many of them since graduating from college have ever reread *Moby-Dick*, *Daisy Miller*, *The Waste Land*, or poems by Wallace Stevens or Emily Dickinson. Some there are no doubt who found that they loved literature so much that they wanted to write or, failing in that aim, to spend their lives in teaching. But the mass of college graduates seem to get their fiction from television and the movies or from paperbacks and the popular magazines. A few of the graduates, chiefly members of women's literary clubs, perhaps do try to read the new American poets; but the men as a rule care nothing for modern poetry. Can one imagine thousands of American men and women crowding into Yankee Stadium to hear Robert

Lowell or James Dickey read his poems? Yet we are told that such things have actually happened in Soviet Russia.

There are fashions in scholarship as in speech and dress. A few years ago dozens of researchers were trying to puzzle out the meaning of the allegory in *Moby-Dick* or seeking to reinterpret "The Turn of the Screw." The scholar who brings out a new book on an American writer feels that he must have a thesis different from those set forth by the scholars who preceded him. In reviewing a new book on William Dean Howells, the veteran Howells scholar Clara Kirk wrote in *American Literature* for March, 1967:

> The first task of such an explorer is to disparage the work of most of the critics who have traveled the well-worn road before him, and his second is to establish a "new" set of guidelines. Mr. Carrington's critical assumptions are those of the neo–New Critics, and they, in turn, are beginning to seem "Old-Fashioned" and "Conventional," for the era of the computer-oriented critic is with us. With a somewhat wry smile, those engaged in American studies must recognize that they will soon be swept into the ash can by the Machine which (who?) will dub us all (Mr. Carrington included) "impressionistic" and "dated."

There are times, however, when even the academic critic finds himself dismayed by the hundreds upon hundreds of critical essays and scholarly explications published in greater numbers in every decade. Then one recalls Anatole France's prophecy in *La Vie littéraire* that "criticism, the youngest of all the literary forms," would "perhaps end by absorbing all the others."

There are fortunately exceptions to the generalizations that I have made about the men and women of my own profession. It is the love of great literature—and in many cases the desire to write—that brought most of us into what is financially still one of the least rewarding of professions. Today those who teach American literature are better prepared—and incidentally better paid—than their predecessors were in the 1920's. Nowadays the professor of English, no matter what his special field may be, is expected to know enough about contemporary literature in England and America to lecture on it to undergraduates. That was not the case in 1922 when so many professors of English disliked or disapproved of *Babbitt* and *Tales of the Jazz Age* and could see nothing of any permanent value in *Ulysses* or *The Waste Land*.

In the introduction to his edition of Poe's *Selected Prose and Poetry* (1950) W. H. Auden emphasized the debt—often unacknowledged—which the critic and the general reader alike owe to the scholar: "The professors are, of course, very necessary, for it is through their devoted labors that Poe may finally reach the kind of reader that every author hopes for, who will read him all, good-humoredly willing to wade through much which is dull or inferior for the delight of discovering something new and admirable." "What every author hopes to receive from posterity," said Auden, "—a hope usually disappointed—is justice." Auden was the first anthologist, I think, to include the neglected *Narrative of Arthur Gordon Pym*, which Poe had been persuaded into calling a "silly book." Auden pronounced it "one of the finest adventure stories ever written." It is, he said, "an object lesson in the art. Every kind of adventure occurs—adventures of natural origin like shipwreck; adventures like mutiny, caused by familiar human beings, or, like the adventures on the island, by strange natives; and, finally, supernatural nightmare events—yet each leads credibly into the next." Poe scholars like Patrick Quinn, Edward Davidson, and others have followed Auden's lead and assigned to *Pym* a place among the masterpieces of American fiction.

The scholars are indeed in Auden's words "very necessary," especially in the case of authors who are no longer living. If William Hazlitt, writing in 1817, could have had access to the findings of modern Shakespeare scholarship, he would not have made the monumental mistake of describing as characteristically Shakespearean certain passages in *Henry VIII* which are now thought to be the work of John Fletcher. If Professor Herbert J. C. Grierson had not brought out his edition of Donne's poems in 1912, how much longer, I wonder, would it have taken Eliot, Ransom, Pound, and the New Critics to discover that, in their view, the main stream of Anglo-American literary tradition runs through the Metaphysical Poets of the seventeenth century? It is the scholars who have discovered or rediscovered unknown or forgotten poets like Edward Taylor, Philip Freneau, Jones Very, Frederick Goddard Tuckerman, and Henry Timrod. The current high standing of such major writers as Poe, Melville, Thoreau, Henry James, and Emily Dickinson is due in large part to the scholars who have edited the texts and written the biographies, the critical studies, and the literary histories.

The modern poet's ranking of his contemporaries is often quite different from that of the professors. Peter Davison, a poet who has observed the academic scene, contributed to the *Atlantic Monthly* for October, 1967, a thoughtful article entitled "The Difficulties of Being Major . . . ," in which he wrote:

> The common lament on our campuses is the dearth of "major poets," and the critics are scuttling to find one. If they cannot find him, surely they can invent him: study someone until he turns out to be major by simply dominating the course catalogues. . . . today critics pick over the contemporary and near-contemporary crops of poetry with all the concentration of cannery workers sorting and grading fruit.

Davison's own opinion was, he said, that "of all American poets of fifty or under, there are only two who could yet be thought in the running": Robert Lowell and James Dickey. They alone, he thought, were "the likely successors to Robert Frost, Wallace Stevens, William Carlos Williams, and Theodore Roethke." In an address at the Library of Congress on April 24, 1967, James Dickey referred to Theodore Roethke as "the greatest poet we have ever had in this country." On the Jackson Bryer poll of academic specialists Roethke and Robert Lowell each got only 8 out of a possible 138 votes. James Dickey apparently got not a single vote.

## YOUTH AND AGE

Young literary critics are generally the best interpreters of the work of writers of their own generation. They are frequently at their worst when writing about the authors of the decades immediately preceding their own. In the 1920's the youthful rebels delighted in ridiculing the eminent Victorians, usually without bothering to read their books. They particularly disliked Tennyson, Longfellow, and Howells. The young intellectuals had little sense of history, and they failed to realize the enormous extent of their own indebtedness to the writers of the past. Their attitude toward the elderly academic critics, upholders of the tradition under attack, was forcefully expressed in some lines written by William Butler Yeats:

> Bald heads, forgetful of their sins,
> Old, learned, respectable bald heads
> Edit and annotate the lines
> That young men, tossing on their beds,
> Rhymed out in love's despair
> To flatter beauty's ignorant ear.

The limitations of the youthful critic are generally obvious enough, and the literary historian knows that he must take them into consideration. My studies, however, indicate that all too many elderly and middle-aged critics seem not to realize that when they undertake to appraise the work of their contemporaries, they do so at the peril of revealing grave limitations in their own literary taste. It is a hard thing to say, but the great danger comes when the literary critic, having passed the half-century mark, feels, perhaps for the first time, that he is now qualified to pass judgment upon the work of poets, dramatists, and writers of fiction of his own time. My generalization applies with peculiar force to the academic critics, whose profession inclines them to conservatism. Professors of English brought up with the notion that Longfellow and Tennyson were major poets, disliked the poems of the Imagists. Carl Sandburg's "Chicago" and John Masefield's "The Widow in the Bye Street" seemed to them merely brutal. Fred Lewis Pattee failed to find truth and beauty in the poems of Emily Dickinson, and Barrett Wendell could find little to praise in Whitman's *Leaves of Grass*. My generalization applies also to all those who read contemporary literature for professional reasons: literary journalists, magazine editors, advisers to publishing houses, literary agents, professional critics, and men of letters.

In his old age Thomas Jefferson, urged by his daughter Martha to read *Ivanhoe*, a best-seller in 1819 and 1820, found himself unable to finish what he said was the dullest and dryest reading he had ever experienced. A few years later Jefferson's friend William Wirt tried to read in manuscript a difficult new poem entitled "Al Aaraaf"; but he could make nothing even of Poe's lovely song to Ligeia. In *Over the Tea-Cups*, the last of the Breakfast-Table series, Dr. Holmes expressed great reservations about *Leaves of Grass*, but he was wise enough to add: "But I suppose I belong to another age, and must not attempt to judge the present by my old-fashioned standards." A better literary critic than any of these, William Hazlitt, in an essay "On Reading Old Books" confessed that the reading of his young friend Keats's "The Eve of St. Agnes" had caused him to regret that he was no longer young:

> The beautiful and tender images there conjured up, "come like shadows—so depart." The "tiger moth's [deep-damasked] wings," which he has spread over his rich poetic blazonry, just flit across my fancy; the gorgeous twilight window which he has painted over again in his verse, to me "blushes" almost in vain "with blood of queens and kings." I know how I should have felt at one time in reading such passages; and that is all. The sharp luscious flavour, the fine *aroma* is fled, and nothing but the stalk, the bran, the husk of literature is left.

## THE ANGLO-AMERICAN LITERARY TRADITION

In the twentieth century critical methods and standards have undergone rapid changes, and not always for the better. For example, as Henry Nash Smith wrote in 1963, Mark Twain's books have had to be tested by a succession of new critical approaches:

Twentieth century criticism of Mark Twain has followed the general course of American criticism. It has been influenced by the impressionism of the years before the First World War, the search for a usable past during the 1920's, the cult of realism and of social significance during the 1930's, the emphasis on technique that became fashionable in the later 1930's and 1940's, and the interest in symbolism, often involving psychological speculation, that has rather paradoxically flourished along with formalism in recent years.

In addition to the slight variations in the status of any major writer that can be expected to show up in every new decade, there are the sweeping changes in both literary taste and critical standards that come about only once or twice in a century. These indicate a shift in the national literary tradition. The new and original writers look for models and direction to foreign writers or to older unfashionable writers of their own country. In England at the time of the Renaissance the great writers turned away from the writers of the Middle Ages to follow the lead of Petrarch, Boccaccio, and Ariosto. In the late seventeenth century John Dryden and his contemporaries, repelled by the extravagance of the Elizabethans and the Metaphysicals, looked to the Latin classics and the Neo-Classical poets and dramatists of France. A century later the Romantic poets and critics repudiated Dryden and Pope. They were attracted to Germany rather than France, and they found models and direction in the older English poets and the writers of popular ballads. American poets and novelists followed in the paths marked out by Wordsworth, Coleridge, Scott, and Byron; and they too repudiated Dryden and Pope. The Romantic movement, like its predecessors, lost its momentum and its vitality; and in the early twentieth century Mencken, Brooks, Untermeyer, and Amy Lowell downgraded the New England poets and promoted the revival of Melville, Thoreau, and Emily Dickinson. There was, however, a second revolutionary wave led by Pound, Eliot, Ransom, and the New Critics, who maintained that the Anglo-American literary tradition stemmed from John Donne and the Metaphysical Poets of the seventeenth century. They were not literary nationalists and with the exception of Hawthorne, Henry James, and Poe they cared little or nothing for the major American writers of the nineteenth century.

The Anglo-American literary tradition as most contemporary critics and creative writers alike would define it seems to me definitely out of line with the larger European-American literary tradition which goes the long way back to Greece, Rome, and Palestine. The modern critics, whether academic or not, place an emphasis for which there is no precedent upon purely aesthetic qualities, and they tend to ignore the many human values that the great classics have always been deeply concerned with. What modern poet would now say with John Keats that it is the function of poetry "to soothe the cares and lift the thoughts of man"? Or who nowadays would salute a new poet as Emerson did Whitman in 1855 when he said of *Leaves of Grass*: "It has the best merits, namely of fortifying and encouraging"? More characteristic of twentieth-century literary criticism is John Crowe Ransom's remark that the "modern" poet "has disdained social responsibility in order to secure this pure esthetic effect. He cares nothing, professionally, about morals, or God, or native land. He has performed a work of dissociation and purified his art." With such an approach to the poetic art Vergil could not have written the *Aeneid*, Dante *The Divine Comedy*, Spenser *The Faerie Queene*, or Milton *Paradise Lost*. Milton's professed purpose was "To justify the ways of God to man." Many of the "modern" poets would have agreed rather with A. E. Housman, who wrote:

> Malt does more than Milton can
> To justify God's ways to man.

A conspicuous characteristic of our twentieth-century fiction, as W. H. Auden pointed out in 1948, is "the denial of free will and moral responsibility. . . . in novel after novel [in America]," he added, "one encounters heroes without honor or history . . . heroes whose sole moral virtue is a stoic endurance of pain and disaster."

The English literary tradition as it has been defined by Matthew Arnold, Ernest Barker, and Ashley H. Thorndike is characterized by energy, honesty, and variety, by fertility in the creation of new art-forms, by a concern with practical matters, and by a compelling desire to explore the meaning of life. Other traits are a deficient sense of artistic form and a propensity for moralizing.

Such is the literary tradition which our nineteenth-century American writers inherited; and it seems to me that they exhibit in greater degree the defects if not the merits of English literature. What Poe called "the heresy of the didactic" is conspicuous in the writings of the New Englanders. Our twentieth-century American writers also display energy, honesty, variety, a fertility in the creation of new literary techniques, and a lively concern with practical affairs. Our modern writers, however, are less concerned with interpreting the meaning of life than they are with aesthetic considerations.

There are of course significant exceptions to my generalization. One finds a great concern with the meaning of life in the poems of Edwin Arlington Robinson and Robert Frost; that concern is very evident also in the later work of T. S. Eliot and William Faulkner. A poem, said Frost, "begins in delight . . . and ends in a clarification of life—not necessarily a great clarification, such as sects and cults are founded on, but in a momentary stay against confusion." In 1950 Faulkner concluded his Nobel Prize Award speech in these words:

It is his [the writer's] privilege to help man endure by lifting his heart, by reminding him of the courage and honor and hope and pride and compassion and pity and sacrifice which have been the glory of his past. The poet's voice need not merely be the record of man, it can be one of the props, the pillars to help him endure and prevail.

In an article entitled "Mirror of a Violent Half Century" in the New York *Times* Lewis Mumford wrote in 1950: "If our civilization is not to produce greater holocausts, our writers will have to become something more than merely a mirror of its violence and disintegration. . . ." The writer, he maintained, "is still a maker, a creator, not merely a recorder of fact but above all an interpreter of possibilities. . . . He must be capable of interpreting life in all its dimensions the last half-century has neglected; restoring reason to the irrational, purpose to the defeatists and drifters, value to the nihilists, hope to those sinking in despair."

If Mumford is right, the twenty-first century will question our present ranking of the major American writers, some of whom were alienated from the society in which they were born and bred. Even if Mumford is wrong, there is still the rising younger generation, many of whom are already at odds with their elders. They can be expected to reinterpret the Anglo-American literary tradition and to frame their own canon of the major American writers.

In a passage that I have quoted in an earlier chapter, Willa Cather wrote in *Not under Forty* (1936): "The world broke in two in 1922 or thereabouts. . . ." She thus described the younger generation which by 1936 had brought about radical changes in the American literary canon:

Eighteen or twenty years ago there were graduated from our universities a company of unusually promising men, who were also extravagantly ambitious. The world was changing, and they meant to play a conspicuous part in this change: to make a new kind of thought and a new kind of expression: in language, color, form, sound. They were to bring about a renaissance within a decade or so. Failing in this, they made a career of destroying the past.

It looks as though history may now be repeating itself and the world once more about to break in two. In January, 1969, President Nathan M. Pusey of Harvard University noted in his annual report that commentators were suggesting that "we are moving through a turning point in history in which old ways of doing things are breaking up. Perhaps," he continued, "we are experiencing shattering fundamental changes the significance of which cannot yet be even dimly discerned." Reluctantly Dr. Pusey conceded "the possibility that our colleges and universities are only among the first of institutions to be shaken by an all-encompassing sea-change now occurring around the world." That was written before the Students for a Democratic Society took over the Administration Building at Harvard and had to be driven out by the police.

In 1869 one of Harvard's most distinguished scholars, George Ticknor, wrote: "It does not seem to me as if I were living in the same country in which I was born." If Ticknor had been alive in 1969, he would have been astonished and chagrined to learn that the students most deeply involved in disturbances on college campuses are not those preparing for professions like law, medicine, and engineering but undergraduates majoring in the humanities. Ticknor would have been astonished also to learn that at Harvard and other universities there are young members of the faculty bent upon converting into agencies for their favorite reforms such respected associations of scholars as the Phi Beta Kappa Society, the American Historical Association, and the Modern Language Association of America. The student and faculty radicals on our campuses are indeed, in the words of Willa Cather, making "a career of destroying the past." For them the past is the System, the Establishment; it is "a bucket of ashes."

Many of the younger generation now in our colleges and universities feel themselves somehow alienated from the society in which they grew up, and they loudly question its traditional values. Their memories do not extend so far backward as the Second World War, but they are acutely aware that the world they live in is not the world of their fathers and grandfathers. Theirs is the age of airplanes, automobiles, freeways, and mobile homes, of television and the computer, of affluent suburbs, of urban ghettoes and a rising crime rate, of air and water pollution, and of an over-populated world in fear of famine. It is the age of the "pill" and of sex morals that frighten and dismay the too-permissive mothers and fathers of college boys and girls. It is also the age of the race to the moon, the Cold War, and the fear of a nuclear holocaust; and it is, above all for young men, the age of the undeclared war in Vietnam.

One cannot of course foresee what the future will bring. It is permissible, however, to hazard the guess that the younger generation now in college will find some of our major American writers irrelevant to their interests and alien to their literary tastes. "The generations of poetry in our age," wrote T. S. Eliot in 1957, "seem to cover a span of about twenty years. . . . I mean that it is about that length of time before a new school or style of poetry appears." In their college English classes students have read too little outside of contemporary literature and have prematurely concluded that most of

English and American literature written before 1920 is of little importance. The younger generation is apparently little interested in aesthetic considerations and not greatly concerned with critical standards.

And yet I should guess that the few who will take the trouble to study some of our well-known authors of the nineteenth century may discover kindred spirits in the antislavery writers. We may in fact see an attempt to restore Lowell, Whittier, and Mrs. Stowe to the rank of major American writers. We may also expect to see a boost in the stocks of Edward Bellamy, George W. Cable, Henry George, Upton Sinclair, and John Dos Passos. If the Black Militants are permitted to dominate the Afro–American Studies programs now proliferating in our universities, an effort will be made to elevate to the status of major American writers William E. B. Dubois, Richard Wright and James Baldwin. The Black Militants, however, have no interest in Paul Laurence Dunbar or Booker T. Washington—they were "Uncle Toms."

How secure in their places on the American Parnassus are the fifteen or twenty writers whom the professors of English now rank as major? Will the new generation find anything to their taste or relevant to their purposes in the writings of Wallace Stevens, E. E. Cummings, Scott Fitzgerald, Sinclair Lewis, Edith Wharton, Willa Cather, John Crowe Ransom, Ezra Pound, or even—outside of *The Waste Land*—of T. S. Eliot? And what will they do with Poe, Melville, Hawthorne, and Henry James? What will the destroyers of the past find to their liking in *The Golden Bowl, Tender Is the Night, Harmonium*, the *Pisan Cantos*, and *The Four Quartets*?

In literary circles the signs of alienation and revolution are not so clearly seen as they are in the fine arts. In that field some of the avant-garde artists and art critics have such an intense hatred for what they call "aristocratic" art that they do not believe in any established scale of values and find no place in the art world for interpretation and criticism. The effort to destroy the past in the interest of "immediacy" goes further than the revolt of the young intellectuals of the 1920's. In the words of Herbert N. Schneidau, "the method is to destroy the System—capitalist, paternalist, rationalist, visualist, elitest [*sic*]—that has prevented full life by perpetuating separations, distinctions, distances."* Jose Ortega y Gasset wrote: "Hatred of art is unlikely to develop as an isolated phenomenon; it goes hand in hand with hatred of science, hatred of State, hatred, in sum, of civilization as a whole." "Pereant isti qui ante nos nostra dixerunt!"

My surmises about the future state of the American literary canon are

---

* I am indebted to Professor Schneidau, of the State University of New York at Buffalo, for permitting me to read a paper that he presented at the December, 1968, meeting of the Modern Language Association, "The Age of Interpretation and the Moment of Immediacy: Contemporary Art vs. History."

likely enough to be proved wrong—there may in fact be a conservative reaction—but beyond question the twenty-first century will make changes in
the ranking of both our major and our minor writers. Eventually the young
literary rebels as they grow older will acquire a better sense of history and,
I hope, a deeper feeling for what in our past is both sterling and inalienably
American. No matter what their social, political, or economic biases may be,
those who love literature can hardly remain indifferent to the merits of Emerson, Hawthorne, Poe, Whitman, and Henry James in the nineteenth century and of Eliot, Frost, Hemingway, and Faulkner in the twentieth. Each
of these writers had a vision of life that is not duplicated elsewhere, and each
of them in a few masterpieces created works of art so perfect in their kind
that our posterity cannot let them die. There will be readers a century hence
for such poems as "Israfel," "Uriel," "When Lilacs Last in the Dooryard
Bloom'd," "Little Gidding," and "The Death of the Hired Man" and for such
works of fiction—to name only the briefest—as "Rappaccini's Daughter," "The
Fall of the House of Usher," "The Death of the Lion," "The Snows of Kili-
manjaro," and "The Bear."

*Unfortunately the* mens aequa et clara *is the rarest of attributes, and dead partisanships have a disconcerting way of coming to life again in the pages of their historians. That the vigorous passions and prejudices of the times I have dealt with may have found an echo in my judgments is, perhaps, to be expected; whether they have distorted my interpretation and vitiated my analysis is not for me to determine.*
Vernon L. Parrington, *Main Currents in American Thought* (1927), Foreword

*My endeavour is to think straight in such terms as are offered to me, to clear my mind of cant and free it from the cramp of artificial traditions; but I do not ask any one to think in my terms if he prefers others. Let him clean better, if he can, the windows of his soul, that the variety and beauty of the prospect may spread more brightly before him.*
George Santayana, *Scepticism and Animal Faith*, Preface

# Afterword

This book is not an autobiography, but it touches my professional life at many points. It deals with writers whose books I learned to love in my youth and have taught to hundreds of students since 1913, when I gave my first course in American literature at Wake Forest University. Perhaps a few of those who have read portions of this book may be interested in a brief account of my long-time involvement with the difficult problem of the proper ranking of American authors. My experiences were not untypical.

In the turbulent 1920's the young intellectuals were radically revising the canon of the major American writers and attacking departments of English as the upholders of an outmoded literary tradition. In the universities and colleges there was something very like a generation gap between older and younger professors. Over protests of elderly professors young rebels were making a place in their courses for the living writers. The late John Owen Beaty and I were among the first to include some of their writings in textbooks designed for college students. In the middle 1920's as one of the editors of the *Southwest Review* I was actively engaged in the discovery and promotion of young writers in the South and West. Within the Modern Language Association in those years there was a small but very able group of younger scholars who were determined to make respectable the study of American literature. In 1928 in *The Reinterpretation of American Literature,*

334

to which I was a contributor, we urged the need for new critical standards and new methods of research. In 1929 we launched our own organ, *American Literature*. As a member of its editorial board from 1928 to 1954 I was conscious of new methods of criticism and aware of important changes in the status of many writers of both the nineteenth and the twentieth centuries. In 1936 and again in 1949 I had to select for my anthology, *American Life in Literature*, those writers who I thought should be taught to college students. In *The South in American Literature* I had to choose those southern writers who seemed to me to have real significance for students of the nation's literature. In 1949 and again in 1950 while lecturing at the University of Vienna I noted that some of our major writers seemed to have much more for Europeans than others. When I returned from Vienna in 1950, I revised my history of southern literature (still in manuscript) in order to make clear the distinction between major writers, like Poe and Mark Twain, and those fascinating lesser figures, William Byrd, John Pendleton Kennedy, William Gilmore Simms, Henry Timrod, Joel Chandler Harris, and Sidney Lanier. In the twentieth century our literature has become a world literature; and when we attempt to rank our writers, we cannot afford to ignore the opinions of Europeans and Latin-Americans. French criticism of Poe and Faulkner has thrown new light upon two of our major authors.

The old New England poets never seemed to me the peers of Poe and Whitman; but still each of them wrote a few poems that I cherished and I was reluctant to see them relegated to the status of fifth-rate minor poets. I was excited by the rediscovery of Herman Melville. It was Carl Van Doren who in 1915 persuaded me to read *Moby-Dick*. I read or reread with delight the work of lesser writers who were being rediscovered: George Henry Boker, William Byrd, Thomas Holley Chivers, William Gilmore Simms, Henry Timrod, Frederick Goddard Tuckerman, and Jones Very.

I early learned to admire some of the writers who made memorable the decades that fall between the two world wars. Edwin Arlington Robinson and Robert Frost seemed to me the best of the new poets. It was Katharine C. Balderston who in 1916 induced me to read *North of Boston*. A review by Bliss Perry in the New York *Times* introduced me to the poems of Robinson. I had a special interest in certain living writers whom I had met or knew by correspondence: Robert Frost, Carl Sandburg, Vachel Lindsay, Witter Bynner, Van Wyck Brooks, DuBose Heyward, Karle Wilson Baker, Ellen Glasgow, and John Hall Wheelock.

In both my teaching and my research I had a special interest in literature as a reflection of American life and thought. This circumstance may explain in part why I found it difficult to appreciate the merits of the expatriates and why I was slow in doing justice to some of the New Critics. I was repelled by the sordid subject matter found in some of the novels written by Dreiser, Dos Passos, Faulkner, and some others. I have never been able to share the enthusiasm that some of my academic friends have for the poems of E. E. Cummings and Wallace Stevens. I still believe that those unfashionable poets, Carl Sandburg, Vachel Lindsay, Sara Teasdale, and John Hall Wheelock, each wrote a few fine lyrics which will find a place in the anthologist's golden treasury of the twenty–first century. Wheelock, whose *Dust and Light* I first read in 1920, still seems to me a major American poet. He is, in the words of Allen Tate, "one of the best poets in English."

The year 1922, as I have pointed out elsewhere in this book, was a turning point in American literary history. That was the year of T. S. Eliot's *The Waste Land*, James Joyce's *Ulysses*, Scott Fitzgerald's *Tales of the Jazz Age*, Sinclair Lewis's *Babbitt*, and that symposium by Thirty Americans entitled *Civilization in the United States*. In that year also John Beaty and I, finding no text suitable for our sophomore English classes, brought out one of our own. In *An Introduction to Poetry* we invited an almost constant comparison between contemporary poetry and the poetry of earlier centuries. We found nothing in the poetry of the twentieth century which seemed to us to rise to the heights reached by Shakespeare and Milton, but we thought the narrative poems of Robert Frost were quite as good as those of Tennyson, and Robinson's sonnets seemed to us better than those of Longfellow. Dr. Beaty and I, however, failed to include any poem by T. S. Eliot in our book, which was published one month before *The Waste Land* appeared. Eliot is represented in the revised edition of *An Introduction to Poetry*, but even in 1936—like most of our academic contemporaries—we did not see Eliot as one of the three or four great poets of the twentieth century.

In reporting the critical estimates of the many persons who have so freely expressed their various opinions I have tried to be objective, and in the main I have kept my own opinions to myself. Let me add that I have not found it easy to view objectively certain mistaken (as they seem to me now) estimates written by old friends no longer living: William Peterfield Trent, Arthur Hobson Quinn, Fred Lewis Pattee, Ralph Leslie Rusk, and Carl Van Doren. They were competent scholars and able critics, and they all contributed notably to filling in the record of American literary achievement. Their critical limitations were chiefly those of the period in which they lived. It is not easy for a reader born in the nineteenth century to bring to the work of writers who have emerged since the end of the Second World War the same degree of sympathy and understanding that he has for *Moby-Dick*, *Leaves of Grass*, *North of Boston*, and *A Farewell to Arms*.

When I planned this book, I thought of giving separate chapters to eight or ten writers of the twentieth century. It is perhaps just as well that, for

336

various reasons, I abandoned that plan. In the last twenty years there have come about notable shifts in the reputations of certain authors who in 1950 were generally rated as major. Critics who a decade or two ago might have suggested my including Sinclair Lewis and Carl Sandburg would now probably suggest Scott Fitzgerald and Wallace Stevens. Even if I had been able to single out the eight or ten best of the modern writers, I could not have discussed some of them with the same degree of sympathy and understanding that I have for Emerson, Hawthorne, Poe, Whitman, and the six others whom I have discussed separately. Perhaps we can be sure now that Frost, Eliot, Faulkner, and Hemingway belong in the rare company of Melville, Thoreau, Emily Dickinson, Henry James, and Mark Twain; but how shall we rank Conrad Aiken, Willa Cather, Ellen Glasgow, Katherine Anne Porter, John Crowe Ransom, John Steinbeck, Allen Tate, Edith Wharton, and Thomas Wolfe?

There were other difficulties. After I gave up teaching in 1961, I was no longer under any compulsion to keep up with the enormous and rapidly increasing mass of published criticism and research in American literature. The condition of my eyes, moreover, warned me that it would be better to bring my book to a conclusion rather than to spend two or three years more on it without any assurance that the result would justify the time and energy expended.

I am fully aware that in my earlier writings I am on record with critical estimates that are at variance with the dominant critical opinion of today. Some of them I would now alter, but I have no apology to make even for those estimates that now seem to me to be wrong. In this book I have rarely obtruded my own critical opinions upon the reader; and where I have done so, the reader I hope will not find them a distraction from the main purpose of the book. My function is that of historian. If the factual record is as accurate as I have tried to make it, a critic of any school will be able to use the materials that I have collected and systematized even though his own estimates of American writers may differ widely from mine.

J. B. H.

# Index

The names of many minor writers and the titles of many books have been omitted.

340

Fletcher, John Gould, 196, 199, 215, 231, 280, 318
Foerster, Norman, 113–114, 173, 174, 181, 251, 303
*For Whom the Bell Tolls*, 203, 225, 227, 297, 313
Franklin, Benjamin, 88, 108, 251, 273, 276, 292, 302, 304, 310
Freneau, Philip, 12, 106, 240, 257
Freud, Sigmund, 156, 256, 305, 307, 308
Frost, Robert, 44, 93, 121–122, 171, 175, 187, 194, 195, 201, 209, 211, 212, 213, 214, 215, 219, 227, 231, 233, 234, 238, 240, 247, 255, 257, 279, 280, 281, 282, 283, 284, 294, 295, 298, 299, 314, 318, 329–330
Fuller, Margaret, 35–36

Garland, Hamlin, 125, 223, 246–247
Garrison, Wendell Phillips, 21
Girson, Rochelle, 312–314
Glasgow, Ellen, 202, 203, 213, 221, 225, 226, 249, 280, 283, 296, 298, 304, 323
Gohdes, Clarence, 41, 98, 164
*Golden Bowl, The*, 133, 134
Goldman, Eric F., 306–308
*Gone with the Wind*, 266–267
*Good Earth, The*, 206, 226, 296–297
Gosse, Edmund, 53, 86, 128
Graduate Students' Poll, A, 226–227
*Grapes of Wrath, The*, 203, 225, 226, 297, 298, 312
"Great American Novel, The" (Herbert Brown), 78–79
*Great Gatsby, The*, 227, 260, 303
*Green Hills of Africa, The*, 144, 275
Griswold, Rufus Wilmot, 19, 32–34, 52
Guérard, Albert, 91, 93, 103

"Hall of Fantasy, The" (Hawthorne), 19, 40
Halleck, Fitz-Greene, 16, 100, 104
Hardy, Thomas, 141, 158, 233, 242
Harris, Joel Chandler, 141, 248, 249, 289
Hart, James D., 89, 181, 317
Hart, John S., 32, 104–105
Harte, Bret, 137, 289
Hawthorne, Nathaniel, 10, 19, 31, 36, 37, 39–42, 45, 46, 56, 57–58, 59, 88, 94, 98, 104, 106, 113, 124–125, 170, 200, 227, 252, 255, 256–257, 262, 271, 273, 274, 276, 277, 279, 289, 290, 292, 301, 304
Hayne, Paul Hamilton, 38, 116
Hazlitt, Henry, 213
Hazlitt, William, 89, 206, 327
Hemingway, Ernest, 112, 144, 167, 168, 202, 203, 205, 206, 212, 213, 217, 224, 225, 227, 228, 247, 257, 275–276, 279,

280, 281, 282, 283, 296–297, 302, 313, 321
Hergesheimer, Joseph, 209, 210, 214, 221, 223, 226, 253–254, 293
H.H. *See* Jackson, Helen Hunt
Hicks, Granville, 183, 224, 255–56
Higginson, Thomas Wentworth, 49, 60, 65, 91, 94n, 145–146
Holland, Josiah Gilbert, 77, 81, 147
Holman, C. Hugh, 190, 276–277, 280, 284, 286
Holmes, Dr. Oliver Wendell, 24, 25–26, 32, 47, 68, 86, 88, 94, 98, 106, 107, 115, 239, 240, 241, 242, 256, 258, 271, 311, 327
Holmes, Justice Oliver Wendell, 42, 62, 264
*House of the Seven Gables, The*, 222, 290
Howells, William Dean, 18, 22, 38, 52–53, 65, 77, 86, 90, 91–92, 96, 105–106, 107, 108, 114–122, 123, 141, 149–150, 164, 170, 177, 208, 253, 255, 257, 271, 273, 274, 276, 277, 289, 290, 302
"Hundred Years of American Verse, A" (Howells), 52–53

*Invisible Man, The*, 228
Irving, Washington, 8, 15, 88, 94, 104, 170, 271, 290, 292, 302

Jackson, Helen Hunt (H.H.), 30, 145, 146
James, Henry, 38, 41, 44–45, 48–49, 74, 87, 90, 97, 107, 117, 118, 122–135, 162, 170, 180, 194, 199, 208, 227, 251–252, 254, 255, 257, 271, 273, 274, 275, 276, 277, 279, 280, 290, 294, 301, 320
James, William, 129, 264
Jarrell, Randall, 72, 233–234, 242
Jefferson, Thomas, 272, 292, 310, 327
Jewett, Sarah Orne, 255, 257, 304
Johnston, Edward W., 14
Jones, Howard Mumford, 50, 190
Jones, William A., 16, 23

Keats, John, xvi, 235, 327
Kellett, E. E., xiii–xiv, 317–318
Kettell, Samuel, 13
Kipling, Rudyard, 90, 142, 293, 294
Kirk, Clara, 120, 324
Knapp, Samuel Lorenzo, 13
Krutch, Joseph Wood, 156, 264

Landor, Walter Savage, 122, 193
Lang, Andrew, 141
Lanier, Henry W., 289–291
Lanier, Sidney, 28, 96, 116, 147, 239, 242, 278
*Last of the Mohicans, The*, 289, 302
Lawrence, D. H., 165